A Short History of Christianity beyond the West

Theology and Mission in World Christianity

Editors-in-Chief

Kirsteen Kim (*Fuller Theological Seminary, USA*)
Stephen B. Bevans (*Catholic Theological Union, Chicago, USA*)
Miikka Ruokanen (*University of Helsinki, Finland/Nanjing Union Theological Seminary, China*)

Editorial Board

Kwabena Asamoah-Gyadu (*Trinity Theological Seminary, Ghana*)
Martha T. Frederiks (*Utrecht University, The Netherlands*)
Dana L. Robert (*Boston University, USA*)
Elsa Tamez (*Latin American Biblical University, Costa Rica*)
Rachel Zhu Xiaohong (*Fudan University, Shanghai, China*)

VOLUME 31

The titles published in this series are listed at *brill.com/tmwc*

A Short History of Christianity beyond the West

Asia, Africa, and Latin America, 1450–2000

By

Klaus Koschorke

BRILL

LEIDEN | BOSTON

 This is an open access title distributed under the terms of the CC BY-NC-ND 4.0 license, which permits any non-commercial use, distribution, and reproduction in any medium, provided no alterations are made and the original author(s) and source are credited. Further information and the complete license text can be found at https://creativecommons.org/licenses/by-nc-nd/4.0/

The terms of the CC license apply only to the original material. The use of material from other sources (indicated by a reference) such as diagrams, illustrations, photos and text samples may require further permission from the respective copyright holder.

Cover illustration: Ghana (Kintampo): Christianity in everyday life (Photo by Klaus Koschorke, with kind permission by the author).

Library of Congress Cataloging-in-Publication Data

Names: Koschorke, Klaus, author.
Title: A short history of Christianity beyond the West : Asia, Africa, and Latin America 1450-2000 / Klaus Koschorke.
Description: Leiden ; Boston : Brill, [2025] | Series: Theology and mission in world Christianity, 2452-2953 ; volume 31 | Includes bibliographical references and index.
Identifiers: LCCN 2024029214 (print) | LCCN 2024029215 (ebook) | ISBN 9789004699823 (paperback) | ISBN 9789004699830 (ebook)
Subjects: LCSH: Christianity–Asia–History. | Christianity and culture–Asia–History. | Christianity–Africa–History. | Christianity and culture–Africa–History. | Christianity–Latin America–History. | Christianity and culture–Latin America–History.
Classification: LCC BR1065 .K67 2025 (print) | LCC BR1065 (ebook) | DDC 270–dc23/eng/20240731
LC record available at https://lccn.loc.gov/2024029214
LC ebook record available at https://lccn.loc.gov/2024029215

Typeface for the Latin, Greek, and Cyrillic scripts: "Brill". See and download: brill.com/brill-typeface.

ISSN 2452-2953
ISBN 978-90-04-69982-3 (paperback)
ISBN 978-90-04-69983-0 (e-book)
DOI 10.1163/9789004699830

Copyright 2025 by Klaus Koschorke. Published by Koninklijke Brill BV, Leiden, The Netherlands.
Koninklijke Brill BV incorporates the imprints Brill, Brill Nijhoff, Brill Schöningh, Brill Fink, Brill mentis, Brill Wageningen Academic, Vandenhoeck & Ruprecht, Böhlau and V&R unipress.
Koninklijke Brill BV reserves the right to protect this publication against unauthorized use.

This book is printed on acid-free paper and produced in a sustainable manner.

Contents

Preface XI
List of Figures and Maps XIII
Technical Notes for Use XVIII

In Place of an Introduction: "Christians and Spices" – or: the Multiplicity of Regional Centers in the History of World Christianity XX

PART 1
1450–1600

1 The Christian World around 1500 3
   1.1 Christian Europe around 1500 3
   1.2 The Islamic World 4
   1.3 Knowledge of Non-European Cultures, Perceptions of Europe from Outside 5
   1.4 Christians and Churches in Africa and Asia 7

2 The Iberian Expansion of the 15th/16th Centuries 11
   2.1 The Portuguese on Their Way around Africa (1415ff) 11
   2.2 Spain, Columbus and the "Discovery" of the "New World" (1492) 12
   2.3 Divided Spheres of Interest ('Inter Cetera' 1493, Tordesillas 1494) 14
   2.4 Encounters: Vasco da Gama and the Indian St. Thomas Christians (1498ff) 17

3 Iberoamerica I: Colonization and Christianization 20
   3.1 American-Indian Cultures on the Eve of the Iberian Invasion 20
   3.2 Stages of the Conquest 21
   3.3 Legal Titles: Patronage and 'Requerimiento' 22
   3.4 Mission Personnel, Duality of Mission and Colonial Church 24

4 Iberoamerica II: Debates and Controversies 28
   4.1 Religious Debates: Franciscans and Aztecs in Mexico 1524 28
   4.2 Controversies over Ethics of Colonialism: Antonio de Montesinos, Bartolomé de las Casas 29

4.3   Experiments on the Formation of an American-Indigenous Church   33
  4.4   Beginnings of Black Slavery in America   35

5 **Mission under the Padroado: Encounters and Conflicts in Africa and Asia**   38
  5.1   Ethiopia: Portuguese as Guests and Allies in the Christian Empire   38
  5.2   Beginnings of Catholic Presence in Sub-Saharan Africa   40
  5.3   Goa as an Ecclesiastical and Political Center   42
  5.4   Francis Xavier: India, Malacca, Moluccas, Japan, Plans for China (1542–1552)   44

6 **Forms of Indigenous Christianity**   48
  6.1   Asia: the South Indian Paravars and the Martyrs of Mannar (Sri Lanka)   48
  6.2   Africa: the Christian Kongo Kingdom in Its Transatlantic Connections   50
  6.3   Iberoamerica: Voices of American-Indian and Mestizo Christians   52

7 **Reception of the Council of Trent Overseas and the End of Local Experiments**   56
  7.1   State of Expansion at the End of the 16th Century   56
  7.2   Trent and Its Impact on Spanish America   57
  7.3   India: the Synod of Diamper 1599 and the Forced Union of the St. Thomas Christians   60
  7.4   Ethiopia: Expulsion of the Jesuits under Emperor Fasilidas (since 1632/33)   61

Illustrations for Part 1   65

PART 2
17th/18th Centuries

8 **Changing Framework**   71
  8.1   Aspects of European Expansion   71
  8.2   Stages in Mission History   72

- 8.3 Enlightenment and Other Debates 73
- 8.4 Regional Centers, Transcontinental Entanglements 74

9 Latin America 77
- 9.1 The Church in the Colonial City 77
- 9.2 Native American and Mestizo Voices 80
- 9.3 Jesuit Reductions (1609–1768) 82
- 9.4 On the Eve of Independence 84

10 Africa 89
- 10.1 Ethiopia: Period of Self-Imposed Isolation 89
- 10.2 Regional Developments 90
- 10.3 Protestant Beginnings 92
- 10.4 Transatlantic Slave Trade, Vision of a Return to Africa 93

11 Asia 97
- 11.1 Japan: the End of the "Christian Century" 97
- 11.2 China: Accommodation Strategies and Rite Controversy 98
- 11.3 Sri Lanka and the Philippines: Resistance in a Colonial Context 100
- 11.4 Korea: Self-Founded Martyrs' Church (1784ff) 102
- 11.5 Tranquebar 1706 and the Beginnings of Protestant Mission in Asia 104

Illustrations for Part 2 108

PART 3
1800–1890

12 The End of the First Colonial Age and the Beginning of the "Protestant Century" 119
- 12.1 Collapse of the Old Colonial Systems (Ibero-America, Africa, Asia) 119
- 12.2 Hitting Rock Bottom of the Catholic Missions (Asia, Africa, America) 120
- 12.3 Developments in the Protestant World 122
- 12.4 Transcontinental Migration Flows, Beginnings of African-American Missions 124

13 Asia 129
  13.1 South Asia: Missions as a Factor of Modernization 129
  13.2 Northeast Asia (China, Japan, Korea): Opium Trade and Bible Smuggling 135
  13.3 Philippines, Vietnam, Indonesia 141
  13.4 Indigenous Versions of Christianity 142

14 Africa 147
  14.1 West Africa: Slave Emancipation and Transatlantic Resettlement Projects 147
  14.2 South Africa: Black Christians and White Settlers 150
  14.3 East and Central Africa: David Livingstone and Other European "Discoverers" 153
  14.4 African Christian Rulers: Madagascar, Uganda, Ethiopia 156
  14.5 S. A. J. Crowther, First Black African Bishop, and Controversies about the "Three Selves" 159

15 Latin America 163
  15.1 Independence Struggle and the Church (1804–1830) 163
  15.2 The Catholic Church and the New States (1830–1890) 164
  15.3 Romanization of Latin American Catholicism 166
  15.4 Forms of Protestant Presence in Latin America 168

  Illustrations for Part 3 172

PART 4
1890–1945

16 Churches and Missions in the Age of High Imperialism 181
  16.1 Growing Colonial Rivalries 181
  16.2 New Missionary Actors 183
  16.3 Indigenous Counter-Movements 185
  16.4 Multiplicity of Transregional and Transcontinental Networks 187
  16.5 The First World War as a Caesura and the End of the 'Christianity-Civilization' Model 190

17 Asia 195
  17.1 Religious Nationalisms and Indigenization Experiments 195
  17.2 Ecumenism as a Protest Movement, National Church Aspirations 197

  17.3 Developments in Catholic Asia 199
  17.4 Between World War I and World War II 201

18 **Africa** 205
  18.1 The Christian Missions and the "Scramble for Africa" 205
  18.2 The Emergence of African Independent Churches 207
  18.3 Themes of the Twenties and Thirties 211
  18.4 Christian Elites and the Political Independence Movements 213

19 **Latin America** 217
  19.1 The Situation around 1900 217
  19.2 Regional Profiles: Brazil, Mexico, Cuba 218
  19.3 World Economic Crisis and Social Question 220
  19.4 Denominational Pluralization, New Religions 221

  Illustrations for Part 4 225

PART 5
1945–1990

20 **Postcolonial Order and Ecclesial Emancipation Movements** 231
  20.1 End of the Second World War, Waves of Decolonization 231
  20.2 New Alliances, Movement of "Third World"-Countries 232
  20.3 Forms of Ecclesiastical and Theological Emancipation 233
  20.4 Growing Importance of the Southern Churches in the Global Ecumenical Movement 236
  20.5 New Actors and Movements 239

21 **Asia: the 1950s** 242
  21.1 Christians as a Minority in the Process of Nation Building 242
  21.2 Loss of Status and Persecutions under Communist Rule 244
  21.3 Search for Christian Identity in the "New Asia" 246
  21.4 Approaches to New Theological Orientation 248

22 **Africa in the 1960s** 251
  22.1 Church and State in New Africa 251
  22.2 'Historical' and Independent Churches 253
  22.3 Approaches to African Theology, Interreligious Initiatives 256
  22.4 South Africa: Christians and Churches in the Apartheid State 258

23 Latin America: the 1970s   263
   23.1 Between Social Revolution and State Repression   263
   23.2 The Second Vatican Council (1962–1965) and the Bishops' Conference of Medellín (1968)   264
   23.3 Liberation Theologies: Characteristics, Controversies, Developments   265
   23.4 Protestant and (Neo)Pentecostal Groups, Revitalization of African American Religions   268

24 "Shift of Centers": Developments in the 1980s   273
   24.1 From a North to a South Majority   273
   24.2 "Return of the Religions", Religious Fundamentalisms   277
   24.3 "Reverse Missions", Impacts on the West   278
   24.4 Regional Developments and Profiles   280

Illustrations for Part 5   286

PART 6
On the Threshold of the 21st Century

25 1989/90 as an Epoch Year in the History of World Christianity   295
   25.1 End of the Cold War, Collapse of Apartheid, Crisis of Liberation Theologies   295
   25.2 Internet, Digital Globalization, Liberalized Travel   298
   25.3 Changing Geographies of Religion, Transcontinental Churches, New Dynamics of Polycentrism   301
   25.4 "The Next Christendom" – Discussions and Expectations around the Turn of the Millennium   304

Outlook, Perspectives   311

Maps   314
Bibliography   332
   Bibliography I: Standard Works, General Surveys   332
   Bibliography II: Complete List of References   335
Illustration Credits   365
Survey of the Digital Appendix: Photos from Selected Regions   366
Index   367

Preface

Since the 1980s, a growing majority of the Christian world population is living in the global South. Any attempt to understand Christianity as a world religion has to pay proper attention to these dramatic changes. Until quite recently, the history of the Christian communities in Asia, Africa and Latin America has often been described more or less as a mere appendix to Western church and mission history. But churches existed in Asia and Africa long before the first European "discoverers" and missionaries entered the scene. Even later, the western missionary movement was just *one* factor, among others, in the worldwide spread of Christianity. Describing world Christianity as a polycentric movement, we have to take into account a multitude of regional centers of expansion, indigenous initiatives, cultural expressions, local forms, global entanglements and multidirectional forms of exchange.

This textbook and study guide has been the result of many years of teaching at various institutions, both in Germany (Munich University LMU) and during multiple guest professorships in Asia, Africa and UK (Liverpool Hope). It is intended for a variety of audiences: students and teachers of church history, religious studies, mission history and World Christianity, contextual theology and ecumenical studies, various area and cultural studies, global history and history of globalization, anthropology of Christianity etc. The volume is designed to be used for different forms of academic instruction: for survey courses, as an extension (or supplement) to traditional period lectures, for courses on the Christian history of individual continents or regions, and for treatment of selected topics. At the same time, this one volume single-authored survey is directed also to a wider public interested in the global dimensions of Christianity and its history.

A special feature of the book is its close connection with a similarly structured documentary source book on the history of Christianity beyond the West from 1450 to 1990 which has been published in English, German and Spanish.[1] This facilitates academic teaching and enables parallel reading of relevant source materials for the individual chapters of his book. Another characteristic of the volume is its rich visual material. In addition to the maps and historical

---

1 Koschorke, K./ Ludwig, F./ Delgado, M. (2007 ff) (eds.), A History of Christianity in Asia, Africa, and Latin America, 1450–1990. A Documentary Sourcebook (Eerdmans: Grand Rapids, MI/ Cambridge, U.K.); for the German and Spanish editions see details on p. XVIII, FN. 3. – This textbook is a revised and updated translation of: Koschorke, K. (2022), Grundzüge der Außereuropäischen Christentumsgeschichte. Asien, Afrika und Lateinamerika 1450–2000 (utb 5934; MohrSiebeck: Tübingen).

illustrations, there is a digital appendix with about 250 photos from various regions and places relevant for the history of Christianity in the global South. They were taken by the author during repeated overseas travels and research stays since the 1980s.

The textbook and study book was developed in various test runs. Thanks are due for critical comments and suggestions to many persons. First of all to my students and collaborators at the Munich Chair of 'Early and World Church History' (which I held from 1993 to 2013) and other places of varied guest professorships in different regions. Special thanks also go to the co-editors of the above-mentioned source volume, my colleagues Mariano Delgado (Fribourg/Switzerland), Frieder Ludwig (now Stavanger) and Roland Spliesgart (Munich). Various colleagues at home and abroad have proofread individual sections or commented on specific aspects. I mention with thanks (in alphabetical order): Afe Adogame (Princeton); Raimundo Barreto (Princeton); Verena Boell (Leipzig); Ciprian Burlacioiu (Munich); Christian Büschges (Bern); David Daniels (Chicago); Adrian Hermann (Bonn); Michael Hochgeschwender (Munich); Klaus Hock (Rostock); Daniel Jeyaraj (Liverpool/Chennai); Thomas Kaufmann (Göttingen); Sebastian Kim (Pasadena); Hartmut Lehmann (Kiel); Johannes Meier (Mainz); Elizabeth Marteijn (Groningen); Andreas Müller (Kiel); Christoph Nebgen (Frankfurt); Peter Tze Ming Ng (Hong Kong); Stanislau Paulau (Halle); Rudolph von Sinner (São Leopoldo); Wolbert Smidt (Mekele); Mira Sonntag (Tokyo); Veit Strassner (Maikammer); Martin Wallraff (Munich); Andrew Walls[†] (Edinburgh/Liverpool); Kevin Ward (Leeds). Library research and technical support was provided by Philipp Kuster (Munich). Special thanks are also due to the editors of the 'Theology and Mission in World Christianity' series and the production team of Brill Publisher. The lively exchange with many colleagues from the worldwide ecumenical community should not go unmentioned. They have opened my eyes – since a first formative guest lectureship in Sri Lanka in 1982/83 – to the richness of Christian history in other cultures and world regions.

Klaus Koschorke
Munich, December 2023
February 2024

Figures and Maps

Figures

1 Ethiopian Orthodox priest with Ge'ez Bible (Lake Tana/Ethiopia 1997)   65
2 Kerala (India): Bishop and clergy of the Syriac Orthodox Church, a branch of the St. Thomas Christian tradition of India (photo taken in 1983) [= Photo A14]   65
3 Bartolomé de las Casas (1484–1566), Dominican monk, missionary and bishop, "defender of the Indians"   66
4 Mexico: Plaque commemorating Las Casas in his former diocese of Chiapas [= Photo M08]   66
5 Mexico: The Lord's Prayer in Nahuatl, the pre-Hispanic lingua franca of the Aztecs and other peoples in central Mexico; translation and representation in pictorial script took place in the 16th century, mainly by Franciscan missionaries   66
6 India (Kochi/Kerala): St. Francis Church, originally built by the Portuguese in 1503, considered as the oldest European church in India   67
7 Japan/ Kagoshima: Monument to the memory of the arrival of Francis Xavier (1506–1552) and his Japanese companion Yajiro (Hanshiro) in 1549 on the southern island of Kyushu [= Photo C01]   67
8 Japan: The Martyrs of Nagasaki (1597), engraving by Wolfgang Kilian (Augsburg 1628)   68
9 Japan/ Amacusa (Kyushu): Trampling on image of the Virgin Mary as test of religious allegiance for underground Christians [= Photo C09]   68
10 From the pictorial chronicle 'Nueva corónica y buen gobierno' of the Inca Poma de Ayala around 1614 y buen gobierno' des Inka Poma de Ayala um 1614 (Explanation taken from: Prien 1978, Geschichte, 222)   108
11 From the pictorial chronicle 'Nueva corónica y buen gobierno' by the Inca Poma de Ayala around 1614 (Explanation taken from: Prien 1978, Geschichte, 228)   108
12 Cuzco (Peru), Plaza Mayor, with cathedral [= Photo J01]   109
13 Cuzco (Peru): "Supper with Guinea Pig": painting by the Christian mestizo artist Marcos Zapata (1710–1773), today in the cathedral [= Photo J04]   109
14 Mexico: Sor Juana Inés de la Cruz (1648–1695), nun, poet, and advocate of women's right to knowledge and education   110
15 (Historical) Kongo empire: Doña Beatriz Kimpa Vita (1684–1706), Kongolese prophetess, leader of the Christian social revolutionary movement of the Antonians, also referred to as the African Joan of Arc (portrait 1710 by Bernardo da Gallo)   111

16 Olaudah Equiano (c. 1745–1797, also known as Gustavus Vassa), former slave from Benin (Nigeria): African Christian, publicist, and champion of the English anti-slavery movement   111

17 An early transatlantic marriage: Christian Jacob Protten "Africanus" (1715–1769), Moravian missionary and linguist in what is now Ghana; and Rebecca Protten (1718–1780), former slave and evangelist from the Caribbean; both married in Herrnhut (Germany) in 1746; with daughter Anna Maria   111

18 Ghana: Elmina Fort, hub of the transatlantic slave trade, successively in Portuguese, Dutch and British colonial possession [= Photo G14]   112

19 Ghana: Jacobus Elisa Johannes Capitein (c. 1717–1747), West African pastor who, after studying in Leiden, was ordained as a clergyman in the Dutch Reformed Church and became a colonial pastor in Elmina (portrait by Pieter Tanjé, between 1742 and 1762)   112

20 Macao, former Portuguese colony: facade of St. Paul's Church from the 17th century   113

21 Beijing (Peking): Astronomical observatory, depicted by the French Jesuit Louis le Comte (1655–1728). Due to their astronomical knowledge Jesuits gained great influence and high positions at the imperial court [= Photo B08]   113

22 China: Matteo Ricci, Italian Jesuit (1552–1610), and Ly Paulos (Xu Guangqui), Chinese bureaucrat, mathematician, and convert baptized by Ricci (1562–1633), in front of an altar (print from Athanasius Kircher's Monumenta of 1669)   114

23 Bartholomäus Ziegenbalg (1682–1719), the first German Lutheran missionary in India (Tranquebar / Tharangambadi) from 1706. He translated the Bible into Tamil, established schools and founded an Indian Lutheran congregation   115

24 The Tamil catechist Aaron (b. Arumugun, 1698/99–1745), the first Indian to be ordained as a Protestant minister in Tranquebar in 1733   115

25 Tranquebar (Tharangambadi, South India), starting point of the Danish-Hall mission and Protestant presence in India. Picture: Fort Dansborg, center of the Danish ("hired") mini-colony   115

26 China: Robert Morrison (1782–1834), first Protestant missionary to China (and the Chinese diaspora) and his team (Li Shigong, Chaen Laoyi) translating the Bible into Chinese (image from ca. 1828)   172

27 Liang Fa (1789–1855), first Chinese Protestant minister and evangelist, who was instrumental in printing and disseminating Morrison's translation of the Bible. His own Bible tracts influenced the later leader of the Taiping movement Hong Xiuquan (see Figure 28)   172

28 Hong Xiuquan (1814–1864), leader and "Heavenly King" of the Christian-inspired Taiping mass social revolutionary movement (1850–1864)   173

29 China: Anti-Christian cartoon (before 1891) showing the worship of a crucified pig and immorality of Europeans   173

FIGURES AND MAPS　　　　　　　　　　　　　　　　　　　　　　　　　　　XV

30　Japan/Nagasaki: First contact of the "Hidden Christians" in 1865 with a French missionary after the "opening" of the country in 1854 (relief in front of the Urakami Cathedral) [= Photo C17]　174

31　Japan: entrance to Doshisha University, founded in 1875 as an English school by Protestant educator Niijima Jo (Joseph Hardy Neesima; 1843–1890) [= Photo C15]　174

32　Miguel Hidalgo (1753–1811), Mexican priest, scholar, and one of the pioneers of Mexican independence　175

33　Official medallion of the British Anti-Slavery Society (since the end of the 18th century), which was strongly supported by evangelical forces within the missionary movement. The medallion was designed by Josia Wedwood in 1795　175

34　Samuel Ajayi Crowther (c. 1806/08–1891), first black African bishop of modern times (in British-colonial West Africa) and symbol of the upward aspirations of modern African elites across the continent　176

35　Ethiopia: The Ethiopian victory at Adwa in 1896 over an Italian invasion force was an event of pan-African significance and fueled emancipation efforts by black Christians on both sides of the Atlantic [= Photo F16]　176

36　South Africa: Mangena Maake Mokone (1851–1931), formerly a Methodist preacher, founded the 'Ethiopian Church' in 1892, one of the first and most successful independent African churches in southern Africa　177

37　Black transatlantic church fellowship (1896): Bishop Henry Turner (of the North American 'African Methodist Epicopal Church' [AME]) welcomes James Dwane (Pretoria) as representative of the "Ethiopian Church" of South Africa and its acceptance into the AME fellowship　177

38　Pandita Ramabai (Saravasti) (1858–1922), Indian social reformer, Christian education activist, and founder of the Pandita Rambai Mukti Mission (image on Indian postage stamp from 1989)　225

39　India: V. S. Azariah (1874–1945), evangelist, first Indian bishop in the Anglican Church, pioneer of the Asian ecumenical movement　225

40　Lilivathi Singh (1868–1909), publicist, college professor, and Christian education pioneer who worked primarily for the rights of Indian women to education　225

41　Japan: Kanzo Uchimura (1861–1930), author, Christian evangelist, and founder of the 'Non-Church Movement' (Mukyokai) in Meiji and Taisho period Japan　225

42　China: Tsinghua University in Beijing, founded in 1911 by U.S. missionaries, today one of China's leading universities [= Photo B16]　226

43　Korea: The Cheamri Massacre of 1919, committed by Japanese soldiers against Christian villagers [= Photo D15]　226

44 Group Photo of the 1938 World Missionary Conference in Tambaram, India (near Madras/ Chennai). This was the first ecumenical assembly with a majority of delegates from Asia, Africa and Latin America   227
45 Seoul (Korea): The 'Yoido Full Gospel Church' is considered Asia's first megachurch, with numerous services every Sunday and thousands of visitors each time (Photo taken in 2010) [see Photo D03–06]   286
46 Beijing (China): the 'Haidian Christian Church' in the university district (Photo taken in 2012) [= Photo B19]   286
47 Sri Lanka: Morning worship (2019) at the Theological College in Kandy-Pilimatalawa. The worship space is designed with elements of traditional Sinhalese culture [= Photo E20]   287
48 Colombo (Sri Lanka): Chapel in the Anglican Cathedral (built in 1973), example of cultural indigenization [= Photo E23]   287
49 "Wonderful Jesus" – street scene in Ghana (1997) [= Photo G03]   288
50 Ghana: Rural Pentecostal church in Nkawkaw (1997) [= Photo G07]   288
51 Albert Luthuli (1898–1967): South African Congregationalist lay preacher, delegate at the Tambaram World Missionary Conference in 1938, president of the African National Congress since 1952, Nobel Peace Prize laureate in 1960   289
52 The pope in Africa: John Paul II (1978-2005) was the first pope to visit numerous African countries (here: 1988 in Botswana)   289
53 Kwame Bediako (1945–2008), prominent West African theologian, emphasized the influence of indigenous cultures on African Christianity   289
54 Desmond Tutu (1931–2021): Fighter against apartheid, Nobel Peace Prize laureate (1984), Anglican Archbishop of Cape Town (South Africa)   289
55 Óscar Romero (1917–1980), Archbishop of San Salvador and prominent proponent of liberation theology, assassinated by the military during a mass on March 24, 1980   290
56 San Salvador: Crowds at the 1994 celebrations for the beatification of Óscar Romero, the archbishop of San Salvador who was assassinated in 1980   290
57 Porto Allegre (Brazil): The Crucified and the Junkie (street scene 2019 [= Photo K01]). The representation of human suffering in the suffering Christ is a constant motif in the history of Christianity in Latin America (cf. already the pictorial chronicle of Poma de Ayala around 1614 [Figure 10])   291

Maps

1 Portuguese on the way around Africa (15th/16th c.)   314
2 Stages of the Spanish Conquista in America (16th c.)   315
3 Portuguese colonial expansion (15th/16th c.)   316

FIGURES AND MAPS

4   Divided spheres of interest ('Inter Cetera' 1493, Tordesillas 1494)   317
5   Historical Kongo kingdom (15th–17th c.)   318
6   Dioceses in Spanish America (16th/17th c.)   319
7   Protestants in colonial Iberoamerica (16th–18th c.)   320
8   Transatlantic slave trade (16th–18th c.)   321
9   Transatlantic remigration to Africa and the founding of freetown (Sierra Leone) in 1792   322
10 West Africa in late 18th/ Mid 19th c.   322
11 Ceylon (Sri Lanka) under Dutch rule (1658–1796)   323
12 Japan in the 16th and 17th Centuries   324
13 The World around 1750   325
14 European colonial possessions around 1830   326
15 European colonial possessions around 1914   327
16 Africa around 1900   328
17 Ethiopia around 1900   329
18 South Africa around 1900   330
19 Global migration circa 1975   331

Technical Notes for Use

This book is distinguished by a number of special references to text and visual material.

1 Running References to the Parallel Documentary Sourcebook

It should be noted that this book can be used in parallel with the similarly themed documentary sourcebook on "A History of Christianity in Asia, Africa, and Latin America, 1450–1990" (Eerdmans: Grand Rapids, ^{R}2021), which was edited by the author and has been published in German, English and Spanish editions.[3] In the ongoing presentation of the textbook, the marking "Text" refers to the corresponding documents in the source volume. The numbering is identical in the English, German and Spanish editions of the source volume.

2 Illustrations and Maps

Illustrations ("Figures") can be found at the end of each part respectively epoch section, maps from page 314 onwards. References to them are inserted at the appropriate place in the text in each case.

3 Digital Appendix with Photos

Special attention should be paid to the digital appendix of this textbook and study book. It contains about 250 photos of the author on different places and topics of the history of Christianity in the global South. A list of the regions concerned can be found on p. 366. These pictures were taken during various international travels and encounters of the author in the years 1982–2019. They are particularly suitable for illustrating relevant academic courses and are licensed for this purpose under a Creative Commons license

---

3 English edition: Koschorke, K./ Ludwig, F./ Delgado, M. (^{R}2021) (Eds.), *A History of Christianity in Asia, Africa, and Latin America, 1450–1990. A Documentary Source Book* (Eerdmans: Grand Rapids, MI/Cambridge, U. K.). – German edition: Koschorke, K./ Ludwig, F./ Delgado, M. (^{5}2021) (Eds.), *Aussereuropäische Christentumsgeschichte (Asien, Afrika, Lateinamerika) 1450–1990* (Vandenhoeck & Ruprecht: Göttingen). –– Spanish edition: Koschorke, K./ Ludwig, F./ Delgado, M. (2012) (Eds.), *Historia del cristianismo en sus fuentes*. Asia, África, América Latina (1450–1990) (Editorial Trotta: Madrid).

(CC BY-NC-ND 4.0).⁴ These photos are referenced in the following chapters with the label "Photo." Accessible via the "Bonus Material" button at https://doi.org/10.6084/m9.figshare.27038062.

4 Bibliography in Two Parts

The general bibliography (Bibliography II, pp. 335–364) is preceded by a selection of standard works and surveys on the non-Western history of Christianity (Asia, Africa, Latin America) (Bibliography I, pp. 332–334). Their acquisition in libraries or provision in seminar apparatuses is particularly recommended.

5 Footnotes/ Endnotes

Footnotes respectively endnotes are generally omitted. They are only used (at the end of each chapter) to identify literal quotations (if not otherwise evident) or to verify individual data. Recommendations for Further Reading can be found at the end of each chapter.

---

4 Commercial use is only possible after consultation with the author. The author can be contacted by e-mail (klauskoschorke@sunrise.ch) or by mail via the publisher at brill.com.

In Place of an Introduction: "Christians and Spices" – or: the Multiplicity of Regional Centers in the History of World Christianity

In 1498, when Vasco da Gama, with the help of a Muslim pilot, "discovered" the direct sea route to India that Columbus had missed on the alternative Atlantic route six years earlier, he met two Arab merchants on the beach at Calicut (now Kozhikode). They greeted him in Genoese and Castilian with the friendly words, "What the hell are you looking for here?". To which he gave the famous reply, "Christians and spices". Access to the spice-producing regions of Asia was indeed the economic motive of Portuguese overseas expeditions, and connection to the fabled realm of the Christian priest-king John in the Far East the ideological one. And it was more by chance that Vasco da Gama had landed in that region of India (today's Kerala), where in fact there existed an ancient and centuries-old indigenous Christian community in the form of the St. Thomas Christians. The subsequent encounter between the Portuguese newcomers and the Indian St. Thomas Christians was, however, marked by a multitude of intercultural misunderstandings. For example, the first service of the Portuguese on Indian soil took place in a Hindu temple, which they mistook for a Christian church. They did wonder, according to an eyewitness, about the priests' peculiar costume (with cords and white ash painting) and the unfamiliar images of the saints – provided with "four or five arms" and large teeth that "stuck out an inch from their mouths" [Text 5a]. It was only in retrospect that the Iberians realized they had stumbled into a "pagan" temple. Later then (since 1500) they met the "real" St. Thomas Christians. The relationship between the Indians and the Portuguese turned out to be very changeable in the following time. St. Thomas Christians exist in modern India until today, although as a frequently divided community.

I have told this episode repeatedly to my Munich students. I think it is also suitable as an introduction to this textbook and study book. For it vividly demonstrates that there already existed Christian communities in Asia or Africa long before the first European missionaries or Western colonists appeared in these regions. Today, as never before in its history, Christianity has become a worldwide phenomenon, present in all six continents and in a multitude of different cultures. However, there is still a widespread belief that this global expansion has been primarily the result of earlier Western missionary activities in the countries of the Southern Hemisphere. Indisputably, the Western missionary movement since the 16th century has been an important factor in the process of this global expansion, both temporally and regionally. However, it has been only *one factor among others* – besides, for example, its spread through (voluntary or involuntary) migration, along trans-regional diaspora networks, in the context of different trade and cultural contacts, or as a result of the activities of local multipliers and indigenous Christian initiatives of different scope.

Elsewhere, Western missionaries encountered ancient Christianities already in existence – as in 16th-century India, where the St. Thomas Christians could look back on an uninterrupted history since the 4th (if not 3rd) century. Such encounters, however, were quickly overshadowed by conflicts. This was the case again in *India,* where the Catholic Portuguese – after initial friendship and mutual support – soon identified deficiencies in the traditional Christianity of their Indian co-religionists. Since the 1550s, they therefore intensified their efforts to Latinize the St. Thomas Christians. In 1598, these were then more or less forcibly integrated into the Portuguese colonial church, from which individual groups have only been able to free themselves again since 1653. Subsequently, the history of Christianity in the country remained characterized by the opposition of a St. Thomas Christian branch and successive Western missionary church undertakings.

A constellation comparable to that in India – indigenous Christians in conflict with the Portuguese newcomers – also developed in the 16th century in the Christian empire of *Ethiopia.* Here, too, in 1540, in the face of Muslim threats, the Iberians were initially welcomed as allies and helpers in need. Their priests were greeted as pastors to the small Portuguese community in the country. When, however, the Jesuit missionaries sought to subjugate the Ethiopian Orthodox Church to the control of Rome from 1555 onwards and rejected its time-honored traditions as "heretical", a rupture occurred. As a result, the Portuguese were finally expelled first from the imperial court and then from the country in 1632. In the period that followed, the country entered a prolonged phase of self-isolation from Christian Europe. At the same time, this self-isolation led to an increased emphasis on specifically ancient Ethiopian traditions, in distinction from Western traditions. From then on, the East African country was almost completely closed to European missionaries, both Catholics and later Protestants.

Ethiopia became important in a global perspective not only as a representative of a seemingly particularly 'archaic' type of African Christianity, which somehow has survived to the present day. In the 19th and early 20th centuries, Ethiopia became the reference point of the so-called Ethiopian movement. This was a widespread and 'modern' emancipation movement of black Christians on *both* sides of the Atlantic, in the slaveholding societies of the Caribbean and USA as well as in the British colonies of West and South Africa. Ethiopia – which had successfully expelled an Italian invading army in 1896 at the height of European imperialism – was now increasingly seen as a symbol both of ecclesiastical and political independence. It inspired diverse pan-African movements as well as transatlantic networks (both religious and political) of African and African-American Christians.

The history of Christianity in *Korea* is also particularly significant. It represents the example of a self-Christianization that is singular even in the Asian context. Its *Catholic* beginnings date back to 1784, when a group of Confucian scholars – who had come into contact with Jesuit tracts in Chinese in the completely isolated country – sent one of their own to Beijing to learn more about the "Western knowledge" respectively Christian teaching. The latter was baptized there, returned to Korea, convinced and baptized there his colleagues. Thus he became the founder of an underground church that subsequently grew steadily despite the rapid onset of persecution. All this happened fifty years before the first European priest (from France) entered the country.

The beginnings of *Protestant* presence on the peninsula a hundred years later (1884) also took place initially from the margins. Even before the arrival of the first U.S. missionaries, it was set in motion by Koreans who had encountered Christianity in the diaspora outside the country. As a result, the newly founded Protestant congregations experienced rapid expansion. Early on, they became the bearers of a national consciousness in times of Japanese oppression. In the catastrophic year of 1910 – when Korea was formally annexed by Japan – Korean evangelists were already active among their compatriots in the diaspora in Siberia, Manchuria, Japan, Hawaii, California, Mexico, and Cuba. The loss of their national sovereignty – as Korean historians interpret this process – was compensated for by Korean Christians, among other things, through extensive evangelistic enterprises. Korea thus developed early into an independent "center of world mission" – a development that continued at an accelerated pace after 1945. Korean activists became active in Northeast Asia as well as in Turkey or Peru and – after the collapse of the Soviet Union in 1990/91 – in numerous areas of the former Soviet empire.

These are all paradigms of a *"polycentric" approach to the history of World Christianity*. In this context, the term "World Christianity", which has been used frequently recently, refers to the diversity of denominational, cultural and contextual forms of the Christian movement in the different stages of its history. It is important to remember here that this polycentricity is not just a phenomenon of the recent past (since the end of the Second World War). Rather, it characterizes the history of Christianity from its very beginnings, and as early as in New Testament times. For example, the Christian community in Rome was not founded by Paul. Rather, it already existed when the "Apostle to the Gentiles" wrote his Epistle to the Christians of the capital city (in which he first felt compelled to introduce himself to them [Rom 1:1–7]). Its beginnings lie in the dark.

It probably arose as a result of the high fluctuation and transregional networks of the Jewish diaspora in the Roman Empire. – In India, as mentioned above, the first Christian communities can be traced back to the fourth, if not already the third century. They had formed in the context of the intensive trade between the Mediterranean region and the Indian subcontinent. Later, Indian Christians placed their beginnings under the authority of the apostles Thomas and Bartholomew. In times of the European Middle Ages, there existed in Asia (along with Rome and Byzantium) a third center of contemporary Christianity which far surpassed the Latin Christianity of Europe just in its geographical extension: the East Syrian (formerly often called "Nestorian") 'Church of the East', which at the height of its expansion in the 13th century stretched from Syria to eastern China and from Siberia to southern India and southern Asia. They had spread along the late antique trade routes through merchants and monks.

The 16th century was not only the era when Catholic pioneer missionaries (like Francis Xavier) set out for the far regions of Asia or (like Antonio de Montesinos) for the new worlds of the Americas. It was also the time when a growing number of already baptized Kongo Christians were taken by the Portuguese as slaves across the Atlantic to their (and others') American possessions. Some of them worked there as evangelists among their compatriots and fellow sufferers. Clear traces of this *transatlantic Kongo Christianity* can be traced in the Caribbean or Brazil until the early 19th century. And the beginnings of Protestant presence in West Africa at the turn of the 18th and 19th centuries are not only linked to the names of Anglican missionaries (from England) or Swabian Pietists (from the Basel Mission). They were preceded by an initiative of African-American returnees from Nova Scotia (on the other side of the Atlantic). Former slaves set out – with the Bible in hand as their charter of liberty – to what is now Sierra Leone to found there a "place of freedom". As a hub in the Christianization process of West Africa, the resulting "Freetown" (with its both English and African speaking indigenous elite) was to play a central role in the subsequent period.[2]

The insight into the polycentric character of the history of Christianity also has consequences for the concrete imparting of knowledge. In the following, the aim of this book is to convey basic information on the history of Christianity in Asia, Africa and Latin America since the end of the 15th century. This history is to be described in its different regional manifestations and global interdependencies. For reasons of space, a pragmatic selection of regions had to be made. North America, as indicated in the title, is not the subject of the

---

2 Individual references to the examples given here can be found in: Koschorke (2010), *Polycentric Structures*; Koschorke (2012), *Phasaes of Globalization*; Koschorke/Hermann (2014), *Polycentric Structures*.

presentation, apart from a few cross-references. This is despite the fact that its missionary history in the colonial phase until the end of the 18th century was in many respects parallel to that of Central and South America (as well as the Caribbean). Oceania, too, can be mentioned only occasionally in the present account, despite the immensely exciting (and partly autochthonous) history of its Christianization. In the Africa chapters, the focus is on sub-Saharan Africa, with repeated reference to West and South Africa in particular, as well as individual regions of East Africa. In the Asia sections, it is specific countries – India, China, Japan, and Korea – whose developments are addressed in each of the successive epochs. Other regions are mentioned rather selectively. The ancient Near Eastern churches are treated paradigmatically with a focus on India's St. Thomas Christianity (for Asia) and Orthodox Ethiopia (representing ancient African Christianity). Other ancient churches in the Near East – such as those of the Copts (Egypt), Maronites (Syria), Armenians or Georgians – are only occasionally discussed.

The division into five epochs (with caesurae around 1450/1500, 1600, 1800, 1890, 1945 and 1989/90) is guided by the endeavor to get a view of analogous and different developments as well as simultaneities and dissimilarities in the Christian history of different regions. The starting point of this book at the turn of the 15th to the 16th century results from the simple circumstance that only since this date one can speak of a developing Christian presence in all three continents mentioned in the title. The earlier – "pre-colonial" – history of the Christianities of Asia and Africa is repeatedly referred to. The volume ends with the 1990s, which in various respects also mark a caesura in the global history of Christianity. For the collapse of the Soviet empire and the end of the Cold War had profound effects not only on the situation of Christians and churches in Eastern Europe and in the former communist sphere of power. They also led to dramatic changes and system changes in Africa and Latin America, by which many churches in the region were directly affected – partly very actively and partly rather passively.

As mentioned in the preface, this structure of the textbook and study book is connected with the possibility of its use in different formats of academic teaching. This is especially true with regard to possible uses in various disciplinary contexts (such as church history, ecumenical and intercultural theology, history of religions, various regional and cultural studies, global history, etc.). Moreover, the volume seeks to contribute to a more integrated view of the history of Christianity in the non-Western world. Despite the upswing in historical 'World Christianity Studies' in recent years, especially in Anglophone academia, there are still too few comparative studies that relate the Christianity history of individual regions to each other. The question of both analogous and specifically different developments in comparable contexts continues to be asked too little. Studies on the history of individual regions or continental developments often follow heterogeneous research traditions or are conducted in mutual isolation.

To give a concrete example: At the turn of the 19th and 20th centuries, mission-independent black churches under African leadership were formed simultaneously, but initially quite independently of each other, in different regions of Africa. These so-called 'African Independent [or: Initiated] Churches' (AIC's) are now – in contrast to fifty years ago – firmly established in the historiography of Christianity on the continent. The research situation is different with regard to Asia, where at the same time around 1900 analogous constellations and conflicts developed between the emancipation efforts of indigenous Christian elites and the growing paternalism (and racism) of Western missionaries. The only difference is that these conflicts – so far only selectively analyzed – led to (mostly evolutionary) national church aspirations rather than to an immediate break with the mission churches (as in Africa). In both continents, however, in Christian Africa as in Christian Asia, the situation at the beginning of the 20th century cannot be described without proper consideration of these protest movements of native Christians. From these, in turn, especially in Asia, came considerable impulses for the early ecumenical movement in the churches of the West as well.

A further challenge will then be the task of integrating the multitude of regional developments into a new overarching perspective. This should also include the Christian history of the West (without, however, being dominated by it, as in traditional mission history). At the same time, it should be able to provide elements of a Christian culture of memory that can increasingly be experienced as a common heritage.

PART 1

1450–1600

∴

CHAPTER 1

The Christian World around 1500

1.1 Christian Europe around 1500

Around 1500, the majority of the world's Christian population lived in Europe. *At that time* (!), the Christian world consisted primarily of what has been called the "Christian Occident", the Europe on the eve of the Reformation, a firmly established system of states, usually headed by princes. These usually derived their legitimacy from dynastic heredity and ecclesiastical sanction. At the center of this Europe was the "Holy Roman Empire of the German Nation," as it was called for the first time in an official document in 1486, with its German, Dutch, Bohemian and northern Italian core countries. In its self-understanding, it was universal, claiming succession to the ancient Roman Empire. At its head was the emperor, elected by the electors and crowned by the pope. This emperor was a Habsburg monarch around 1500: Maximilian I (1493–1519), as was his successor, who as Spanish king was called Charles I and as German emperor (1519–1556) bore the name of Charles V. Charles V was also the person with whose name the two main events of 16th century church history would later be associated: the rise of the Reformation movement and the resulting confessional division of Western Christendom on the one hand, and its worldwide expansion on the other. For as a Spanish monarch, Charles would command possessions in Europe, North Africa and America (and later in Southeast Asia) "where the sun never sets." As emperor, however, he was at the same time the person before whom Luther stood at the Diet of Worms in 1521 and who, even more than the changing Renaissance popes in Rome, was to become the decisive opponent of the Reformation movement. – Outside the empire (and next to the Habsburg hereditary lands) stood the other states of the European state system, some – like France – with a centralized monarchy, others – like Tudor England or the Polish elective monarchy – with extensive rights of participation of nobility and estates. The pope, as "pater communis christianitatis," tried in changing constellations to assert his spiritual authority as a normative force vis-à-vis the community of states. His entanglement in the territorial disputes over the Papal States and in the political power game proved to be an obstacle. – In Scandinavian northern Europe, large areas are still untouched by Christianity. In the east, the Muscovite Empire is an Orthodox power center that is expanding in an easterly direction. The Iberian powers of Portugal and Spain in the west of the continent were in charge of Europe's overseas expansion that began in the 15th century.

1.2 The Islamic World

The increasing limitation of the Christian world to Europe – often lamented by churchmen after the fall of Constantinople in 1453 – was anything but self-evident. At the beginning of antiquity, the Christian world had encompassed the entire Mediterranean region. At the same time, its focal points lay precisely in the south or east of the Mediterranean world. This changed with the rise of Islam, which overran the Christian core regions of Egypt, North Africa, Syro-Palestine and parts of Asia Minor as early as the 7th century and also established itself on the Iberian peninsula in the 8th century. Before that, it had already reached Persia in the east, from where it gradually spread to Central and South Asia along maritime and land-based trade routes over the centuries. The expansion of Islam did not lead to the immediate disappearance of the Christian churches of the Orient, but it resulted in their growing marginalization. They survived for the most part, but as a shrinking minority with reduced legal status. At the same time, they were exposed to growing pressure to assimilate. Outside Islamic lands, they were largely cut off from connection with other centers of contemporary Christianity. This affected, for example, the Christian churches in India, in Central Asia, and (to a lesser extent) in Ethiopia. In the 15th century, the Islamic world formed, as it were, a kind of barricade that extended from present-day Mauritania through Syria and Persia to India and to individual parts of the Indonesian archipelago, cutting off Christian Europe from the rest of the then known world. In the words of Pope Pius II (c. 1460), Europe was now the last homeland left to Christendom ("Europa id est patria"). A hypothetical visitor from Mars – as the missionary historian Stephen Neill once remarked – would certainly have given the Prophet's religion the greater chance of a future on Earth at that time.

Admittedly, a change in trend had been apparent for some time. On the Iberian Peninsula, the *Reconquista* (re-conquest) had been underway for some time, leading to the expulsion of the last "Moors" from Spanish soil with the fall of Granada in 1492. 1492 was also the year of the "discovery" of America by Christopher Columbus. The expulsion of the Muslims from Western Europe and the beginning of Europe's overseas expansion thus are simultaneous processes. However, it cannot be said that Islam or Islamic powers in general were in retreat in Europe. The opposite was the case. In 1453 Constantinople had fallen. Thus the Christian Byzantine Empire – which had withstood the Muslim onslaught for centuries – had come to an end. But it did not stop there. The Turkish Ottomans (originally just one among numerous particular princely houses of Anatolia) established themselves as the strongest power in the Islamic world. In 1516/17 they conquered Syria and Egypt (1517 fall of Jerusalem) and subjugated North Africa to their suzerainty before advancing westward again under Suleyman I (1520–1566). They overran the Balkans, conquered Hungary, and stood before Vienna for the first time in 1529. This is the "Turkish danger" that was to play such an important role in the controversies of the Reformation period and which led Martin Luther, for example, to make statements about how one should behave as a Christian if one fell into the hands of the "infidels" – namely the Turks. At the same time as the European model of Christianity began to be exported to the newly discovered regions of America, Africa and Asia, Christian Europe in the 16th century was still involved in a defensive struggle against a non-Christian religion – Islam. At the same time, however, this conflict also gave rise to a variety of intercultural relationships in the 16th century. Incidentally, Martin Luther was one of the proponents of a Latin translation of the Koran.

1.3 Knowledge of Non-European Cultures, Perceptions of Europe from Outside

In the course of the late 15th and 16th centuries, European explorers encountered numerous countries and cultures whose existence had previously been completely unknown in the West. But even where direct relations had existed earlier – as between the Roman Empire and India – knowledge of the world beyond Europe was fragmentary and largely overlaid with legends. To an astonishing extent, the geographical ideas of early modern Europe were still influenced by ancient authors. Thus, the writings of Claudius Ptolemy, who in the 2nd century A.D. had quasi-canonically summarized the geographical knowledge of antiquity, were still considered an authority in the 15th century. At the same time, however, the Alexander novel of late antiquity also enjoyed great popularity, with its fantastic descriptions of India as a world of miracles and a kind of land of milk and honey. It was translated into numerous languages, existed – later also in print – in various vernacular versions, and was one of the most widely read books in Europe in the Middle Ages, along with the Bible.

The *Crusades* stimulated renewed interest in the East. Travel accounts such as those of the Venetian Marco Polo – who in 1298, while in Genoese custody, dictated his experiences in China and other Asian countries to a fellow prisoner – met with an ambivalent fate. On the one hand, contemporaries did not believe him. On the other hand, his book became a literary success, admittedly primarily as entertainment reading in the manner of invented travelogues. But geographers and cartographers also evaluated his detailed descriptions. Christopher Columbus later used the book as a kind of travel guide, in his vain search for a direct sea route to "India". In the 13th and early 14th centuries, there was a proliferation of journeys to Asia by Franciscan monks such as William of Rubruck (who in 1253/54 reached the court of the Great Khan Möngke Khan in Mongolian Karakorum), John of Montecorvino (who in 1294 reached Khanbalik, today's Beijing), and Father Odorico da Pordenone, who visited northern China between 1322 and 1328. Admittedly, their reports became available only to a limited audience. With the end of Mongol rule in China in 1368, this intermediate phase of direct contacts with the Middle Kingdom came to an end.

The figure of the legendary priest-king John gained enormous importance in the imagination of late medieval Europe. He was associated with the idea of a rich Christian ruler in the Far East, from whom one hoped for support against the Islamic arch-enemy. This legend was first mentioned in the time of the Crusades around 1145 by the historian Otto von Freising. In 1177, under Pope Alexander III, the Roman Curia even attempted to contact the mythical ruler in the Far East. In the following period, this idea continued to waft through Christian Europe. In particular, it inspired the voyages of discovery by the Portuguese in the 15th century, who sought to track him down in "India" – which was assumed to be in Ethiopia, in southern Africa or finally on the Indian subcontinent. Even Vasco da Gama, who set foot on Indian soil for the first time in 1498 in the region of present-day Kerala, initially believed that he had arrived there in the realm of the priest-king.

The idea of the spherical shape of the earth was widespread among the humanist educated of the late 15th century. It was the decisive prerequisite for the enterprise of Columbus, who for the first time sought to reach the Asian empires once described by Marco Polo not on the way around Africa, but on the alternative Atlantic route. In 1492 or 1493, Martin Behaim of Nuremberg (in Germany) made the oldest surviving terrestrial globe showing the world known in Europe at the time. This included Europe itself, a curiously flattened Africa, and an Asia that was also greatly shortened. Remarkably, the America "discovered" shortly before by Columbus was still missing on this globe, which the Genoese himself considered to be the shores of East Asia until the end of his life. Other contemporaries, such as the Florentine Amerigo Vespucci, however, quickly realized that Columbus had indeed reached a continent previously unknown in Europe. This "new world" was then titled "America" for the first time on the world map produced by the German cartographer Martin Waldseemüller in 1507.

The perception of Europe in non-European cultures also reflected in many cases earlier relationships or selective encounters at the time of the Crusades. The 'Kebra Nagast', for example – the Ethiopian national epic from the 13th century – knows of two sons of King Solomon and the Queen of Sheba (according to 1 Kings 10; 2 Chr 9). One of them (Menelek) was portrayed as the progenitor of the "Solomonic" dynasty that ruled Ethiopia since the 13th century, while the younger one – and thus *subordinate* – became the ancestor of the Byzantine rulers in *'Rum'*.[1] Within the framework of a biblically narrative, the claim of the African rulers to supremacy over the Christian brother nations of the West was thus expressed.

1.4 Christians and Churches in Africa and Asia

Despite the expanding Ottoman Empire, ties between Christian Europe and the Oriental churches were by no means completely severed. By 1500, for example, Rome was home to a sizeable Ethiopian diaspora. Martin Luther, for example, was well aware that there were Christians also "in Persia, India, and throughout the Orient."[2] They were important to him as representatives of a Christianity that was not under the rule of the pope. In 1534, there was even a visit and theological exchange between an Ethiopian monk and the reformers in Wittenberg. Three regions are to be considered here: the Near East, northern Africa and South Asia.

From 1517/18 onward, the various churches of the southern Mediterranean and neighboring areas increasingly came under Turkish rule. While in the Ottoman possessions in the Balkans around 1520 more than 80% of the population were still Christians, *Anatolia* – with the exception of the region around Trabzon – was already majority Islamized around this time. In *Constantinople,* the ecumenical patriarch resided again since 1466 as the head of the remaining Greek Orthodox Christians. In the Ottoman Empire, these Christians lived as second–class citizens and were exposed to the ups and downs of relative tolerance and fanatical persecution. The same was true for the members of the Oriental churches in *Syria, Lebanon and Palestine* (such as the so-called Jacobites [Syriac Orthodox], Maronites, etc.), who had separated from the Byzantine imperial church in the dogmatic controversies of the 6th and 7th centuries. They had, of course, already been under Islamic rule for many centuries. The conquests of the Ottomans since the 15th century brought a change from Arab to Turkish sovereignty. The ancient Armenian Church was particularly hard hit, as its homeland was reduced to rubble by the advancing Ottomans. However, the Armenians were also active in long-distance trade outside their areas of origin at an early stage. There were colonies of Christian Armenians in numerous regions of Asia, an early stage of the later developing global Armenian diaspora. Georgia, which had also been Christian since the 4th century, had not yet recovered from Timur Lenk's raids at the end of the 14th century and disintegrated into several dominions.

Mesopotamia was the center of the East Syrian – formerly often called "Nestorian" – 'Church of the East'. Here resided its head, the catholicos-patriarch, and from here bishops were sent to distant church provinces for a long time. At the height of its expansion in the 13th and 14th centuries, the Church of the East stretched from eastern Syria to eastern China and from Siberia to southern India. It thus encompassed an ecclesiastical territory that, just in terms of its geographical extent, was larger than that of contemporary Western Christianity. In recent times, numerous new evidences of its astonishingly wide spread in China, Central, Western and Southern Asia have been discovered. As late as 1504, a delegation of Indian clerics returned to India from the official residence of the East Syrian Catholicos in Mesopotamia [Text 1b]. Subsequently, the former "world church" shrank to a regional church in Kurdistan (in the border region of present-day Turkey/Iraq). Internal divisions further weakened the 'Church of the East'.

In early church times, *North Africa* was also one of the core countries of Christianity. Prominent church fathers and theologians such as Clement of Alexandria, Origen, Cyprian of Carthage and Augustine of Hippo came from there. By 1500, nothing remained of this splendor in Tunisia and Algeria – former centers of the Latin-speaking African church. The last evidence of Christian presence in these regions dates from the 12th century. The situation was quite different in *Egypt*, where the Christian community had become the bearer of an Egyptian (this is "Coptic") self–confidence at an early stage. Despite the enormous losses caused by the long-lasting Islamic rule, the Coptic church was still vital and numerous in the 13th century. In the 16th century it experienced a low point. However, it has maintained its own language and traditions to this day and is present primarily in Upper Egypt (as well as in the global ecumenical movement). – In contrast, by 1500, virtually nothing remained of the glory days of early Christianity in Nubia – south of Egypt, in what is now *Sudan*. Around 1540, the Portuguese explorer Francisco Alvarez reported on a visitor to Nubia who found 150 old churches there. However: "The inhabitants are neither Christians, Muslims nor Jews, but live in the opinion that they would like to be Christians" [Text 1n].

Christian *Ethiopia* found itself in a precarious situation around 1500. Proud of its Christian past – which historically dates back to the 4th century and in Ethiopian self-perception even goes back to the Old Testament King

Solomon – this isolated mountainous country also faced growing Muslim threats. This led to the renewal of earlier contacts with Rome and Portugal. In Jerusalem and other Christian pilgrimage sites, Ethiopian monks were still part of the street scene in the 16th century. Until the 20th century, Ethiopians obtained their metropolitans from Egypt.

In *southern Asia*, too, there were still clear signs of an earlier Christian presence around 1500. For example, the Portuguese – who in 1498 under Vasco da Gama found the sea route to India that Columbus had sought in vain on the alternative western route – encountered St. Thomas Christian communities in *southern India* that had existed continuously in the region for more than 1000 years [Texts 4–7]. They belonged to the network of the (formerly so-called "Nestorian") East Syrian 'Church of the East' and drew their bishops from Mesopotamia. In other regions of South Asia, however, the Christian communities attested there earlier had died out by 1500 – for example, in Sri Lanka (Ceylon), for which both archaeological and literary sources attest an East Syrian Nestorian presence between the 6th and 10th centuries [see Photo A15/16]. – In *Central Asia*, too, only a few remnants of the once flourishing East Syrian communities along the various routes of the Silk Road had survived by 1500. They had become victims of, among other things, the devastating persecutions under Timur Lenk (1336–1405), who put an end to Christian and Jewish presence in his domain. As late as 1298, Marco Polo had given the percentage of Christians in the city population of Samarkand, Timur Lenk's capital in present-day Uzbekistan, as about 10%. – In 16th-century *China*, too, there existed only a few traces of the earlier, quite considerable Christian presence in the Middle Kingdom. Christianity had already found its way there in 635 at the latest, as the famous so-called "Nestorian Stele" of Xian, erected in 781, reports [see Photo A01–04]. It experienced a second peak under the Mongol emperors of the Yuan dynasty in the 13th and early 14th centuries. With the change to the Ming dynasty in 1368, however, the Christian–friendly policy of the Chinese emperors came to an end. The Jesuit Matteo Ricci found Jewish families around 1605, but no remains of ancient Chinese Christianity [Text 3].

On the other hand, European travelers at the beginning of the 16th century still encountered remnants of this early pre-Portuguese era of Asian Christianity in many places. The Italian Ludovico di Varthema, for example, traveled through Egypt, Persia and India between 1503 and 1507. Through Varthema, more precise knowledge of the trade routes of the Indian Ocean reached Europe. At the same time, he repeatedly reported about scattered Christians ("Nestorians", Armenians) in various regions of South Asia such as India, Burma [Myanmar] and Thailand at the beginning of the 16th century [Text 2].

Notes to Chapter 1

1. Budge (1932), *Queen of Sheba*, LXVII.16.42 (= *Kebra Nagast* Chapter 19 + 20 + 34).
2. Martin Luther (Weimarer Ausgabe 2,236,14–17).

Further Reading for Chapter 1

1.1–3 (*Global Situation of Christianity around 1500*)

Kaufmann (2017), *Latin-European Christianity*, 149–204; Ward (2017), *Christianity in Africa*, 129–147; Hastings (1994), *Church in Africa*, 46–70; Moffett (1991), *Christianity in Asia* I, 470–509; Moffett (2005), *Christianity in Asia* II, 3–16; Baum/ Winkler (2003), *Church of the East*, 84–134; Salvadore (2017), *Ethiopian-European Relations*, 19–152; Böll (1998), *Von der Freundschaft zur Feindschaft*, 43–58; Armanios, (2011), *Coptic Christianity;* Gumilev (1987), *Kingdom of Prester John;* Ducellier (1995), *Frühzeit der türkischen Herrschaft*, 6–49; Bryner (2004), *Orthodoxe Kirche*, 53 ff.; Kellermann (2001), *Islam;* Schilling (2017), *1517;* Ludwig (2019), *Reformation in the Context of World Christianity;* Irvin (017), *Reformation and World Christianity;* Schilling/ Seidel Menchi (2017), *Reformation in a Context of Global History*. 8

1.4 (*Oriental Churches before 1500*)

Jenkins (2008), *Lost History;* Moffett (1991), *Christianity in Asia* I, passim; Gillman/ Klimkeit (1999), *Christians in Asia before 1500;* Neill (1984), *Christianity in India* I, 1–110; Standaert, (2001), *Christianity in China;* Baum/ Winkler (2003), *Church of the East;* Andrade (2018), *Journey of Christianity;* Hastings (1994), *Church in Africa*, 46–70; Sundkler/ Steed (2000), *Church in Africa*, 1–41; Kalu (2005), *African Christianity*, 1–139; Hage (2007), *Orientalisches Christentum*, 1–68 and passim; Lange/ Pinggéra (2010), *Altorientalische Kirchen;* Angold (2006), *Eastern Christianity;* Baumer (2005), *Seidenstrasse* (with many pictures); Bays (2012), *New History*, 1–16 (on China); Iliffe (^{3}2017). *Africans*, 58–64; Salvadore (2017), *Ethiopian European Relations;* Krebs (2021), *Medieval Ethiopian Kingship;* Paulau/ Tamcke (2022), *Ethiopian Orthodox Christianity*, 2–80.

CHAPTER 2

The Iberian Expansion of the 15th/16th Centuries

2.1 The Portuguese on Their Way around Africa (1415ff)

Overseas mission was almost exclusively a Catholic enterprise in the 16th century until well into the 18th century. One of the reasons was geography. Initially, the Iberian powers – Portugal and Spain (created in 1479 by uniting the crowns of Castile [Ferdinand] and Aragon [Isabella]) – were the main sponsors of expansion. In the confessional conflicts of the 16th century, they were firmly on the side of the Roman Catholic Church led by the Pope. The Reformation movement in the center of Europe, on the other hand, initially had to fight simply for its survival. Moreover, by abolishing the monastic orders, it had deprived itself of a crucial missionary instrument. – Exposed by its position, the first advances took place from the Iberian Peninsula in order to bypass the Islamic barricade and to find a sea route to "India". One goal – two paths: Portugal felt its way further and further along the African coast. Only when the Portuguese lead had become unassailable did the "Catholic Kings" of Spain agree to the project of the Genoese adventurer Columbus to sail to Asia along the alternative western Atlantic route. Columbus was seemingly successful, and although he did not discover "India" or East Asia in 1492 (as he believed to the end of his life), he reached a new continent. Six years later, a Portuguese fleet under Vasco da Gama succeeded in sailing around Africa and reaching India by sea for the first time in 1498 [see Map 1].

For a long time, the Portuguese were ahead in this race. The beginning of their involvement in Africa is generally dated to 1415, when they conquered Ceuta, their first possession on North African soil. In the following period, they advanced further and further south along the African coast and the offshore islands (Madeira, Cape Verde) in regular expeditions until they reached Sierra Leone around 1460, the Congo River around 1482, Walvis Bay (in present-day Namibia) in 1485 and the southern tip of the continent in 1487/88. At Christmas 1487, they arrived in the region that has since been called Natal. However, South Africa was only of interest to the Portuguese as a transit point to India. In the East African coastal cities, which had become rich through trade with India, they encountered strong Arab competition. At the same time, however, they encountered Indian Thomas Christians for the first time in the port city of Malindi (in present-day Kenya) and Mozambique [cf. Text 115], who had arrived there as sailors.

© KLAUS KOSCHORKE, 2025 | DOI:10.1163/9789004699830_003
This is an open access chapter distributed under the terms of the CC BY-NC-ND 4.0 license.

What made this rapid advance possible? One important prerequisite was the enormous technological advances in shipbuilding and navigation. The Portuguese further developed caravels and the astrolabe, acquired knowledge of Atlantic currents and changing winds, and used magnetic compasses, nautical charts, and log boards. Seafarers from other nations also took part in the regular expeditions, but only within the framework of the monopoly that the Portuguese had had confirmed by the Pope in various bulls since the 1450s which they strictly enforced. Why it was the comparatively small and poor Portugal that succeeded in opening up the African coasts and eventually establishing an Asian maritime empire, and not one of its larger and more populous European neighbors (such as Spain or France), is a question much discussed in research. The same applies to the broader question of why, finally, as a result of these activities, Europe "discovered" Asia and not, conversely, China, for example, Europe. After all, Chinese naval ventures had already reached the entrance to the Persian Gulf and the Red Sea as well as the East African coast in the early 15th century. After that, however, the Middle Kingdom ended its western expeditions.

The Portuguese explorers along the African coast were driven by a variety of motives, including their crusading mentality, the fight against Muslim rivals and the search for the legendary priest-king John. Among the economic incentives, the trade in gold, slaves, pepper and ivory was the main lure. For a long time, sections of the West African coast were named after these "goods" exported to Europe by the Portuguese: the Pepper Coast in Liberia, the Ivory Coast in the state still so named today, the Gold Coast in current Ghana, and the Slave Coast in Togo, Dahomey and Nigeria. The contacts of the Portuguese with the African population varied greatly. They ranged from so-called "silent trade" (without direct encounters in the exchange of goods) to cooperation with local rulers to violent conquest and enslavement. But there were also many encounters in what was still, as it were, a pre-colonial contact zone, from which – as in the Kongo Kingdom – independent African Christianity variants later developed [see chapter 6.2].

2.2 Spain, Columbus and the "Discovery" of the "New World" (1492)

On the Spanish side, it was the Genoese navigator Christopher Columbus who set out from the port of Palos on August 3, 1492, with a flotilla of three ships to discover and acquire "certain islands and countries" in the Atlantic Ocean on behalf of the Castilian crown – for the "spread of the right faith as well as for our advantage and benefit." Such were the provisions of the "Letter of

Protection" issued to him by the Catholic Majesties Ferdinand and Isabella on April 17, 1492. His project of crossing the Atlantic was by no means uncontroversial. Experts at court had already pointed out in advance the – in the end "fruitful" – geographical errors of Columbus, who, like leading contemporary cartographers, had miscalculated the circumference of the earth (and thus the distance to the shores of East Asia).

After a crossing of a good ten weeks, the small fleet reached the island of Guanahani in the Bahama group on October 12, 1492, which Columbus named San Salvador. Further stops were the coasts of Haiti and Cuba before the Genoese, appointed "Admiral of the Indian Seas" and Viceroy of the newly discovered lands, set off on his return journey on January 16, 1493. He received a triumphant reception in Spain. As early as September 25, 1493, he set out on his second voyage with a large fleet of 17 ships and a crew of about 1,400 men, which lasted until June 1496. In Santo Domingo (today the capital of the Dominican Republic), the oldest European city still existing in the New World was founded in 1498. On his third (1498–1500) and fourth (1502–1504) expeditions, his caravels touched the coasts of South and Central America for the first time at the level of present-day Venezuela and between Honduras and Panama. Columbus considered them to be a previously unknown part of East Asia. Fittingly, he was given a letter for Vasco da Gama, who had just sailed around the Cape of Good Hope to India for the second time in 1502. In addition to Columbus, the Spanish crown soon authorized other – privately financed – expeditions. This accelerated the influx of Castilian colonists and adventurers to the Caribbean [see Map 2].

Contact with the indigenous population was initially peaceful. Columbus' description of the first meeting on the island of Guanani resembles a description of paradisiacal conditions. The Indians were peaceful and knew no weapons. "They walk naked, just as God created them. Both men and women ... have beautifully formed bodies and winsome features." "They gave and took everything heartily".[1] "Idolatry," was an opinion repeatedly expressed by Columbus, was not to be found among the natives. Therefore, he was convinced that they could easily be won over to Christianity, and he soon proposed to the crown the sending of "pious and devout men" who "knew their language" in order to be able to "convert such great peoples and incorporate them into the bosom of the Church" [entries in the ship's log of Oct. 14 and Nov. 6, 1492; cf. text 218]. This peaceful idyll, however, did not last long. As early as 1493, there were acts of violent resistance by the indigenous people against the booty-hungry conquistadors, which intensified in the following period. At least rudimentary communication with the indigenous population took place, among other things, through the capture of individual Indians, who then had to learn "our [Castilian] language". Later, it was repeatedly the American Indian companions of Spanish adventurers or stranded settlers who acted as interpreters. Famous is the story of Malinche, called Doña Marina by the Spaniards. She was a Mayan slave and became mistress of the conqueror of Mexico Hernán Cortés, who served him as translator during the negotiations with the Aztec ruler Moctezuma in 1519 [see Photo M07].

Columbus' travelogues aroused enormous interest in Europe after his return. His letter to the 'Catholic Kings' of Spain of 1493 appeared in no fewer than 17 different editions and translations between 1493 and 1497 thanks to the new printing technology. The news from the New World was also intensively discussed in German humanist circles, admittedly without initially recognizing its implications. The six Indian companions that Columbus brought with him from his first expedition to Spain in 1493 also caused a great stir among the European public.

2.3 Divided Spheres of Interest ('Inter Cetera' 1493, Tordesillas 1494)

Immediately after Columbus returned from his first voyage of discovery in 1493, the Spanish and Portuguese crowns negotiated the demarcation of their spheres of interest. Spain had the pope confirm its ownership rights for its overseas discoveries, both present and future. This procedure followed an established tradition that ultimately goes back to the medieval idea of the Pope's world dominion, who, as the supreme feudal lord, conferred political rights of dominion on Christian princes – even if the Spanish and Portuguese crowns saw themselves as anything but feudal recipients of the Pope. On May 4, 1493, Pope Alexander VI issued the *bull 'Inter Cetera'* addressed to the Spanish royal couple Ferdinand and Isabella, the core sentences of which read:

> In order that you may enter upon so great an undertaking [sc. as that of Columbus] with greater readiness and boldness … *We hereby give, grant and confer* – … from the fullness of Our apostolic authority, which has been conferred upon Us by Almighty God … and by virtue of the Vicarship of Jesus Christ on earth, to you and to your heirs and successors *all islands and mainlands found or to be found, discovered or to be discovered*, together with all dominions, cities, camps, places and villages and all rights … in so far as these islands and mainlands are situated west or south of a line to be drawn from the Arctic to the Antarctic pole at a distance of 100 miles west and south of one of the islands commonly known by the names of Azores and Cap Verden … Moreover, We charge

you in your holy obedience that you appoint ... in the said mainlands and islands worthy, God-fearing, trained, skillful, and experienced men, that they may instruct the aforesaid inhabitants in the Catholic faith and educate them to good morals. [Text 223a]

This document had an enormous impact and marked out essential stages of the following developments. First of all, the following points are important:

a. *Division of the Atlantic world* into a Castilian and Portuguese territory. The Bull of 1493 established a *demarcation line* (extending from the North Pole to the South Pole), which was specified and moved westward a year later in the State Treaty of *Tordesillas in 1494*. It now ran 370 nautical miles (1170 km) west of the Cape Verde Islands. This enabled the Portuguese later to claim dominion over Brazil. The territories west of this line, as well as south of a previously established north-south boundary, included effectively all of Central and South America (apart from Brazil) and were assigned to the Spanish Crown. The territories east of this line (in Africa, Asia as well as Brazil) were henceforth attributed to the Portuguese dominion. In 1529, the Treaty of Saragossa also drew a line of separation on the other side of the globe, barely 300 miles east of the Moluccas (with the result that the Philippines became a Spanish colony). Thus the boundaries between Portuguese and Spanish spheres of interest in Asia were also demarcated [see Map 4]. – Other European countries (France, England, later also the Netherlands) were not involved in this division of the world among the Iberian powers and saw little reason to recognize it. However, this had concrete consequences only later.

b. *Transfer of power versus missionary mandate.* In the colonial ethical debates that followed, the legitimacy of the Pope's transfer of political power over non-Christian peoples was by no means undisputed [see chapter 4.2]. It was justified in the bull Inter Cetera with the missionary mandate to the Catholic majesties: These had to ensure that the non-Christian inhabitants of the newly discovered territories were "instructed in the Catholic faith" and that a corresponding ecclesiastical infrastructure was established. This subsequently developed into the royal missionary patronage (*patronato real* – Spanish, *padroado real* – Portuguese). The emerging colonial churches overseas were placed under the responsibility, but at the same time under the control, of the respective crown. The Catholic rulers thus not only held supreme political power in their colonies, but also acted as heads of the colonial church. In 1501, the pope granted the Spanish crown the church tithe and, in 1508, the right of presentation for ecclesiastical offices in all existing or newly established bishoprics in the mission territories. The colonial Indian Council became the supreme arbitration body in spiritual matters as well. State power was increasingly permitted to intervene directly in church matters.

c. The vigorous exploitation of patronage rights by the respective crowns led to the development of a colonial state ecclesiasticism in both Spanish America and Portuguese Asia, which increasingly *blocked even papal attempts at intervention*. In 1538, Emperor Charles V decreed a sovereign placet for papal decrees that could be published only after prior permission in his American possessions. This placet was also initially denied to Pope Paul III's remarkable bull 'Sublimis Deus' – in which he had condemned the enslavement of the indigenous peoples of the Americas in 1537 [Text 226]. Secret copies of the bull were confiscated. In Portuguese Asia, too, the colonial authorities jealously guarded their monopoly position. They also suppressed missionary activities not authorized by them – even as Portuguese influence in the region increasingly waned and the crown was less and less able (and willing) to fulfill its evangelizing obligations. And when in 1622 the Roman Curia, in the form of the Propaganda Fidei, set up its own mission headquarters to send non-Portuguese mission personnel to Asia, this led to protracted disputes with the Portuguese crown, often referred to as the Propaganda-Padroado conflict which lasted into the 19th century. In India, they even escalated into a formal schism at the end of the 19th century [cf. chap. 17.3].

d. To the astonished indigenous Americans encountered by the Spanish conquistadors in the New World, specially brought notaries announced the news of their new Spanish overlords in a language incomprehensible to them. The Indians were then presented with the alternative: Submission or war. This was done in a formalized summons, the so-called *'Requerimiento'* [Text 225a; cf. chapter 4.2], which had been in effect since 1513. The Portuguese, too, were by no means squeamish in their ventures in Africa and Asia. A characteristic difference between the Spanish and Portuguese overseas empires, however, was in the different forms of colonial rule. The Spanish very soon moved to territorial rule in the Americas, seeking to colonize entire swaths of land. The Portuguese strategy, on the other hand, has often been described as naval base colonialism. They were content – if only because of their limited human resources – with a network of bases along the African and especially Asian coasts and were primarily interested in controlling maritime trade routes [see Map 3]. Extensive territorial rule occurred only in individual regions.

2.4 Encounters: Vasco da Gama and the Indian St. Thomas Christians (1498ff)

On May 20, 1498, Vasco da Gama and his fleet became the first Europeans to reach by sea the destination that Columbus had missed on the alternative Atlantic route: India. He did so, as discussed at the outset [page XVIII], in search of "Christians and spices" [Text 4]. What followed was, at first, a series of cross-cultural misunderstandings. For example, the first service of the Portuguese on Indian soil took place in a Hindu temple. Despite the peculiar "images of saints" – with "four to five arms" and teeth that "protruded far from the mouth" – the Iberians initially mistook it for a Christian church [Text 5a]. The encounter with the – "real" – St. Thomas Christians did not occur until the following expeditions to India by the Portuguese (in 1500 under Cabral and again in 1502 under Vasco da Gama) [Text 5c]. Initially, cordial relations prevailed between the Indian Christians and the Portuguese, "our Christian brethren in truth," as a St. Thomas Christian source from 1504 referred to the newcomers [Text 1b]. For both sides knew themselves to be dependent on each other – the Iberians, unfamiliar with the country, on the help of local co-religionists, and the St. Thomas Christians, beset by Hindu princes and Muslim rivals, on support from the "Franks" from the far West. Later, with a more entrenched Portuguese presence on the subcontinent, the relationship was to cool rapidly.

The St. Thomas Christians themselves traced their beginnings back to the apostle Thomas. Historically, there is evidence of a continuous Christian presence in India at least since the 3rd, if not the 2nd century – originated in the context of late antique trade relations between the Mediterranean and the Indian subcontinent. Later, as mentioned, the Indians became part of the all-Asian network of the East Syrian (so-called "Nestorian") 'Church of the East'. This had separated from the Byzantine imperial church in the West in the 5th century and gradually spread along continental as well as maritime trade routes to Central Asia, China, and South Asia. The liturgical language of the St. Thomas Christians was Syriac (as in the other East Syrian ecclesiastical provinces). Their areas of settlement were primarily (but not exclusively) in the region of present-day Kerala. There, in the context of South Indian caste society, they occupied an elevated position – as merchants, in agriculture (with a monopoly in pepper cultivation), and as warriors in the service of local rulers. In some cases, they enjoyed a considerable degree of autonomy. During the European Middle Ages, individual travelers such as Marco Polo, the Franciscan John of Montecorvino or Nicolò de' Conti [Text 1a] established occasional contacts with Latin Christianity.

The St. Thomas Christians obtained their bishops from "Babylon", the seat of their head (the Catholicos-Patriarch) in Mesopotamia. The latter resided around 1500 in a monastery near Alqosh north of Mosul (northern Iraq). The letter of 1504 already mentioned above is also addressed to the patriarch, in which the newly ordained Syrian bishops returning from Mesopotamia report on the current situation in India. "There are here about thirty thousand families of Christians," we learn, "our co-religionists ... They have begun to build new churches and are prosperous in every respect." Mention is made of 20 towns near Calicut that are "home to Christians and churches." Initial contacts with the Portuguese in the Indian city of Cannanore were gratifying. "We [the bishops] went to them and told them that we were Christians and told them our story. They were pleased with us." Mutual visits were made to each other's Mass celebrations – Latin and Syriac [Text 1b; 7]. Differences of the respective ecclesiastical traditions did not play a role at first. The Portuguese priests, who in the following period increasingly flocked to the South Indian coastal region, had free access to the churches of the St. Thomas Christians. The East Syrian bishop Mar Jacob also gave the Portuguese access to the pepper trade in the region.

Gradually, however, the climate changed. Increasingly, the Portuguese discovered supposed deficiencies in the ecclesiastical practice of the Indian Christians, who knew neither a pope nor the seven sacraments nor mandatory celibacy for priests. Thus, the Iberians also doubted the validity of their baptisms. Instead, they emphasized the superiority of the Latin tradition. In addition, the St. Thomas Christians were drawn into the struggles of the Portuguese with the Muslims of the region. They responded, according to Indian historian A.M. Mundadan, "[by] avoiding the Portuguese as far as possible".[2] And as early as 1516/18, the Portuguese priest Penteado described the change of mood as follows:

> The St. Thomas Christians do not care for communication with [us] Portuguese. This is not because they are not happy that they are Christians as we are, but because we are among them what the English and Germans are among us. As regards their customs, their will is corrupted by their priests who say that just as there twelve Apostles, even so, they founded twelve [different form of ecclesiastical] customs, each different from the others ... [Text 18]

Notes to Chapter 2

1. Bitterli (1981), *Dokumente* I, 35 f. (Columbus' logbook of Oct 14, 1492).
2. Mundadan (1984), *Christianity in India* I, 351.

Further Reading for Chapter 2

2.1 (*The Portuguese on their Way around Africa, 1415 ff*)

Boxer (1991), *Portuguese Seaborne Empire*, 15–38; Russel-Wood (1992), *World on the Move*, 8–57; Gumilev (1987), *Kingdom of Prester John;* Gründer (2003), *Expansion*, 25–35; Reinhard (1983), *Expansion* I, 28–49; Schmitt (1986–1988), *Dokumente* I, 50–94. II,126–159.

2.2 (*Spain, Columbus and the "Discovery" of the "New World"* [1492])

Bakewell (²2004), *History of Latin America*, 66–77; Prien (2013), *Latin America*, 1–52; Abernethy (2000), *European Overseas Empires*, 45–63; Fernández-Armesto (1991), *Columbus*; Provost, F. (1991), *Columbus*; Gründer (2003), *Expansion*, 36–54; Reinhard (1985), *Expansion* II, 32–51; Schmitt (1984), *Dokumente* II, 95–134; Pietschmann (1994), *Handbuch* I, 207–313; Goodpasture (1989), *Cross and Sword*, 5–13 (documents).

2.3 (*Divided Spheres of Interest* [*'Inter Cetera' 1493, Tordesillas 1494*])

Bakewell (²2004), *History of Latin America*, 76–77; González/ González (2008), *Christianity in Latin America*, 40 ff.64 ff; Prien (2013), *Latin America*, 30f. 60–108. 111–113; Reinhard (1985), *Expansion* II, 43 ff; Delgado (1991), *Gott in Lateinamerika*, 23–34. 66–84; Pietschmann (1994), *Handbuch* I, 235 ff. 376 ff; Konetzke (1991), *Süd- und Mittelamerika* I, 27 ff.220 ff; Gründer (1992), *Welteroberung*, 86 ff.92 ff.

2.4 (*Encounters: Vasco da Gama and the Indian St. Thomas Christians, 1498 ff*)

Neill (1984), *Christianity in India* I, 68–110. 185; Mundadan (1984), *Christianity in India* I, 242–282; Mundadan (1967), *Arrival of the Portuguese*, 67 ff.; De Souza (1998), *Indian Christians*, 31–42; Hage (2007), *Orientalisches Christentum*, 315–378; Zupanow (2005), *Jesuit Mission*, 284–325; Thaliat (1958), *Synod of Diamper*.

CHAPTER 3

Iberoamerica I: Colonization and Christianization

3.1 American-Indian Cultures on the Eve of the Iberian Invasion

The "New World" encountered by the Spanish conquistadors was by no means a cultureless space. Rather, it presented an extremely diverse picture ethnically, linguistically, culturally and geographically. The indigenous population referred to by the conquistadors as "Indians" or "Indios" was not a homogeneous group. It included the Caribs and Arawaks encountered by the Spanish in the Caribbean, the Mexica (Aztecs), Tarasques, and Maya in present-day Mexico, the various Inca groups in Peru, the jungle Indians in the Amazon, the Guaranís in Paraguay, or the Araucans in Chile. These groups differed in almost every way. They built great civilizations, like the Maya, Aztec and Inca, or were warlike cannibals, like the Tupí in northern Brazil. Their languages varied considerably and often differed from village to village. Researcher speak of about 100–150 language families with 400 to 2,000 different languages on the double continent, depending on the criterion of distinction. Religious practices and beliefs were also diverse. Simple belief in spirits was widespread. In other societies, there were highly developed theological doctrines with complex cosmogonies. This jumble of peoples, languages and cultures was later to pose enormous challenges to the Iberian missionaries.

In addition to nomadic groups of hunter-gatherers, there were impressive examples of state organization. Two empires – those of the Aztecs and Incas – experienced their greatest territorial expansion precisely at the time of the Spaniards' arrival. The Aztec empire consisted of 38 provinces in the area of present-day Mexico. The capital Tenochtitlán with about 150 000 to 200 000 inhabitants on about 12 km^2 was the center of the empire and the largest urban center of the hemisphere. The "Empire of the Four Lands" of the Incas, on the other hand, at the height of its expansion around the year 1500, stretched over 4000 km, roughly from today's Quito (Ecuador) to areas south of modern Santiago de Chile. Thus, it reached an extent greater than that of today's European Union. A system of long-distance roads and relay runners enabled communication as well as effective administration of this vast territory. This organizational feat is all the more remarkable because major technical discoveries – such as the wheel, which had been used in other cultures for millennia – were unknown to the Incas.

Most Native American cultures were scriptless. In pre-European times, autochthonous writing was limited to Mesoamerica (especially Maya, Aztecs). In the Andes, although knotted cords called *quipu* were in use in the administration of the Inca state, they were not used to designate textual content. Indigenous historical textual sources from pre-Hispanic times are thus extremely rare. In Mesoamerica, however, numerous pictorious manuscripts were still produced in the early colonial period, as well as textual sources written in indigenous languages but using Latin letters. This was less common in other regions. Indian traditions, however, have been handed down in many cases through the later writings of mestizo chroniclers and European authors (colonial officials, missionaries).

3.2 Stages of the Conquest

The Spanish were able to establish themselves in the New World surprisingly quickly. In 1492, Columbus first set foot on American soil on the Caribbean island of Guanahaní. In 1501, the Spanish landed on the Venezuelan coast and in 1510 established the first permanent European settlement on the Mesoamerican mainland in Panama. In 1519, Hernán Cortés (1485–1547) set out from Cuba with 10 ships and 608 men to conquer Mexico. Already on November 8, 1519 he entered – accompanied by the later captured Aztec ruler Moctezuma II (*ca.* 1476/78–1520) – without a fight the capital Tenochtitlán. Despite a superior force of about 200,000 warriors, the Aztec empire fell into the hands of the Spanish. Even smaller was the force (200 men plus 37 horses) with which the Castilian adventure Francisco Pizarro (1476/78–1541) took control of the huge Inca Empire in 1532/33. Along with the Spanish, the Portuguese soon became active on the South American continent. More by chance on their way to India, they discovered in 1500 under Pedro Alvares Cabral what was later named Brazil. Finally, in 1520, it was Ferdinand Magellan (*ca.* 1485–1521), a Portuguese navigator in Spanish service, who circumnavigated the southern tip of South America in the first circumnavigation of the globe. By the mid-16th century, Castilian conquistadors had already reached the southwest of what is now the United States, and southern Chile [see Map 2].

What explains the rapid advance of the Spanish conquerors? Apart from their technological superiority – firearms, steel swords, mobility through horses – they encountered no united opponents in many places. The resentment of various indigenous peoples, forcibly subjugated by the Aztecs and Incas only a short time before, against their new masters had by no means faded. The Spaniards in Mexico as well as in Peru knew how to take advantage of these internal antagonisms and recruited Indian auxiliaries. In addition, the Inca Empire was weakened by a civil war around 1532/33. Diseases introduced by the Europeans also had a devastating effect early on. In addition, intercultural misunderstandings and psychological factors often played a decisive role. For example, at the time of the arrival of the Spaniards around 1519, the Aztecs – already worried by bad omens and the gloomy prophecies of their priests – expected the return of their god Quetzalcoatl from the West. Were the bearded white men who came in ships from the Atlantic Ocean his emissaries? Were the gods now returning? This uncertainty – according to a later source [cf. Text 220] – paralyzed the Aztec ruler Moctezuma II, who offered no resistance to the invaders. Also caught off guard was the last Inca ruler, Atahualpa (*c.* 1500–1533), who was overpowered and captured by the Spaniards in 1532 amid his entourage in a hand coup. Despite the enormous amounts of gold extorted as ransom, Pizarro later had him executed after a mock trial.

Who came to America from Spain? It was a colorful mix of differently motivated immigrants who were drawn to the New World (with which future conflicts were already pre-programmed). They included adventurers and soldiers of fortune, unemployed veterans of the Reconquista, failed existences, convicts, or mission-inspired Franciscans in search of alternative forms of community. Not everyone was allowed to come. Rather, the Castilian crown operated a strict emigration and population policy. Early on, the entry of Jews, Moors, and Protestant "heretics" into the West Indies (Caribbean) was prohibited, and the Casa de la Contratación, established in Seville in 1503, was charged with controlling Spanish immigration to the Americas. In 1538, for example, all non-Spanish subjects of the Crown (Germans, Genoese) were again prohibited from entering the country, after having been permitted only in 1526. One of the reasons was the concern about the invasion of heretical – that is, Protestant – movements. The number of men far exceeded that of women, although the Crown, with the transition to settlement colonialism, encouraged the emigration of families and different occupational groups since 1501. In total, about 300,000 Spaniards may have emigrated to the New World in the 16th century. In Portuguese America, the number of Europeans at the end of the 16th century was probably about 30,000.

3.3 Legal Titles: Patronage and 'Requerimiento'

The Spanish kings saw their rule in the New World legitimized by the papal bulls of 1493 (especially 'Inter Cetera' of May 5, 1493 [Text 223a]). Later bulls (such as 'Universalis ecclesiae' of July 28, 1508 [Text 228] led to the further elaboration and consolidation of the 'Royal Patronage' in Spanish America. The seizure of possession on the ground then took place through the proclamation of the infamous *'Requerimiento'*. In it, the indigenous peoples of the Americas were called upon to submit to the rule of the Castilian crown, with reference to the rights granted to them by the pope. This text was read out – mostly in Spanish or Latin (!) as well as under formal authentication by a notary – since 1513 in each case in a situation of the first contact with the different indigenous ethnic groups. If they refused the request, which was already linguistically completely incomprehensible to them, they were declared outlawed and could be subjected to war. This practice persisted until the 1550s. After a long sermon dealing with Adam and Eve, Jesus Christ and the apostle Peter, the world domination of the popes, and the transfer of the American lands to the Castilian crown, the indigenous peoples were presented with the following alternative:

> If you act accordingly [sc. and submit], you will do right and fulfill your duty to their Highnesses, and we [sc. the respective conquistador] in their name will treat you with love and kindness ... You will not be compelled to become Christians in this case, unless you yourselves desire to do so ... But if you do not do so, and maliciously delay, then we shall ... make war against you in all ways and manners ... We shall treat you as vassals who do not obey, and refuse to receive their lord, and resist and contradict him ... [Text 225a]

The controversies over colonial ethics were then to be based precisely on the 'Requerimiento'. Theologians such as the Dominican Francisco de Vitoria (1483–1546) would sharply criticize the Requerimiento, as would his fellow friar Bartolomé de las Casas (1484–1566), who rejected it as "unjust, absurd, and legally invalid." Both disputed the legal force of the papal bulls for legitimizing Spanish rule in the New World. For the Pope was supreme authority in spiritual matters, but not in temporal matters, and had no 'potestas directa in temporalibus' to rule over foreign lands. Therefore, he could not transfer the West Indies to the Spanish crown. Even pagan princes, the Dominicans say, taking up the natural law argumentation of the Thomistic tradition, are legitimate authorities. Why should the peoples of the Americas, Las Casas criticized, have accepted the Spanish king "as a lord whom they had never seen, never known ... and of whom they did not even know whether he was good or evil"? Without prior "agreement, treaty, or understanding," no obedience to "a foreign king" could be demanded from the indigenous people [Text 225b].

3.4 Mission Personnel, Duality of Mission and Colonial Church

Missionary work in the New World was initially almost exclusively the responsibility of the so-called mendicant orders (above all Franciscans, Dominicans, Augustinian Hermits). For a long time, the secular clergy hardly played a role. They had little motivation to undergo the hardships of an overseas journey and were initially viewed rather critically by the colonial authorities. It made no sense, Cortés wrote in a letter to Charles V in 1524, to import the cost-intensive ecclesiastical apparatus of Europe with bishops and diocesan clergy to Mexico, "who will only follow their habit of squandering the goods of the church with pomp and ceremonies and other vices" and "would discredit our faith here".[1] Not so the religious, who were committed to the ideal of apostolic poverty and quickly tried to adapt to the living conditions on the ground. The beginning of systematic missionary activities is generally considered to be the year 1500 (Franciscans on Hispaniola/Haiti) or 1524, when the first officially sent group of twelve Franciscans, the so-called "doce apóstoles," arrived in Mexico. Already the number of twelve was programmatic, symbolizing the dawn of an apostolic era in the evangelization of the newly discovered continent. The Dominicans also arrived in Hispaniola in 1510 and in Mexico in 1526, and the Augustinians later in Peru, as a group of twelve. For a large part of the Franciscans, this was also connected with a utopian vision: to realize in the New World the dream of a return to the ideals of the early church, which had failed in the encrusted structures of Europe. This included the renunciation of worldly possessions. Many Spanish Franciscans belonged to the reform wing of their order. Papal pronouncements (since Pope Hadrian VI's bull 'Omnimodo' of May 9, 1522) conferred far-reaching powers on the mendicant orders, including episcopal powers. The Jesuits (founded in 1534 and papally recognized in 1540), pioneers of the Catholic mission in Asia, became active in America first in Portuguese Brazil (since 1549) and in Spanish America (here first in Peru) since 1568.

There were considerable differences over the question of an appropriate missionary strategy, both within the various orders themselves and vis-à-vis other colonial actors. This concerned in particular the question of violence. In contrast to the aforementioned Las Casas, who in principle excluded any form of use of force and recognized peaceful evangelization as the "only method" ("unico vocationis modo"), other voices, even from the Franciscan camp, were less dismissive. In view of the monstrosities of Indian "idolatry" and especially of the ritual human sacrifices practiced on a large scale by the Aztecs (well attested also in indigenous sources) – thus a frequently repeated justification – a moderate degree of violence was quite legitimate, at least in the initial phase.

A Peruvian source from the end of the 16th century distinguishes three ways or stages in the Christianization of the Inca Empire: a first one, which took place "with [military] power and force"; a second one of voluntary acceptance of Christianity, due to the positive example of individual religious or lay people as well as after an elementary catechization; and a third phase of self-Christianization and transmission of the new faith by converted natives [Text 231]. Franciscan missionaries stood for both: on the one hand, the destruction of pagan temples, systematic eradication of "idolatry," and a *tabula rasa* method of mission (according to Juan de Zumárraga, first bishop in Mexico [1530–1548]); and, on the other hand, a high regard for the non-religious aspects of Aztec culture and careful recording of its heritage (according to Bernardino de Sahagún [1499–1590], who has often been called the first anthropologist and ethnographer of Spanish America). In an effort to protect the Indians from exploitation by the conquistadores, both sides agreed.

The collapse of the old religious and social order led to mass conversions in many places in the late 1520s. Mexican sources of the 16th century report – quite credibly – thousands of baptisms in one day and hundreds of thousands in one year. According to a chronicler of the time, "the baptismal candidates were so numerous that the priests ... were often no longer able to lift the jar with which they baptized, because their arm was tired".[2] Even at that time, however, there were differing opinions among the participating orders about the quality of such mass baptisms. Dominicans tended to insist on the need for more intensive preparation. In other regions, however, the fierce resistance of indigenous tribes to both the advance of the Spanish conquistadores and the activities of the missionaries continued unchanged. Not all missionary success stories held water. In many cases – as self-critical observers among the Catholic clergy and orders noted toward the end of the century – the old gods were still hidden among the new Catholic saints.

Ever since the Spanish crown moved on to settlement colonialism and the establishment of territorial rule over the discovered territories, there was a latent tension between the exercise of colonial rule, Christianization and economic exploitation. At the same time, a *structural conflict* developed that would also characterize later eras of mission history: the opposition between a "mission church, that is, a church disinterestedly concerned for the welfare and salvation of the Native Americans, and the colonial church, which served the interests of the colonial power and its settlers."[3] This conflict cannot be reduced to the opposition between the episcopate and the monks, as was commonly assumed for a long time (especially since initially the majority of bishops in Spanish America came from the ranks of the mendicant orders). Arguably, however, tensions between the *frayles* on the one hand and the secular clergy and episcopate on the other increased from the 1550s onward. In parallel, the conflict was intensified by the colonial state's tightened control of the church under the 'Patronato Real'. Essential functions – such as the right to select and send missionaries, collect tithes or divide bishoprics – had already passed to the crown earlier. Bishops increasingly became state functionaries. The church's autonomy decreased and the extent of state intervention increased.

In contrast, the Fransciscans developed the *vision of an Indian church* as a rebirth of the original church [see chapter 4.3] and sought to keep the indigenous people away from the harmful influence of the European settlers – partly with, partly without state support. Thus, for example, Toribio de Benavente OFM (1482–1568), better known by his Indian (Nahuatl) name "Motolinia," expressed himself:

> For for this new land and for this simple generation, nothing was fitting but that the bishops lived as in the original Church, poor and humble, that they sought no income but souls, and that they carried no more than their pontificals, and that the Indians did not see pampered bishops in soft robes sleeping in beautiful beds...[4]

This recourse to the early church was at the center of numerous controversies and met with resistance from the colonial church establishment. In 1556, for example, the second archbishop of Mexico, Alonso de Montúfar OP (1498–1569), sought to introduce tithing among the Indians as well. Until then, they had been exempt from this tax. He opposed the Frayles, who stood on the side of the Indians and spoke out against the burden of the ecclesiastical tithe. According to the archbishop, their appeal to the original church was nonsense, because there was no *iglesia primitiva* in this sense in Mexico.[5]

In Brazil, until the middle of the 16th century, there was hardly any question of an ecclesiastical organization. In 1551, the first Brazilian bishopric was established in Salvador da Bahia. It remained the only one until 1676. Because of the relatively small number of priests, lay people played a considerable role in the religious life of the colony from the very beginning.

Notes to Chapter 3

1. Lippy/ Choquette/ Poole (1992), *Americas*, 31.
2. Baumgartner (1971), *Liturgie* I, 162.
3. Prien (1978), *Geschichte*, 107.
4. Cayota (1993), *Indianische Kirche*, 79.
5. Beckmann (1971), *Utopien*, 396.

Further Reading for Chapter 3

3.1 (American-Indian Cultures on the Eve of the Iberian Invasion)
Garrard-Burnett/ Freston/ Dove (2016), *Religion in Latin America*, 22–33 (by D. Tavárez); González/ González (2008), *Christianity in Latin America*, 12 ff.; Bakewell (²2004), *History of Latin America*, 25–43; Prien (2013), *Latin America*, 12–16; Meltzer (2009), *First peoples*; Dussel (1992), *Church in Latin America*, 23–42; Pietschmann (1994), *Handbuch* I, 101–206; Reinhard (1985), *Expansion* II, 9–31; Mills/ Taylor (1998), *Documentary History*, 3–80.

3.2 (Stations of the Conquest)
Bakewell (²2004), *History of Latin America*, 95–108; Burkholder/ Johnson (1994), *Colonial Latin America*, 35–69; Reinhard (1985), *Expansion* II, 32–68; Pietschmann (1994), *Handbuch* I, 207–312; Konetzke (1991), *Süd- und Mittelamerika* I, 27–108; Leon-Porttilla/ Heuer (1986), *Rückkehr der Götter*; Gründer (2003), *Expansion*, 43–54; Delgado (2017), *Catholicism*, 17–37; Parry (1990), *Spanish Seaborne Empire*, 39–136.

3.3 (Legal Titles: Patronage and 'Requerimiento')
Prien (2013), *Latin America*, 21–24. 110–124; Williams (1990), *Discourses of Conquest*; Garrard-Burnett/ Freston/ Dove (2016), *Religion in Latin America*, 87–106. 173 ff; Reinhard (1985), *Expansion* II, 58 ff.; Delgado (1996), *Abschied*, 43 ff.57–67; Delgado (1995), *Las Casas. Werkauswahl* II, 246–267; Delgado (1991), *Gott in Lateinamerika*, 74–80; Pietschmann (1994), *Handbuch* I, 256 ff.; Parry (1990), *Spanish Seaborne Empire*, 137–172; Goodpasture (1989), *Cross and Sword*, 28–52 (documents).

3.4 (Mission Personnel, Duality of Mission and Colonial Church)
González/ González (2008), *Christianity in Latin America*, 40–103; Prien (2013), *Latin America*, 53–108; Prien (1978), *Geschichte*, 79–261; Bakewell (²2004), *History of Latin America*, 137–159; Lippy/ Choquette/ Poole (1992), *Americas*, 17–70; Delgado (2017), *Catholicism*, 17–37; Meier (2018), *Ränder*, 145–281; Konetzke (1991), *Süd- und Mittelamerika* I, 220–281; Goodpasture (1989), *Cross and Sword*, 53–78 (documents). – (References to primitive Christianity as a counter-model:) Prien (1978), *Geschichte*, 143 ff; Phelan (1956), *Geronimo de Mendietta*, 5 ff.37–60; Beckmann (1971), *Utopien*, 380–403; Mérida (1994), *Kirche und Mission*, 380 ff.; Sylvest (1975), *Motifs*, 36 ff.

CHAPTER 4

Iberoamerica II: Debates and Controversies

4.1 Religious Debates: Franciscans and Aztecs in Mexico 1524

Despite the violent nature of the conquista, there were also many forms of peaceful contact and intercultural exchange between Spaniards and indigenous people early on. Religious discussions were also among them. The most famous is the debate that Franciscan missionaries held in Mexico in 1524 with the "nobles" and priests of the Aztecs. There is a record of it in Mexican (Nahuatl) and Spanish by the ethnologist and missionary Bernardino de Sahagún OFM. Although it was not completed until 1564 – many years after the event – it is based on older notes in the Aztec language. The historicity of the course of the conversation and the terminology used is disputed in detail. Even if the elaborated version of the *colloquios* now available was primarily intended to serve as a model of conversation for future missionaries, it nevertheless provides important insights into the interreligious disputes in 16th-century Mexico.

The basic tenor on the part of the Aztec nobles is deep dejection. "After all, our gods died too," is their bitter summary after the violent downfall of their empire.

> You [the Franciscans] say that we do not know the Lord of *Mit* and *Bei* [Aztec term for the Supreme God], the Lord of heaven and earth. You say that not true gods are our gods. It is a new unheard word that you spoke, and we are dismayed by it. For our creators …, they did not speak so. They gave us their custom and their law … Shall we now destroy the old law? The law of the Chichimecs, the law of the Toltecs, the law of those of Colhuacan, the law of the Tepanecs [various indigenous peoples of Mexico]? [Text 235]

In contrast, the Franciscans point, among other things, to the universality of the worship of God as a criterion of true religion. "Please hear it: if [your] gods were really true gods, would we not also worship them divinely?" Would not the deities of the Aztec pantheon then also be "invoked everywhere on earth"? This is the case with "the Book of God, the Word of God" (i.e., the Christian Bible), which is heard "everywhere on earth [and] in the world." Since the indigenous peoples who had fallen into idolatry had not previously received "the precious word" of the true God of the Christians, their "sin [so far] has not been too great." It would be different, however, if they now refused to listen to the missionaries' preaching. – The Franciscans, like other mendicant orders, were in the tradition of medieval religious discussions. Elsewhere, too – as in Japan in 1551 between Buddhists and Jesuits [see chap. 5.4; Text 15] – detailed interreligious debates occurred early on even in situations of first contact.

Formal and informal religious discussions existed in various forms. In Nicaragua, for example, a record of a three-day interview with local caciques "to find out what they thought about [their] faith" is preserved from 1557.[1] The later, the more frequent such conversations reveal longer-lasting contact and more intensive interactions between the two sides. Noteworthy, for example, is the report by the Spanish priest Francisco Hernández around 1546 of his encounter with a Mayan prince:

> He had met a [Mayan] prince who, when asked about his faith and his traditional religion, which they used to have in the [Mayan] kingdom, told him that they knew and believed in God, who dwelt in heaven, and was ... Father, Son and Holy Spirit. The father is called *Içona*, who created the people and all things. The Son is called *Bacab* [...] [and the Holy Spirit *Echuac*] [...] Moreover, he added that at one time all men must die, but of the resurrection of the flesh they knew nothing ... The princes [of the Maya] knew [many] special traditions, but the common people believed only in these three persons, Içona, Bacab and Echuac, and in Chibiria, Bacaba's mother ...[2]

Içona, Bacab and Echuac correspond to certain Mayan deities. To what extent such analogies between the Christian faith and the religion of the indigenous people were mere syncretistic adaptation (or "satanic imitation". in missionary terminology) or at least also contained buried, albeit later "darkened", traces of a previous Christian primal revelation to the inhabitants of the Americas, was a question controversially discussed in detail among the missionaries of Mexico.

4.2 Controversies over Ethics of Colonialism: Antonio de Montesinos, Bartolomé de las Casas

A significant feature of Latin American Christianity's history is the intensity of the debates on colonial ethics, which began remarkably early. Unlike Asia and Africa, Christianity arrived in the Americas exclusively in a colonial context.

On the one hand, as discussed, it served there to legitimize the *conquista*: the first thing the Spanish did in many places on American soil was to erect a cross. At the same time, however, from the very beginning – and also in the name of the cross – the sharpest protest was voiced against the excesses of colonial rule on the double continent. This ambivalence was to mark a characteristic feature of Latin American Christian history in the following centuries as well.

a. 1511: Advent sermon of *Antonio de Montesinos*. Santo Domingo on Hispaniola (today: Dominican Republic/Haiti) was the first Spanish city founded in the New World. Dominican missionaries arrived there in 1510. Just one year later, an incident occurred there with far-reaching consequences. It was the Fourth of Advent in 1511, when the Dominican friar Antonio de Montesinos ascended the pulpit to preach a penitential sermon of unheard-of severity to the assembled community of settlers. He spoke about the Bible word John 1:23 ("I am the voice of one crying in the wilderness"):

> This voice,'[he said,] 'will be one you never heard before ... You are all in mortal sin because of the cruel tyranny you work on these innocent people ... By what right ... do you hold these Indians in such cruel and horrible servitude? By what authority have you made such hideous wars on these people? They were living on their own lands in peace and quiet. By what right have you wasted them, so many, many of them, with unspeakable death and destruction? By what right do you keep them so oppressed and exhausted? You give them no food, you give them no medicine ..., you kill them. Just to get at gold, ... day by day. Are they not human beings? Do they not have rational souls? Are you not required to love them as yourselves? ... Take this for certain that in the state you are in you cannot be saved any more than the Moors [Muslims] or Turks who lack faith in Jesus Christ ... [Text 224]

The reaction of the settlers: "all were dismayed, some as if out of their minds," but in the end – according to the report – no one was converted. Instead, they sued Montesinos (who had spoken on behalf of the entire Dominican community) for sedition before the governor of the crown. This was the city's resident admiral, Don Diego Columbus, son of the famous "discoverer." The friars, however, refused any recantation. This marked a constellation of conflict that was to be repeated many times in the following periods: between the religious orders, the conquistadors – who possessed a license from the crown, but otherwise carried out their campaigns of conquest and discovery mostly on their own account and at their own risk – and the representatives of the (regional or overseas) colonial government.

b. *Bartolomé de las Casas* as the "protector of the Indians". Inspired, among other things, by the "prophetic" example of Antonio de Montesinos was a man who, more than any other, was to be at the center of the controversies surrounding the legitimacy of Spanish rule in the New World: his later fellow religious Bartolomé de las Casas (1484–1566) [Figure 3]. Himself initially a prospector, 'encomendero' and field chaplain in Hispaniola and Cuba, he experienced a conversion in 1514. He then gave up his *encomienda* (landed property with forced Indian labor) and devoted himself in the future to defending the rights of Native Americans. He did this in various capacities: as a lobbyist and officially appointed "protector of the Indians" at the court of Charles v (1517–1520), as a Dominican friar on Hispaniola, Nicaragua, Guatemala, and Mexico (1522–1546), as a bishop in Chiapas in Mexico (1544–46), and after his return to Spain in 1547 through numerous interventions at the court of Charles v and Philip II (1547–1566). Like Antonio de Montesinos, he has been rediscovered in the 20th century and recognized as "father of liberation theology" in Latin America.

His extensive writings cannot be presented here. His "Short Account of the Destruction of the Indies" (*Brevísima relación*) of 1542 (printed in 1552), which was addressed to the crown, achieved an enormous impact. It is a single indictment against the brutal exploitative system of the Spaniards (or "Christians," as they are called in his "account"). This had already led in some regions to the extermination of entire indigenous peoples in the 1520s, as a result of warlike actions and economic enslavement. What Las Casas could not take into account in his horrendous descriptions were the deadly effects of the infectious diseases introduced by the Europeans. But even so, his report is frightening enough:

> Among these gentle sheep [sc. the Indians], whom their Creator and Originator created [without falsity and arg], the Spaniards drove ... like wolves, tigers and lions ... For forty years they have done nothing else among them, and still to this day they do nothing else but tear them apart, strangle, torment, martyr, torture ... Thus they have achieved it that at present, of more than three million people, whom I formerly saw with my own eyes on the island of Hispaniola, only 200 are left. The length of the island of Cuba stretches almost as far as the road from Valladolid to Rome; today it is almost completely denuded of people ... [etc.; in the same way Las Casas goes through region by region in the Caribbean and Mesoamerica].[3]

Censuses documenting the dramatic decline of the indigenous population had been conducted in Spanish America since 1508 (first on Hispaniola). Modern estimates assume a reduction from about 1.5 million to 325,000 people between 1519 and 1570 for colonial central Mexico alone.[4] The enslavement of Indians had been officially prohibited by a decree of Queen Isabella since 1500 or 1503 [Text 223b]. However, it was replaced by the system of encomiendas, in which a certain number of Indians were "recommended" to the Spanish settlers by the colonial administration or assigned to forced labor in gold mines or agriculture. This system was the subject of Las Casas' lifelong struggle. He did this through his publications, sermons, memoranda, legal opinions and petitions to the local authorities, to the "Council of the Indies" (quasi the Spanish overseas ministry), directly to the Castilian monarchs and finally, in one of his last letters in 1566, also to Pope Pius V. His repeated (a total of five) journeys across the Atlantic also served this mission.

Las Casas' struggle (and the efforts of other religious before him) was not without effect. In the end, however, he achieved only pseudo-success, since pro-Indian measures of the central government were repeatedly undermined by the local settlers. This was also the case with the "New Laws" (Leyes Nuevas), which Charles V enacted in 1542/43, largely under the influence of (or in response to) the Dominican's interventions. They provided for the permanent abolition of the encomienda system as well as an improved legal status of the Indians as free subjects of the Spanish crown (subject to certain tribute payments). In 1545, however, the king largely revoked the New Laws in response to strong protests and sometimes violent resistance from the Spanish *encomenderos*, especially in Peru.

Las Casas emphasized the *unity of the human race*. The Indians, too, are rational creatures of God. The "only" legitimate form of proclaiming the faith – "De unico modo vocationis," the title of his writing from 1526 – was therefore for him that of non-violence. In the suffering Indio – according to Las Casas – *Christ himself suffers*. This is a motif that was to play an important role in the Indian-Christian literature and art of the following periods. For example, in a fresco in the church of Parinacota (Chile, 17th century), which shows a crucified Christ with Indian features being pierced by the lances of the conquistadors.[5] The enslavement of the indigenous population was consequently a "mortal sin" for the religious. "No one can be saved who owns Indians" – this principle Las Casas preached again and again since his "conversion" in 1514. In 1546, as one of his last official acts as bishop of Chiapas, he wrote a confessional instruction that obligated the clergy of his diocese to refuse absolution to all Spaniards if they did not first release their Indians and make full restitution to them.

The controversies over Spanish rule overseas reached a climax in the great *dispute of Valladolid in 1550/51*. Ordered by the emperor himself, this dispute dragged on for months. Las Casas faced the court chronicler Juan Ginés de

Sepúlveda, who sought to justify the violent conquest of the "West Indian lands" as a "just war" – using arguments from scholastic legal philosophy that Las Casas picked apart one by one [cf. Text 227]. If either party could invoke the legal figure of just war at all, it was not the Spaniards but the Indians (in their resistance to the Spaniards) – an astonishing statement by the friar. What is even more astonishing is that Las Casas was initially able to prevail across the board, and Sepúlveda's writing to the contrary was banned from printing by the Inquisition. But this, too, was ultimately only a sham victory. The theory of the Conquista was indeed shaken. But little changed in the concrete situation of the American Indians in the New World.

Towards the end of the century, Las Casas' writings were banned, as being detrimental to the reputation of the Castilian crown. Even during his lifetime, he had been severely attacked by the colonists as a "high traitor" (and even a "Lutheran" heretic). Conversely, his "Short Account" (quoted above) was translated into various Western European languages (including German) from 1579 onward. It was to play an important role in the colonial and confessional debates of the time.

4.3 Experiments on the Formation of an American-Indigenous Church

In the years between 1524 and 1570, a considerable literature in various indigenous languages was produced in Mexico, which in the 16th century was referred to by the collective term *"Theologia Indiana"*. It was an expression of the efforts of the Franciscans in particular to form an "Indian church". Intensive language studies were an essential part of this endeavor. A wealth of texts and translations in various regional languages and literary genres (such as model sermons, catecheses, pastoral handouts, biblical texts such as the Lord's Prayer or the Psalms, devotional literature, dictionaries, but also ancient works such as Aesop's Fables) as well as pictorial catechisms based on Aztec pictorial script have been preserved. Sermons in Native American idioms (such as Nahuatl) have been the subject of intense study for some time. Researchers occasionally even speak of a "Nahuatlization of Christianity."[6] The Santa Cruz Indian College of Tlatelolco (now Mexico City), established in 1536, represented a remarkable project. The goal was to educate an intellectual elite from the children of the native aristocracy and also to lead suitable youths to the priesthood [Text 239]. Despite considerable initial success, the Franciscans felt compelled to abandon this prestigious project after 1546, partly in the face of strong opposition from the Spanish settlers. The simple church architecture of the Franciscans in the 16th century did not only correspond to local conditions. It was also an expression of their ideal of apostolic simplicity. They employed local craftsmen and artists to build their churches. In Peru, for example, they introduced Andean symbols and local motifs into the design of the church interior and the baptismal fonts.

The Franciscans' statements in the colonial discourse were also particularly important. In the face of voices among the settlers and colonial officials who regarded the indigenous peoples as inferior or even as mere animals. *Bernardino de Sahagún* (c. 1499–1590), for example, emphasized the full humanity of the Indians: "It is most certain that these peoples are our brothers, stemming from the stock of Adam, as do we. They are our neighbors, whom we are obliged to love, even as we love ourselves." Whatever they may have been in the past – now they are skillful in learning all the crafts and "liberal arts and sacred theology" [Text 236]. In part, the Indians are virtually idealized. They are described as gentle, peaceful, humble, and incapable of any sin, comparable in this to angels. Unlike the Spaniards, the kingdom of heaven is therefore certain for them. Thus, for example, the already mentioned *Motolinía* (*Toribio de Benavente*, 1482–1568), one of the "doce apóstoles" of Mexico: "These Indians know no obstacle that prevents them from entering heaven, while we Spaniards have many of them".[7] For that reason, however, they should be kept away from the corrupting influence of the European colonists. Even the idea of a separate episcopate for the Indians was discussed. This high esteem for the Indians was, of course, linked to a decidedly patriarchal attitude that saw them – under the care of the Frayles – in a state of diminished autonomy. Finally, contrary to original intentions, they were also denied access to priestly ordination and religious orders [Text 240].

A particularly revealing source is the 'Historia eclesiástica indiana' written in 1596 by *Geronimo de Mendietta* (1525–1604), a Franciscan missionary of the second generation. Here he describes the history of the "Indian Church" in its various stages as a movement predestined in God's plan of salvation. Its golden age, however – according to Mendietta – was long gone. He saw the present as gloomy, in view of an increasingly centralized church regiment, comparable to the Babylonian captivity of the church. This pessimistic judgment applied all the more to the future. Conversely, the idea of an Indian church met with little approval from the colonial administration in times of the intensifying Hispanization policy under Philip II. Just like the writings of Las Casas, the works of the Franciscan protagonists – both Motolina's 'Memoriales' and Sahagún's 'Historia general de las cosas be la Nueva España' as well as Mendietta's 'Historia eclesiástica indiana' – were banned. They could only be printed in the 19th or 20th century.

4.4 Beginnings of Black Slavery in America

Native American slavery had been theoretically prohibited in Spanish America since 1500/03 respectively since the "New Laws" of 1542. The import of African forced laborers, on the other hand, played a subordinate role in the colonial ethical debates of the time, although it assumed gigantic proportions, especially from the 17th century onward [Map 8]. It is estimated that in the five centuries since the beginning of the Iberian invasion, about 10–15 million Africans were taken to the New World as slaves.[8] Already on the first ships of the Spaniards, Africans were carried in small numbers. Admittedly, they came initially as so-called house slaves or as laborers for the construction of public buildings, and still from Spain itself. With the growing number of sugar plantations in the Caribbean and in view of the mass death of the American Indians, the need for other – and at the same time more resilient – labor increased. This need was increasingly met by imports directly from Africa. In 1518, a license granted by the Spanish crown resulted in the first direct import of 4,000 slaves from West Africa to the Antilles. The suppliers were the Portuguese, who were to maintain a monopoly in the transatlantic slave trade for a long time. Around the middle of the 16th century, the population of the Caribbean islands (in addition to those of mixed blood) was composed of three groups: Europeans, Indians, and – at the bottom of the social ladder – a growing number of African Americans. In Cuba, the decimation of indigenous peoples was particularly advanced. There, by 1608, blacks already made up about 44.5% of the total population.[9]

Las Casas had accused himself – wrongly, since this development had long since begun – of being partly responsible for the importation of African slaves into the Caribbean. In order to relieve the physically weaker American Indians from the harsh pressure of work, he had supported the importation of blacks, who were considered more robust, in the period before he entered the order. He later bitterly regretted this move, condemning the enslavement of Africans as "as unjust as that of the Indians."[10] Other ecclesiastical voices were less decisive. Doubts such as those of the Mexican archbishop Alonso de Montúfar in 1560 in a letter to King Philip II ("We know not what reason there is that the Negroes should be more slaves than the Indians")[11] remained restrained: Rather, in the late 16th and 17th centuries, the Iberian colonial church was to be among the profiteers of the system, and the secular clergy in particular among the largest slaveholders in colonial society. Voices of protest were raised only sporadically.

Notes to Chapter 4

1. Text in: Delgado (1991), *Gott in Lateinamerika*, 117–120.
2. Quoted from: Nebel (1992), *Missionskatechismen*, 259 f.
3. Quoted from: Enzensberger (1981), *Bericht von der Verwüstung*, 11 ff.
4. Reinhard (1985), *Expansion* II, 62.
5. Meier/ Langenhorst (1992), *Bartolomé de las Casas*, 157.
6. Klaus (1999), *Franciscan Sermons … in Nahuatl*, 11.
7. Sylvest (1975), *Motifs*, 44.
8. Prien (2007), *Lateinamerika*, 147; Zeuske (2013), *Sklaverei*, 456 f.
9. Meier (1991), *Anfänge*, 275.
10. Meier/ Langenhorst (1992), *Las Casas*, 112.
11. Meier (1991), *Anfänge*, 281; cf. Konetze (1991), *Süd- und Mittelamerika*, 80.

Further Reading for Chapter 4

4.1 (Religious Debates: Franciscans and Aztecs in Mexico 1524)
Tavárez (2017), *Indigenous Christianities*, 5–26; Klaus (1999), *Franciscan Sermons … in Nahuatl*, 45–47; Mills/ Taylor (1998), *Documentary History*, 19 ff; Wissmann (1981), *Religionsgespräch der Franziskaner mit den Azteken*; Lehmann (1949), *Sterbende Götter*; Saranyana (1986), *Catecismos hispanoamericanos*, 251–264; Edmonson (1974), *Sahagún*, 224–233; De Alva/ Jorge (1988), *Work of Bernardino de Sahagún*, 65–92. 321–340; León-Portilla (2002), *Bernardino de Sahagún*; Nebel (1992), *Missionskatechismen*, 242–270; Delgado (1991), *Gott in Lateinamerika*, 132–144; Lockhart (1992), *Nahuatl Accounts*; Christensen (2014), *Translated Christianities*.

4.2 (Controversies over Ethics of Colonialism: Antonio de Montesinos, Bartolomé de las Casas)
Prien (2013), *Latin America*, 110–125; Dussel (1992), *Church in Latin America*, 43 ff.; Delgado (2017), *Catholicisms*, 21ff; Goodpasture (1989), *Cross and Sword*, 11f (de Montesinos); Sanderlin (1993), *Bartolome de Las Casas* (Writings); Wagner/ Parish (1967), *Bartolomé de Las Casas* (Life and Writings); Hanke (1994), *All mankind is one*; Meier/ Langenhorst (1992), *Bartolomé de las Casas*; Delgado (1991), *Gott in Lateinamerika*, 145–165; Delgado (1994/95), *Las Casas. Werkauswahl* Vol. 1–2; Prien (2000), *Evangelium*, 207–292; Schilling (2020), *Karl V.*, 261–284; Gillner (1997), *Las Casas*.

4.3 (*Experiments in the Formation of an American-Indigenous Church*)

For literature see titles under ch. 3.3; see also: Phelan (1956), *Geronimo de Mendietta*; Klaus (1999), *Franciscan Sermons ... in Nahuatl*, 11 ff; Baumgartner (1992), *Indianische Sprachen*, 313–347; Beckmann (1971), *Utopien*; Frost (1993), *Tlatelolco-Projekt*, 126–144; Nebel (1992), *Missionskatechismen*, 242–27; Prien (2013), *Latin America*, 83–85; Garrard-Burnett/ Freston/ Dove (2016), *Religion in Latin America*, 87–106 ("Indigenous Religious Reactions", by M. Aguilar-Moreno).

4.4 (*Beginnings of Black Slavery in America*)

Prien (2013), *Latin America*, 125–139; Garrard-Burnett/ Freston/ Dove (2016), *Religion in Latin America*, 198–206 (by J. Bristol); Iliffe (^{3}2017), *Africans*, 135–169 ("The Atlantic Slave Trade"); Meier (1991), *Anfänge*, 267–290; Paquette (2010), *Handbook of slavery*; Drescher (2009), *Slavery and antislavery*; Adiele (2017), *Transatlantic enslavement;* Zeuske (2022), *Sklaverei und Sklavenhandel;* Pietschmann (1994), *Handbuch* I, 326 ff; Reinhard (1985), *Expansion* II, 90 f.140 ff; Hurbon (1992), *Afro-American Society*, 363–375.

CHAPTER 5

Mission under the Padroado: Encounters and Conflicts in Africa and Asia

5.1 Ethiopia: Portuguese as Guests and Allies in the Christian Empire

Unlike the Spaniards in the New World, the Portuguese encountered in Asia and Africa countries, some of which had ancient indigenous churches for centuries. In India, these were the St. Thomas Christians, and in Africa, Christian Ethiopia. Around 1500, the East African country was at a political, cultural and religious peak that it would not reach again for a long time. In the preceding centuries of relative isolation from the other centers of the Christian world, Ethiopian Orthodox Christianity had developed a very specific profile. This included its own church language (the ancient Semitic Ge'ez), a biblical canon that was expanded compared to the Western tradition, and its own ecclesiastical hierarchy, headed by an abuna ordained by the Coptic patriarch in Egypt [see Map 1; Figure 1; Photo F01–09].

At the beginning of the 16th century, however, the country faced renewed threats from its Muslim neighbors. This led to increased contacts with Rome and Portugal. In 1520, at Ethiopian invitation, a Portuguese delegation arrived at the court of the Ethiopian ruler Lebna Dengel. There they were questioned about their faith and then pompously welcomed as fellow Christians ("we are all Christians"). Talks followed about an economic and military alliance. The king was disappointed to see how small Portugal looked on a map of the world (*mapa mundi*) presented to him as a gift. These events (as well as the subsequent six-year stay of the Portuguese in Ethiopia) are described in detail in the travelogue of one of the participants of this delegation, the priest Francisco Alvares. He describes, with numerous details about its liturgical and monastic life, Ethiopia as a country full of churches and monasteries, which was proud of its long and uninterrupted Christian past. This history did not only reach back to the time of the New Testament (Acts 8) ("We were the first Christians"), but began already long before with the legendary union of King Solomon with the Queen of Sheba. This is the Solomonic narrative, which was broadly unfolded and legendarily embellished in the Ethiopian national epic 'Kebra Negast' from the 13th century [Text 109]. At the same time, it served to underline the independence of Ethiopian Christianity.

© KLAUS KOSCHORKE, 2025 | DOI:10.1163/9789004699830_006
This is an open access chapter distributed under the terms of the CC BY-NC-ND 4.0 license.

In 1524, Emperor Dengel (Dawid II, 1508–1540) wrote to the Pope in Rome. In it, after a few phrases of devotion, he asked him to ensure unity among the Christian rulers of Europe in order to establish a united front against Islam [Text 123]. Then, from 1529, the Ethiopian Empire itself became a victim of its Muslim neighbors. Ahmed Gran of the neighboring Adal Sultanate opened a jihad. Within ten years, Ethiopia was almost entirely defeated, its churches and monasteries reduced to rubble, and numerous Christians forced to convert by force [Text 124]. Historian Adrian Hastings has characterized Ahmed Gran's campaigns, conducted with extreme brutality, as a systematic campaign of cultural and national genocide.[1] Help came in 1541 from a Portuguese expeditionary force led by Christopher da Gama, youngest son of the famous India navigator Vasco da Gama. The latter fell in the fighting but was able to save the Ethiopian empire from ruin.

In return, the Portuguese now expected the Ethiopian church to be more closely tied to Rome. But the Ethiopians refused. The new emperor Galawdewos (1540–1559) rejected in particular the subordination of his church to a Latin patriarch. In 1555, the first Jesuits arrived in Ethiopia. Their presence triggered manifold debates, and the emperor, who was quite versed in theology, defended the peculiarities of the Ethiopian tradition against Jesuit criticism in a famous writing – later known in Europe as the 'Confession of Galawdewos' (Confessio Claudii). In 1557 the arrival and a work of the Jesuit Andrea da Oviedo entitled "The Primacy of Rome and the Errors of the Ethiopians" led to a scandal. Oviedo had previously been appointed (Latin) Patriarch of Ethiopian by Rome. The emperor then forbade the Jesuits to preach among his countrymen, and conversely Oviedo declared the emperor excommunicated. The military situation remained volatile, and Galawdewos fell in one of the battles. By his successor, the Jesuits were assigned a separate field of activity in Fremona among the small Portuguese community there.

The so-called Galawdewo's Creed ('Confessio Claudii') of 1555 [Text 125] breaks down into two parts. In the first part, the emperor declares his belief in the Trinity and Incarnation and affirms the validity of the first three Ecumenical Councils (of 325, 381 and 431), without criticizing the Fourth Council (Chalcedon 451), which was so important for the Western tradition. In the second part, without any polemical sharpness, he defends three Ethiopian practices that had been criticized by the Jesuits as a reversion to Judaism: the celebration of the Sabbath (in addition to Sunday), the rite of circumcision, and the abstention from pork. These customs were by no means to be equated with the practice of the Jews as condemned in the New Testament, he said, but were declared expressions of local conventions. For example, "the circumcision we have is custom of the land like the scarring of the face in Ethiopia and Nubians and the piercing of the ears among Indians." Christianity – according to this remarkable African voice – is understood here as a universal religion, but open to different cultural expressions.

5.2 Beginnings of Catholic Presence in Sub-Saharan Africa

In West Africa, the Catholic mission, supported by the Portuguese crown, widely followed the routes of the Lusitanians' strategic conquests along the coasts as well as on the offshore islands. It was a peculiar mix of economic, political, religious and ideological motives that drove the Portuguese in their voyages of discovery. Among them were crusading ideas, fighting the Muslim arch-enemy, direct access to the gold of "Guinea" (i.e. sub-Saharan Africa) and the spice-producing regions of Asia, the search for the legendary priest-king John, and the spread of the Christian faith. The latter had already been stipulated in a series of papal bulls in the 1450s as a condition for granting far-reaching privileges to the Portuguese crown. This was the case in Pope Nicholas v's bull "Romanus pontifex" of 1455, which has often been referred to as the "Charter of Portuguese Imperialism." It granted the Portuguese king the exclusive right to carry out discoveries and conquests as well as settlements on the west coast of Africa, and gave him patronage over the church that was established in the newly discovered territories.

Missionary personnel included members of the Portuguese Order of Christ, as well as (from the 1460s or 1480s) Franciscans and Dominicans. Later, Augustinians and Jesuits joined them. On the whole, the missionaries' radius of action was quite limited. They mostly stayed near the Portuguese fortresses. In addition to members of the religious orders, secular priests were also part of the basic equipment of all ships leaving Lisbon for Africa (or India). The latter mostly did not enjoy a good reputation. Sporadically, in West Africa (less so in East Africa), there were also beginnings of the formation of a native clergy. Repeatedly, the Portuguese brought Africans home from their voyages of discovery and trade – mostly as slaves, but also as freemen (or later freedmen) – some of whom received a religious education and later returned to Africa. Thus, as early as 1490, we learn of a sending of black priests from Lisbon to São Tomé. The colored clerics received their training in seminaries first in Portugal and later in isolated cases in Africa. In 1518, the Roman Curia authorized the royal chaplain in Lisbon to ordain "Ethiopians, Indians and Africans".[2] Theoretically, therefore, there were certainly possibilities for the formation of an indigenous clergy, but in practice they were hardly used.

The Portuguese presence in the coastal regions of Africa consisted primarily of a network of fortified bases, which were established by force if necessary, but often also with the consent of local rulers. This required mutual cooperation, including slave trade, which played a major role in the economic activities of the Portuguese. The Portuguese built their first fort on West African soil in 1482 at Elmina in present-day Ghana [see Figure 18; Photo G14]. Elmina soon functioned as a central transshipment point for transporting African slaves from the region to the New World (especially Brazil); and the first Catholic church built in tropical Africa was located right in the middle of this fort. Gradually, other trading posts were established, in line with the Portuguese advance south along the coast. In 1482/84 they reached the Congo River, in 1485 the Walvis Bai (in present-day Namibia) and in 1487/88 under Bartolomeu Dias the southern tip of the continent, which they euphemistically named the "Cape of Good Hope". From there, they continued along the East African coast, where the Portuguese increasingly encountered Arab competition, some of which they eliminated with brutal force.

In all this, the resources of the Portuguese were limited, and cooperation with local rulers – wherever possible – was urgently needed. It led to a variety of exchange relationships. The example of *Benin*, one of the largest non-Muslim empires on the territory of present-day Nigeria, is noteworthy. Here, diplomatic activities were lively in 1514/16. The king (Oba) of Benin sent an ambassador to Lisbon and expressed interest in buying arms and sending Christian missionaries to his country. The Portuguese crown then sent a legation accompanied by clergymen to Benin, where it was also received with great respect [Text 117–118]. The intended alliance between the two countries did not materialize, since the Oba refused to convert to Christianity and the Portuguese refused to sell firearms. However, the latter were allowed to establish a trading post and three churches in Benin. In addition, several nobles and a prince were baptized. However, this success did not last. In 1532, the trading post was closed again and the Portuguese presence in the country ended for the time being.

Conversion of native rulers was the primary goal of Catholic missionaries elsewhere as well. It corresponded to their *top-down strategy*: as soon as the king's baptism was accomplished, it was offered more or less en masse to the subjects as well. Catechesis and instruction in Christian mores were, if at all, left for later. According to historian Kevin Ward, the Portuguese in Africa were not primarily interested in conquest. "Most important for them was to establish good relations with local rulers, to be formalised in treaties of friendship and cooperation. A mark of these alliances was the acceptance of the Catholic faith, the baptism of the ruler, his wife and family, and the adoption of a Portuguese Christian name, often that of a present or former Portuguese ruler. For many African rulers, the significance of baptism was not primarily 'religious' but diplomatic".[3]

A more consistent Catholic presence in the region in the 1570s, for example, was brought about by the baptism of the ruler of *Warri,* another independent kingdom in what is now Nigeria. A counter model is presented by the short-lived conversion and baptism in 1561 of the king of Mutapa (in present-day Zimbabwe) and his mother. At the whispers of rival Muslim merchants, however, who suspected the missionaries of being sorcerers, the king soon reversed this move and had the missionaries murdered, which he later regretted. "These people," said, disillusioned, the Jesuit Monclaro, who doubted the convertibility of Africans, "are very unfit for baptism, and even those who grow up among us and become Christians always leave us … because they greatly value their own customs. They become Christians easily and leave Christianity just as easily because they do not understand its meaning."[4]

On the whole, the sporadic missionary attempts of the Portuguese in 16th century Africa were not very successful. On the other hand, many encounters between Portuguese and Africans took place in a contact zone that was not yet characterized by unilateral colonial power structures. This allowed a momentum of its own to develop that led, among other things, to the formation of an independent African Catholicism. This was the case in the *Christian Kongo*, whose ruler Mvemba Nzinga (Afonso I, 1465?–1543) took the initiative in Christianizing his empire – partly even against the resistance of the Portuguese, who were primarily interested in the slave trade [see chap. 6.2].

5.3 Goa as an Ecclesiastical and Political Center

In India, Vasco da Gama's first sea voyage (1498) was followed by a second expedition led by Cabral (1500) and a third, again led by Vasco da Gama (1502). In the meantime, the Portuguese had learned to distinguish Hindus from Muslims. Since 1500 they had also got in contact with the real (and not only the imagined) St. Thomas Christians. Subsequently, regular shipping between Lisbon and Goa began. It brought a growing number of settlers to India (and from Goa to the other Portuguese possessions in Asia). At the same time, the number of Portuguese clerics and religious (initially mainly Franciscans) increased steadily. In 1503, the first Roman Catholic church on Indian soil was built in Cochin (modern: Kochi) [see Figure 6].

Goa, conquered in 1510, became the ecclesiastical and political center of the Portuguese colonial empire in India. In 1530, the Portuguese established the headquarters of their *Estado da India* there. In 1534 Goa was elevated to the status of episcopal see [Text 9a] and in 1558 designated metropolitan church for all of Asia, with suffragan dioceses in India, Malaysia, China, and Japan under its jurisdiction until the end of the 16th century. With its magnificent churches, monasteries and buildings, the city soon gained the reputation of a "new Rome." The city is beautiful, Francis Xavier reported in 1542 after his arrival, it is crowned by a great cathedral and is inhabited almost entirely by Christians. "It has a Franciscan monastery with many friars, and several other churches. There is good reason for thanking God that the Christian religion flourishes so much in this distant land in the midst of heathens" [Text 10a].

On the other hand, complaints were made early on about the immorality of the colonists, who "buy droves of girls and sleep with them" [Text 9b]. It was largely the "dregs" of Portuguese society – according to the Indian historian Teotonio de Souza – who sought their fortune in faraway India. Here, too, members of the secular clergy often had a bad reputation. By their immoral lifestyle, they discredited the reputation of the Christian faith among the "heathens," according to repeated complaints by the religious [Text 9b]. In 1543, the Inquisition was introduced in Goa to combat Judaizing or heretical tendencies among the Christian population [Text 9d]. The prohibition of forcible conversion of dissenters was repeatedly inculcated, but at the same time the public practice of non-Christian cults was forbidden. In the 1540s, the Hindu temples in the city were destroyed [see Text 9c]. Some of their assets were used to build hospitals for Indian Christians or assigned to religious orders.

At the same time, Goa was (until its capture by Indian troops in 1961) the center of the Portuguese colonial empire in Asia and East Africa ('Estado da India'). As mentioned, the Portuguese were primarily concerned with maritime supremacy and securing their trade monopolies, not with large-scale settlement. This "naval base colonialism" led to the establishment of a network of fortified stations along the coasts of Africa and Asia, and only sporadically to more extensive territorial possessions [see Map 3]. At no time did Portuguese personnel in 16th century Asia probably exceed 6000 or 7000 men capable of bearing arms. In 1511 the Iberians conquered Malacca, in 1514 they advanced for the first time to the Moluccas (Ternate), and in 1557 they established a semi-official (and unfortified) settlement in Macao, initially still under Chinese sovereignty. On neighboring Ceylon (Sri Lanka) they had already established themselves since 1505. Even though large areas of the vast Asian continent remained permanently outside their influence, the Portuguese jealously insisted on exclusive access to their sphere of Asian interests – redefined in the Treaty of Saragossa in 1529. Only Portuguese ships were permitted (and required to be the first) to call at Goa. Only with the permission of the

Portuguese crown were Catholic missionaries allowed to operate (at least officially) in other regions of Asia. The only exception was – also according to Saragossa 1529 – the island kingdom of the Philippines, where the Spaniards established a permanent presence since 1565. In 1594, different regions were assigned to the various missionary orders active there [Text 21].

5.4 Francis Xavier: India, Malacca, Moluccas, Japan, Plans for China (1542–1552)

The beginnings of Catholic missions in Asia are closely associated with the name of Francis Xavier (Francisco de Jassu y Janvier). Born in 1506, the Basque was one of the founders of the Societas Jesu in 1534, approved by the Pope in 1540. A modern, highly mobile form of religious order directly subordinate to the pope – sent out to spread the faith among "infidels" overseas and to combat "heretics and schismatics" in the Old World – the Society of Jesus was among the most important actors in the globalization of Catholicism in the early modern period. In 1542, Xavier arrived in Goa, from where he soon left to work among the Parava fishing caste – already Christianized – on the southeastern tip of India (1542–1544; cf. chap. 6.1). In 1545, he traveled to Malacca and from there on to the – partly already Islamized – Moluccas (in today's Indonesia). In 1547, on his way back, he received news of the recently "discovered" Japan in Malacca for the first time. In 1549, together with three Japanese baptized in Goa and two fellow Jesuits, he set out from India for the island kingdom, finally on a Chinese junk. Although he spent only 27 months in the Land of the Rising Sun, a flourishing church subsequently arose there. In 1552, Xavier died on the island of Sanzian (Shangchuan) off the Chinese mainland, his last unachieved goal – the Chinese Empire – before his eyes [Text 10–13; cf. Map 12].

An important role in the Japan enterprise was played by the first Japanese convert named *Anjiro* (also: Angero, Yajiro, later "Paul of Japan"). As a refugee who had had to leave his country because of a murder charge, but who could not find peace of mind, he heard about the "holy priest" from Europe and decided to wait for Xavier in Malacca. Later, he accompanied the group of three Jesuits who first set foot on Japanese soil in his hometown of Kagoshima (on the southern island of Kyushu) in 1549. Anjiro acted as interpreter, translator and was able to win many relatives and acquaintances for the new faith [see Figure 7; Photo C01/02] – Next stop was the imperial city of Miyako (Kyoto). Xaver tried in vain to get here an audience with the emperor who, however, was a person without influence. At that time, Japan was fragmented. The emperor was a mere symbolic figure and puppet, and power lay with the 214 or so feudal lords (*daimyo*). Xaver found friendly reception with one of these regional lords, the daimyo Ouchi Yoshitaka in the residence city of Yamaguchi. He impressed with his erudition and rich gifts (including items hitherto unknown in Japan, such as a watch, glasses, music box, mirror, flint gun, and a Latin Bible). He received permission to preach in public and was busy day and night disputing with curious visitors about questions of the natural and supernatural world. Here, too, the number of baptized Christians increased rapidly – Significantly, he was invited to the court of the feudal lord Otomo Yoshishige in Bungo (now Oita, on Kyushu). This would later become the first Japanese convert from the higher nobility and set off a chain reaction. In 1551/52, Xaver returned to Goa to seek – unsuccessfully – access to the Chinese Empire (as the cultural hegemonic power of Northeast Asia).

About the civilization of the Japanese Xaver expressed himself in tones of highest admiration. Above all, according to his letter of November 5, 1549, this people is by far

> the best who have yet been discovered, and it seems to me that we shall never find among heathens another race to equal the Japanese. It is a people of very good manners, good in general, and not malicious; their sense of honor is particularly pronounced, honor is above everything to them. [...] They listen with great avidity to discourse about God and Divine things ... They do not have idols in the form of animal figures [sc. as in Indian Hinduism], most Japanese worship the spirit of great ancestors [...] They listen willingly to things consonant to nature and reason; and although they are not free from vices and wicked practices [sc. such as homosexuality], if you show them that their sin is contrary to reason, they readily acknowledge their guilt and obey the law of reason. [Text 12b]

Xaver changed his missionary method under the impression of these new intercultural encounters. No longer the goal of quick mass baptisms, but adaptation to the given cultural context was now considered the appropriate way. In Japan, this was mainly done in contrast to the prevailing Buddhism. Of course, it was important to avoid the impression that Christianity was just another of the numerous Buddhist sects. Critical here, as in later stages of mission history, was especially the question of an appropriate name for God. Xavier therefore rejected the Buddhist designation for God he had previously used, *Dainichi* – name of the Varicocana Buddha and "Lord of Light" – and replaced it with the Latin word *Deus*.

After Xavier's departure, a *religious debate* took place in 1552 in Yamaguchi, a cultural and religious center of the country with over 100 monasteries and temples. The discussion was held between the two Jesuits he had left behind and representatives of different Buddhist schools. A protocol originally written in Japanese by the linguistically skilled brother Juan Fernández has been preserved [Text 15]. The subject matter was a variety of issues in dispute between the two sides, such as the spiritual nature of the soul, theodicy, or sexual ethics. This conversation has been appreciated as a highly significant "first documentation of the clash of Asian and European ways of thinking". "The Jesuits proved to be masters of the Aristotelian-Scholastic way of reasoning, while their interlocutors apparently had little room in their worldview based on the unity of the cosmos for the dualism of spirit and matter and the personal conception of God and man."[5]

When Xavier left the island kingdom at the end of 1551, there were between 800 and 3,000 baptized Christians there. In the period that followed, their number increased steadily. For the year 1570, their number is given as about 30,000, and for 1581, already more than 100,000. The "Christian century" of Japan began, as the historian C.R. Boxer described the period between 1549 and 1650 in a study that has become a classic until today. Around 1600, about 300,000 of approximately 20 million Japanese were probably Christians.[6] At the same time, in a changed political constellation, a series of persecutions of Christians began, which led to the formation of a Japanese underground church [see chap. 11.1].

Notes to Chapter 5

1. Hastings (1994), *Church in Africa*, 137.
2. Boxer (1978), *Church Militant*, 4.
3. Ward (2017), *Christianity in Africa*, 136
4. Marx (2008), *Handel und Mission*, 31.
5. Schmitt (1987), *Dokumente* III, 475–481 (Wolfgang Reinhard).
6. Boxer (1993), *Christian Century*, 320 f.

Further Reading for Chapter 5

5.1 (Ethiopia: Portuguese as Guests and Allies in the Christian Empire)

Hastings (1994), *Church in Africa*, 3–70.136–147; Kalu (2005), *African Christianity*, 104–116; Sundkler/ Steed (2000), *Africa*, 34–41. 73 ff; Paulau/ Tamcke (2022), *Ethiopian Orthodox Christianity*, 2–80; Salvadore (2017), *Ethiopian-European*

Relations; Hock (2005), *Christentum in Afrika,* 27–31.50–54; Böll (1998), *Von der Freundschaft zur Feindschaft,* 43–58; Hage (2007), *Orientalisches Christentum,* 200–221; Lange/ Pinggéra (2010), *Altorientalische Kirchen,* 41–50; Paulau (2021), *Verflechtungsgeschicht*e (early links with Protestant Europe); Daniels (2019), *Luther and European Christianity,* 21–32.

5.2 (*Beginnings of Catholic Presence in Sub-Saharan Africa*)
Hastings (1994), *Church in Africa,* 71–86; Ward (2017), *Christianity in Africa,* 139–142; Hock (2005), *Christentum in Afrika,* 36–39; Boxer (1978), *Church Militant,* 2–12 („The Indigenous Clergy"); Baur (1994), *Christianity in Africa,* 44–50; Sundkler/ Steed (2000), *Church in Africa,* 42 ff; Reinhard (1983), *Expansion* I, 28–49; Schmitt (1986–1988), *Dokumente* I, 218–243; Marx (2008), *Handel und Mission,* 12–43; Hodkin (1975), *Nigerian Perspectives,* 105–152.

5.3 (*Goa as Ecclesiastical and Political Center*)
Neill (1984), *Christianity in India* I, 111–140; Tekkedath (1982), *Christianity in India* II, 310–331.353–364, Frykenberg (2008), *Christianity in India,* 127ff; Reinhard (1983), *Expansion* I, 50–80; Meier (2018), *Ränder,* 48–52; De Souza (1998), *Indian Christians,* 31–42.

5.4 (*Francis Xavier: India, Malacca, Moluccas, Japan, Plans for China [1542–1552]*)
Moffett (2005), *Christianity in Asia* II, 9–13.63–75; Schurhammer (1973), *Francis Xavier;* Mormando (2006), *Francis Xavier;* Neill (1984), *Christianity in India* I, 134–165; Mundadan (1984), *Christianity in India* I, 155–163; Ross (1994), *Vision Betrayed,* 13–31; Boxer (1993), *Christian Century,* 36–90; Morris (2018), *Christianity in Japan,* 93–178; Mullins (2003), *Christianity in Japan;* Hsia (2004), *Promise: China;* Friedrich (2022), *The Jesuits;* Meier (2018), *Ränder* 52–60.75–82.122–124; Clossey (2008), *Salvation and Globalization;* Molina (2013), *To Overcome Oneself* (Global vision); O'Malley (2017), *The Jesuits;* Županov (2019), *Oxford Handbook of the Jesuits.*

CHAPTER 6

Forms of Indigenous Christianity

It is one of the remarkable phenomena of the period under discussion here that multiple developments leading to the formation of new indigenous Christianities were already taking place in numerous regions outside Europe in the 16th century. They emerged partly within and partly outside a given colonial context and were supported by local groups who turned to the new faith for a variety of reasons. However different the individual motives for turning to Christianity may have been, they often led to the formation of a new and lasting religious identity that survived rapid persecutions or changes of the colonial context. In the earlier – mission history oriented – research mostly ignored, the investigation of these groups forms an important topic for studies in the history of Christianity beyond Europe. These "indigenous Christianities"[1] are also of growing interest to social anthropologists and cultural studies scholars. Later developments in the respective regions often cannot be understood without these early forms of an independent appropriation of Christianity.

6.1 Asia: the South Indian Paravars and the Martyrs of Mannar (Sri Lanka)

In Asia, the example of the Paravars is noteworthy. This was a fishing caste on the south coast of India that converted to Christianity as a closed group between 1535 and 1537 on their own initiative. The formerly privileged caste of the Paravars, who were engaged in pearl fishing, had increasingly become dependent on Indo-Arab traders. At the same time, they faced growing pressures from local Hindu rulers. Therefore, they sought to place themselves under the protection of the Portuguese, which finally led to their adoption of Christianity.

A special role was played by an Indian Christian named João da Cruz. He had been sent to the court of King Manuel I in Lisbon in 1513 as a fifteen-year-old by the prince of Calicut and converted there. Returning to India, he worked with great zeal to spread his new faith, combining religious, economic and political interests in a most peculiar way. On his advice, a 70 persons-strong delegation of Paravars traveled to Cochin (Kochi, in present-day Kerala). They secured Portuguese support, were baptized and returned to their villages on the fishing coast. They were accompanied by some priests who performed mass baptisms there and soon disappeared again [Text 16].

© KLAUS KOSCHORKE, 2025 | DOI:10.1163/9789004699830_007
This is an open access chapter distributed under the terms of the CC BY-NC-ND 4.0 license.

When the famous Francis Xavier – later celebrated as the "Apostle of Asia" – left Goa in 1542 and began his missionary work on the southern tip of India, outside the Portuguese-controlled territories, he thus encountered there already existing Christian communities. They numbered about 20,000 people. Although the majority of these new Christians were baptized, they possessed only rudimentary knowledge of their new faith. "Since the Christians of this area have no one to instruct them, they are completely ignorant and know nothing else to say except that they are Christians. There is no one to say mass for them; no one to teach them the Creed" or the commandments. Faced with a lack of language skills, Francis Xavier opted for a method of evangelization that was as simple as ultimately effective. He had native collaborators translate central texts and prayers – such as the Lord's Prayer, the Hail Mary, the Ten Commandments and the Apostles' Creed – into Tamil. He had the children memorize these texts, which they passed on to adults, parents, relatives and neighbors. Together, these prayers were then practiced regularly. "On Sundays, I gathered the inhabitants of a neighborhood, men and women, young and old, to repeat the prayers in their own language. They showed great joy and came very gladly," Xavier wrote in one of his letters [Text 10b]. After a year he moved on. Only irregularly did other Catholic priests come to the region. The transmission of the new faith took place mainly within the community itself.

However, the Paravars' initially very superficial acceptance of the Catholic faith proved durable. It survived changing colonial constellations such as the transition to the rule of the Calvinist Dutch (who took over parts of South India in the 17th century) and the Anglican British in the 19th century. The Paravars established themselves as a "Christian caste in the Hindu society" of South India – a situation that continues to the present day.

From the beginning, however, the fishing coast became also a center of regional self-propagation. The Christianized Paravians did not stay in one place. As fishermen they changed, depending on the season respectively the monsoon winds, their location and moved regularly to the opposite northwest coast of Sri Lanka, in the region around Mannar. Thus, the beginnings of a Catholic Christianity also occurred here early – before the Portuguese gained a foothold in the region. These early beginnings are all the more impressive because they soon led to violent reactions from local rulers. In 1544, the Hindu king of Jaffna (in the north of the island) launched a punitive expedition against the inhabitants of Mannar. The new Christians were mercilessly massacred and all "executed without distinction of age or status – women and men, children and infants." This is the report of a chronicler of the 16th century, who gives the number of victims as 600 to 700 [Text 17]. At the same time he emphasizes the steadfastness and intrepidity of these "martyrs of Mannar".

Their veneration flourished in the centuries that followed, and the region around Mannar remains a stronghold of Sri Lankan Catholicism to this day.

6.2 Africa: the Christian Kongo Kingdom in its Transatlantic Connections

While the Paravers of southern India were a marginalized group, elsewhere it was local rulers who promoted the Christianization of their territories. The most fascinating example of this kind, which has been intensively explored in recent research, is the Christian Kongo Kingdom. Here, according to the historian of modern history Horst Gründer, "the phenomenon of a Christianization carried out by the natives without pressure from outside" can be observed, "which, moreover, was pushed forward by the Africans more strongly than by the Europeans, sometimes even against their resistance".[2] At the same time, according to social anthropologist John Thornton, a "distinctly Kongo version of Christianity" and independent African form of Christianity developed here.[3] Brought to the New World by enslaved Kongolese Christians, this was later to become an important factor in the spread of Christianity among their African compatriots and fellow sufferers in the Americas.

The first peaceful contacts between the Portuguese and Kongo rulers had occurred as a result of Diogo Cão's voyages of discovery along the coast of West Africa in the 1480s [see Map 1 + 5]. In 1491, the Kongo king Nzinga Nkuvu was baptized [Text 120]. But it was the long reign of his son *Mvemba Nzinga, with baptismal name Afonso I* (1506–1543), who was committed to the program of modernizing and Christianizing his kingdom, that became decisive. To build up a native church in the Kongo, he sent his son Dom Henrique to Portugal for theological training. From there he returned to his homeland in 1521 as Africa's first – and until the 19th century last – black bishop, but soon died there. Portuguese missionaries came to the country, but as invited guests. Symbols of the old religion, such as fetishes, were replaced by crosses. Conversely, Christianity was integrated into traditional Kongolese ideas about the universe. European visitors of the 16th and 17th centuries took no offense at this 'inclusive' understanding of Christianity. In his capital Mbanza Kongo (renamed "San Salvador" by him), the king had a large church built, where he occasionally preached himself – "better" than the local European priests, as an enthusiastic missionary reported back home.

What has survived is an extensive correspondence between the African monarch and his Portuguese counterparts in Lisbon as well as the Curia in Rome between 1540 and 1542, in which Afonso, "king of the Kongo by the grace of God," repeatedly asked for suitable missionaries and craftsmen to be sent. However, the religious personnel who came from Portugal were largely unfit. Instead of fulfilling their duties as educators of princes or teachers of the numerous sons of the nobility at court – according to his complaint to King Manuel on Oct. 5, 1514 – the freshly arrived clerics preferred to run their own businesses, filling their houses even "with women of bad living" and thus making the people "to mock and to laugh" at the king, in his religious zeal [Text 121]. In general, the Portuguese were less interested in evangelizing the country than in gaining access to the region's copper deposits and, above all, in the slave trade. The latter to an extent that threatened to "depopulate" his empire – according to Afonso already in 1526 in another letter of complaint [Text 122]. Nevertheless, he succeeded in advancing Christianization not only at court but also among the rural population. His successors were able to maintain the avowedly Catholic character of the Kongo Empire, which later increasingly disintegrated, for about 300 years. They even adorned themselves – like the Kongo ruler Pedro IV, who ruled from 1695–1718 – with the title of defenders of the church's orthodoxy ('Defensor fidei').[4] Remnants of this Kongo Catholicism still existed in the early 19th century.

The Christian Kongo also gained great importance in particular through its *transatlantic connections*, which have only recently been intensively researched. Slaves abducted from the Kongo in the 17th and 18th centuries reached the New World colonies partly already as baptized Christians. Some acted there as informal evangelists among their compatriots and fellow sufferers – with the result that groups with a recognizable Kongo-Christian identity formed among blacks in Brazil, the Caribbean or in the south of what is now the United States. "Kongo black Christians," for example, played a role in several significant slave revolts, such as the Stono Rebellion of 1739 in South Carolina and the Haitian Revolution of 1793, and in northern Brazil a "black aristocracy" developed among the Catholic population of enslaved Africans, composed primarily of Kongolese.[5] In folklore-such as the annual coronation of a Kongo king in Carnival-music, dance, processions, or oral tradition, memories of the African homeland were kept alive or reconstructed. The black brotherhoods (partly within and partly outside the existing ecclesiastical structures), which can be traced back to the mid-16th century in Brazil, were also particularly important. They functioned not only as contact points for newcomers and semi-autonomous centers of social and religious life in colonial society. In isolated cases, they also formed networks that connected black Christians on both sides of the Atlantic. The conversion of African Americans, according to the aforementioned John Thornton, was thus a "continuous process" that began early "in Africa and continued in the New World." "Much of the Christianity of Africa reached America across the ocean."[6]

6.3 Iberoamerica: Voices of American-Indian and Mestizo Christians

In Latin America, many testimonies from an indigenous perspective, reflecting the view of the conquered, date from the second half of the 16th century and the first decades of the 17th century. This is also true of indigenous Christian voices, mostly writings by mestizos who felt the clash of the world of the conquerors and the conquered within themselves, rearticulating pride in the submerged culture. For example, the *Inca Garcilaso de la Vega* (1539–1616), son of a Spanish father and an Inca princess, whose "Chronicle" and "Commentaries" on the history of Peru have been called one of the most impressive indigenous voices in Spanish America. He portrays the Incas as benevolent rulers who governed an empire where everyone was well fed and happy before the Spanish arrived. The Incas were already seeking the true God, albeit under a different name [Text 246]. At the same time, the author justifies Spanish rule and welcomes the Christianization of his people. The same applies to other historical works written in the cultural centers of New Spain (Mexico) and Peru since the middle of the 16th century, many of which were published only in the 19th or 20th century. According to the cultural scientist Richard Nebel, they are to be seen as an expression of the search for a new "Christian-Indigenous-Spanish identity" and illustrate the genesis of a mestizo mixed culture.[7]

Other surviving Indian testimonies, however, are voices of *continuing resistance* to the Spaniards or lamentations over the demise of the old world. For example, the dirge written in Nahuatl by an anonymous author in Mexico in the 1520s about the conquista experienced as a catastrophe [Text 221; cf. Text 247] or the report ("Instruction") of the penultimate Inca ruler Titu Kusi Yupanki (c. 1570), written in local Ketschua and then translated into Spanish by an Augustinian monk. A shrewd diplomat, head of the Indian resistance, and even a baptized Christian, he gives insight into the shaking of the Inca world in the final phase of their struggle against the Spaniards.

Early beginnings of a *self-organization* of American-Indian Christians in the colonial cities of Spanish America were represented by the *brotherhoods*. These were lay organizations that served the veneration of a particular saint and at the same time the mutual support of their members. They were so popular that as early as 1582, the Third Provincial Council of Lima sought to reduce their number and place them under greater episcopal control. Children of the nobility were taught the Christian faith in the schools of the Franciscans, Dominicans and later the Jesuits, and soon in many cases also acted as translators and multipliers. They possessed, according to a report from 1596, "such a good memory that they remembered a sermon or the story of a saint after hearing it once or twice, and repeated it later with good humor, boldly and correctly" [Text 230].

Sacred art was one of the fields where indigenous traditions found their way in early on. In addition, the Christian Indians were skilled craftsmen, good musicians and in many cases actively involved in shaping the life of worship. "In our country," said the Peruvian chronicler Poma de Ayala around 1600, "the Indians are just as gifted as Castilians in their artistry and workmanship. Some of them are excellent singers and musicians. They make themselves masters of the organ, fiddle, flute, clarinet, trumpet, and horn without any difficulty. ... Indians are skilful at all decorative arts such as painting, engraving, carving, gilding, metalwork, and embroidery. They make good tailors, cobblers, carpenters, masons, and potters ... On Sundays and holy days they conduct the ceremonies as well as any Spaniard. In default of a priest, they baptize the babies with holy water, reciting the proper forms of words... On Wednesdays and Fridays, Indians conduct the morning service".[8]

The school of Cuzco (Peru), which was to reach its zenith in the 17th and early 18th centuries, achieved particular importance in the field of sacred art. However, it is attested as early as 1545. This indigenous school of art was, to be sure, at first essentially a European foundation. In the course of time, however, the creative possibilities of indigenous artists steadily increased. They integrated Andean motifs – such as landscapes, local flowers, fruits, animals or people in native costume – into their paintings, certainly also as a sublime protest against the dominance of European traditions. Christ and the saints were given mestizo facial features. Even a guinea pig – a popular delicacy in Peru to this day – has not been missing in a depiction of the Last Supper by the mestizo artist Marcos Zapata (*c.* 1750, now in Cuzco Cathedral) [see Figure 13; Photo J04/05].

The cult of the *Virgin of Guadelupe* became a central symbol of national identity in colonial and independent Mexico at the end of the 18th and 19th centuries. According to legend, she appeared several times before the Indian peasant Juan Diego in 1531 and demanded a shrine for herself – as a sign of God's special providence for ordinary Mexicans. The legend itself came later and was first attested in writing in 1648 [Text 242]. However, the existence of the Guadelupe cult per se is attested as early as the mid-16th century. It was also the subject of early critical commentary on the part of the Franciscans, who suspected in it the continued worship of the Aztec goddess Tonantzin in Christian guise. What is remarkable about the tradition of this and other Marian apparitions in Ibero-America is, among other things, the reversed roles: it was not the native Indian, but the European bishop who had to be "converted" in the legend.

One of the most remarkable testimonies of early encounters with Christianity is found around 1563 in the writings of *Pedro de Quiroga* (1520–1588). The text is characterized by the combination of sharp criticism of Spanish colonial rule with a deep devotion to Jesus. The figure of the Inca Tito presented here is not a historical but a literary figure. However, it is probably representative of many Indian biographies of the time. Tito, born in Cuzco, a relative of the Inca kings, encounters three Spaniards – conquistador, merchant, hermit – who represent different types of Christian presence in conquered Peru. "With hostility you have attacked us" – Tito's opening statement – and yet preached the Christian God. Tito first comes up against a soldier, in the midst of intra-Spanish fighting: "Then I realized that you were wise, brave and warlike people, that you had a God and a holy and good religion. But I saw that your brazen actions were contrary to what you recommend to us". Next, Tito meets a merchant who can only give him a superficial knowledge of the new faith. Finally, he encounters a hermit living in poverty and piety. Thus "I understood," is his summary, "that there were good and bad people among you... This good man abhorred your evil works ... and introduced me to the holy faith in Christ" [Text 238].

Notes to Chapter 6

1. Terminology used, e.g., by: Tavárez (2017), *Indigenous Christianities*.
2. Gründer (1992), *Welteroberung*, 58.
3. Thornton (1984), *African Catholic Church*, 155.
4. Hastings (1998), *Pedro IV of the Kongo*, 69.
5. Daniels (2014), *Kongolese Christianity in the Americas*, 216.
6. Thornton (^{2}1998), *Atlantic World*, 254. 262.
7. Nebel (2006), *Indigen-christliche Autoren im kolonialen Mexiko*, 145–152.
8. Goodpasture (1989), *Cross and Sword*, 47 ff.

Further Reading for Chapter 6

6.1 (Asia: The South Indian Paravars and the Martyrs of Mannar [Sri Lanka])

Mundadan (1984), *Christianity in India* I, 391–401; Neill (1984), *Christianity in India* I, 140–147; Schmitt (1987), *Dokumente* II, 456–459; Schurhammer (1963), *Bekehrung der Paraver*, 215–254; Kaufmann (1981), *Christian Caste in Hindu Society*, 203–234; Lindenfeld (2021), *Indigenous Experience*, 178–187.

6.2 (Africa: The Christian Kongo Kingdom in its Transatlantic Connections)

Thornton (2024), *Transatlantic Connections*; Thornton (²1982), *Atlantic World*, 235 ff. 262–271; Thornton (1984), *African Catholic Church*, 147–167; Heywood/ Thornton (2007), *Atlantic Creoles*; Hastings (1994), *Church in Africa*, 79–86.109–118.635–639; Hastings (1998), *Pedro IV of the Kongo*, 59–72; Ward (2017), *Christianity in Africa*, 137–139; Lindenfeld (2021), *Indigenous Experience*, 97–106; Hock (2005), *Christentum in Afrika*, 39–44; Gründer (1992), *Welteroberung*, 50–65; Baur (1994), *Christianity in Africa*, 55–62; Daniels (2014), *Kongolese Christianity in the Americas*, 215–226.

6.3 (Iberoamerica: Voices of American-Indian and Mestizo Christians)

Adorno (2000), *Writing and Resistance*; Hamilton (2009), *Guaman Poma*; Prien (1978), *Geschichte*, 221–228 (Poma de Ayala); Mills/ Taylor (1998), *Documentary History*, 153–164 (Poma de Ayala); Prien (2013), *Latin America*, 223–242 (popular religiosity); Ardanaz (1992), *Pedro de Quiroga*; Tavárez (2017), *Indigenous Christianities*, 31–49; Christensen (2014), *Translated Christianities*; Lockhart (1992), *Nahuatl Accounts;* Edmonson (1974), *Sahagún;* Nebel (2006), *Indigen-christliche Autoren*, 142–161; Delgado (1991), *Gott in Lateinamerika*, 167–170. 233–237; Granados (2003), *Bild und Kunst*; Del Pomar (1964), *Cuzco School of Painting*; Martin/Pettus (1973), *Scholars and Schools*; Nebel (1992), *Virgen de Guadelupe*; Poole (1995), *Lady of Guadalupe*; Lindenfeld (2021), *Indigenous Experience*, 31–49.

CHAPTER 7

Reception of the Council of Trent Overseas and the End of Local Experiments

7.1 State of Expansion at the End of the 16th Century

What did the map of Catholic presence in Asia, Africa and America look like at the end of the 16th century? Parallel to the establishment of colonial rule by the Iberian powers overseas, colonial ecclesiastical structures had also consolidated in the territories under their control. In Spanish America, a network of dioceses stretched from Mexico to the south of the double continent, with archbishoprics in Santo Domingo, Mexico and Lima (each since 1546). In Brazil, Salvador da Bahia was for a long time the only episcopal see (and was elevated to archbishopric in 1676) [see Map 6]. West Africa was organizationally under the two bishoprics of Cape Verde Island and São Tomé, established in 1534. In Asia, Goa was the ecclesiastical and political center of the Portuguese possessions. In 1557, Goa was elevated to an archdiocese whose jurisdiction extended from the Cape of Good Hope and the East African coast to Japan – encompassing numerous territories where Portugal exercised no de facto control. The Philippines (Spanish-controlled since 1565) were divided among the various missionary orders active in the island kingdom in 1598 [Text 21].

But as the example of Francis Xavier shows, Catholic missionaries were active from the beginning also outside the respective colonial dominions. This was the case in Asia, where early on a broad variety of intercultural encounters can be observed. Jesuits, for example, took part in inter-religious discussions at the court of non-Christian princes (as in the Lahore of the Mughal Muslim rulers [Text 21]) or at intellectual centers such as the Japanese residential city of Yamaguchi (where they held debates with Buddhist representatives) [text 15]. Elsewhere (as in southern India and Ethiopia), Europeans got in touch with already existing ancient Churches, whose representatives were quite self-confident in their encounter with the Portuguese (whom they welcomed, but as guests). Again, in other places – in a context not yet characterized by asymmetrical power relations of later periods, still outside the colonial sphere – there were manifold contacts with regional rulers and indigenous people, which (as in the Christian Kongo) led to the formation of local versions of Christianity. In other cases, early sporadic missionary activities resulted in the establishment of permanent congregations and a continuous missionary presence only generations later.

Protestant missionary activities overseas did not play a role in the 16th century. There were isolated and short-lived forays (such as those of the French Huguenots in Brazil and Florida in the 1550s and 1560s [Text 233b; Map 7]). On the whole, however, the Protestant movement was still too preoccupied with its survival in Central Europe and, at the same time, cut off from many overseas connections. Only towards the end of the 16th century this picture should gradually change. However, the Catholic overseas mission played an important role in the confessional controversies of Europe. Catholic polemicists – such as the Jesuit Cardinal Roberto Bellarmin (1542–1621) – and missionaries (such as the Franciscans Bernardino de Sahagún and Gerónimo de Mendieta in Spanish America) developed a theory of compensation. They saw missionary gains in the New World as compensation for losses in the Old. At the same time, Bellarmin, for example, sought to prove the superiority of the Roman Church precisely from the criterion of its geographical catholicity: For unlike the Protestant "heresies" confined to a "corner of Europe," the Roman Church was now represented "in all four corners of the world." Confessionalization in the Old World and overseas missions thus presented themselves as two sides of the same coin. "The more the Catholic Church lost souls in Europe, the greater was the zeal for winning souls among non-European peoples".[1] Lutheran theologians in Germany, in turn, looked with great interest at the Christian empire in Ethiopia and emphasized the similarities between Orthodox tradition and Protestant principles vis-à-vis Roman "tyranny."

7.2 Trent and its Impact on Spanish America

One of the central events of the 16th century was without any doubt the Council of Trent (1545–1563). Here, Roman Catholicism reformed itself after the massive loss of ground to the Reformation, corrected various grievances, introduced reforms and defined itself as strictly anti-Protestant. At the same time, it was a purely European event. Not a single representative of the overseas episcopate took part in the deliberations (if only because the Spanish crown knew how to prevent it); and not a single one of the numerous issues arising from the situation in the New World – such as the bitter colonial-ethical debates in Spanish America – was on the council's agenda. Nevertheless, it had profound effects on the development of the emerging churches overseas. One of these effects was the abandonment of various local experiments and initiatives to develop an indigenous church, as had been sought especially in mendicant circles. Instead, centralist tendencies and the model of a church controlled by the colonial state became entrenched. While the myth of a quasi-monolithic Tridentine Catholicism in Europe itself has been increasingly destroyed in recent years, the effects of the Council on the emerging church structures overseas were in part much more direct.[2]

The canonical reception of Trent in Spanish America is initially most tangible in the *provincial councils* held in Mexico and Lima since the 1550s. Relevant here, in addition to the second provincial council in Mexico (Mexico II; 1565) and Lima (Lima II; 1567/68), are especially the third ones in Mexico (Mexico III; 1585) and Lima (Lima III; 1582/83). The latter has repeatedly been called the Tridentine of South America. Enormous importance has also to be attattached to the Junta Magna of 1568. This advisory body to the Spanish crown defined the conditions under which Trent was to be applied in the New World. At the same time, it set out to centralize colonial church policy, preventing dissenting initiatives by the bishops and direct interference by Rome in American affairs. This was accompanied by the consistent application of state censorship as well as growing discrimination against the indigenous people as a human race without culture, which increasingly rendered obsolete the goal of building an Indian church as well as training an indigenous clergy. Writings by pro-indigenous missionaries (such as Las Casas or Sahagún) were denied permission to print or placed on the index of forbidden books. The ban on ordaining Indians or mestizos as priests had already been pronounced at the first Mexican provincial council of 1555. It was confirmed in 1565 or – as in the case of Mexico III (1585) – only slightly modified (as a "temporary" regulation) and reveals the transfer of the Spanish *limpieza* ideology ("purity of blood") to the colonial context of the Americas.

Considerable importance was also attached to the *mistrust of vernacular languages* as the "mother of all heresies" – a mistrust that was reinforced by the opposition to the European Reformation movement. As mentioned elsewhere, a considerable body of ecclesiastical literature in various Indian languages had emerged before 1570. In Mexico, for example, at least 109 Indian-language works in a variety of regional languages (Nahuatl, Tarascan, Otomí, Pirinda, Mixtec, and others) have survived from the period between 1524 and 1572. These were largely produced in connection with the efforts of the Franciscans in particular to form a 'theologia indiana' [see chap. 3.1]. This experiment was never undisputed. Now, however, anti-indigenist tendencies intensified, and the uncontrolled circulation of Bible texts in the vernaculars called into action in Mexico the Inquisition, founded there in 1571. "We find it very harmful," the first Mexican provincial council of 1555 alreadydeclared, "when Indians are given sermons in their language because they do not understand them, and because of the errors that creep in during transmission," and decreed their confiscation. The second Mexican provincial council of 1565, convened for the purpose of promulgating and adapting the Trent resolutions, decided that "Indians shall not be permitted to possess manuscripts of collections of sermons, quotations, and other parts of the Scriptures, but only the Doctrina Christiana, approved by the bishops and translated by religious who know the language".[3] These restrictions were repeatedly justified, among other things, by refering to the danger of a "Lutheran" heresy. In any case, censorship and controls tightened considerably in the period that followed, and catechisms in indigenous idioms were increasingly replaced by those of European origin (for example, by Bellarmin). Use of catechisms other than the new Unity Catechisms was made punishable by excommunication, as Lima III decreed.[4] Although various council decisions continued to make it obligatory for Spanish and Creole clergy to learn indigenous languages, they did so with diminishing success. Other (and positive) impulses of the Tridentine Council – such as the provisions for greater use of vernacular languages in pastoral care [cf. Text 234b] – had only limited effect in the face of intensifying centralism.

The replacement of priests from the religious orders by *secular priests* had a particularly serious impact. For a long time, missionary work among the indigenous people had been primarily in the hands of the mendicant orders (Franciscans, Dominicans). Sometimes at great personal sacrifice, they had become intensively involved in their living conditions and were able to work largely independently of the colonial church hierarchy. As a result of the provisions of Trent, they were now to be placed under the jurisdiction of the respective bishops or replaced by the secular clergy, which as a rule was less experienced in the local languages and mostly disinterested in missionary work. Earlier exceptions, which were in contradiction to Trent, were now revoked by the Pope (so in the bull 'In Principiis Apostolorum Sede' of 25.4.1565). Protests by the Franciscans against the enforcement of the corresponding Tridentine decisions were unsuccessful.[5] A growing number of American Indian congregations (*doctrinas*) passed to secular priests after the great councils of the 1580s, while the earlier missionaries, with all their experience and language skills, were displaced to the city convents.

It was not so much specific decrees of the Council of Trent, according to historian Hans-Jürgen Prien, as the "Tridentine spirit" that determined the reorganization of the Roman Church in Spanish America. "With the adoption of the decisions of Trent, a more religiously uniform society emerged in Latin America than had ever existed in medieval Europe." At the same time, "a cultural Catholicism developed that permitted the continuation of medieval popular piety and its blending with Indian and African elements."[6]

7.3 India: the Synod of Diamper 1599 and the Forced Union of the St. Thomas Christians

In India, the antagonisms between Portuguese colonial Catholicism and native St. Thomas Christians intensified in the second half of the 16th century. At the same time, the Catholic hierarchy became less tolerant of local traditions and customs of the surrounding Hindu society. This was certainly also a consequence of the consolidated Portuguese presence on the subcontinent. In any case, this tendency intensified with the reception of the council of Trent by a series of provincial councils between 1567 and 1592 in Goa, the center of the Portuguese colonial empire in Asia.

Tendencies toward Latinization of the Indian St. Thomas Christians were already evident in the 1520s. In particular, the Portuguese sought to interrupt the Indians' connection to the East Syrian patriarch in "Babylon" (Mesopotamia) – which was only partially successful. Thus, around 1550, the activities of an Indian priest (ordained by the East Syrian patriarch) who "is going about teaching the St. Thomas Christians the Babylonian [i.e., East Syrian] customs without fear of God or the Holy [Roman] Mother Church" caused great concern [Text 19]. At the same time, the Council of Trent, which ended in 1563, experienced an intense reception, especially in Portuguese India. The Goanese provincial councils of 1567 (Goa I), 1575 (Goa II), and 1585 (Goa III) played an important role in this. This reception affected many aspects of church life, including combating "pagan" customs as well as deviant traditions of the St. Thomas Christians. Points of difference were, above all, the different understanding of marriage and marriage impediments, the question of an obligatory priestly celibacy – unknown to the St. Thomas Christians – the number of seven sacraments as well as the recognition of the East Syrian patriarch as ecclesiastical head, which was considered heretical by the Portuguese. The Syriac ("Chaldean") church language was identified as the source of numerous "heresies".

In 1599, the infamous *Synod of Diamper* (Udiyamperur) near Cochin (Kochi) took place, which led to the more or less violent incorporation of the St. Thomas Christians into the Portuguese colonial church. As a traumatic event, it has remained in the long-term memory of Indian Christianity, regardless of denominational affiliation. The synod was convened by the Catholic Archbishop of Goa, the Jesuit Alexis de Menezes, in violation of canon law. The goal was to abolish the separation between Latin and Syriac Christians and to establish the fullest possible conformity with Rome and Roman practice. This was done with constant reference to the council of Trent. The St. Thomas Christian clergy were urged to unconditional obedience to the pope. The Creed, to which the participants committed themselves by oath, emphasized in particular those articles of the Tridentine faith that had previously been unknown to the St. Thomas Christians. They now had to renounce all "Nestorian errors" and especially all allegiance to the patriarch in Babylon, "whom I condemn, reject, and anathematize, as a Nestorian heretic and schismatic, and out of obedience to the holy Roman Church, and therefore for the attainment of [eternal] salvation." All ecumenical councils of the Roman Catholic tradition – and especially the third one in Ephesus (in 431), which had pronounced the condemnation of Nestorius – were to be recognized. All other decisions of the Council of Trent also had to be obeyed [Text 20]. The Syriac church records were partly "purged" and partly burned. The St. Thomas Christians were indeed permitted to continue using their own liturgy. But their rite was to be "cleansed" of everything that did not conform to Tridentine standards.

The synod of Diamper sealed – temporarily – the end of ecclesiastical independence of the St. Thomas Christians. It was not until 1653 that at least some of them succeeded in breaking away again from the forced union with Rome. In the turmoil of the following period, however, they were not able to re-establish the old connection with the East Syrian (dyophysite) patriarch in "Babylon". Instead, they joined another Oriental church community, the "Jacobite" (miaphysite) Patriarchate of Antioch. This led to the formation of the Malankarian Orthodox Church, or the Syrian Orthodox branch of Indian Thoma Christianity. "From courtship to rape" – this is how the Indian historian Teotonio de Souza described the history of the St. Thomas Christians with the Portuguese in the 16th century.[7] The initially friendly encounter between Indian and European Christians grew first into mutual distrust and finally into the forced submission of one side by the other.

7.4 Ethiopia: Expulsion of the Jesuits under Emperor Fasilidas (since 1632/33)

A constellation analogous to that in India – local Christians in conflict with the Portuguese newcomers – also existed in Ethiopia in the 16th century. The only difference was that this conflict ultimately led to the expulsion of the Jesuits and the breaking off of contacts between Christian Ethiopia and Catholic Europe. "From friendship to enmity" – this is how the historian Verena

Böll described this development in the East African country.[8] As early as 1557, Rome's efforts to place the Ethiopian church under the control of a Latin patriarch led to a clash. The Jesuits and Andrea da Oviedo, appointed by Rome as patriarch for Ethiopia, were still allowed to remain in the realm of the Negus. But from then on they were essentially limited to pastoral care of the small Portuguese community in the region around Fremona.

In 1603, after a temporary Jesuit absence in Ethiopia, Pedro Paez was the first Jesuit priest to arrive in the country again. He came during a period of renewed political instability. The highly learned Spaniard, filled with the spirit of the Counter-Reformation, succeeded in persuading Emperor Za Dengel to recognize papal authority and make changes in liturgical life (such as Sabbath observance). This sparked a first bloody revolt. Despite opposition from conservative clergy andmonks", a sizable Catholic party formed at court, and the new emperor Susenyos (r. 1607–1632) formally converted to the Catholic faith in March 1622. A new Latin patriarch appointed by Rome – Alphonsus Mendes – arrived at the royal court in 1626 with great military pomp. He denied the validity of the Ethiopian sacraments and ordered a renewed baptism of the faithful as well as the re-ordination of the Ethiopian clergy. Feasts and fasts were to be celebrated in the future according to the Roman calendar. Mass could continue to be celebrated in the traditional Ge'ez, but it was to conform to the Roman rite. Not only the monks and parts of the nobility, but also the peasants rebelled. The mass of the simple faithful saw their religious identity threatened by the Latinization of the church demanded by the Jesuits. Finally, the emperor felt compelled to revoke the union with Rome. This act was celebrated by contemporaries as the "liberation of the sheep of Ethiopia" from the "evil lions from the West".

In 1632, Susenyos abdicated and his son Fasilidas (r. 1632–1667) took over. He restored the Ethiopian Orthodox Church as a national institution and expelled the Jesuits first from the court and then from his realm. Illegal residence in the country was henceforth punishable by death. Ethiopian Catholics loyal to Rome were banished and the "books of the Franks" were burned. Following ancient tradition, Fasilidas had a new head (*abuna*) of the Ethiopian church consecrated by the Coptic patriarch in Alexandria. Faced with the threat of Portuguese intervention, tensions continued to escalate. In 1640, the emperor had three French Capuchin monks sent by Rome intercepted and executed while still on Ottoman territory before their arrival in Ethiopia [Text 139]. No longer, as before, the Christian brothers from overseas, but Muslim neighbors were now considered allies. In 1653, a last underground native Catholic priest was executed. This ended any established Catholic presence in the country for a long time to come. For two centuries, Christian Ethiopia largely cut itself off from the outside world and almost completely from ties with Latin

Christendom in Europe. Contacts with other Oriental churches (especially Copts and Armenians), however, continued.

The expulsion of the Jesuits from Ethiopia also played a significant role in the confessional controversies of Europe. Protestants welcomed the defeat of their common adversary. As early as 1534, the Ethiopian deacon Michael had visited the reformators Luther and Melanchthon in Wittenberg, who confirmed agreement with him on central questions of faith. Subsequently, Protestant circles repeatedly pointed to Ethiopia as evidence that Christ's true church was not found "in this narrow corner of Europe" alone, but in various parts of the globe. Thus the prominent Lutheran theologian David Chytraeus (1530–1600) was unable to discern any essential difference between Lutheranism and Ethiopian orthodoxy. The Ethiopian emperor Galawdewos's 1555 defense against Jesuit critics (discussed in chapter 5.1) attracted particular attention. As "Confessio Fidei Claudii Regis Aethiopiae" his tract was rapidly disseminated in Protestant Europe in the mid-16th century.[9]

Notes to Chapter 7

1. Hsia (1995), *Mission und Konfessionalisierung*, 158.
2. For the reception of Trent beyond Europe, see the essays in: Koschorke (2002), *Transcontinental Links*, 20 ff.163–202; and in: Francois/ Soen (2018), *Council of Trent* III, 156–320.
3. Quoted from: Baumgartner (1992), *Indianische Sprachen*, 341.
4. Nebel (1992), *Missionskatechismen*, 257.
5. Sylveste (1975), *Motifs*, 41.
6. Prien (1978), *Geschichte*, 255; Prien (2002), *Trienter Konzil*, 187; cf. Prien (2013), *Latin America*, 30f.
7. De Souza (1998), *Indian Christians*, 31–42; De Souza (2002), *Council of Trent ... in Portuguese India*, 189–202.
8. Böll (1998), *Von der Freundschaft zur Feindschaft*, 43–58.
9. For details see: Paulau (2021), *Verflechtungsgeschichte*; Daniels (2019), *Luther and Ethiopian Christianity*, 21–32.

Further Reading for Chapter 7

7.2 (*Trent and Its Impact on Spanish America*)

Prien (2013), *Latin America*, 171–184; Prien (1978), *Geschichte*, 119–124. 255–261 ("reception of Trent in Latin America"); Prien (2002), *Trienter Konzil*, 163–188; François/ Soen (2018), *Council of Trent* III, 277–299 (reception in Peru);

Garrard-Burnett/ Freston/ Dove (2016), *Religion in Latin America*, 107–132 ("Tridentine Piety in the Americas", by B. Larkin); Villegas (1971), *Durchführung*, passim; Baumgartner (1992), *Indianische Sprachen*, 313–347; Henkel/ Pietschmann (1984), *Konzilien in Lateinamerika* I; Henkel/ Saranyana (2010), *Konzilien in Lateinamerika* II; De La Rosa (1992), *„Reinheit des Blutes"*, 271–292; Konetzke (1991), *Süd- und Mittelamerika* I, 230–237; O'Malley (2000), *Trent and all that*; Jedin (1957/1961), *Council of Trent*; Cushner (2000), *Jesuits in Colonial America*; Tavárez (2017), *Indigenous Christianities in Colonial Latin America*, 82 ff.85–87; Delgado (2017), *Catholicism*, 17–37. 45ff; Kaufmann (2017), *Latin-European Christianity*, 184–188.

7.3 (India: The Synod of Diamper 1599 and the Forced Union of St. Thomas Christians)

Neill (1984), *India* I, 191–219.316–321; Wicki, J. (1976), *Auswirkungen des Konzils*, 213–229; Thaliat (1958), *Synod of Diamper*; De Souza (1998), *Indian Christians*, 31–42; De Souza (2002), *Council of Trent ... in Portuguese India*, 189–202; Paiva (2019), *Impact of Luther*, 287–291.

7.4 (Ethiopia: Expulsion of the Jesuits under Emperor Fasilidas [since 1632/33])

Hastings (1994), *Church in Africa*, 139–172; Sundkler/ Steed (2000), *Africa*, 75–80; Salvadore (2017), *Ethiopian-European Relations*; Ward (2017), *Christianity in Africa*, 133–135; Beshah/Aregay (1964), *Question of the Union*; Böll (1998), *Von der Freundschaft zur Feindschaft*, 43–58; Böll (2012), *Gescheiterte Katholisierung*, 157–170; Hock (2005), *Christentum in Afrika*, 50–54; Hage (2007), *Orientalisches Christentum*, 210 f; Lange/ Pinggéra (2010), *Altorientalische Kirchen*, 45–47; Cohen (2009), *Jesuits in Ethiopia*.

Illustrations for Part 1

FIGURE 1   Ethiopian orthodox priest with Ge'ez bible (Lake Tana/Ethiopia 1997).

FIGURE 2   Kerala (India): Bishop and clergy of the Syriac Orthodox Church, a branch of the St. Thomas Christian tradition of India (photo taken in 1983) [= photo A14].

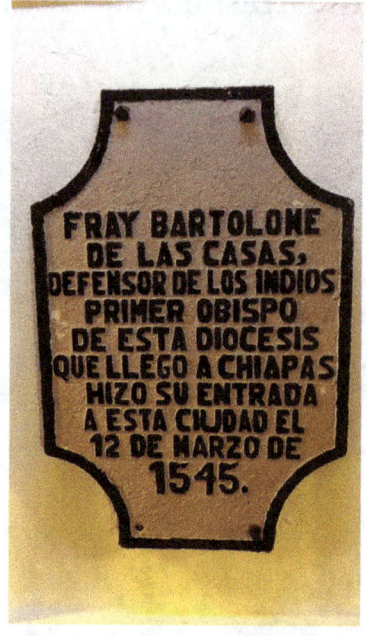

FIGURE 3
Bartolomé de las Casas (1484–1566), Dominican monk, missionary and bishop, "defender of the Indians".

FIGURE 4
Mexico: Plaque commemorating Las Casas in his former diocese of Chiapas [= photo M08].

FIGURE 5 Mexico: The Lord's Prayer in Nahuatl, the pre-Hispanic *lingua franca* of the Aztecs and other peoples in central Mexico; translation and representation in pictorial script took place in the 16th century, mainly by Franciscan missionaries.

ILLUSTRATIONS FOR PART 1

FIGURE 6   India (Kochi/Kerala): St. Francis Church, originally built by the Portuguese in 1503, considered as the oldest European church in India.

FIGURE 7   Japan/ Kagoshima: Monument to the memory of the arrival of Francis Xavier (1506–1552) and his Japanese companion Yajiro (Hanshiro) in 1549 on the southern island of Kyushu [= photo C01].

FIGURE 8   Japan: The Martyrs of Nagasaki (1597), engraving by Wolfgang Kilian (Augsburg 1628).

FIGURE 9   Japan/ Amacusa (Kyushu): Trampling on image of the Virgin Mary as test of religious allegiance for underground Christians [= photo C09].

PART 2

17th/18th Centuries

CHAPTER 8

Changing Framework

Until about 1800, overseas missions remained essentially a Catholic enterprise. It is true that Protestant West European powers became increasingly involved in overseas activities from about 1600 onward. In terms of mission history, however, their presence was initially of little significance. The colonial church structures they established were generally geared at best to the care of European settlers. Only with the rise of the Pietist movement (Halle, Moravians) in the early 18th century (and subsequent movements like the Methodists), a phase of targeted Protestant missionary activities among indigenous people began, for example in Asia. The transregional cross-links of indigenous actors also played an important role early on.

8.1 Aspects of European Expansion

Toward the end of the 16th century, the Iberian overseas monopoly was crumbling. Increasingly, other (mostly Protestant) European powers entered the lucrative overseas trade – in search of slaves (Africa), spices (Asia) or sugar (Brazil, Caribbean). In addition to nations such as France, smaller European countries (such as Denmark, Brandenburg [Prussia] or Sweden) also participated in colonial trade ventures from the early 17th century onward. A leading role was initially played by the Netherlands, which replaced the Portuguese as colonial rulers in numerous areas from the mid-17th century onward. This was especially true in the coastal regions of West and Southern Africa (Elmina in present-day Ghana, Cape of Good Hope, etc.), in South Asia (Southern India, Sri Lanka, Malacca/Malaysia, parts of present-day Indonesia) and temporarily also in Brazil (Pernambuco). The freedom struggle of the Netherlands against Spain played an essential role. Since Spain was united with Portugal in a personal union from 1580 to 1640, the conflict with Portugal was also aimed at securing the country's own independence (which was then recognized under international law in the Peace of Westphalia in 1648). At the same time, the Dutch were consolidating their rule overseas. Historian Wolfgang Reinhard has described this global conflict as the "first world war in Europe."[1] The political conflict was accompanied by a religious one: the Portuguese were Catholics, the Dutch Reformed Calvinists. Overseas, too, the confrontation between rival European powers thus took on the character of a confessional conflict.

The British initially played only a subordinate role in Africa and Asia at that time. In the 19th century, they were a global hegemonic power, but in Africa and Asia in the 17th century, their importance was limited. However, their influence grew steadily in the North Atlantic, in the Caribbean (e.g. in Jamaica) and on the east coast of North America (in the core area of the later USA and parts of Canada). In the second half of the 18th century, its influence increased in the coastal regions of Africa and southern Asia.

8.2 Stages in Mission History

In terms of mission history, the increased presence of Protestant powers overseas was initially of little relevance. They were mainly active in the form of so-called 'companies'. These were semi-public joint-stock companies, which – since they were primarily commercially oriented – showed only limited interest in missionary activities. The charters of these colonial trading companies, which were regularly renewed, stipulated the obligation to spread the Christian religion. For example, the charter of the English East India Company of 1698 contained the provision that from a ship size of 500 tons, a chaplain was to be carried on board of each ship "in order to be able to train the sovereigns and the servants or slaves of the same company in the Protestant religion" [Text 29b]. In practice, however, such provisions were often circumvented – for example, by building ships that were just below this 500-ton limit.

In the Dutch colonial empire in Asia, on the other hand, with its administrative center in Batavia (Jakarta/Indonesia), considerable efforts were made to build up a colonial church infrastructure. In the 17th and 18th centuries, for example, Holland sent a total of 254 *Predikanten* ("preachers") and about 800 lower-ranking church employees ("pallbearers") to the Southeast Asian island empire.2 In the Dutch-controlled parts of Sri Lanka, there were also some remarkable experiments, such as the establishment of seminaries for the training of a native clergy (for example, in Jaffna in 1692 and in Colombo in 1696). Ultimately, however, such initiatives had no long-term effect because they were too tightly constrained within a colonial ecclesiastical corset. The idea of a targeted spread of the gospel among the indigenous population was hardly developed or implemented. – A turning point in the Protestant context came at the beginning of the 18th century with the *Hallean or Moravian Pietist movement*, which in turn inspired similar efforts in the anglophone world (for example, among the Methodists). Usually viewed with suspicion by the respective authorities, this internationally active movement began work among the Hindus of South India, the Khoisan of South Africa, black slaves in the Caribbean, the Inuit ("Eskimos") of Greenland, German emigrants in North

America or Oriental Christians in the Ottoman Empire. Numerically modest as the number of their converts was at first, their work nevertheless became an important prerequisite for later growth.

In the Catholic context, the founding of the 'Congregation for the Propagation of the Faith' (*'Propaganda Fide'*) in Rome in 1622 marks a caesura. It was established as the central missionary authority of the Roman Curia by Pope Gregory XVI. One of its aims was to gain access to the extra-European mission territories independently of the traditional patronage rights of the Spanish and Portuguese crowns (which prevented Rome from communicating directly with the churches in their dominions) and to regain a certain degree of control over the Catholic missions overseas. In doing so, their autonomy was emphasized over colonial political objectives. "What would be more absurd than to import France, Spain, Italy, or any other part of Europe into China? ... Therefore, never exchange customs of those people for European ones," it says, for example, in 1659 in an instruction of the Propaganda to the missionaries sent to China and Indochina [Text 26]. In this context, missionary orders from non-Iberian countries (such as Italy and especially France) became increasingly active. The Iberian patronage powers, however, stubbornly insisted on their traditional prerogatives, which led to numerous conflicts, especially in Asia.

Increasingly, confessional rivalries between European missionaries arose in various regions (such as West Africa or South Asia). Conversely, the Catholic model was not without influence on early Protestant missionary initiatives. In Germany, for example, it was the philosopher Gottfried Wilhelm Leibniz (1646–1716) who was impressed by the Jesuits' work in China in his 'Novissima Sinica' of 1697. His program of a 'propagatio fidei per scientias', in turn, strengthened the conviction of August Hermann Francke (1663–1727), the father of Halle's Pietism, of the necessity of Protestant missionary undertakings. At the same time, in faraway Boston (New England, today USA), the Puritan Cotton Mather (1663–1728), referring to the global Jesuit competition, developed proposals for an interdenominational Protestant world mission. In doing so, he also came into contact with Francke and Halle's emissaries in Tranquebar, South India [cf. chap. 11.5]. The latter, in turn, knew how to make use of the linguistic preparatory work of earlier Catholic missionaries to India in their translation work on site.

8.3 Enlightenment and Other Debates

In the 18th century, the intellectual climate in large parts of Europe changed. With the advance of the Enlightenment and the spread of ideas critical of religion in educated circles, interest in missions declined. This had repercussions overseas as well. In the Catholic mission to Africa, for example, according to Adrian Hastings, the 18th century differed markedly from the 17th century "because the European church had changed". "Rome became both more rigid", in its attitude, and, at the same time, "less zealous", in its missionary commitment[3] In Latin America, a considerable reception of Enlightenment ideas among the Creole upper class can be observed toward the end of the 18th century. Writings by British natural scientists, French philosophers or Spanish reformers reached the New World at ever shorter intervals. This no longer happened primarily through book smuggling – as it had been the case at the beginning of the 18th century, due to the censorship measures of the Inquisition – but increasingly also through the officially tolerated book trade. In universities and seminaries, the new ideas of Voltaire, Rousseau, Newton and Locke were the subject of lively discussion. At the same time, however, the "tolerantism" of the Enlightenment continued to be widely condemned as "Lutheran heresy".

Enlightenment ideas increasingly determined the religious policy of the Spanish and Portuguese crowns in 18th-century Ibero-America. A leading aspect of this – in times of absolutist rule – was the emphasis on complete state authority over the Catholic Church. In contrast to the earlier Habsburg rulers, church patronage was now understood less as a consequence of papal concessions than as an expression of the state's own sovereignty. Competing transnational organizations such as the Catholic missionary orders no longer fit into the picture. This was one of the factors that eventually led to the breakup and expulsion of the Jesuit order from the Portuguese (1759) and Spanish (1767) possessions in the New World [see chap. 9.3].

8.4 Regional Centers, Transcontinental Entanglements

Diverse regional developments shape the picture of Christian history in the global South of this time. These include movements such as that of the African prophetess Kimpa Vita [Figure 15] (as the embodiment and voice of St. Anthony [sic!]) in the Congo in the early 18th century as well as actions of solidarity by Goanese Oratorians for their persecuted Catholic co-religionists in colonial Sri Lanka. However, early evidence of a supra-regional or global consciousness of indigenous Christians can also be found. The Japanese martyrs of Nagasaki (1597), for example, were not only cultically venerated in the Philippines or Catholic Central Europe, but also in Mexico, Paraguay or Peru [see Figure 8; Photo C05/06]. Around 1745, an African pastor in the Dutch colony of Elmina (Ghana) complained to his political and ecclesiastical superiors in Amsterdam about discriminatory treatment on the part of the local colonists. In doing so, he referred to the incomparably better treatment enjoyed by his Indian colleagues in the Danish mini-colony of Tranquebar in far-off southern India [Text 141; see Figure 19]. Examples of transcontinental marriages of indigenous Christians are also attested. One of the best known is the marriage of the former slave and lay evangelist Rebecca from the Caribbean island of St. Thomas to the West African pastor Christian Protten "Africanus" [see Figure 17]. Both belonged to the Moravian *Brüdergemeine* and had met in Germany and married there in 1746. Later, Rebecca traveled with Christian to his West African home in Christiansdorf (in present-day Ghana).

The marriage of Rebecca and Christian Protten is just one particularly striking example of the connections now accumulating between African Christians on both sides of the Atlantic. The term *'Christian Black Atlantic'* has recently been coined to describe the Atlantic world as a space of communication and exchange among black Christians from different regions. An early example of such transatlantic interactions – Kongo Christians as evangelists among their countrymen and fellow slaves in the New World – has already been mentioned. Their involvement found a continuation from about the 1730s in the activities of black Moravian missionaries among African American slaves in the Caribbean. At the same time, since the end of the 18th century, efforts to return freed – often already Christian – slaves to Africa increased. In the 19th century these were to swell further. Black transregional networks were also very important in the Catholic area. Particularly important were Afro-Brazilian brotherhoods, some of which operated in transcontinental connections. One important representative was Lourenço da Silva de Mendouça, an Afro-Brazilian of presumably royal Congolese descent and, at the same time, a recognized leader of the black community in Lisbon and Madrid. Around 1684, he traveled to Rome to deliver a petition to Pope Innocent XI against the mistreatment of Christian slaves by Christian masters in the Americas [Text 255]. As a result, the Propaganda Fide issued two statements condemning the transatlantic slave trade and the forms of its organization.

Exchange relations of various kinds developed through the cultural transfer between East and West, in both directions. Quite remarkable has been, for example, the so-called *Chinese rite controversy* [see chap. 11.2]. It had its origin in the internal disputes of the Catholic orders active in China (especially between Jesuits and Dominicans). But the longer the more it occupied the attention first of the ecclesiastical and later also of the philosophical-enlightened public in Europe. At the same time, it increased there doubts about traditional believes and the credibility of the biblical chronology, and shook previously unchallenged claims to validity of Western Christianity. So here it was not Europe that set the issues overseas. Rather, it saw itself and its traditions challenged by contact with an advanced Asian culture.

Further Reading for Chapter 8

8.1–3 (Steps of European Expansion, Stages in Mission History, Enlightenment and Other Debates)
Reinhard (1983), *Expansion* I, 108–155; Boxer (1972), *Dutch Seaborne Empire*; Abernethy (2000), *European Overseas Empires*, 45–63. 206–224; Gründer (2003), *Expansion*, 55 ff. 74–89. 90–97; Gensichen (1976), *Missionsgeschichte*, 5–13; Elphick/ Davenport (1997), *Christianity in South Africa*, 15–50 (Dutch Period); Moffett (2005), *Christianity in Asia* II, 213–235; Koschorke/ Mottau (2011), *Dutch Reformed Church* (in Sri Lanka); Müller-Krüger (1968), *Protestantismus in Indonesien*, 39–59 (Dutch Colonial Church in Indonesia 17./18. c.); Metzler (1971), *Propaganda Fide*; Mettele (2009), *Brüdergemeine als weltweite Gemeinschaft* (on the Moravians); Beck (1981), *Mission der Brüdergemeine*; Prien (2013), *Latin America*, 243–270 ("The Enlightenment in Ibero-America").

8.4 (Regional Centers, Transcontinental Entanglements)
Thornton (2024), *Transcontinental Links*; Thornton (1998), *Kongolese Saint Anthony;* Sensbach (2005), *Rebecca's Revival*; Andrews (2013), *Native Apostles*, 87–105; Gray (1990), *Black Christians*; Koschorke (1998), *Catholic Underground Church in Ceylon*, 106–116; Steiner (2012), *Japanische Märtyrer von 1597*, 135–156; Merkel (1920), *Leibniz und die China-Mission;* Rowe (2020), *Black Saints*.

CHAPTER 9

Latin America

9.1 The Church in the Colonial City

Hispanic colonization of the Americas bore essentially urban features. During the reign of the Spanish, some 1,000 urban centers were founded as the starting point of their wider conquests and permanent presence in the New World. Uniformly laid out in a checkerboard pattern from the outset – and thus more "modern" than the winding downtowns of medieval Europe – the colonial Spanish settlements were mostly developed in the 16th or early 17th century in the imposing Baroque style. Magnificent churches and spacious monasteries dominated the cityscape. In the center of the colonial metropolises (such as Mexico, Lima or Quito) there was a mostly rectangular or square square, the plaza mayor or *plaza de armas*, seat of the political, ecclesiastical and municipal powers. Around it were grouped the cathedral, the bishop's residence, the governor's palace and the town hall. In the streets that branched off at right angles from the plaza mayor were the houses of the nobles. Further away were the streets of the artisans and merchants. In the outskirts lived the lower service personnel and the poor of the city – mestizos, blacks and Indians, the majority living around their own churches. Even the simple country towns were always built around a large square with a church as the center.

The central plaza functioned at the same time as an arena of public life and the scene of colorful processions. These also served the self-representation of the different groups of colonial society, in a strictly regimented hierarchical sequence. The great festivals of the ecclesiastical year (such as Corpus Christi), civil commemoration days, the name days of the local saints – in Lima, for example, around the middle of the 17th century, 35 in number –, the holding of monastery chapters, the entry of a new bishop, and (in Mexico, Lima or Cartagena) occasionally the macabre ceremonies of the Inquisition provided the occasion for celebration. The processions ended with the entry of the ecclesiastical and secular dignitaries into the cathedral, followed by the various estates, guilds, and lay congregations. These included the various congregations of Indians, mulattoes or blacks, who marched at the end of each. The pageants were accompanied by music, singing, theater (such as on the stages of local Jesuit schools), or evening fireworks. [cf. Photo J01/02; J10]

Not only in the organization of processions, but quite generally, the various lay congregations or brotherhoods played an important role in the religious and social life of the colony. These were associations of lay people dedicated to the veneration of a particular saint, cultivating a "work of mercy" and organizing various forms of mutual support among their members. They owned land, flocks, and (comparable to later credit unions) money. Public welfare was largely in the hands of these religious brotherhoods. The construction of countless chapels and churches was also their initiative. In colonial times, almost every Christian belonged to one or more brotherhoods or guilds. These initially started with the whites, but by the end of the 16th century included all social classes. The mestizos, the mulattos, the Indians and the blacks were also organized in a growing number of their own brotherhoods. The Council of Lima in 1582 sought to reduce and regulate their number "as far as possible," but this did not diminish their popularity.

Particular importance was attached to the black brotherhoods in Brazil. The first examples are attested there since 1552. They achieved a significant presence between 1650 and 1700, especially in the coastal cities. In a country with only a weakly developed colonial church apparatus, they developed in many cases into "autonomous or semi-autonomous organizations" within the church.[1] They became instruments of ethnic solidarity and demands for greater social justice. They repeatedly facilitated the ransom of enslaved members, represented them even to colonial authorities, built transregional networks, and kept alive the memory of the African homeland. Thus, alongside the Catholicism of the white masters, an Afro-Brazilian Catholicism was formed, which had a decisive influence on the subsequent development.

Along with men's convents, women's convents occupied a prominent place in the layout of Spanish colonial cities. There were "six famous and excellent convents for women" in Lima in the 1620s [Text 241a] and more than twenty in Mexico City at the end of the century (Brazil lagged behind; the first convent did not open until 1677). Between 10 and 20% of the female urban population, according to individual estimates, could live in the houses of the women's congregations. The women's convents also reflected the social structure of colonial society, with lavishly furnished rooms for the "brides of Christ" from the upper classes, each with their own servants, and modest cells for members of the lower classes.

Probably the most famous nun of the Spanish colonial period is *Sor Juana Inés de la Cruz* (1648–1695), who was celebrated early on as the "tenth muse of Mexico" [Figure 14]. An illegitimate child from a humble provincial family, she soon attracted attention for her insatiable thirst for knowledge. She gained attention and encouragement from the Viceroy's wife and decided to enter a convent at the age of 18. Life there seemed to her preferable to marriage, as it allowed her – with her own library – to pursue her broad intellectual interests in a self-determined manner. These ranged from mathematics to philosophy and from theology to poetry. She wrote secular and religious poems and dramas and corresponded with leading scholars of her time. Her growing fame sparked criticism in circles of the church hierarchy. To them, she defended women's "God-given" right to education:

> I wish these interpreters ... of St. Paul would explain to me how they understand this: 'Let women keep silence in the church' [1 Cor. 14:34]. For they must understand it either materially, to mean the pulpit and the lecture hall, or formally, to mean the community of all believers. If they understand it in the first sense ... – then why do they rebuke those who study in private? But if they understand it in the second sense and wish to extend the apostle's prohibition to all instances without exception, so that women are not even permitted to write or study privately – why then did the Church permit a Gertrude, a Theresa [of Avila], a Brigid, the nun of Agreda, and many others to write? [Text 243b]

Eventually, she came into conflict with the bishop of Puebla. She was forced to dissolve her library and give up her scientific instruments. A short time later, she died in the service of plague patients. Tragic as her end was, this biography is nevertheless remarkable as an example of a woman in a colonial context who consciously preferred life in a convent to conventional marriage.

As early as 1551, Emperor Charles v had two *universities* established in Mexico City and Lima. They were endowed with the same privileges as the famous University of Salamanca in metropolitan Spain [cf. Text 241c]. In total, 26 universities were established in Spanish America throughout the colonial period. In contrast, no universities were founded in colonial Brazil. Prominent thinkers and authors who had received an education there, for example at the Jesuit College in Bahia, then went on to Portugal to acquire academic degrees at the universities of Coimbra or Évora. In general, school education in Ibero-America was in the hands of the church. The Dominican and Jesuit orders were particularly prominent in this regard. In the smaller towns, the monasteries often fulfilled this task. In the capitals, each order had secondary schools (*colegios*) for the education of future friars. It was especially the Jesuits who very soon opened schools also for the preparation of secular professions. This with considerable success; large parts of the future Creole elite received a qualified education there. This was an essential reason, conversely, for the rapid social and economic rise of the Society of Jesus in colonial America. Initially open also to selected individual youths from the Indian nobility, universities, colleges and finally even elementary schools were later increasingly closed to them.

Beginning around 1600, the church in Spanish and Portuguese America experienced an enormous *financial boom*. It benefited from the rising economy in mining (precious metals), agriculture and trade, and itself became one of the most important players in the colonial economy. It owned extensive landholdings in the cities and countryside and produced sugar, wine, textiles, pottery and other products on its estates. In some regions, more than half of all Spanish-owned land was in the hands of the various orders. The Franciscans were still the least involved. In Brazil, "the Jesuits maintained agricultural estates that were run according to strict rules and economic principles as model estates, but could not do without the labor of black African slaves, which had initially been avoided."[2]

9.2 Native American and Mestizo Voices

For a long time, the history of Christianity in Ibero-America has been described primarily from the perspective of missionary or colonial sources. Yet there is a wealth of testimony from local actors documenting the broad spectrum of indigenous (and African American) responses to the introduction of Christianity. They range from complete acceptance to bitter resistance. As the "beginning of our misery," for example, a Mayan priest in the early 17th century laments the activities of Spanish missionaries [Text 247]. Conversely, texts such as the "Morning Prayer" of a Christian Ketschua (*c.* 1600) impress with their lyricism and the combination of Indian nature mysticism with the language of the Psalms [Text 245]. The Mexican historian and anthropologist David Tavárez speaks of a multitude of "indigenous Christianities" in the process of merging ancient American and Christian traditions.[3]

One of the best known indigenous Christian voices from colonial Spanish America is the famous pictorial chronicle of *Felipe Guamán Poma de Ayala* (ca. 1535/1550 to after 1616) from Peru. 'El Primer Nueva Corónica y Buen Gobierno' (The New Chronicle and Good Government) is the title of his work – written in Spanish and partly in Ketschua – which Guamán Poma, who came from an Inca family, wrote towards the end of his life to draw the attention of the Spanish king Philip III to the crying grievances in his empire [Text 249]. The "Chronicle," a world history from an Inca perspective, begins with Adam and Eve and leads first to the appearance of "our Lord and Savior Jesus Christ." This was born – so it is said – when "Julius Caesar" ruled in Rome and the "Inca Cinche Roca" in the Peruvian Cuzco. Thereafter, both lines of tradition – that of the Roman emperors and popes on the one hand and the Inca rulers in Cuzco on the other – continue until they are joined again at the time of the conquest of Peru by the Spaniards. The preaching of the Christian faith by Catholic missionaries is expressly welcomed (and at the same time the importance of the Spaniards is relativized by reference to an earlier "pre-evangelization" of the Andean empire already by the apostle Bartholomew). At the same time, however, sharp criticism is voiced both of the Spanish colonial rule and the realities of the colonial church. For the (Creole or Mestizo) clergy repeatedly make common cause – so the accusation – with the colonists and other members of the colonial establishment. They torture, rob and abuse the Indians as the "poor of Jesus Christ", they impregnate their women and exploit them. In the suffering Indio – surrounded by the commensal owner as well as the functionaries of the crown and the church, *Christ himself suffers* [Figure 10]. But there are also God-fearing and holy men among the Europeans; and if the Gospel is preached free from imperiousness and greed, a new Pentecost could dawn for the Latin American Church [Figure 11].

The section on "Good Government" then contains the reform proposals of Guamán Poma. These are based on the social and economic structures of Inca society, the adoption of positive elements of Western culture and Christianity, adapted to the practical needs of the Andean population. For the Inca rulers once treated their subjects far better than the Spaniards do at present; and King Philip III is being asked to reinstate Indians in positions of responsibility. Indigenous Christians, unlike most Spaniards, are portrayed as pious and merciful. They are good artists, sculptors, musicians, church singers, and familiar with all aspects of the worship life. If they were not constantly hindered by the corrupt colonial elite, there would be among them "saints and great scholars and the most Christian of Indians."[4] Guamán Poma's work, discovered only in 1908 in a Danish archive, has become famous primarily because of the approximately 400 drawings that depict social, economic and religious life in Peru in the early 17th century. They are regarded as outstanding historical and ethnographic documents and have meanwhile also found their way also into the pop culture of Latin America.

Performing arts were also an important medium for articulating indigenous perspectives. In the cathedral of Cuzco (Peru), for example, there is a representation of the Last Supper (*cena ultima*) by the Indian-Christian artist Marcos Zapata (1710–1773). In addition to Andean flora and fauna, it shows a guinea pig – still considered a delicacy in Peru today – as a communion dish and the local *chicha* as a drink [Figure 13; Photo J04/05]. Marcos Zapata was an outstanding representative of the so-called Cuzco School, whose paintings were not only popular in colonial Peru, but also in other regions of Spanish America. Their beginnings date back to the middle of the 16th century. After a dispute with their Spanish colleagues at the end of the 17th century, the Indian and mestizo artists withdrew from the joint corporation and developed their own forms of expression [see also Text 248].

9.3 Jesuit Reductions (1609–1768)

One of the most remarkable experiments in the entire colonial period of Ibero-America was the establishment of the so-called Reductions in the border region of today's Paraguay, Argentina and Brazil in the 17th and 18th centuries [see Text 250–252]. These were protective settlements established by the Jesuits for the semi-nomadic Guaraní Indians living there. These were "brought together" in permanent villages and settled – under paternalistic control of the Fathers, but shielded from the rest of colonial society. Within the Spanish colonial empire, the Reductions, being directly subordinate to the Crown, enjoyed extensive autonomy. Spanish settlers were forbidden to stay there. Foreign traders were only allowed to stay in the reduction area for up to three days and to negotiate with the Indians in the presence of a missionary. Above all, however, the Reductions were removed from the commend system and the associated system of serfdom and forced labor. The reduction Indians were thus not available to the Spanish landowners as cheap labor – which led to fierce conflicts between the Jesuits and the *encomenderos* from the beginning.

The founding of reductions in itself was not a new invention. First attempts to form closed mission territories, protected from the arbitrariness of Spanish colonists, but under the sovereignty of the Spanish king, had already taken place in the 16th century (for example, by Las Casas in the 'Verapaz' in the area of present-day Guatemala). In the face of the resistance of the European settlers, they failed, as did other earlier undertakings of this kind. In 1604, the Jesuit Province of Paraguay was founded. Shortly thereafter, the first reductions were established there. In the first half of the 18th century, the region between the Rio Paraná, the Rio Uruguay and the Rio Paraguay included 30 reductions with up to 104,000 inhabitants. Other mission settlements were also established in the lowlands of present-day Bolivia and Peru. In 1767 – when the Jesuits were expelled from South America – about 200,000 indigenous people lived in the approximately 70 Indian settlements that still existed at that time.

Individual villages (or rural towns) contained up to 8,000 or more inhabitants. Here, too, magnificent churches with bell towers formed the center and towered over the marketplace and the simple houses of the indigenous people, which were built of rammed earth and had thatched roofs [Text 251]. The church architecture combined forms of the European baroque with local architecture and Indian decoration. The Jesuits specifically promoted the musical and manual skills of their protégés. Missionary work was carried out exclusively in the native language. As one of the consequences of this, Guaraní (in a modernized form) is still the second official language alongside Spanish in Paraguay. In addition to Christianization (through preaching, church festivals and schooling), the Jesuits sought to promote the material well-being of their communities and introduced technical innovations (such as plows, draft animals or mills). In most cases, only two Fathers (as the only whites) lived in the settlements. They were entrusted with spiritual and secular administration and were assisted by a select group of indigenous inhabitants.

The economic and social constitution of the Reductions combined traditional Indian structures with social patterns introduced from Europe. It has been described as "an agrarian collectivism, but one in which private property was not entirely absent."[5] Most of the land was communal, and to cultivate it each Indian had to work two to three days a week. The proceeds were used to pay royal tribute, maintain the church and its institutions, and care for orphans, widows, the aged, and the sick. The own land – which could not be inherited – ensured that the families were provided for as equally as possible. Regular work on the communal land was strictly controlled, although the Jesuits relied more on educational measures than on coercion. The most severe punishment was expulsion from the reduction.

The Jesuit reduction system has been judged quite controversially. As a "holy experiment", a "Christian alternative to colonialism and Marxism", and a model of careful cultural change under the conditions of Spanish colonial rule, it has received admiration and recognition. For others, it has been the object of sharp criticism as a clerical-paternalistic theocracy and a kind of "spiritual concentration camp." In any case, it is remarkable that no case of revolt against the Jesuits is known in the Reductions. In view of the numerical proportions – a total of about 60 fathers faced more than 100,000 men there, some of them armed – this speaks for the inner authority of the Jesuit clergy.

The end of what its opponents called the "Jesuit state" in Paraguay came from the outside. Not only to the Spanish settlers, but also to the colonial government, the political and economic autonomy of the Reductions was increasingly becoming a thorn in the flesh. In the face of growing centralist tendencies in the now prevailing bureaucratic state absolutism (as well as in times of fierce anti-Jesuit propaganda in enlightened Europe), the Jesuits' relative commercial autonomy no longer fit the picture. The immediate trigger of the conflict was the Treaty of Madrid in 1750, which provided for corrections in the boundary between the Spanish and Portuguese possessions in the Americas. The settlements of the Guaraní Indians were directly affected. When they resisted the threat of resettlement, the Spanish crown took action. The

Jesuit order was banned in 1767, and its members were expelled from Spain and its colonies in a cloak-and-dagger operation. In Portuguese America they had already suffered this fate in 1759 (and in French territories in 1764). In Paraguay, the reduction territories were now opened for colonial settlers, and the former reduction Indians often became bondmen of Spanish or Creole landowners in the 19th century.

In the 17th and 18th centuries, there were also protective villages for Indians in other regions, for example in Brazil, established by Jesuits and other orders. Comparable institutions for African-American slaves were lacking there, although a Catholicism of its own character was able to develop in the refugee villages of runaway black slaves (*quilombo*).

9.4 On the Eve of Independence

Until the end of the Spanish (and Portuguese) colonial era, Protestantism played hardly any role on the South American mainland. It was present there more as an enemy image (as result of considerable counter-Reformation propaganda) than as a physical presence. It is true that there were short-term colonial advances (especially by the Calvinist Dutch in Pernambuco, Brazil, in 1630–1654) and repeated trials (and death sentences) by the Inquisition against stranded Protestant sailors or Western European corsairs. In addition, strict book censorship sought to prevent the penetration of Protestant ideas into Hispano-America. On the periphery of the Spanish colonial empire, however, in the Caribbean as well as some enclaves on the neighboring mainland, Western European Protestant powers established themselves from the mid-17th century. In 1655, the English conquered Jamaica, and in 1666, the Danes occupied the Virgin Islands. The Dutch established themselves in Dutch Guiana. Protestant colonial churches were formed there, as well as missionary activities by German Moravians or English Methodists among African slaves in the later 18th century. The latter led to the formation of Afro-Caribbean congregations there.

In the monarchies of Spain and Portugal, the spirit of enlightened absolutism had taken hold in the mid-18th century. This had a direct impact on the respective colonies. In Spain, under King Charles III (r. 1759–1788), there were numerous reforms in administration, trade and the economy. The driving force behind similar changes in Portugal was the prime minister Marquis of Pombal, de facto holder of governmental power (r. 1750–1777). Both Iberian crowns sought to increase access to their overseas territories in order to better exploit resources there. Both governments considered the colonial church an obstacle in this path. The expulsion of the Jesuits from the Portuguese (1759) and Spanish (1767) possessions (and from French territories in 1764) was one of the consequences of this development. The determining ecclesiastical concept was that of regalism: the rights of the Crown vis-à-vis the Church were no longer understood as the granting of papal privileges, but as the expression of state sovereignty. As a result, the colonial church was increasingly subjected to state control. Ttraditional privileges and freedoms of clergy and religious orders were dismantled, and the linguistic assimilation of indigenous people (by obliging clergy to teach in Spanish) was advanced. The Inquisition was reformed (and at the same time increasingly used as an instrument of state surveillance). Leading positions in the ecclesiastical hierarchy were increasingly filled by Spaniards born in the mother country (the so-called *peninsulares*). Thus, under Charles III, earlier tendencies toward the formation of a Creole ecclesiastical ruling class were reversed.[6]

The latter in particular was one of the measures that met with sharp criticism in the Spanish colonies. The structural discrimination of the Creoles (i.e., the Spaniards born in America) was opposed, for example, in a petition from the city of Mexico dated May 5, 1771, addressed to King Charles III. Remarkably, it includes the self-designation as "Americans." "It is not the first time," the protest letter states,

> that ill-will and prejudice damaged the reputation of Americans and made them look as if they were unworthy of attaining any honors. This war was led against us since the discovery of America. In the case of the native Indians, one even questioned their ability to reason. With no less injustice it is pretended that we, born of European parents in this country, possess scarcely sufficient intellect to be human beings [...] We have been excluded from the episcopal and other high ecclesiastical dignities and, in the secular sphere, from the first-rate offices in the army, administration, and judiciary. [Text 259]

This was associated with the demand that Spaniards born in the mother country had be treated as foreigners in Mexico. The Creole upper class of Hispanoamerica had increasingly developed its own sense of identity in the course of the 18th century. Resentment against newly arriving *peninsulares* – often less educated but claiming higher positions – intensified. In Portuguese America, too, the contrast between 'Portuguese' and Brazilians increasingly determined the course of events.

Growing discontent also arose in other groups of colonial society. The Andes were shaken by a multitude of peasant rebellions in the 18th century.

The largest uprising is associated with the name of Tupac Amaru II, whose revolutionary movement in 1780/81 shook Spanish rule in much of present-day Peru and adjacent regions. The leader was the Ketschua Indian (or mestizo) José Gabriel Candorcanqui (1738–1781), who named himself after the last legitimate Inca ruler, Tupac Amaru, beheaded by the Spanish in Cuzco in 1572. His nativist revolt was directed against intensified economic and fiscal oppression (as a result of recent reforms by the Spanish crown). Initially, he sought to achieve a broad alliance between Creole bourgeoisie, mestizo petty bourgeoisie, and Native American peasants "against the [Spanish] pharaoh who persecutes, mistreats, and abuses us" [Text 260b]. However, the unchecked actions of his peasant armies developed their own momentum, and Creole supporters turned away. In 1781, Tupac Amaru II was executed along with his family in Cuzco – in the same square as his "predecessor" in the 16th century. His example, however, inspired later revolutionary movements in Latin America in the 19th and 20th centuries.

The spokesmen of the Creole elite often included local clerics. A prominent example is provided by the Dominican Servando Teresa de Mier (1763–1827), whose sermon on the Guadalupe feast of 12 December 1794 in Mexico – in the presence of the archbishop and viceroy – caused a scandal. Mier was subsequently banned from preaching for 10 years and sent to monastic arrest in Spain. The jumping point of his sermon was the connection of two traditions that were significant for the formulation of an independent – non-Spanish – Creole-Christian identity: the tradition of the apparition of the Virgin of Guadalupe to the Indian Juan Diego [cf. chap. 6.3] and the legend of the work of the Apostle Thomas in Old America long before the arrival of the Spaniards. It was not in the shadow of the Spanish Conquista and evangelization that the Gospel and the Virgin of Guadalupe came to Mexico. Rather, according to the preacher, this happened "already 1750 years ago," that is, already in apostolic times – just as (according to Iberian local tradition) the Virgin had also appeared to the Apostle James in Spain at that time [Text 262]. So – and this was the decisive point – one could be a good Christian and still be against the rule of the Spaniards. Political emancipation was thus preceded by historical-theological emancipation.

Notes to Chapter 9

1. Daniels (2014), *Kongolese Christianities in the Americas*, 219; Dussel (1992), *Church in Latin America*, 75.
2. Meier (2018), *Ränder*, 258.
3. Tavárez (2017), *Indigenous Christianities,* 5(ff).

4. Thiemer-Sachse/Kunzmann (2004), *Guamán Poma de Ayala*, 820.
5. Konetzke (1991), *Süd- und Mittelamerika* I, 273; vgl. Gründer (1988), *„Jesuitenstaat"*, 10 ff.
6. González/ González (2007), *Christianity in Latin America*, 105–112.

Further Reading for Chapter 9

9.1 (*The Church in the Colonial City*)

Burkholder/ Johnson (1994), *Colonial Latin America*, 113 ff.285 ff; Keen (1996), *Latin America*, 120 ff.148–152; González/ González (2007), *Christianity in Latin America*, 74 ff.86 ff; Cushner (2000), *Jesuits in Colonial America*, 92–119; Dussel (1992), *Latin America*, 53–80; Garrard-Burnett/ Freston / Dove (2016), *Religion in Latin America*, 160–172; Mills/ Taylor (1998), *Documentary History*, 153–262; Merrim (1999), *Sor Juana Inés de la Cruz*; Pietschmann (1994), *Handbuch* I, 505–510; Thomas (1994), *Das portugiesische Amerika*, 597–662; Terraciano (2014), *Early Latin America*, 335–352; Osterhammel (20), *Colonialism*, 88–92.

9.2 (*Native American and Mestizo Voices*)

Thiemer-Sachse/ Kunzmann (2004), *Guamán Poma de Ayala*; Prien (1978), *Geschichte*, 221–228 (Poma de Ayala); Hamilton (2009), *Guaman Poma;* Adorno (2000), *Writing and Resistance*; Meier (2018), *Ränder*, 219 ff.225–232; Steiner (1992), *Poma de Ayala*; Dilke (1978), *Letter to a King*; Mills/ Taylor (1998), *Documentary History*, 153–164; Adorno (2000), *Writing and Resistance*; Tavárez (2017), *Indigenous Christianities in Colonial Latin America*; Fane (1996), *Converging Cultures*; Nebel (2006), *Indigen-christliche Autoren im kolonialen Mexiko*, 142–161; Lockhart (1992), *Nahuatl Accounts;* Christensen (2014), *Translated Christianities*; Lindenfeld (2021), *Indigenous Experience*, 31–49; Merrim (1999), *Sor Juana Inés de la Cruz* .

9.3 (*Jesuit Reductions* [1609–1768])

Dussel (1992), *Church in Latin America*, 351–362; Prien (2013), *Latin America*, 186–197; Cushner (2000), *Jesuits in Colonial America*, 118–123. 164ff; Caraman (1976), *The lost paradise*; Gründer (1988), *„Jesuitenstaat"*, 1–25; Hartmann (1994), *Jesuitenstaat;* Meier (2018), *Ränder*, 234 ff.313 ff; Meier (1998), *Chiquitos-Reduktionen*, 117–131; Hoornaert (1982), *Brasilien*, 112–121; Lippy/ Choquette/ Poole (1992), *Americas*, 98–100.

9.4 (*On the Eve of Independence*)

Bakewell (^{2}2004), *History of Latin America*, 285–318. 368–376; González/ González (2007), *Christianity in Latin America*, 109–114; Prien (2013), *Latin*

America, 243–270 ("The Century of the Enlightenment"). 253 ff (Tupac Amaru II); Garrard-Burnett/ Freston/ Dove (2016), *Religion in Latin America*, 220–230 (by J. Lynch); Keen (1996), *Latin America*, 152–155; Buisson/ Schottelius (1980), *Unabhängigkeitsbewegungen*; Pietschmann (1994), *Handbuch* I, 396–398.448 ff; Meier (2018), *Ränder*, 311 ff; Delgado (2002), *Kreolische Emanzipationsbestrebungen*, 315–328; Goodpasture (1989), *Cross and Sword*, 79–104 (documents); Mills/ Taylor (1998), *Documentary History*, 263–346.

CHAPTER 10

Africa

10.1 Ethiopia: Period of Self-Imposed Isolation

In Christian Ethiopia, the expulsion of the Jesuits by Emperor Fasilidas (since 1632/33; see chapter 7.4) was followed by a long phase of self-isolation from the rest of the world and especially from Catholic Europe. The city of Gondar became the new political center of the empire, which was increasingly shrinking in size. A central goal of the ruler was the restoration of Ethiopian orthodoxy in a new and yet traditional form. Emperor Fasilidas had the cathedral in Aksum, destroyed since the Jihad of Gran, restored and numerous new churches built in Gondar. For the last time, the empire experienced a period of cultural and intellectual flourishing in the following years. In literature, architecture and religious painting, a courtly culture developed that emancipated itself from popular traditions. Even after the expulsion of the Portuguese, foreign cultural influences continued to have an impact (for example, from Portuguese India, as shown by the palaces in Gondar). Even motifs by the German painter Albrecht Dürer found their way into Ethiopian art. Economically, Gondar initially remained connected to the trade routes in the Red Sea and Nile Valley, although the important port city of Massawa (in present-day Eritrea) was now under Ottoman control. The last great ruler of the Gondar period was Emperor Iyasu I (1682–1706). After him, a period of disintegration set in, leading the country into a state of complete anarchy until 1755.

The reasons for this decline were manifold: Palace revolutions, tensions between different ethnic groups, invasion by nomadic tribes, advance of the Ottoman Turks, loss of access to the Red Sea. Disintegration was further fueled by ongoing disputes between two rival monastic parties. At their center was a Christological debate, an echo of early church controversies over the divine and human natures of Christ. Synodal attempts at unification led to opposite results. They were complicated by the fragile balance between imperial central authority, the rights of the *abuna* (the ecclesiastical leader), and the largely autonomous monasteries. Finally, the control of the Ethiopian rulers was more or less limited to the region immediately around Gondar. This epoch of anarchy went down in Ethiopian annals as the "time of the judges," when there was "no king in Israel," using biblical terminology. Ethiopia, formerly a heavyweight in Christian Africa, entered the 19th century extremely weakened.

Rome never gave up hope of restoring its influence in Ethiopia. Several missions failed, including the dispatch in 1788 of an Ethiopian educated in Rome and consecrated as a Catholic bishop. Isolated advances from the Protestant side were also unsuccessful. Still in the time of Fasilidas, Peter Heyling, a German Lutheran, stayed temporarily as a teacher, doctor and theologian at the imperial court in Gondar around 1634. More lasting in Protestant Europe was the impact of Hiob Ludolf (1624–1704), founder of Ethiopian studies in Germany, who worked closely with an emigrated Ethiopian scholar. An attempt by the Herrnhut (Moravian) missionary Friedrich Hocker to reach Ethiopia from Cairo in 1752 and 1761 failed, as did various initiatives by the Anglican Church Missionary Society (CMS) at the beginning of the 19th century. They did not aim at conversion, but rather at fraternal support of the Ethiopian Christians. In 1830, Samuel Gobat, a missionary from Basel sent by the CMS, succeeded in reaching Gondar. However, all efforts to establish a permanent presence in Ethiopia were unsuccessful, which is why the CMS finally ended the experiment.

10.2   Regional Developments

Ethiopia was not an isolated case. In other regions of Africa, too, the dominance of the Portuguese (and at the same time the presence of Catholic missionaries) collapsed in the course of the 17th century. Around 1620, there still existed what Adrian Hastings called a network of African Christian rulers extending across the continent.[1] In Ethiopia, as already mentioned, this was Emperor Susenyos (r. 1606–1632). In Warri (in present-day Nigeria), the "Olu" Sebastian (1597–1625), a zealous promoter of the Christianization of his small kingdom, ruled. In 1600, he was even sent to Portugal for training as a priest. Although he did not return as a consecrated clergyman, he was still active in catechetical work among his countrymen at an advanced age. In Mombasa (in what is now Kenya), it was a young (and married to a Portuguese woman) Christian baptized ruler, Dom Jeronimo Chingulia, who was elevated to king around 1626. He had previously received an education for years in Goa by the Augustinian monks there.

Soon, however, the picture changed. In 1631, Chingulia broke with Christianity, massacred the Portuguese garrison in the city and ordered his subjects to convert to Islam. About 150 African Christians also fell victim to his persecution in Mombasa. In Ethiopia, the abdication of Emperor Susenyos (in favor of his son Fasilidas) in 1632 ended the brief Catholic interlude in the country's Christian history. In what is now Zimbabwe, Changamire

Dombo (r. ca. 1660–1695) drove the Portuguese (along with missionaries) from the high plateau in the 1680s and founded the Rozvi warrior empire. In 1698, Mombasa and its strategically important port, which had been reconquered by the Portuguese in the meantime, fell permanently into the hands of the Arab Omani. In Warri (in present-day Nigeria), King Dom Domingos II complained bitterly in a letter to the prefect of the Capuchin mission in São Tomé in 1692 about the severe shortage of priests in his kingdom. Catholic missionaries were coming into the country only very irregularly. Therefore, according to the African ruler, things were bad "in the vineyard of the Lord" [Text 133]. Warri, however, remained an isolated island of Christian presence in the region.

The once important Christian Kongo Empire was also in ruins [see Map 5]. Endless disputes over the throne, military defeat by the Portuguese in neighboring Angola (Battle of Abuila in 1665) and the increasingly dramatic effects of the Atlantic slave trade were the reasons. Christianity, however, had long since gained a foothold not only at the royal court but also among the rural population. Prophetic movements like the one around St. Anthony enjoyed great popularity at the beginning of the 18th century. In reality, "Anthony" was a young woman, Doña Beatriz Kimpa Vita (1684–1706), who saw herself as the mouthpiece of the popular saint [see Figure 15]. She propagated the restoration of the old Christian kingship by returning to the abandoned capital of São Salvador, as well as the destruction of the symbols of the cross, which by now had degenerated into a fetish. For them, Jesus was a Kongolese; and not only the Europeans, but also the Kongolese church now had its own saints. Even after the execution of the Kimpa Vita in 1706 by the victorious Kongo ruler Pedro IV (r. 1695–1718), the Antonian movement persisted. This was a conflict between two currents within traditional Kongolese Christianity, which continued in remnants into the early 19th century. Pedro IV did succeed in restoring the unity of the Kongo Empire. But from then on it was little more than a confederation of small states held together only by the symbol of a single monarchy.

The decline of Catholic missionary activities in 18th century Africa was not only a consequence of the shrinking colonial presence of the Portuguese. It was also caused by internal factors. For example, the Portuguese crown's stubborn adherence to its outdated Padroado privileges, For that reason it denied access to its possessions to Catholic missionaries from other countries whenever possible. Rome's growing intolerance of local versions of Christianity also played a role. This was, among other aspects, a consequence of the Chinese Rites Controversy [see chap. 11.2], as well as waning missionary enthusiasm in wide circles of the Catholic establishment. Finally, de facto only parts of present-day Angola and the coastal region of Mozambique remained under

Portuguese control. However, on Mozambique Island – an important stopover on the way to Goa – a magnificent church was still built in the 18th century, and Goanese Dominicans taught African students in the town's seminaries.

10.3 Protestant Beginnings

In addition to the Portuguese, other European countries also established themselves on the West African coast toward the end of the 17th century. Around 1700, more than 30 fortresses of different nations were counted along a stretch of about 400 km. These included the Portuguese, the Spanish, the French, the Dutch, the Danes, the Swedes and the Brandenburgers (Prussians), who often replaced each other and sought to take over the profitable trade in slaves (and other valuable "goods").

This led to the modest beginnings of colonial church structures in the West African possessions of Protestant powers. In the course of the 18th century, black pastors began to be employed in some of these outposts. Of course, these African pastors did not have much room for maneuver, and in the correspondence received from them they raised many complaints about discriminatory treatment by the local settlers and colonial authorities. But these complaints were nevertheless expressed in a remarkably broad international horizon, by reference to conditions in other regions and mission fields that were perceived as exemplary. Thus, as mentioned earlier, in the case of Jacobus Elisa Johannes Capitein (1717–1747) in the Dutch station of Elmina (in present-day Ghana), who refers to the incomparably better working conditions of his Indian colleagues in Tranquebar in southern India [Text 141; Figure 18]. Capitein, a former slave from the Fante ethnic group, had studied in Holland, earned his doctorate at Leiden University, and in 1742 had become the first African to be ordained as a pastor in the Dutch Reformed Church. Another example is represented by Christian Jacob Protten "Africanus" (1715–1769). Married to the Caribbean mulatto, former slave, and evangelist Rebecca Protten, he became a Danish Lutheran pastor in Christiansborg (Ghana), among other places [Text 142c + d; Figure 17]. Philipp Quaque (c. 1741–1816) had received theological training in England. In 1765 he was the first African to be ordained a priest in the Anglican Church and worked for a long time in what is now Ghana as a "missionary, schoolmaster and catechist for the Negroes on the Gold Coast."

As mentioned above, it was mainly the Dutch who replaced the Portuguese as colonial rulers in various coastal regions in the mid-17th century. For a time, they even succeeded in establishing themselves in Luanda (Angola). Only in the Dutch Cape colony in southern Africa this resulted in a permanent ecclesiastical presence on a significant scale, which has lasted until the present day. Cape Town had been founded in 1652 by the Dutch East India Company ('Vereenigde Oost-Indische Compagnie', VOC), initially only as a stopover on the way to India. Since 1657 a growing number of Dutch colonists arrived in the country. Later, Huguenot religious refugees from France (since 1688) and other Europeans were also welcomed. The ecclesiastical monopoly in the gradually expanding Cape Colony was held by the Dutch Reformed Church, which was under the control of the local political authorities to a much greater extent than in the mother country. There were hardly any missionary activities among the indigenous population. This changed only with the arrival of the German Moravian Georg Schmidt from Herrnhut in 1737, who became active among the Khoikhoi (formerly known as "Hottentots"). However, he soon met with resistance and had to leave the colony again in 1744 [Text 142a + b]. The reason for this was the concerns of the Dutch Reformed Church authorities (in the form of the "Amsterdam Pastoral Letter" of 1738), which regarded the pietistic Moravian 'Brüdergemeine' as a seditious movement. It was not until 1792 that Moravian missionaries were able to resume their work in the Cape.

10.4 Transatlantic Slave Trade, Vision of a Return to Africa

In the 18th century, the transatlantic slave trade reached its peak. During this period, an estimated 6,133,000 Africans were trafficked to the New World. These were more victims than in the centuries before and after combined. For the period 1450–1600 the figures are 367,000, in the 17th century 1,868,000, and 3,330,000 in the 19th century.[2] Slaves came from all western coastal regions of Africa between Senegambia and Angola (and partly also from East Africa and Madagascar). The main supply area was the Kongo-Angola region, with about 40% of all slaves shipped across the Atlantic. 42% of the forcibly exported Africans were taken to the Caribbean, 38% to Brazil and just under 5% to North America. In the beginning, it was mainly the Portuguese who were involved in the lucrative slave trade. But since the 17th century, all European powers active in the African business have participated. The interplay between European merchants, regional (African or Arab) middlemen or slave hunters and African chiefs, who were usually paid with European goods, varied greatly from region to region [see Map 8].

Slavery itself was by no means unknown in "old" Africa and existed in many forms. However, it had a completely different character there – for example in the form of domestic slavery, which could be linked to integration into traditional kinship structures – than the forced export of African human capital overseas, which was increasingly being carried out by Europeans on a quasi-industrial basis. Moreover, Europeans' rising demand for slaves increasingly fueled intra-tribal wars. The effects of the slave trade were particularly devastating in the Angola/Kongo area. This was not only because of the disproportionately high number of slave exports from this region. In addition, the Portuguese also went on slave hunts here themselves, penetrating far into the hinterland and into neighboring areas. These raids were also one of the reasons for the collapse of the Christian Kongo Empire in the mid-17th century.

Many Portuguese clerics and missionaries also owned slaves. Some of them themselves actively participated in the slave trade in Angola and elsewhere. The only way to travel to and from Angola was often on a slave ship. There were, of course, also voices of protest, which became louder with the growth of the slave trade in the 17th century. For example, the Capuchin friars (mostly of non-Iberian nationality), who were active in the Kongo and tried to work as independently as possible from the Portuguese Padroado. In 1685 they presented a memorandum to the Roman Congregation for the Doctrine of the Faith (the 'Propaganda Fide') against the excesses of the slave trade, which was fully approved by it in 1686. Already in 1684, Lourenço da Silva – an Afro-Brazilian of Kongolese descent and spokesman for black brotherhoods in Madrid and Lisbon – had succeeded in intervening with the Curia in Rome and obtaining a condemnation of the "eternal slavery" of black Christians [Text 255]. This condemnation by the Curia, however, did not lead to any lasting results. It was simply blocked by the governments of Portugal and Spain – and a church system that was dependent on these governments.

A powerful testimony to the horrors of the transatlantic slave trade is before us in the account of a former slave, Olaudah Equiano (1745–1797), a native of southeastern Nigeria. Captured as a child in Africa, he was deported to the Caribbean and Virginia and sold as a slave to a British officer. He changed hands twice, finally arriving in London and gaining freedom there in 1766. He writes about the horror of being carried off on the slave ship, among other things:

> The closeness of the space and the heat of the climate, added to the number in the ship which was so crowded that each had scarcely room to turn himself, almost suffocated us. [...] The shrieks of the women and the groans of the dying rendered the whole a scene of horror almost inconceivable. [...] One day, when we had a smooth sea ... two of my wearied countrymen who were chained together ... , preferring death to such a life of misery, somehow made through the nettings and jumped into the sea. Immediately another ... followed their example; and I believe that many

more would very soon have done the same, if they not been prevented by the ship's crew, who were instantly alarmed. [Text 146]

Published in 1789, this "Interesting Account of the Life of Olaudah Equiano" is remarkable not only as one of the first printed autobiographies of a former African slave. It also became a literary success and played an important role in the propaganda of the early British antislavery movement. The book went through nine editions during his lifetime. Translations into other European languages soon followed. Baptized Anglican in 1759 and strongly committed to religion, Equiano became a leader in the African diaspora of the English capital [Figure 16]. He supported initiatives to return the "poor blacks of London" to West Africa.

Toward the end of the 18th century, remigration efforts also increased on the other side of the Atlantic, among black Christians in the Caribbean and the later USA. There, the "Great Revival" movement had also led to a wave of conversions among African-American slaves, often against the will of their white masters. Biblical motifs – such as the Exodus paradigm, the return from the Babylonian exile, and especially the promise of salvation addressed to "Ethiopia" (in Psalm 68:31) – played an important role. Thus black congregations such as the 'First Ethiopian Baptist Church' founded in Jamaica in 1783 by a former slave labelled themselves as "Ethiopian". In 1780, the first association of free African Americans in what is now the United States was founded in Newport, Rhode Island. It counted "the earnest desire of a return to Africa" among its goals.[3] Concrete first steps were taken in 1792 by the resettlement project of African American remigrants in Sierra Leone [see chap. 14.1; Map 9 + 10].

Notes to Chapter 10

1. Hastings (1994), *Church in Africa*, 127.
2. Figures according to: Iliffe (1997), *Geschichte Afrikas*, 177.
3. Campbell (2006), *Middle Passages*, 20.16 ff; cf. Martin (2002), *African Mission Movement*, 56–72.

Further Reading for Chapter 10

10.1 (Ethiopia: Period of Self-Imposed Isolation)
Hastings (1994), *Church in Africa*, 87–129; Paulau/ Tamcke (2022), *Ethiopian Orthodox Christianity*, 122–142; Sundkler/ Steed (2000), *Africa*, 75-80; Hock (2005), *Christentum in Afrika*, 36–39.

10.2 (*Regional Developments*)

Hastings (1994), *Church in Africa*, 102–118; Hock (2005), *Christentum in Afrika*, 44–46; Thornton (1998), *Kongolese Saint Antony*; Hastings (1998), *Pedro IV of the Kongo*, 59–72; Sanneh (1983), *West African Christianity*, 39–52; Hodkin (1975), *Nigerian Perspectives*, 176 ff.188 f; Boxer (1991), *Portuguese Seaborne Empire*, 128–149 („Stagnation and Contraction in the East"); Irvin/ Sunquist (2012), *World Christian Movement* II,319-336.

10.3 (*Protestant Beginnings*)

Hastings (1994), *Church in Africa*, 173–221; Kpobi (2005), *African Chaplains*, 155–170; Beck (1981), *Mission der Brüdergemeine*, 98–106; Hofmeyr/ Pillay (1994), *South Africa*, 8–35; Elphick/ Davenport (1997), *Christianity in South Africa*, 16–30.

10.4 (*Transatlantic Slave Trade, Vision of a Return to Africa*)

Iliffe (^{3}2017), *Africans*, 135-169 ("The Atlantic Slave Trade"); Hastings (1994), *Church in Africa*, 123–126. 173–188; Gray (1990), *Black Christians*, 11–27; Hanciles (2005), *Back to Africa*, 191-216; Walvin (1998), *Olaudah Equiano*; Stanley (2005), *Christian missions (and) antislavery*; Hock (2005), *Christentum in Afrika*, 34–39; Marx (2004), *Geschichte Afrikas*, 19–46; Paquette (2010), *Handbook of slavery*; Zeuske (2022), *Sklaverei und Sklavenhandel*; Drescher (2009), *Slavery and antislavery*; Jakobbson (1972), *Am I not a Man*; Fountain (2010), *African American slaves and Christianity*; Adiele (2017), *Catholic Church and transatlantic enslavement*; Campbell (2006), *Middle Passages*, 15–39; Martin (2002), *African Mission Movement*, 56–72.

CHAPTER 11

Asia

The history of Christianity in Asia in the 17th and 18th centuries presents a very mixed picture. It varied according to socio-cultural, political or colonial context. Alongside regions of astonishing growth, emerging Christian communities elsewhere were subject to fierce repression and persecution.

11.1 Japan: the End of the "Christian Century"

By 1600, the number of baptized Christians in Japan was estimated at about 300,000. The new faith had gained a foothold not only among local feudal lords and members of the nobility. It was also widespread among the peasant population on the southern island of Kyushu, for example. Regions with sometimes considerable Christian presence also existed on the main island of Honshu [see Map 12]. The missionary successes of the earlier decades had been facilitated in part by the political fragmentation of the empire. There were a multitude of rival principalities and no central authority to deny foreign nations access to the island kingdom. Trade with the Portuguese seemed as profitable to many regional rulers (*daimyo*) as contact with the Jesuits, which repeatedly led to conversions. The local Catholic princes later held fast to their newly acquired Christian identity, often under the pressure of fierce persecution.

The turnaround occurred under three rulers who promoted the unification of the country under a central authority. Under Shogun Toyotomi Hideyoshi (r. 1582–1598), the second of these "Great Unifiers," the first persecutions of Christians occurred, at first sporadically. The crucifixion of the 26 martyrs of Nagasaki in 1597 attracted attention far beyond the borders of the country, and they were soon venerated in the Catholic world (in Central Europe as well as in Mexico or Peru) [see Figure 8; Photo C05/06]. In the following period, the anti-Christian measures increased in Japan. In addition to the defense against "foreign" influences, domestic political motives may also have played a role, such as the fear of the growing influence of the Christian *daimyo*s (as a threat to the new central power). The missionaries – increasingly suspected of being the fifth column of the Iberian powers – were expelled, Christianity was banned, and native Christians were forced into apostasy or executed. Between 1614 and 1636, the Christian Church of Japan was almost completely destroyed in a wave of the cruelest persecutions. In 1638, a widespread peasant revolt occurred in

© KLAUS KOSCHORKE, 2025 | DOI:10.1163/9789004699830_012

This is an open access chapter distributed under the terms of the CC BY-NC-ND 4.0 license.

Kyushu. It probably began as a social conflict and ended as an open rebellion often inspired by Christianity (and led with Christian symbols). Only with the greatest effort (and the support of Dutch [!] ship artillery) did the central government succeed in putting down the uprising.

Subsequently, the Far Eastern empire almost completely isolated itself from the outside world for the next 200 years. As early as 1636, an "Edict on the closure of the Land" had been issued [Text 23a]. From then on, all contacts with Catholic nations were forbidden. No Japanese were allowed to travel abroad or return from there on pain of the death penalty. Only the Protestant Dutch were permitted (as the only Europeans) to establish a small trading post near Nagasaki in 1641. Systematic hunts were made for smuggled-in priests, and the native population was subjected to a rigorous system of religious surveillance and denunciation. Those suspected of Christianity had to prove their "innocence" or completed apostasy by taking an "oath of apostasy" and stepping on images of saints and the Virgin Mary [Text 23b; Figure 9; Photo C08/09]. This procedure was repeated regularly. Nevertheless, the discovery of Christian groups and subsequent mass executions occurred time and again.

Despite intensive surveillance and severe persecution, a Christian minority managed to survive underground until the 19th century. Outwardly conformist, these "hidden Christians" (*Senpuku Kirishitan*, formerly usually referred to as *Kakure Kirishitan*) knew how to pass on their faith in secret. They celebrated services in hiding in their private homes. Lay Christians assumed priestly functions. Thus, the baptism of children and their religious instruction continued. The Bible and other liturgical texts were passed on orally, since printed works could be detected and confiscated by the authorities. Prayers were said in front of a statue of Buddha with a crucifix carved on its back, or in front of a statue of *Kannon*, a sacred Buddhist image of a woman and child that the "hidden Christians" venerated as the Virgin Mary with the infant Jesus [see Photo C11]. Their prayers sounded like Buddhist chants, spiked with untranslated words from Latin, Portuguese and Spanish. When, after the forced "opening" of Japan in the mid-19th century, European priests were allowed to enter the country again for the first time, the Frenchman Bernard Petitjean encountered a community of about 30,000 of these underground Christians near Nagasaki in 1865 [see Figure 30; Photo C17]. The Our Father, Hail Mary, Apostles' Creed and various prayers in Japanese were still quite familiar to them [Text 59a; see chap. 13.4.1].

11.2 China: Accommodation Strategies and Rite Controversy

In 1552, Francis Xavier had died on an island off the coasts of China without having achieved his final goal – access to the Chinese empire. Later attempts by his comrades in the order to reach this destination were also initially unsuccessful. Only the work of the Italian Matteo Ricci (1552–1610) marked the beginning of a longer-term presence of the Jesuits in the Middle Kingdom. In 1583 Ricci, together with his compatriot Michele Ruggieri, received permission to stay in the southern Chinese coastal region. In 1601, he then succeeded in settling in Beijing and gaining access to the imperial court. "Door openers" here were initially his mathematical, astronomical and geographical knowledge as well as his growing familiarity with Chinese etiquette. In particular, his *mappamundo* (world map) – which showed China for the first time in global perspective – caused a tremendous sensation [Text 24a]. In subsequent years, Jesuits became active at the imperial court in prominent position as astronomers (important for the production of the imperial calendar), advisors and mediators of western knowledge [see Figure 21 + 22; Photo B05–07].

Ricci has been probably the most important representative of an "accommodative" approach to the advanced civilizations of Asia. His procedure was determined by the goal of winning over the educated classes of China. Scholarly disputations, but not public preaching, were his method. Unlike the Jesuits in Japan, his reference system was not Buddhism, which he rejected as idolatry, or popular Taoism, but the Confucian tradition. In doing so, he referred above all to the Confucian classics, in which he believed (in contrast to the prevailing neo-Confucianism of his time) to find a monotheistic faith. Their translation into Latin was therefore one of Ricci's tasks, as was the production of theological writings in Chinese. Among these, especially his writing "The True Meaning [of the Doctrine] of the Lord of Heaven" (*Tianzhu shiyi*) from 1603 – a catechism in the form of a dialogue – was to be widely distributed [Text 24c]. Ricci aimed at a synthesis of natural philosophy, Confucianism and Christian faith, analogous to the combination of Christian theology and Aristotelianism (as its preliminary stage) in Thomas Aquinas. He dressed himself in the manner of Confucian scholars.

Ricci's method of far-reaching "accommodation" (or cultural adaptation, according to 1 Cor 9:22) was by no means uncontroversial within his own ranks. The great controversy, however, came only after his death. The main objections were on two points: the evaluation of the ceremonies in honor of Confucius (and the ancestors) and the question of an appropriate rendering of the concept of God in Chinese. Objections were raised to the "civil" (rather than religious) understanding of the Confucius rites as advocated by Ricci, as well as to his theistic interpretation of the "Heavenly King" of the Confucian texts. This controversy, which lasted for more than a century, has gone down in history under the title "Rites Controversy". Its importance lies, among other things, in the fact that here a local dispute gained significance for the entire church. For now not only the rival orders in China itself (above all Jesuits,

Dominicans, Franciscans) took part in the quarrel. From 1645 at the latest, Rome also became involved in the dispute. It expressed itself with a series of contradictory statements, at the end of which was the definitive ban of Chinese rites (and thus of a church model related to the cultural traditions of China) by Pope Benedict XIV in the bull 'Ex quo singulari' of 1742. Already in 1704, Pope Clement XI had forbidden the use of certain Chinese terms (tian, shangdi) as designations of God, as well as a participation of native Christians in ceremonies in honor of Confucius [Text 28]. This led to the break between Rome and Beijing. For only shortly before, the Chinese Emperor Kangxi (1654–1722) had approved of the Jesuits' work in his empire [Text 27]. He now perceived the Pope's intervention as a snub. In 1724, an official ban on Christianity followed. Missionaries had to leave the Middle Kingdom, and the number of Chinese believers decreased drastically. Individual congregations survived in isolation.

The rites controversy in China (and India, where there were analogous controversies [see Text 25]) had far-reaching effects, both in Asia and in Europe. In China, it solidified the image of the incompatibility of Christianity as a foreign religion with the cultural traditions of the country. It was not until 1939 that Rome lifted the compulsory oath against Chinese rites, which all missionaries active in the region had been obliged to take since 1742. In Catholic Europe, the controversies surrounding the events in faraway China made waves. Increasingly, they also stimulated debates in the philosophical public of the continent (Leibniz, Voltaire and others). Enlightened critics saw in the Middle Kingdom – once idealized by the Jesuits as a rational community – a counter-model to the feudal despotism of old Europe. With its ancient civilization, China also challenged established ecclesiastical world views and traditional biblical chronology.

11.3 Sri Lanka and the Philippines: Resistance in a Colonial Context

In contrast to China and Japan, European colonial rule was established in other regions of Asia. This was the case in the coastal regions of *Ceylon (Sri Lanka)*, where the Dutch got stuck since the mid-17th century and established the ecclesiastical monopoly of Dutch Calvinism. They replaced the Portuguese, who had established a foothold on the island since 1505 and introduced Catholicism there. Later came the British (1796–1948), with whom the wide range of Anglo-Saxon missionary Protestantism also arrived on the island. In this respect, Sri Lanka could serve as a prime example of the parallelism of Western colonial and missionary expansion [see Map 11].

At the same time, however, the country's Christian history also illustrates the independent dynamics of a version of Christianity once established in a colonial context. For with the end of Portuguese rule in 1658, insular Catholicism also seemed to have come to an end. The practice of the "papist" religion was made punishable, and en masse the Catholic faithful fell back into – be it Buddhist or Hindu – "paganism" or filled the now reformed churches. Soon, however, the Catholic community was able to regenerate itself underground. Increasingly, it also made itself visible in the colonial public sphere of the country. Goanese members of the Oratorian Congregation, such as Joseph Vaz (1651–1711), played an important role in this development. Unlike the Portuguese missionaries, the Indian priests were able to pass unnoticed through the strict controls of the Dutch. Unlike the Dutch colonial pastors [Text 31a], they were well acquainted with the language and habits of the native Catholics. This is thus, as it were, an early example of an intra-Asian solidarity action. Increasingly, Catholic believers were now taking the offensive. Their underground priests, according to the complaint of a Dutch source,

> openly by day practice their seductive religious exercises with the pealing of the bells and the exposition of their idolatrous images; yes, and they even baptize and marry the people in the land ... and incite them to openly blaspheme the doctrine and the teachers of the Reformed religion. [Text 32]

In Catholic centers like Negombo [see Photo E01–03], demonstrators even hindered the Dutch preachers from performing their duties. An emergency meeting of the central Reformed church council in Colombo on Dec. 2, 1751, only reveals the helplessness of the colonial church officials. Already around the middle of the 17th century, the number of Catholic believers far exceeded that of the members of the Dutch colonial church. With the end of Dutch rule on the island in 1796, the church then collapsed completely [see chapter 12.1].

The situation was quite different in the *Philippines*, today the "most Catholic country in Asia," which had been gradually occupied by Spain since 1565. The evangelization – and to a large extent also the so-called "pacification" – of the island kingdom was in the hands of the various missionary orders, among which the country was divided in 1594 [Text 21]. In the period that followed, the chronicles report a variety of conflicts: between the church and the colonial government, between the traditional religionists and Christians, between the church hierarchy and the missionary orders, rivalries within the missionary orders themselves, and between secular and religious clerics.

As for the lay people in the church, historian Reinhard Wendt has drawn attention to the ambivalent function or "the anti-colonialist potential" of the Catholic-Iberian festive culture introduced by the Spaniards in the Philippines.

> Implanted Catholicism and indigenous traditions had given rise to a Marian piety with a considerable amount of local flavor that had taken a firm place in the everyday reality and cultural self-understanding of at least the inhabitants of Central Luzon.

On the one hand, this Iberian Catholic festive culture served to legitimize colonial rule. At the same time, however, it increasingly functioned as a link between the various – previously unconnected – ethnic groups of the island kingdom, who discovered in the Fiesta Filipina a forum for exchange and the development of overarching identities. In particular, it was the spectacular passion plays that in many cases had a "latent system-disrupting effect." "Spectators and participants may have equated the Roman soldiers with the colonial rulers and identified themselves with Christ, who suffered under the weight of his cross".[1] The peak of this development does indeed fall into the 19th century, at the end of which the Philippines then liberated itself from Spanish rule. Its beginnings go back to the earlier colonial period.

11.4 Korea: Self-Founded Martyrs' Church (1784ff)

Along with the Philippines, *Korea* is the Asian nation with the highest percentage of Christians in the population (2015: 27.66%). The country's churches – first the Catholic, and later (in the late 19th century) the Protestant – are the result of a self-Christianization to an extent that is unique even in the Asian context. This is especially true of the beginnings of Korean underground Catholicism in 1784. Earlier sporadic encounters of Koreans with Christianity (in the diaspora in China or as prisoners of war in Japan) had remained without longer-term effect. The events of 1784 can be traced back to an initiative of Confucian scholars at the end of the 18th century. They had come into contact with Christian teachings in hermetically sealed Korea, initially in the form of Jesuit tracts in Chinese that had been circulating in the country for some time. A group of these Confucian *literati* now sought to learn more about the "Western knowledge". They succeeded in sending one of their members – named Yi Seung-hun (other spelling: Seung-Hoon Lee) – to Beijing (Peking) in 1783 as a member of the annual tribute commission of Korea, where he received further texts and information from the Jesuit fathers still working there. He was baptized in the "Northern Church" (with baptismal name "Peter"), returned to Korea in 1784, discussed the books he had brought with him with his colleagues, convinced and baptized them, whereupon they in turn now spread the new teaching. They began to produce a Christian theological literature, first in Chinese, later – a momentous innovation – in Korean. Despite the rapid onset of bloody persecution, by 1794 the Catholic community already numbered about 4,000 members. All this happened about fifty years before the first European priest, the Frenchman Pierre Maubant, entered the country in 1836 [see Photo D10/12; B09/10].

What has survived is a 1789 letter from "Peter" Yi Seung-hun to the Catholic fathers in Beijing. It provides a fascinating insight into both the self-organization of the nascent church and the accompanying uncertainty about the legitimacy of the path it was taking. Many new Christians, according to this account, he baptized "according to the rite that had been followed at my own baptism in Beijing." He instructed others to do likewise. At a congregational meeting in 1786, it was decided,

> that I should celebrate Holy Mass and confer the Sacrament of Confirmation: not only did I yield to their request, but I conferred the same power to celebrate Holy Mass on ten other persons. For these ceremonies, I followed the procedure laid down in various books [which I had brought with me from Beijing], both prayer books and books of hours (primers) – adding certain parts and omitting others. For the prayers, I made selections from our prayer books. [Text 33a]

At the same time, Yi Seung-hun repeatedly asked for regular priests to be sent to Korea. Finally, in 1794, a Chinese priest (James Zhou Wen-mo; in Korean: Chu Mun-Mo) succeeded in having himself smuggled into the country disguised as a horse trader. He worked there in secret until his execution in 1801.

The emerging underground church grew rapidly. It also spread to the countryside and among ordinary people without education. Women played a prominent role, already accounting for two-thirds of all church members by 1800. Later trial records repeatedly emphasize the "women in the congregation" and their diverse evangelistic and social activities. The use of the native Hangul script (instead of Chinese characters) in the production of underground religious literature was also particularly important in the rapid spread. Thus, the "Essentials of the Lord's Teaching" (*Chu-Gyo Yo-Ji*) by "Augustin" Jeong Yak-jong (Chóng Yak-jong), who died as a martyr in 1801, is the first Christian theological work in the Korean language. Visibly inspired by Matteo Ricci's "True Doctrine," it explored Confucian, Buddhist, Taoist, and shamanistic views [Text 33b]. As the basic catechism of the Catholic Korean Church, the text was to remain in use for more than a century.

In 1791, the first martyrdoms took place [see Photo D10–12]. The central charge in the previous trial, the files of which are preserved in Chinese, was the accusation of sedition and violation of religious duties. Thus, the defendants had refused sacrifices in honor of the ancestors [Text 33c]. In 1801, the royal dowager issued a general ban on Catholicism. According to a summary by Sebastian and Kirsteen Kim in their already classic history of Christianity in Korea, the decisive factors were four main accusations: 1. the Christian faith places God above king and parents; 2. belief in life after death leads to neglect of social duties; 3. inclusion of different classes and genders in Christian communities threatens the Confucian system; 4. encouragement of celibate female piety endangers social reproduction.[2] As a result, there were systematic persecutions of Christians, some of which were carried out with extreme brutality. The numerous martyrdoms of the 19th century, as a result of successive waves of persecution (1801, 1815, 1827, 1839, 1846), were accurately documented by local Christians. The persecution of 1866/67 claimed the most victims, at which time the Catholic community numbered about 23,000 believers in all provinces of the country.

11.5 Tranquebar 1706 and the Beginnings of Protestant Mission in Asia

One can speak of the beginning of Protestant missionary work in Asia in a qualified sense (instead of mere colonial church presence) only since 1706. This is the year in which the Germans Bartholomäus Ziegenbalg (1682–1719; Figure 23) and Heinrich Plütschau (1677–1746) became active in the Danish tenant and mini-colony of Tranquebar (today: Tharangambadi; see Figure 25) on the southeast coast of India. Their arrival initiated the period of the Danish-Halle mission in India. This is characterized by the interaction of various factors: as, for example, the initiative of the Danish King Frederik IV. (1671–1730); the provision of suitable personnel by Halle's Pietism; a mission theology oriented toward the salvation of the individual; and – as a consequence – a preoccupation with the regional culture, hitherto unique in Protestant missions, which aimed at the emergence of a native church. Intensive language studies [Text 34], bible translations (including the first complete translation of the New Testament into Tamil), religious discussions, corresponding – and repeatedly obstructed by Halle's headquarters – literary activities (such as the denied printing permission for Ziegenbalg's writing 'Genealogy of the South Indian Deities' [Text 37]) as well as manifold conflicts with the local colonial authorities were characteristics of this program. With the ordination of the first Indian Protestant pastor Aaron in 1733 [Text 38; Figure 23], an important milestone was reached.

The beginnings in Tranquebar were anything but easy. There was considerable resistance from the European colonists. In 1708/09, Ziegenbalg was even thrown into prison for several months by the local commander. The reason was his protest against the treatment of baptized Christian slaves [Text 37]. In 1707, a first Lutheran Tamil congregation was established, the starting point of the 'Tamil Evangelical Lutheran Church' (TELC) of South India, which still exists today. The Tranquebar mission was ecumenically oriented from the beginning. It soon cooperated with Anglican congregants in neighboring (and British-controlled) Madras (today Chennai). Such early examples of interdenominational cooperation were not limited to southern India. Rather, the Tranquebar experiment took place in an extended international communication context from the very beginning. For the missionary reports from Tranquebar (printed continuously since 1710 as "Halle'schen Berichte") circulated not only in awakened circles in Denmark, Germany and on the European continent. Translated into English early on (as "The Propagation of the Gospel in the East, London", 1709–1718), they also found readers in Britain and on the American East Coast. Cotton Mather (1663–1728), a Puritan from Boston, then developed ideas for a coordinated Protestant world mission. The Tranquebar experiment also attracted attention among native pastors in West Africa, as mentioned above [Text 141].

In the debates of the Tranquebar missionaries with the "Brahmins" of South India, many topics can be found that are still relevant in the Hindu-Christian dialogue today. Although Ziegenbalg rejected South Indian Hinduism as idolatry, he also saw considerable common ground. Among these he counted the belief in a God as well as in a compensatory justice after death – a conviction that he saw on the wane in the Europe of the Enlightenment in view of increasing "atheistries" [Text 37]. His fourth "Conversation with a Malabar Priest" states:

> The priest said: 'There are many religions and sects in this world. Among us Tamil people alone there are 360 sects. We see that many such sects are found among you Christians ... As only one God rules this world, we can say nothing else than that such differences of religion come from God. Correspondingly, all religions point to salvation ... If someone has firmly resolved to attain salvation, he could attain it – no matter which religion he belongs to. But it happens easier in one religion than in another ... 'The following reply was given to him: 'The fact that so many kinds of religions

and sects are found among the people in this world, does not come from God, as you think, but through the delusion of Satan' [...] They asked us, whether we consider the entirety of their religion as false and erroneous or only some aspects. The following response was given [sc. by the missionaries] to them: 'Due to the light of nature, some general truths are indeed found among you. You have written about them in your books. ... For example, you say that there is only one God, who should be known, loved, feared and worshipped. [Further you say that] the soul is immortal ... [and] that after this present time [here on earth] there will be another life, in which people receive either reward or punishment... [Text 35]

As the first stage and "beginning of Protestant Christianity in India," the Tranquebar Mission has been widely acknowledged. Beyond the limited area of the small Danish colony (which was taken over by the British in 1845), it was active in the area of present-day Tamil Nadu. Its legacy was continued in the 19th century by various missions (such as the Leipzig Mission) and churches in southern India.

Notes to Chapter 11

1. Wendt (1997), *Fiesta Filipina*, 357. 65. 356. 360.
2. Kim/Kim (2015), *Korean Christianity*, 32.

Further Reading for Chapter 11

11.1 (Japan: The End of the "Christian Century")

Moffett (2005), *Christianity in Asia II*, 79–104; Ross (1994), *Vision Betrayed*, 47 ff.67–117; Cooper (2004), *Japan*, 393–410; Boxer (1993), *Christian Century*, 308–400; Yasutaka (2021), *Senpuku Kirishitan*; Morris (2018), *Christianity in Japan*; Ward (2009), *Women Religious Leaders*.

11.2 (China: Accommodation Strategies and Rite Controversy)

Moffett (2005), *Christianity in Asia II*, 105–142; Hsia (2004), *Promise: China*, 375–392; Ross (1994), *Vision Betrayed*, 118–154; Zupanow/ Fabre (2018), *Rites Controversies*; Reinhard (1983), *Expansion I*, 184–195; Meier (2018), *Ränder*, 95–120; Menegon (2009), *Ancestors, Virgins and Friars*; Merkel (1920), *Leibniz und die China-Mission*; Minamiki (1985), *Chinese Rites Controversy*; Mungello

(1994), The *Chinese Rites Controversy*; Bays (2012), *New History*, 17–40; Zhang, Qiong (2015), *Chinese encou*nters.

11.3 (*Sri Lanka and the Philippines: Resistance in a Colonial Context*)

Moffett (2005), *Christianity in Asia* II, 222–235.150–174; Boudens (1957), *Catholic Church in Ceylon*; Koschorke (1998), *Catholic Underground Church in Ceylon*, 106–116; Koschorke (2011), *Dutch Reformed Church in Colonial Ceylon*; Perera (1942), *Joseph Vaz*; Wendt (1997), *Fiesta Filipina*; Ileto (1979), *Pasyon and Revolution*; Irvin,/ Sunquist (2012), *World Christian Movement* II,405416.

11.4 (*Korea: Self-Founded Martyrs' Church* [*1784ff*])

Moffett (2005), *Christianity in Asia* II, 143–149.309–321; Kim/Kim (2015), *Korean Christianity*, 14–53; TRE 19 (1990), 615–620: „Korea II" (Won Yong Ji); Diaz (1986), *A Korean Theology*; Kim (2014), „*Non-Missionary Beginnings*", 73–98.

11.5 (*Tranquebar 1706 and the Beginnings of Protestant Missionary Work in Asia*)

Neill (1995), *India* II, 28–58; Moffett (2005), *Christianity in Asia* II, 236–250; Gross/ Kumaradoss/ Liebau (2006), *Beginning of Protestant Christianity* I–III; Jeyaraj (2012), *Transcontinental Communications*; Cañizares-Esguerra/ Maryks/ Hsia (2018), *Jesuits and Protestants in Asia*, 195–213.

Illustrations for Part 2

The image shows an Indian dressed in rags, praying on his knees, with the caption "Poor Indian" and the signature "Poor Jesus Christ". The Inca thus identifies the suffering native American with the Lord. The maltreated Indian is the suffering witness of the foundation of the Church of the New World. Like St. Barbara at the mercy of the lions, "our converted Indian is hunted by six beasts: the dragon is the '*corregidor*'; the lion is the owner of the *commenda*; the tiger is the Spaniard of the rest houses, that is, the functionary of the crown to whom the rest houses were subject and who treated the Indian porters with brute force." The rat on the lower left is not so much a beast as a noxious animal; it represents the Indian *cacique* who submitted to the Spaniards and supported their system of exploitation, and on the right the hypocritical cat, the scribe, a kind of "tax collector" of the New World. Finally, in the center right, the Father of the '*doctrina*' appears in the form of a fox.

FIGURE 10

From the pictorial chronicle 'Nueva corónica y buen gobierno' of the Inca Poma de Ayala around 1614 y buen gobierno' des Inka Poma de Ayala um 1614 (Explanation taken from: Prien 1978, *Geschichte*, 222).

"Nevertheless, so many excesses and abuses do not confuse the committed and ardent faith of our chronicler. The graphic that concludes those comments is a message of hope. We are in the chapter about the '*doctrinas*', and it is about the sermon of the '*padre cura*'. He is in the pulpit; from his mouth come only words in *quechua* (already not in Spanish), which may be regarded as the realization of the desire expressed in the previous graphic ...: Gospel and Holy Scripture. The natives no longer show fear and trepidation, on the contrary, half of the image is filled by a gathering of men and women, no longer in rags, but with properly worn, clean ponchos, in collected posture. As a sign of meditation, some have closed their eyes, others are looking at the lips of the Father, drinking his *quechua* words, others show tears, no longer of pain but of emotion. A ray of light enters through the window of the church, directed toward the assembly. In it flies a dove. Flames of fire descend. The conclusion, not written by Guaman, is evident: if the Fathers in the '*doctrinas*' had preached only the Gospel without Spanish admixture, it would have been a pure Pentecost for the Latin American Church."

FIGURE 11

From the pictorial chronicle 'Nueva corónica y buen gobierno' by the 120 around 1614 (Explanation taken from: Prien 1978, *Geschichte*, 228).

ILLUSTRATIONS FOR PART 2

FIGURE 12   Cuzco (Peru), Plaza mayor, with cathedral [= photo J01].

FIGURE 13   Cuzco (Peru): "Supper with Guinea Pig": painting by the Christian mestizo artist Marcos Zapata (1710–1773), today in the cathedral [= photo J04].

FIGURE 14   Mexico: Sor Juana Inés de la Cruz (1648–1695), nun, poet, and advocate of women's right to knowledge and education.

ILLUSTRATIONS FOR PART 2

FIGURE 15
(Historical) Kongo empire: Doña Beatriz Kimpa Vita (1684–1706), Kongolese prophetess, leader of the Christian social revolutionary movement of the Antonians, also referred to as the African Joan of Arc (portrait 1710 by Bernardo da Gallo).

FIGURE 16
Olaudah Equiano (c. 1745–1797, also known as Gustavus Vassa), former slave from Benin (Nigeria): African Christian, publicist, and champion of the English anti-slavery movement.

FIGURE 17   An early transatlantic marriage: Christian Jacob Protten "Africanus" (1715–1769), Moravian missionary and linguist in what is now Ghana; and Rebecca Protten (1718–1780), former slave and evangelist from the Caribbean; both married in Herrnhut (Germany) in 1746; with daughter Anna Maria.

FIGURE 18   Ghana: Elmina Fort, hub of the transatlantic slave trade, successively in Portuguese, Dutch and British colonial possession [= photo G14].

FIGURE 19

Ghana: Jacobus Elisa Johannes Capitein (c. 1717–1747), West African pastor who, after studying in Leiden, was ordained as a clergyman in the Dutch Reformed Church and became a colonial pastor in Elmina (portrait by Pieter Tanjé, between 1742 and 1762).

ILLUSTRATIONS FOR PART 2

FIGURE 20   Macao, former Portuguese colony: facade of St. Paul's Church from the 17th century.

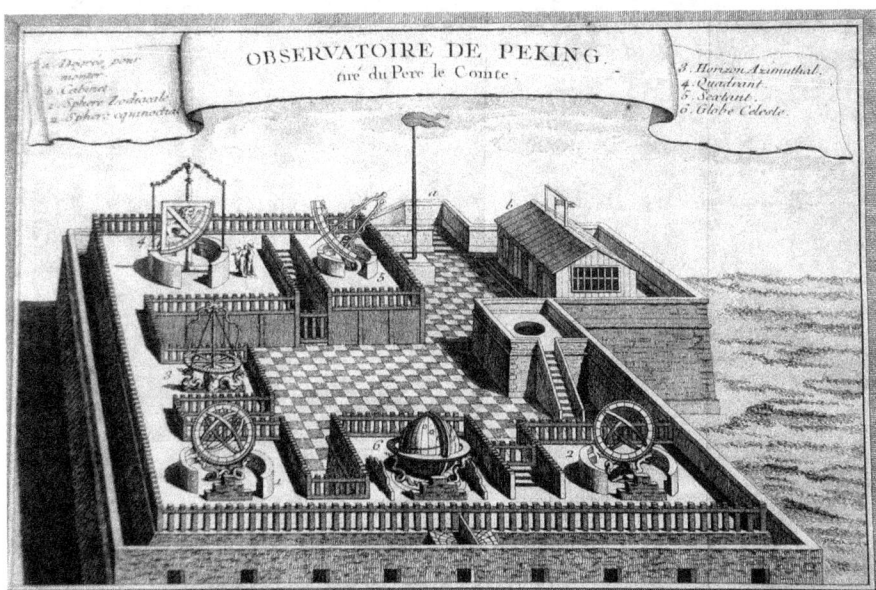

FIGURE 21   Beijing (Peking): Astronomical observatory, depicted by the French Jesuit Louis le Comte (1655–1728). Due to their astronomical knowledge Jesuits gained great influence and high positions at the imperial court [= photo B08].

FIGURE 22   China: Matteo Ricci, Italian Jesuit (1552–1610), and Ly Paulos (Xu Guangqui), Chinese bureaucrat, mathematician, and convert baptized by Ricci (1562–1633), in front of an altar (print from Athanasius Kircher's *Monumenta* of 1669).

ILLUSTRATIONS FOR PART 2

FIGURE 23
Bartholomäus Ziegenbalg (1682–1719), the first German Lutheran missionary in India (Tranquebar / Tharangambadi) from 1706. He translated the Bible into Tamil, established schools and founded an Indian Lutheran congregation.

FIGURE 24
The Tamil catechist Aaron (b. Arumugun, 1698/99–1745), the first Indian to be ordained as a Protestant minister in Tranquebar in 1733.

FIGURE 25   Tranquebar (Tharangambadi, South India), starting point of the Danish-Hall mission and Protestant presence in India. Picture: Fort Dansborg, center of the Danish ("hired") mini-colony.

PART 3

1800–1890

CHAPTER 12

The End of the First Colonial Age and the Beginning of the "Protestant Century"

12.1 Collapse of the Old Colonial Systems (Ibero-America, Africa, Asia)

At the turn of the 18th and 19th centuries, the old colonial order collapsed [Map 14]. The changes were most dramatic in Central and South America. There, Spain and Portugal lost all their colonial possessions on the mainland between 1810 and 1825. Instead, numerous independent nation-states with often shifting borders formed – Mexico, the Central American countries, Colombia, Peru, Bolivia, Paraguay, Uruguay, Argentina, and Chile. Until the end of the 19th century, remains of the former Spanish rule existed only on the periphery, i.e. on the islands of the Caribbean (Cuba, Puerto Rico) and in the Pacific region (Guam, the Philippines). In 1822, Brazil also declared its independence from Portugal. The Iberian country thus lost its only possession in the Americas and, at the same time, its most important overseas territory.

In Africa and Asia, the decline of the Portuguese colonial empire had begun long before. By 1800, the Portuguese presence in Asia was limited to a few enclaves (Goa, Diu, Macao, and parts of Timor in present-day Indonesia). Shipping between Lisbon and Goa was also reduced to a few trips annually. But also the colonial empire of the Dutch – who had replaced the Portuguese as colonial masters in large parts of Africa and Asia around 1650 – was increasingly dissolving. In 1798, the heavily indebted 'Dutch East India Company' (VOC) went bankrupt, and the Dutch possessions along the African coast and in South Asia were taken over – temporarily (Java) or permanently (South African Cape, Ceylon [Sri Lanka], Malacca) – by the British.

Historians speak of the end of the first – Iberian-dominated – colonial age. Various factors were decisive for this development: Economic backwardness, corruption and inefficiency of local colonial administrations, 'overstretching' of limited resources, growing competition from other European powers (such as Britain and France) in the Atlantic, and growing aspiration for autonomy in the American colonies themselves were such factors. In Africa and Asia, the Portuguese empire had already passed its peak by 1650. This process was accelerated by the loss of maritime dominance in the Indian Ocean to the Omani Arabs (and the Marathas of Western India). Subsequently, Portuguese influence there steadily declined. In Ibero-America, the Enlightenment, the North

© KLAUS KOSCHORKE, 2025 | DOI:10.1163/9789004699830_013
This is an open access chapter distributed under the terms of the CC BY-NC-ND 4.0 license.

American War of Independence, and the French Revolution had spread liberal ideals and emancipatory ideas. Especially in circles of the Creole elite, i.e. the white settlers born in the colonies themselves, the beginnings of a new – now "American" – self-awareness intensified. The effects of the Napoleonic Wars were particularly serious. Portugal and Spain were occupied by France in 1808. The colonies thus lost their imperial center. In this power vacuum, open revolt occurred in various regions of Hispano-America beginning in 1810. When finally the relative autonomy enjoyed by the Spanish overseas territories during this transitional phase was to be reversed – after liberal reforms had been repealed and the old order restored in Spain since 1814 – this only further accelerated the revolutionary process and separatist tendencies overseas.

Even before these events, the Netherlands had lost large parts of its colonial empire. After the occupation of the mother country by French troops in 1796, the British took over numerous Dutch possessions in Africa and Asia to get ahead of their French rivals. After 1815, the victorious Great Britain was initially the only colonial power worthy of the name. What other European nations still retained in terms of overseas territorial possessions, they now kept by England's grace. For a long time, Great Britain itself was less interested in formal colonial rule rather than in unhindered access to overseas markets. The era of so-called free trade imperialism began.

12.2 Hitting Rock Bottom of the Catholic Missions (Asia, Africa, America)

The collapse of the old colonial empires had a direct impact on the history of the Christian communities in the respective regions. For with the colonial rule of the Europeans, in many cases also the established colonial church structures disintegrated. In Ceylon (Sri Lanka), for example, the Dutch Reformed colonial church, which had already been in a process of constant decline, collapsed with the end of Dutch rule on the island in 1796. The Dutch clergy left the country; and in large numbers the native believers fell back into Buddhist or Hindu "paganism." "The religion of Christ has never been so disgraced in any age of the Church", the English chaplain Claudius Buchanan, for example, had to conclude around 1812 after a tour through the island [Text 40].

However, it was primarily the Catholic missions that were affected by the decline. The year 1815 marked a low point from which they were not to recover – globally and locally – for a long time. In *Europe*, the French Revolution and the Napoleonic reorganization of the continent had shattered the Church of the Ancien Regime. The great secularizations since the late 18th century destroyed the economic basis of the Catholic church system and its missionary orders. In France, the clergy had been drastically decimated by the revolutionary terror of the 1790s. In Germany, the ecclesiastical principalities had been dissolved since 1803; and in Italy, the Papal States were occupied by French troops in 1798. In the same year, the Roman missionary headquarters – the 'Propaganda Fide' founded in 1622, which had directed the evangelizing activities of the Curia overseas for almost two centuries – was also abolished. 1808 saw the renewed occupation of the Papal States and the capture of the Pope by French troops. The Congress of Vienna in 1814/15 did reverse many of the changes of the Napoleonic era. But the situation of the Catholic Church remained precarious.

But long before that, the Catholic missionary system had already been decisively weakened by the *abolition of the Jesuit order*. Under pressure from the absolutist regimes in pre-revolutionary France and Spain, Pope Clement XIV had dissolved the Societas Jesu, the largest and most successful missionary order of modern times, in 1773. The Jesuits had already been expelled from Portugal (1759), France (1764), Spain (1767) and their overseas possessions. Thus the most important instrument of Catholic missionary activities was broken up, with long lasting impact. In 1852, for example, there were only 10 Catholic priests left in Angola and Mozambique, the two pillars of the Portuguese Padroado in Africa.

In *China*, the Christian religion had been banned since the days of Emperor Yongzheng (r. 1723–1735) as a result of the so-called Rites Controversy. In 1724, all Catholic missionaries except some court astronomers had been expelled from the country. An imperial edict of 1800 confirmed the long-standing ban. In 1811 and 1827, two, respectively three, of the four famous churches once built by the Jesuits in Peking (Beijing) were destroyed. *Japan* had been a "closed country" since the beginning of the 17th century anyway; and in *India,* the French clergyman Abbé J.A. Dubois (1770–1848), who had been a missionary in the country for many years, lamented the almost complete decline of Catholicism in the subcontinent around 1815 as follows:

> The Christian religion of Catholic persuasion was introduced into India a little more than three hundred years ago, at the epoch of the Portuguese invasions [in the sixteenth century] [...] The low state to which it [the Christian religion] is now reduced, and the contempt in which it is held, cannot be surpassed. There is not at present in this country more than a third of the Christians who were to be found in it eighty years ago, and this number diminishes day by day by frequent apostasy. It will dwindle to nothing in a short period; and if things continue as they are going on, within less than fifty years there will, I fear, reman no vestige

of Christianity among the natives. The Christian religion, which was formerly the object of indifference, or at most contempt, has now become, I dare say, almost an object of horror. It is certain is that during the last sixty years no new adherents, or very few, have been gained. [Text 39]

The situation was particularly dramatic in *Ibero-America*. Here, complaints about the moral decadence and low level of education of the colonial clergy already had multiplied at the beginning of the 19th century [e.g., Text 273]. Then, with the end of Spanish rule in the 1820s, there was a mass exodus of loyalist bishops and priests. "Religious orders are non-existent in many places," was how a European visitor around 1825 described the situation in Chile and the Plata region. "Where they still exist, the members are generally beyond all observation of the rule . ... All the Franciscan fathers who were sent from Spain ... have fled or have had to remain as prisoners" [Text 269]. In Mexico, for example, between 1810 and 1834, the number of secular clergy decreased from 4,229 to 2,282 and the number of religious from 3,112 to 1,726. By the end of the independence process, most of the episcopal sees in Latin America were vacant. Religious orders were in decline, large numbers of priests laicized, hundreds of smaller monasteries gone, and numerous seminaries closed.

12.3 Developments in the Protestant World

In the 19th century, by contrast, the Protestant missionary movement, which had previously played a limited role at best regionally, experienced an enormous upswing. For them, this century became the "great century of missionary advance" (K.S. Latourette). In the course of this century, the Protestant missionary movement reached numerous areas that had previously been closed to Europeans and founded congregations in regions that had previously not been shown on any map. The Protestant missionary movement was by no means only evangelizing, but also a factor of modernization in many places. Missionaries built not only chapels, but also – and sometimes first – schools, hospitals and orphanages. They studied (and alphabetized) the regional languages, translated the Bible and other texts, introduced the first printing presses in many places, or gave impetus to the development of a native press. They criticized social grievances – such as the practice of widow burning in India or child abandonment in Africa – and were in turn partly responsible for consolidating the image of the "savage" African in Europe. Without the "mission school" factor, certain modernization processes in 19th century Asia or the anti-colonial liberation struggle of African elites in the 20th century cannot be understood.

Even where the emerging Protestant congregations lagged numerically behind their Catholic competitors (as in India or China), Protestant missions set the tone in many places in the eyes of the non-Christian public. This is shown, for example, by various religious revival movements in different Asian regions at the end of the 19th century, which – such as the so-called "Protestant Buddhism" in Sri Lanka – were often related to the model of missionary Protestantism, both in protest against, and as imitated example.

It is no coincidence that the starting point of this new stage in Protestant missionary history was *Great Britain*, the mother country of the Industrial Revolution and the hegemonic power of the early nineteenth century. The Baptists (since 1792), Methodists (since 1813) and other evangelical groups such as the Anglican-Lower 'Church Missionary Society' (CMS, since 1799) deserve special mention. Their leading representatives were also prominently involved in the fight against the slave trade. Initially, the CMS was mainly active in West Africa and India, and later in numerous other regions in Asia, Africa and Oceania. The form of organization of these early mission organizations was that of an association, the voluntary union of pious individuals; and the promotion of missions was no longer considered a matter for the colonial state, but primarily for the commitment of responsible citizens and pious laymen. In the process, people cooperated widely across denominational and national boundaries. The same applies to the missionary societies on the *continent*, such as the Basel Mission (founded in 1815), whose German or Swiss alumni became active in West Africa in English service or in Indonesia under Dutch sovereignty. Not to spread one specific denominational form of Christianity, but to proclaim "Christ himself" (and not "Luther, or Calvin, or Zwingli") and to preach the "pure doctrine of the gospel" was the goal of the Basel emissaries. In doing so, they saw their missionary commitment as part of a global movement and embedded in the "blowing of the Spirit of God over the whole world," as it says in the first Basel appeal from 1815.

This Basel "Mission Institute" had emerged from a circle of awakened Christians in the southern German-Swiss region and was supported by a network of regional aid societies. In 1828, the Rhenish Missionary Society in Wuppertal-Elberfeld emerged from one of these "aid societies" ("Hilfsvereine") – initially a mere feeder institution for Basel. Other Basel aid societies merged in 1836 in Hamburg to form the interdenominational North German Missionary Society. In a later phase, there was also an increase in the formation of church-connected denominational missions in Germany, such as the founding of the strictly Lutheran Leipzig Mission in 1847 or the Hermannsburg Mission in 1849. But also quasi-private initiatives – such as the one-man missionary seminar of the Berlin pastor Johannes Jänicke, from which, for example, the later famous

China missionary Karl Gützlaff emerged [Text 54] – belong to the picture of early German missionary Protestantism. Parallel to these developments, Protestant societies were founded also in other regions of continental Europe. For example, the Paris Mission (Société des Missions évangéliques de Paris) was established in 1811, and corresponding societies were founded in Denmark (Det Danske Missionsselskab, 1821) and Norway (Det Norske Missionsselskab, 1842).

In 1810, the 'American Board of Commissioners for Foreign Missions' (ABCFM) was founded in Boston. It was first an interdenominational and later a congregationalist organization. As early as 1812, it sent eight missionaries of its own to Bengal (where, however, they were immediately expelled by the British colonial administration). Among them were three missionary women who had been ordained specifically for their task as teachers in the "heathen" world before being sent overseas. In general, women played an important role in the *American missionary movement* from the beginning in various capacities. By 1855, the ABCFM was active in Africa, Europe, the Near East, South and Northeast Asia, the Pacific, and among native Indians. A prominent representative of the ABCFM was Rufus Anderson (1796–1880). Concurrently with, but independently of, Henry Venn (1796–1873) of the British Anglican CMS, he developed the concept of the "Three Selves" – the vision of a self-propagating, self-financing, and self-governing "native church" as the goal of missionary work. Since mid-century, this concept became the guiding principle of numerous Anglo-Saxon missions.

In 1814 the Baptists, in 1819 the Methodists, in 1821 the Episcopalians, in 1837 the Presbyterians and in the course of time other American denominations founded their own missionary societies. Presbyterian and Baptist missionaries from the U.S. also became active in Latin America (Mexico, Brazil, etc.) beginning in the 1850s on a larger scale. The role of *black missionaries*, who were active as evangelists in Africa in particular, is of particular importance in the history of American missions in the 19th century. Initially, most of them worked on behalf of white-dominated missionary societies and, since the 1870s, increasingly as emissaries of black churches or African-American societies from the USA [see below chap. 12.4].

12.4 Transcontinental Migration Flows, Beginnings of African-American Missions

The Western missionary movement was, however, only one factor among others in the worldwide spread of Christianity in the 19th century. The global migration flows of that time also played an important role. They led to changes in religious and denominational geographies in many places. This includes numerous examples of first-time Protestant presence in regions where it had not existed before. The 19th century saw successive waves of *European emigration overseas*. Between 1800 and 1925, one in five Europeans left the old continent. German emigrants went to the United States, Latin America (especially Brazil, Argentina, Chile), in smaller numbers to South Africa and, toward the end of the century, to the new German colonies. Irish immigrants fled from the 1840s to the U.S. to escape the famines in their homeland and strengthened the Catholic element there. Conversely, in Brazil, for example, the immigration of entire village communities from Germany, which began in 1824, led to a legal Protestant presence for the first time. It marked an important first stage of denominational pluralization in a country that previously had been officially purely Catholic. Other versions of Protestantism – such as North American mission churches since the mid-19th century and various Pentecostal and neo-Pentecostal movements in the 20th century – did not play a significant role in South America until later. In the process of the global spread of the churches of the Reformation, the transcontinental migration movements of the 19th century are of considerable importance.

Less studied so far (and hardly researched systematically), but also relevant, was the voluntary or forced *migration of indigenous Christians* within the colonial worlds of the 19th century. In numerous British overseas possessions and other regions of the global South, the institution of so-called 'indentured labor' replaced the officially abolished slavery system from the middle of the century onwards. This led to increased fluctuation and circulation of, for example, Indian coolies within (and outside) the colonies of the British Empire. At the same time, this resulted in various forms of religious export. It led, for example, for the first time to a considerable Hindu presence in the Caribbean, where it had previously been unknown. On the other hand, it also led to the establishment of Tamil Christian communities in various regions of South Asia or East Africa, where no Western missionaries had been active before. Among the first 350 Indian immigrants to Natal, South Africa, in 1860, there were already 50 Catholics and 4 Protestants. In the course of time, the number of Protestants (Methodists, Anglicans, Lutherans) among the Indian immigrants in South Africa increased significantly. Spontaneous spread of faith by Christian migrants could also be observed in the tea plantations of Sri Lanka, where British colonists were surprised by the religious services of their "coolies" imported from South India [Text 60].

In general, the importance of *ethnic diasporas* as networks for a non-missionary spread of Christianity can hardly be overestimated. This is true especially for the 19th century Asia. In China, for example, Western missionaries had no official access at all before 1842 (and only limited access thereafter). The beginnings of Chinese Protestantism thus developed in the wide ring of Chinese diaspora communities between Thailand, Malacca and Indonesia. From there, activists such as the famous evangelist Liang Fa [see Figure 27] made forays into the Middle Kingdom beginning in the 1820s. Through his tracts, he exerted considerable influence on the later indigenous mass movement of the T'aiping [see Text 61]. Also in the final phase of the Chinese Qing dynasty, toward the end of the 19th century, a modern (and at the same time often Christian) intelligentsia was formed, initially mainly in the Chinese foreign diaspora. From there, they carried their revolutionary ideas into the motherland. One prominent example has been Sun Yat-Sen (1866–1925), a baptized Christian, later (1912) to become the first (provisional) president of republican China.

Of great importance in the given context have been the interactions and entanglements between colored Christians within the so-called *'Black Atlantic'*. Transatlantic networks of African-American Christians already played an important role in the 17th and 18th centuries, as discussed elsewhere [see chapter 10.4]. Toward the end of the 18th century, remigration efforts of former black slaves from the United States intensified. In 1792, these efforts led to the establishment of a settlement of African-American repatriates in Sierra Leone [discussed in more detail in chapter 14.1]. As a result, the first Protestant church under the leadership of black Christians was founded on West African soil. The early 19th century then saw the beginnings of African American missionary work in Africa. At first, it was mainly individual black Baptist and Methodist preachers from Jamaica or the American East Coast who became active in West Africa – initially still in the service of white-dominated societies. Increasingly, however, independent African-American initiatives and the founding of their own black missionary societies proliferated. This was especially true since the 1870s, when – after the American Civil War and the disappointing outcome of the subsequent "Reconstruction" period – hopes for an equal coexistence of black and white in the USA were dashed. Now interest turned again to Africa in a new way.

The example of the African Methodist Episcopal Church (AME), the oldest and largest black church in the United States, is particularly noteworthy. Founded in 1816 in Philadelphia, it spread rapidly among African-Americans in North America. From the 1870s, it also had an offshoot in West Africa, reaching

South Africa a little later, where it merged in 1896 with a local black church. This was the 'Ethiopian Church' founded by the former Methodist preacher Mangena Mokone in 1892 [see Figure. 36–37; Photo H11–12]. Thus a durable transatlantic church organization was established. By the late 19th century, African American missionaries were active in southern Africa, Liberia, Sierra Leone, the Gold Coast, Nigeria, and the Belgian Congo. Smaller in number and equipped with far fewer resources than their white missionary counterparts, they nevertheless exercised considerable influence. They stimulated, for example, independence movements among African Christians, which intensified toward the end of the century.

Further Reading for Chapter 12

12.1 (Collapse of the Old Colonial Systems)
Boxer (1972), *Dutch Seaborn Empire*, 268–294; Boxer (1991) *Portuguese Seaborne Empire*, 200ff; Parry (1990), *Spanish Seaborne Empire*; Abernethy (2000), *European Overseas Empires*, 64–80; Bakewell (^{2}2004), *History of Latin America*, 312 ff. 382–410; Osterhammel (1997), *Colonialism*, 23–38; Rothermund (2006), *Decolonization*, 222ff; Reinhard (1985), *Expansion* II, 203–258; Reinhard (1996), *Kolonialismus*, 97–132. 178ff; Gründer (1992), *Welteroberung*, 315–323; Fieldhouse (1991), *Kolonialreiche*, 11–136; Ansprenger (^{4}1981), *Auflösung;* Wendt (2007), *Globalisierung*, 177 ff; Osterhammel (2009), *Verwandlung der Welt*, 565–673; Jansen/ Osterhammel (2017), *Decolonisation*.

12.2 (Hitting Rock Bottom of Catholic Missions)
Moffett (2005), *Christianity in Asia* II, 175–192; Gründer (1992), *Welteroberung*, 315–429; Jedin (^{R}1985), *Handbuch* VI/1, 3–105. 229–247. 615–649; Schmidlin (1925), *Katholische Missionsgeschichte*, 387 ff.

12.3 (Developments in the Protestant World)
Ward (2017), *Missionary Movement*, 223–246; Walls (1996), *Missionary Movement*; Robert (2011), *Christian Mission*; Latourette (^{R}1980), *Expansion of Christianity* IV + V (1800–1914); Gründer (1992), *Welteroberung*, 315–367; Gensichen (1976), *Missionsgeschichte*, 26–48; Raupp (1990), *Mission in Quellentexten*, 231–411; Warneck (1880), *Missionsjahrhundert*; Tyrell (2004), *Weltmission*, 13–136; Christ-Von Wedel/ Kuhn (2015), *Basler Mission*; Ward/ Stanley (2000), *Church Mission Society*; Robert (1997), *American Women in Mission*; Cox (2008), *British Missionary Enterprise*, 77–168.

12.4 (*Transcontinental Migration, Beginnings of African-American Missions*)

Hastings (1994), *Church in Africa,* 173–188; Walls (2002), *Sierra Leone,* 45–56; Hanciles (2014), *Black Atlantic*; 29–50; Hanciles (2005), *Back to Africa,* 191–216; Campbell (2024), *Origins of the Back-To-Africa Movement*; Burlacioiu (2024), *Sierra Leone*; Koschorke (2024), *Transatlantic Ethiopianism*; Campbell (1998), *Songs of Zion*; Walvin (1998), *Olaudah Equiano*; Oltmer (2012), *Globale Migration* 45–78; Martin (1989), *Black Baptists and African Missions*; Williams (1982), *Black Americans,* 3–85; Russel (2000), *Jamaican Baptist Missions*; Fountain (2010), *African American slaves and Christianity*; Martin (2002), *African Mission Movement,* 57–72.

CHAPTER 13

Asia

13.1 South Asia: Missions as a Factor of Modernization

13.1.1 New Beginning in Serampore (1800ff)

In Asia, the beginnings of this new stage in Protestant mission history are associated with the name Serampore. Serampore was a small Danish trading post in Bengal, India. It was here that the pioneer Baptist missionaries around William Carey settled from 1800 onward – rather than in British-ruled Calcutta just a few miles away. This was a consequence of the anti-missionary attitude of the British colonial authorities at the beginning of the 19th century, which only gradually loosened. As a result, Serampore developed into a missionary center with an pan-Asian appeal.

William Carey (1761–1834), the founder of the Serampore Mission, came from a weaving family in Northampton, England. Originally a shoemaker, Carey educated himself as an autodidact and learned numerous languages – first various classical and living languages of Europe and later different Indian idioms. In 1783, Carey joined the Baptists. Reports of the South Sea voyages of James Cook (1728–79) aroused his interest in the world outside Europe – and in the millions of people who had not yet been reached by the gospel. With his tract "An Enquiry into the Obligations of Christians to use Means for the Conversion of Heathens," he gave impetus to the founding of the 'Baptist Missionary Society' in 1792. In 1793 he set out for India. He first made his way in Calcutta and moved on to Serampore in 1800. Other Baptist activists followed.

The goal was to establish a voluntary, self-sustaining "faith mission" independent of the colonial authorities. Its features were intensive language study, street preaching (to reach the mass of illiterate people) and interreligious disputes (with the Brahmin elite). This included the translation of sacred scriptures such as the Hindu epic Ramayana. Successes (in the sense of formal conversions) were initially few. Serampore's importance lay above all in the variety of impulses emanating from this center. Particular attention was paid to Bible translations and – closely related to this – the establishment of a printing press. By 1820, the New Testament was available in Bengali translation as well as in Sanskrit, Oriya, Hindi, Marathi, Punjabi, Assamese, and Gujurathi. In all, portions of the Bible have been translated into forty languages of India and neighboring countries – such as the Maldives, Burma, Java, and China. For some Indian and East Asian languages, printing types were produced at

Serampore for the first time. In a letter from William Ward, a close associate of Carey's, dated late 1811, there is the following account:

> As you enter, you see your cousin, in a small room, dressed in a white jacket, reading or writing, and looking over the office, which is more than 170 feet long. There you find Indians translating the Scriptures into the different tongues, or correcting proof-sheets. You observe, laid out in cases, types in Arabic, Persian, Nagari, Telugu, Panjabi, Bengali, Marathi, Chinese, Oriya, Burmese, Kanarese, Greek, Hebrew and English. Hindus, Mussulmans and Christian Indians are busy, composing, correcting, distributing. Next are four men throwing off the Scripture sheets in the different languages; others folding the sheets and delivering them to the large store room; and six Muslims do the binding. Beyond the office are the varied type-castors, besides a group of men making ink; and in a spacious open-walled-round place, our paper-mill, for we manufacture our own paper. [Text 44]

Another focus of his work was education. In 1818, the Serampore College was founded, which still exists today. The goal was to "the instruction of Asiatic and other youth in Eastern literature and European science" [Text 45]. Teaching was primarily in Sanskrit (as well as Arabic and Persian), and for certain students also in English. The subject matter included the "Shastras of the Hindus" and the Bible, as well as various scientific and other disciplines. The college was attended by both Christian and Hindu students. In 1827, the college was granted the right to confer academic degrees.

The wide global ecumenical horizon in which the Serampore pioneers located their own work can already be seen in the large number of Bible translations. As early as 1806, Carey also drew up the plan for a world mission conference, which was to take place for the first time in 1810 – and thus a hundred years before Edinburgh in 1910 – at the Cape of Good Hope. Such a "general association of all denominations of Christians, from the four quarters of the world" was to become – according to Carey's unfulfilled vision – a regular event and take place about every ten years [Text 46b].

13.1.2 *Further Developments (1813ff)*

The Baptists did not remain the only Protestant missionaries active in India. Despite all obstacles, other Protestant societies soon got engaged on the subcontinent. In 1813, British India was opened to missions from the United Kingdom – against the fierce resistance of the English 'East India Company' (EIC), which was primarily interested in commercial matters [Text 41]. The company, endowed with a state monopoly, united vast areas of India under its control. In 1833, at the next regular renewal of this charter for the EIC by the British Parliament, this restriction also fell, and British India was now open to missionaries of other nationalities as well. Subsequently, the broad range of Euro-American missionary Protestantism made its way to the subcontinent. Anglicans, Methodists, Baptists, Presbyterians, Congregationalists, Lutherans and other denominations sent their messengers of faith to the South Asian country. At the same time, they also introduced different national versions of the same confession (such as English and American Methodism or German and Scandinavian Lutheranism) on the subcontinent.

In 1834, for example, the German-Swiss 'Basel Mission' began its work in Mangalore, India. Gradually, also Catholic religious congregations – such as the Jesuits, who were reconstituted by the pope in 1814 but were severely depleted in number – became active again in India. At the same time, the organizational reconstruction of Indian Catholicism was promoted by the Roman Curia. The Protestant missionaries saw in the Rome-free St. Thomas Christians of Kerala potential allies and a possible instrument for the evangelization of all India. After all, they were free – in Protestant eyes – from numerous errors of the Catholic tradition [Text 46]. Thus, British Anglicans sought to support them in a "brotherly" manner – rather than "tyrannically" appropriating them (as the Portuguese had done). This was tried, for example, by printing and distributing a translation of the Bible in the native Malayalam and by setting up a theological college for the St. Thomas Christians in Kottayam. On the whole, however, the Anglican missionaries massively underestimated the differences between the two church traditions. Tensions arose, and in 1836 the Syrian Orthodox metropolitan put an end to this early phase of cooperation with the Anglicans.

In neighboring colonial Ceylon (Sri Lanka), various Anglo-Saxon missions (Anglicans, Methodists, Baptists and American Congregationalists) had been active since the 1810s. In Burma (Myanmar) – which was only gradually subjected to British rule in the course of the 19th century – larger Baptist congregations were formed among various ethnic minorities. The starting point here was the work of the American Baptist Adoniram Judson (1788–1850), who had originally set out for India but was deported to Burma (Myanmar) by the British colonial authorities immediately after his arrival in Calcutta in 1812. There he then worked – in the then still independent upper part of the country – as a pioneer missionary below the Karen ethnic group.

The "great uprising" of 1857/58, later transfigured into the first national revolution, shook British rule in India. It led to the end of the British East India Company. British India – a conglomerate of directly ruled territories and limited autonomous princely states – now became a crown colony and "jewel" in the empire of Queen Victoria, who proclaimed herself Empress of India in 1877. In terms of religious policy, her government took the line of strict neutrality toward the country's various religions. The Christian communities suffered setbacks as a result of the uprising, but continued to grow steadily in the period that followed. The number of Catholics around 1860 is estimated at just over one million. In 1900, there were about 1,920,000. The emerging Protestant communities were naturally smaller. However, they subsequently experienced dynamic growth: from about 139,000 around 1860 to about 1,200,000 around 1900. Around 1900, about 650,000 Christians belonged to the Orthodox or St. Thomas Church communities in India.

13.1.3 *Mission as a Factor of Modernization*
The Protestant missionary movement not only led to the establishment of denominationally separate (and usually modest in numbers) missionary congregations. It was also present in the public sphere in many ways: through its journalism, its social (and socio-political) activities, the introduction (or use) of new technologies, and its involvement in the medical and educational fields. In many cases, missionaries were perceived as pioneers and multipliers of Western modernity. To mention, for example, the printing press: It was part of the basic equipment of almost every major mission station. In early 19th century Madras, for instance, most privately operated presses were owned by Christian missions. Their techniques of religious journalism inspired the Hindus, and foundations such as the 'Hindu Tract Society' followed the example of the Christian 'Madras Religious Tract Society'. Issues such as caste, child marriage and other traditions condemned as 'social evils' of Hindu society were not only the subject of concerned deliberations at missionary conferences. They also became the subject of public campaigns and advances to the colonial government. The early example of a successful campaign was the fight against "Sati", the custom of burning widows, the abolition of which in Bengal was called for in particular also by the great Hindu reformer Ram Mohan Roy. In 1829, this practice was banned. Medical mission – that is, the operation of hospitals and dispensaries, the sending of doctors and the medical training of native helpers – was a central aspect of missionary work from the very beginning. Later, it became the hallmark of American societies in particular.

The influence of the missions was particularly far-reaching in the field of education. Non-Christian rulers – such as the Burmese king in Mandalay in 1868 – called on missionaries to build schools [Text 50]. In British India, Christian colleges – such as the 'Scottish Church College' in Calcutta or the 'Wilson College in Bombay' – played an important role in spreading Western education. Graduates of these colleges found good posts in the state administrative service, but also as judges, lawyers, teachers and professors. From the middle of the century, the missionary foundations faced stronger competition from state institutions such as Madras University, established in 1857, and increasingly from the 1880s onward from school foundations by the Theosophists. Nevertheless, the missions maintained their strong position in the education sector, and the Indian Christian community could boast the highest literacy rate, especially in southern India, right after the traditional Brahmin elite and despite its heterogeneous composition. A renowned institution like the 'Madras Christian College' – founded in 1837 for the upper Hindu classes – functioned as an elite forge not only for the majority of Hindu students. Future Christian leaders like V. S. Azariah (1874–1945), later the first Indian bishop, studied there as well.

Toward the end of the 19th century, successes in the area of female education were particularly phenomenal. Indian Christian women in Madras in southern India had the highest level of education. For Indian Christians, their leading role in the field of female education was a sign of Christian progressiveness. A Christian personality like Pandita Ramabai (1858–1922), an educator and social activist from a Brahmin family, enjoyed respect and recognition beyond religious boundaries. Not only in Christian circles she was regarded as visible proof of the emancipatory power of Christianity [see Figure 38].

13.1.4 Reception Outside the Mission Churches, Indigenous Interpretations of Christianity

One of the characteristics of the history of Indian Christianity is that the reception of missionary impulses often took place outside the channels of the missionary churches. An early example is the Bengali reformer Raja Ram Mohan Roy (1772–1833). He was one of the leading figures in the cultural life of Bengal in the early 19th century and has often been called the "father of modern India." A Hindu all his life, he called Jesus the "perfect teacher" and sought to reform popular Hinduism, which he rejected, in the light of Christ's ethics and the Sermon on the Mount, among other things. "The Commandments of Jesus, the Leader for Peace and Happiness," was the title of a book he published in Bengali and English in 1820. It contains excerpts of the ethical (but not dogmatic) passages of the New Testament [Text 51]. He rejected the invitation of the Serampore missionaries to become a Christian. Instead, he founded the 'Brahmo Samaj', a movement that was to play an important role in the Hindu revival of the 19th century. On the other hand, individuals also found their way to the Bible through him (and later also to the Christian church).

Other Hindu reform movements were also marked to varying degrees by both Christian impulses and opposition to missionary Protestantism. Since the 1870s, these have included groups such as the 'Prarthana Samaj' founded in Bombay, the 'Ramakrishna Mission' (with its teaching that all religions are ultimately one), militant organizations such as the 'Arya Samaj', or a personality such as Swami Vivekananda (1863–1902) – internationally known since his appearance at the World Parliament of Religions in Chicago in 1893. As a wandering monk, he had previously always carried two favorite books with him: the Bhagavad Gita and a treatise on the "Imitation of Christ". Christianity contained nothing of value – so his message – that could not be found equally and better in Hinduism. Indian Christians, for their part, saw the "ferment" of the Christian message at work in the diverse social and religious reform movements toward the end of the 19th century. The return to the ethical dimensions of the Hindu tradition – according to an opinion frequently expressed around 1900 even by reform-oriented Hindus – was a consequence of the confrontation with the message of Jesus.

Early on, there was an independent reception of biblical impulses among Indian Christians. Krishna Mohan Banerjea (1813–1885), for example, one of the first converts of the Scottish pioneer of education Alexander Duff, stated: "Having become Christians, we have not ceased to be Hindoos. He pointed to parallels between the Old Testament and the Vedas, the sacred scriptures of the Hindus. Similarly, A.S. Appasamy Pillai (1848–1926) described the Rigveden, the oldest part of the four Vedas, as an "anticipation" of Christianity. Voices like these have been appreciated as "Pioneers of Indigenous Christianity" by historian Kaj Baago.[1] Their rediscovery in the 1960s set in motion a systematic securing and research of their literary legacy. – Beginning in the 1860s, there were early local efforts to establish Christian communities or churches free from missionary control. Early examples were the 'Hindu Church of the Lord Jesus Christ' (1858), the 'Bengal Christian Association for the Promotion of Christian Truth' (1868) or the 'Bengal Christian Samaj' (1887). Since 1886, the project of a 'National Church of India', which was started in Madras, gained supra-regional importance [see chapter 17.2].

The missions were successful not only among Western-educated Indians. Since the 1860s, there has been an increase in the conversion of entire ethnic or social groups in various regions of the subcontinent. This happened usually quite independently of each other, especially among the Dalits (members of the lowest castes). Such "mass conversions" were not in themselves a new phenomenon. Similar movements had already taken place in the 16th century. But they now changed in various places the social profile of the emerging Protestant communities, which had previously relied more on the principle of individual conversion. Remarkably, these group conversions were mostly the result of local non-missionary initiatives. By the outbreak of World War I, one million Dalits had embraced Christianity. Such mass movements took place, for example, in present-day Andhra Pradesh, Punjab, Chota Nagpur or the border region between India and China.

13.2 Northeast Asia (China, Japan, Korea): Opium Trade and Bible Smuggling

China, Japan and Korea were "closed" territories for Europeans (and especially for Western missionaries) around 1800. What these three countries also have in common is that they were forcibly "opened" to trade with the outside world in the course of the 19th century – China since 1842, initially by the British, as a consequence of the Opium Wars and the system of "unequal treaties" (with massive restrictions on sovereignty for the empire); Japan since 1854/55 by American gunboats; and Korea since 1876. In Korea, however, it was not Western powers but the newly awakened Japanese imperialism that forced the opening of this "shut off" nation – and finally also formally occupied the country in 1910. In this process, the Protestant communities that emerged in the country developed in a unique way into the bearers of a Korean national consciousness.

13.2.1 *China*

In China, only remnants of the former Catholic communities existed around 1800. While there had still been about 800,000 Catholic Christians in the Middle Kingdom around 1700, their number probably declined to about 187,000 around 1800. They survived under the most difficult conditions. In 1800, an edict by Emperor Jiaqing renewed the ban on Christianity that had existed since the early 18th century. Two severe persecutions in 1805 and 1811 also ended the 200-year presence of Catholic scholars at the imperial court. As a result, repression continued to increase. Even language instruction for foreigners was punishable by death.

The beginnings of Protestant presence among the Chinese therefore initially lay largely outside the Middle Kingdom. Since missionary activities were strictly forbidden in China itself, the Briton Robert Morrison (1782–1834; Figure 26), often referred to as the pioneer of the Protestant mission to China, advocated the training of lay evangelists outside the country – in the broad belt of Chinese diaspora communities abroad that stretched from present-day Thailand through Singapore and Malaysia to the Indonesian archipelago. In 1817, one such base was established in Malacca. It quickly developed into a center for missionary translation, press and educational activities. The German Karl Gützlaff (1803–1851) also acquired his Chinese language skills initially in diaspora communities in Java, Singapore, and Thailand before undertaking his famous travels along the Chinese coast between 1831 and 1833 [Text 54]. In the process, he smuggled Christian tracts into the country, if necessary, on opium boats. Gützlaff's translation of the Bible and especially his translation of parts of the Old Testament were later to play an important role in the genesis of the revolutionary Taiping movement in China [see below ch. 13.4.2].

Since 1842, Western missionaries (as a consequence of the First Opium War 1840–1842) were allowed for the first time to stay in five so-called "treaty ports" as well as in Hong Kong, which had now become British [Text 55a]. In order to spread the "glorious gospel" in the interior of the country as well, Gützlaff developed the project of evangelizing the giant empire through native actors. Admittedly, the project failed in the form he imagined. However, in the 1860s it provided the impetus for the founding of the interdenominational 'ChinaInland Mission' by the Briton T. Hudson Taylor, which – open to men and women of different denominations and nationalities – developed into the largest Protestant mission organization in China by the end of the 19th century. By 1880, the number of Chinese evangelists exceeded that of foreign missionaries. The Second and Third Opium Wars led to the Treaties of Tianjin (1858) and Peking (Beijing) (1860) [Text 55b], which allowed missions of both denominations free access even to the interior of the country. The Treaty of Beijing became sadly famous when a clause granting additional special rights was smuggled into the Chinese text through a forgery by the French Catholic missionary Abbé Delamarre, who acted as translator. The effects of the forced opening were ambivalent. On the one hand, the number of Protestant and Catholic societies or orders active in China now increased by leaps and bounds. On the other hand, the principle of extraterritoriality, which removed the missionaries (and in many cases their native subjects) from the legal supervision of the Chinese authorities, led to numerous local conflicts. Above all, however, the "unequal treaties" have remained in China's collective memory to this day as a national humiliation. France in particular used the instrument of the "Catholic Protectorate" to pursue its own imperial and economic interests in the country.

Around 1860, there were only a few baptized Protestants in China. For the year 1870, the number of Catholic Christians is given as 404,000. By 1900, the number of Protestants had probably risen to about 436,000 and the number of Catholics to 1,200,000. In the Catholic communities, which had long survived underground, European clergymen increasingly took control again after 1860. This repeatedly led to conflicts and complaints from local Christians, as some recently discovered documents in the Vatican archives once again show.[2] In addition to their evangelistic activities, the established Protestant missions also became active in the educational and social sectors. Beyond the establishment of congregations, they thus had an impact on a broad public. Numerous renowned educational institutions were established in the 1880s, originally as missionary foundations, ranging from St. John's College in Shanghai (founded in 1879) and Shantung Christian University (established in 1904) to Tsinghua University in Beijing (founded in 1911) [see Figure 42; Photo B17] and other institutions of multidisciplinary knowledge transfer. The same is true for founding hospitals and journalistic ventures. One of the most prominent secular Chinese journals in the 1880s called *Wangua gongboa*, for example, had developed from missionary journalism.

In 1895, China experienced further national humiliation with its defeat in the First Sino-Japanese War. The backwardness of its political, economic and social structures was obvious. It triggered a variety of reform efforts as well as fierce disputes between reform advocates and their opponents at the imperial court and in public. In 1905, the traditional Confucian examination system was abolished. Large numbers of Chinese students now flocked abroad, for example to Tokyo. Even before that, a Western-educated elite had formed in the Chinese diaspora outside the empire that increasingly sympathized with Christianity as a vehicle for social modernization. Sun Yat-sen, for example, the first provisional president of Republican China in 1912, was a baptized Christian. He had been educated in an Anglican school in Hawaii in the 1880s and had subsequently joined a Christian church, as had several of his revolutionary companions.

The so-called *Boxer Rebellion* of 1899/1901, directed against foreign barbarians in general and Western Christianity in particular, was admittedly a xenophobic counter-movement. About 250 foreign missionaries and 30,000 Chinese Christians fell victim to it. At the same time, however, it accelerated the indigenization of the country's Protestant churches. Independent Christian communities were formed; and in 1903 a 'Chinese Christian Union' (*Jidutu hui*) was established in Shanghai under Chinese leadership. At the first World Missionary Conference in Edinburgh in 1910, Chinese delegate Cheng Ching Yi made a highly publicized plea for a united Chinese church, free from the denominationalism of Western missionaries. A year later (1911/12), the Qing (Manchu) dynasty, which had ruled the Middle Kingdom for over 350 years, collapsed. In the government of the now republican China, Christians played an important role in various positions.

13.2.2 *Japan*

Japan, too, was a "closed" country until the middle of the 19th century. It was not until 1853/54 that an American naval squadron forced the gradual opening of Japanese ports for trade (and as a stopover on the sea route from San Francisco to Shanghai). From the 1870s onward, the Land of the Rising Sun sought to join the Western world on its own initiative. In the process, it modernized at a breathtaking pace. At the beginning of the 20th century, Japan had become a model of Asian progressiveness, often admired and imitated by the elites of the vast continent.

Before the appearance of American gunboats in 1853/4, the Dutch were the only European nation permitted to trade with Japan, limited to a single post (Dejima) off Nagasaki [see Photo C12]. Castaways were deported at the earliest opportunity, and the import of Christian books was strictly forbidden. In 1848, for example, a stranded American businessman had to prove that he did not belong to Catholicism by stepping on a picture of the Madonna, which was the usual religious test for Japanese under suspision. He survived the subsequent interrogation by the governor of Nagasaki only because the interpreter deliberately mistranslated the American's answers about his religion, according to the transcript preserved [Text 56a]. Even after the first treaties with Western powers, the ban on Christianity initially remained in place. American missionaries who began arriving in the country in 1859 were at first allowed to work only as teachers or doctors in the foreigners' quarters of the port cities. The "hidden Christians" of Japan (*Sempuku Kirishitan* or *Kakure Kirishitan*), who had survived underground for more than two centuries and first revealed themselves to a European priest in 1865, initially continued to be persecuted [see chapter 13.4.1 below].

A fundamental change only became apparent as a result of the so-called Meiji Restoration of 1868. In a coup, the Tokugawa shogunate – the feudal military government that had ruled since 1603 – was deprived of power and the emperor was restored as the country's ruler. For nearly 300 years, he had functioned only as a powerless symbol of national identity. The reformers were not at all concerned with restoring the old system, but with comprehensively reshaping Japan into a nation that could stand up to the West. The new slogan was "(Western) Civilization and Enlightenment." Japanese delegations traveled to Europe and the United States in 1871 to study the legal, governmental, economic and educational systems there and to learn about modern technologies. Among other things, they returned with the realization that religious freedom was an indispensable prerequisite for Japan's international recognition as a "civilized" nation. In 1873, public plaques banning Christianity were removed [Text 56d]. This was not formally lifted, however, until the Meiji Constitution, promulgated in 1889, established the principle of religious freedom for the first time [Text 56e]. At the same time, however, the "Rescript on Education" issued in 1890 saw emperor worship as the spiritual center of modern Japan, firmly intertwined with state Shinto.

The missionaries, who began to arrive successively in 1859, came from various countries. Among the Catholics, they were especially French-including the priest Bernard Petitjean (1829–1884), who had first encountered the underground Catholics in 1865 [see chap. 13.4.1; Text 59a; Figure 30; Photo C17]. Protestant pioneers came first from America, followed later by missionaries of other nationalities. In 1861, the Russian Orthodox Church also began a mission. By 1873, a total of 53 Protestant, Catholic, and Orthodox missionaries were working in Japan.

More important, however, were the initiatives of Japanese converts. From the beginning, 19th-century Japanese Christianity was primarily an urban movement among upper-middle-class students and intellectuals. 30% of early Protestant Christians came from the ranks of the *samurai* – the still influential class of warrior nobility that had been disempowered as a result of the Meiji Restoration. Masahisa Uemura (1858–1925), along with some fellow students (or classmates) who had been secretly baptized, founded the first Protestant congregation in Yokohama in 1872. From the 'Union of Confessors of Jesus', a Christian student fraternity in Sapporo (Hokkaido), came Kanzo Uchimura (1861–1930), who later launched the Japanese non-church movement (*Mukyokai*) [Text 78; Figure 41]. Niijima Jo (Joseph Neesima, 1843–1890), who founded the Doshisha, the largest of the early Christian schools, in Kyoto in 1875, achieved international fame. Later, the Doshisha was given the status of a university [see Figure 31; Photo C15/16]. "Christianity as wave of the future" and as channel of modern knowledge, indispensable to overcome outdated backwardness – this was a widespread idea among educated Japanese. Occasionally, there were even considerations (for example, by the influential educationalist Fukuzawa Yukichi) to declare Christianity the national religion. Christianity was "spreading like fire on a grassy plain, so that in capital and country there is no place where it is not preached," lamented a Buddhist anti-Christian tract from 1881 [Text 53]. In the early 1890s, however, there was a nationalist backlash against the uncritical adoption of Western models, combined with a revival of Buddhism and Shinto. Among Protestants and Catholics alike, the sometimes enormous growth rates of the 1870s and 1880s declined significantly. Overall, Japanese Christians remained a small, but in many cases influential minority.

13.2.3 *Korea*

The history of Korean Christianity is singular in many respects. Korea, along with the Philippines, is the Asian country with the highest percentage of Christian population (2005 census: 29.32%). In its two main branches, Catholic and Protestant, this was largely the result of a process of self-Christianization.

The beginnings of Catholic Christianity date back to 1784, as already discussed [see chap. 11.4]. It was a group of Confucian scholars who, dissatisfied with the political and cultural situation of the country, made contact on their own initiative with Catholic clergy in Beijing. Thereupon, they accepted the Christian faith, baptized each other and founded an underground church, which was soon subjected to fierce persecution. All this happened about 50 years before the first European priest, the Frenchman Pierre Maubant, entered the country in 1836. The numerous martyrdoms of the 19th century, as a result of successive waves of persecution (1801, 1815, 1827, 1839, 1846), were accurately documented by local Christians. The persecution of 1866–67 claimed the most victims. At that time, the Catholic community numbered about 23,000 believers in all provinces of the country.

The beginnings of Protestant Christianity are traditionally attributed to the activity of American missionaries since the year 1884. But even before that, Korean Christians who had accepted the new faith outside the country (in Manchuria or Japan) had brought it to Korea. For example, it was the Korean pioneer evangelist Suh Sang-Yun, who founded a first house church in his native village of Sorai in 1883. The first American missionaries – the physician Dr. Horace Allen, the Presbyterian Horace G. Underwood and the Methodist Henry G. Appenzeller – quickly gained recognition for their initiatives in health and education. In fact, the ban on Christianity was not lifted until the early 1890s. The establishment of schools (from 1886 for the first time also for girls), of hospitals as well as the spreading of western medicine were among the missionaries' important fields of work. Bible translations and the production of Christian literature in Hangul, which reached a broad readership, were central. Gradually, the denominational spectrum of missionary work expanded, and other missions became active in the country alongside Presbyterians and Methodists.

Initially, Christianity spread mainly in circles of the urban intelligentsia and reform-oriented groups. Many of them saw Protestant Christianity as a modernizing force and a prerequisite for social change. "The Protestant Jesus appeared to be more activist than Buddha, more progressive than Confucius, more powerful than the spirits of traditional religion and more modern than the Catholic Lord of Heaven".[3] Beginning around 1900, the number of Protestant Christians exceeded that of Catholics. A major factor in the rapid growth of Christian congregations was the so-called Three-Self Principle. This was as such an older missionary concept aimed at the rapid establishment of self-financing, self-propagating, and self-governing indigenous congregations. In Korea, it was followed with particular resolution. From 1891 on it was official policy, first among the Presbyterians and later among other denominations (such as the Methodists) [Text 58b].

Since the end of the first Japanese-Chinese war in 1894/95, Korea had increasingly come under Japanese control. In 1905, the country was declared a

Japanese protectorate and was formally annexed in 1910. From the beginning, Korean Christians played a disproportionately important role in the gradually formation of a national movement. This occurred due to their high degree of self-organization, their international connections, and despite the often rather restraining influence of conservative American missionaries. The formal annexation of the country in 1910 triggered a new wave of resistance. A crucial date after the end of World War I was the Korean independence movement of March 1, 1919, which the Japanese violently suppressed [see Photo D15/17]. Its manifesto was proclaimed simultaneously in various places inside and outside the country, such as the Korean YMCA in Tokyo. The Declaration of Independence was signed by 33 religious leaders, including 16 Protestants [Text 80].

13.3 Philippines, Vietnam, Indonesia

The *Philippines* were under Spanish rule until 1898. In the development of Philippine national consciousness in the 19th century, the intra-Catholic conflict between the privileged Spanish orders and the lower Filipino clergy played an important role. Tensions intensified from the 1860s onward, when the Jesuits, expelled in 1768, returned to the island kingdom. In many places they took back their old congregations, which had previously been led by indigenous priests. Any advocacy for the rights of the indigenous clergy was increasingly understood as criticism of Spanish rule. In 1872, there was an armed revolt, as a result of which three prominent Filipino priests were also sentenced to death. This spurred a new wave of patriotism and anticlericalism, directed primarily against the Spanish hierarchy and the European-dominated monastic orders. With the overthrow of Spanish rule in 1898 came the hope of a Philippine national church with its own hierarchy. When Rome refused to appoint Filipino bishops, the 'Iglesia Filipina Independiente' (IFI) was founded in 1902, which temporarily included a quarter of the island's population [Text 79]. Under the new American rule (1902 to 1946), a large number of Protestant missions also entered the country.

In today's *Vietnam,* Catholic beginnings date back to the 16th century. Around 1800, the number of Catholics there is estimated at about 300,000. The new faith spread primarily among the peasant population in protest against the Confucian-educated upper class, which was culturally oriented toward China. In the course of the 19th century, however, there were fierce persecutions of Christians [see Text 57]. These were motivated in part by defensive reactions against the growing presence of the French in the region. Conversely, these persecutions triggered calls from French missionaries for military protection.

In 1859, Saigon and the Mekong Delta fell into French hands. Since 1884, all of Vietnam was occupied by France. At the beginning of the 20th century, an anti-colonial national movement was formed, in which the local Catholic intelligentsia became increasingly active. In 1909, three Catholic priests were convicted as ringleaders in Saigon.

In the coastal regions of *Indonesia*, Dutch rule was re-established in 1816 (after a brief British interlude). The Dutch were able to bring the entire archipelago under their control only in the course of the 19th century and at the beginning of the 20th century. The Dutch Reformed Church was reorganized and in 1817 was almost given the status of a colonial state church [Text 42]. At the same time, however, vast areas such as the island of Java were sealed off against Christian missionary activity. Mass conversions occurred, initially still outside the Dutch-controlled territories, among the Minahasa in North Sulawesi and especially among the Batak in the mountainous regions of North Sumatra. This led there to the emergence of one of the largest folk churches in Asia and the largest Protestant denomination in Indonesia, the 'Christian Protestant Batak Church' (HKBP). The work of the German Lutheran missionary Ingwer Nommensen (1834–1918) had a formative influence.

13.4 Indigenous Versions of Christianity

The Western missionary movement was just one factor among others in the emergence and development of Asian Christianities. Churches and Christian communities existed in some regions long before European missionaries set foot on the continent, and they emerged or spread repeatedly in areas far from any Western missionary presence or after the end of European colonial rule. Even where they had been established in a colonial context, Christian communities could subsequently develop a momentum of their own that distinguished them from their colonial beginnings. In each case, it was ultimately the indigenous actors who decided whether to accept, reject, selectively appropriate, or modify the missionary message. Some examples of pre-colonial presence (such as the Indian St. Thomas Christians) or of non-missionary origins (such as in Korea) have already been discussed in this book [see chapter 2.4; 7.3; 11.4]. Two paradigms that are particularly noteworthy for the 19th century will be examined in the following.

13.4.1 *Japan's "Hidden Christians" (Sempuku Kirishitan/Kakure Kirishitan)*

In Japan, too, the European missionaries or priests who had been streaming back into the country since the 1860s encountered a long-established community of local Christians: the *Sempuku Kirishitan* or "Hidden Christians," who had survived 250 years of the cruelest persecution underground, in complete isolation from the rest of the Christian world. Famous is the scene that occurred in Nagasaki on March 17, 1865: in the church built for foreign residents by French priest Bernard Petitjean, 15 residents from the nearby village of Urakami identified themselves as Christians. "The hearts of all us here do not differ from yours," an old woman whispered to him, asking him about a statue of the Virgin Mary and the celebration of Christmas [Text 59a; see Photo C17]. Nagasaki on the southern island of Kyushu had been a center of the Catholic mission in the 16th century. There Petitjean now encountered first hundreds and later thousands of "Hidden Christians." In total, there were probably about 30,000 *Sempuku Kirishitan* in the vicinity of Nagasaki and on the offshore Goto Islands at that time.

The *Sempuku Kirishitan* were the descendants of Japanese Christians who had kept their faith "in secret" and passed it on from generation to generation in a form familiar to them. They celebrated services in secret rooms of their private homes, passed on biblical stories and parts of the liturgy orally – since the possession of printed books was too dangerous – and, after the expulsion of all foreign Catholic clergy in the 17th century, depended on lay leaders to perform their celebrations and rites. In the course of time, the Virgin Mary took the form of a bodhisattva (Maria Kannon), and the veneration of her martyrs took the form of popular ancestor worship. Petitjean, in his first encounters with these underground Christians, was impressed by their knowledge of Catholic beliefs: they knew about the Trinity, the Fall, the Incarnation, and the Ten Commandments. Many knew the Lord's Prayer, the Hail Mary, the Apostles' Creed, the Salve Regina, and the Sacrament of Penance. Their religious organization at that time consisted essentially of two offices: that of the *chokata* – a man who could read and write and lead the congregation and speak the Sunday prayers – and the *mizukata*, who performed baptisms.

Later, Petitjean also received from the *Sempuku Kirishitan* a copy of their holy book, the *Tenchi Haijmari no Koto* ("Beginning of Heaven and Earth"). In this text – interspersed with Latin and Portuguese loanwords – the biblical account of creation was combined with Buddhist mythology and various local traditions. Originally transmitted orally, this collection of partly folkloric tales was later set down in writing and increasingly gained dogmatic significance [Text 59b]. In research, this text has been described as an attempt of Christianization of Japanese traditions and, at the same time (for example by the anthropologist Christal Whelan), of the "Japanization of Christianity".

In 1865, news of the reappearance of the "Hidden Christians" caused a great stir. But by no means all *Sempuku Kirishitan* rejoined the Roman Catholic Church and discarded some of the practices criticized by it as unorthodox. Others could not recognize in the Catholicism of the French missionaries the faith of their ancestors. They continued to live in communities of their own. Centuries of isolation had transformed their faith and made seclusion an integral part of their self-understanding. Even today, especially on the Soto Islands in the south of the country, there exist independent communities of "Hidden Christians," referred to in scholarly literature now as *Kakure Kirishitan*. Some of them have since lost awareness of their Christian origins.

The Hidden Christians of Urakami (now a district of Nagasaki), who came out to the French priest Petitjean in 1865, continued to face persecution until 1873. Many were sent into exile, from which they did not return until 1873. In 1895 they began building their own church – the Urakami Cathedral – which was completed in 1910. Exactly over this church the second atomic bomb of the Americans exploded on August 9, 1945 and destroyed it almost completely [see Photo C18/19].

13.4.2   *China: the Taiping Movement*

The Taiping movement emerged under quite different conditions in 19th century China. It was a Christian-inspired mass movement (1850–1864), the Chinese version of the German Peasants' War, so to speak, which temporarily brought the Qing dynasty, which had ruled since 1644, to the brink of collapse. It had arisen in the troubled areas of southwestern China, in a quasi extra-colonial context, and initially had only a very indirect connection with the Western missionary movement. Initially, this connection was established only through Christian tracts circulating in the interior of the country. The Taiping leadership saw itself as decidedly Christian, and preached the biblical message to the exclusion of all other doctrines, despite all syncretistic elements. They advocated puritan ethics, sought friendly contact with the missionaries, but remained independent in theology and action. Their suppression (eventually supported by Western powers) in 1864 claimed millions of lives.

The leader was a certain Hong Xiuquan (1814–1864), who had a series of visions since 1837 [see Figure 28; Photo B14/16]. Under the influence of the study of the Chinese Bible – which he had become acquainted with through tracts of the Chinese convert Liang Fa [see Figure 27] and later through the study of Gützlaff's translation of the Bible – he began to understand these visions as revelations of the Christian God and to interpret them in the light of the Old Testament promises. From this he derived for himself the mission to overthrow the old gods of China in the land of Canaan, as Joshua had once done, and to establish a "Heavenly Kingdom of Peace" instead. Knowledge of this vision and its interpretation was just as obligatory for his rapidly growing following as that of a catechism consisting of the Ten Commandments, the Lord's Prayer and other texts, which – according to a contemporary report – "every rebel in the year 1854 possessed and which is today still in countless hands" [Text 61 a + b]. Hong Xiuquan called himself a younger brother of Jesus Christ. In 1853, he had himself proclaimed king in Nanjing, the "New Jerusalem". He proclaimed the equality of all people, organized state examinations based on the Bible, and made the transgression of the Decalogue and other vices such as opium smoking punishable by death. Hong welcomed European visitors as "transoceanic brothers", and sought an equal position for his China in the circle of "Christian" – i.e. Western – "nations".

How Christian was the Taiping movement? This question is answered controversially today, as it was back then. An authority such as the American historian John K. Fairbank has called it a Chinese "variant of Old Testament Protestant Christianity." The sinologist Daniel H. Bays speaks of "China's first indigenous Christian movement."[4] The Chinese historian Lee Chee Kong states: "The Taiping Movement started as a Christian-influenced movement with elements also from Chinese writings, but it ended as a revolutionary movement."[5] Missionaries of the 19th century initially welcomed it as a sign of the worldwide outpouring of the Holy Spirit and hoped for a new China under Christian leadership. Later, their voices became increasingly critical, especially when the movement turned into open rebellion. Chinese contemporaries and bitter opponents such as the Hunanese Zeng Guofang interpreted the war between the Taiping and the Qing dynasty as a conflict between two civilizations, the Confucian and the Christian (or the "religion of the Western barbarians"). The Taiping themselves saw themselves as called by the Christian God and as children of "the same heavenly Father" as their Western visitors. For the foreigners also knew – as the Taiping were pleased to note – the "heavenly laws" in the form of the Ten Commandments [Text 61.d]. In any case, Taiping monotheism with its egalitarian and universalist tendencies shows what revolutionary consequences an even partial reception of biblical impulses could have in the social conflicts of the time – shaking the fundaments of a centuries-old hierarchical social order.

Notes to Chapter 13

1. Baago (1969), *Pioneers of Indigenous Christianity*.
2. Bays (2012), *New History*, 52 f.
3. Kim/ Kim (2015), *Korean Christianity*, 81.
4. Fairbank (1989), *China*, 82 ff; Bays (2012), *New History*, 53.
5. Fairbank (1989), *China*, 82 ff; Bays (2012), *New History*, 53; Kong (2001), *Taiping Rebellion*, 814.

Further Reading for Chapter 13

13.1 (*South Asia: Missions as a Factor of Modernization*)
(Asia in general:) Moffett (2005), *Christianity in Asia* II; Sunquist (2001), *Dictionary of Asian Christianity*; Koschorke (2017), *Asia,* 267–300; Ward (2017), *Late 18th Century,* 129–137. – (Southern Asia): Frykenberg (2013), *Christianity in India,* 169–418; Neill (1985), *Christianity in India* II; Baago (1969), *Pioneers of Indigenous Christianity*; Kopf (1979), *Brahmo Samaj*; Jensz (2022), *Missionaries and Modernity.*

13.2 (*Northeast Asia: China, Japan, Korea*)
Bays (2012), *New History*; Bays (1996), *Christianity in China*; Lutz (2010), *Pioneer Chinese Christian Women*; Metzler (1980), *Synoden in China, Japan und Korea*; Mullins (2003), *Christianity in Japan*; Iglehart (1960), *Japan*; Thelle (1987), *Buddhism and Christianity in Japan*; Kim (1996), *Modern Korean Nationalism*; Kim/ Kim (2015), *Korean Christianity,* 14–106.

13.3 (*Philippines, Vietnam, Indonesia*)
Schumacher (1981), *Revolutionary Clergy*; Ileto (1979), *Pasyon and Revolution*; Anderson (1969), *Philippine Church History*; Hermann (2016), *Philippines,* 337–446; Keith (2012), *Catholic Vietnam*; Müller-Krüger (1968), *Protestantismus in Indonesien*; Aritonang/ Steenbrink (2008), *Christianity in Indonesia.*

13.4 (*Indigenous Versions of Christianity*)
Moffett (2005), *Christianity in Asia II,* 502–504. 298–300; Whelan (1996), *Japan' Hidden Christians*; Barron (2020), *Kakure Kirishitan*; Yasutaka (2021), *Senpuku Kirishitan*; Mullins (1998), *Christianity Made in Japan;* Wagner (1982), *Taiping Rebellion*; Spence (1996), *God's Chinese Son*; Kilcourse (2016), *Taiping Theology*; Bays (2012), *New History,* 53–56; McGrath/ Russell (2022), *Global Indigenous History,* 302–324; Lindenfels (2021), *Indigenous Experience,* 178–192. 210–225. 225–230(ff).

CHAPTER 14

Africa

14.1 West Africa: Slave Emancipation and Transatlantic Resettlement Projects

In West Africa, too, the early 19th century marked a turning point and the beginning of a significant Protestant presence. Unlike in India, however, not only two European missionary societies – the Anglican Church Missionary Society (CMS) and the Swiss-German Basel Mission – were involved. The third important factor was an African-American initiative: the return of former African-American slaves who had become Christians in the New World and were now coming back to Africa. Two locations are to be considered: Sierra Leone and Liberia.

"African Protestant Christianity was already very much a reality around 1780. The one place, however, where it did not exist was Africa" (Adrian Hastings)[1] – apart from its sporadic presence in the aforementioned trading posts of various West European powers (Dutch, British, Danish, etc.) along the West African coast. However, it existed in considerable numbers on the other side of the Atlantic, in the Caribbean and especially in North America. In the English colonies on the North American east coast, the core area of the later USA, there were already numerous African-American slaves or freedmen who had accepted the Christian faith. Of particular importance was the so-called Second Great Revival of late 18th and early 19th centuries, which affected both whites and blacks. Among other things, it led to the emergence of the first black churches (such as the 'First African Baptist Church', which was founded in Savannah, Georgia, in 1788). Enthusiastic piety, biblical faith and trust in the promises of the God of the Exodus, who had once "led Israel out of the slave house of Egypt", were characteristics of this African-American evangelical Christianity.

During the American War of Independence (1776–1783), the British had tried to draw African American slaves to their side. They raised black regiments and promised freedom and land ownership to those who rose up against their American masters. After the American victory, the British then had to deal with a considerable number of black troops who could not be demobilized locally. Some of these found accommodation in other places that were still under British control, such as the Caribbean or Nova Scotia (Nova Scotia, in what is now Canada). There, a community of African American Christians thus formed – legally free, often literate, Protestant, and with the Bible in hand as "the charter of their freedom and dignity."[2]

London developed into another focal point of African presence outside Africa. There, too, there was already a considerable diaspora of African immigrants. It included, in addition to the city's black proletariat, prominent figures such as Olaudah Equiano, originally from Nigeria [see Text 146; Figure 16], and Ottoba Gugoana, whose journalism attracted considerable attention in England's nascent anti-slavery movement. Friend Granville Sharp, one of the pioneers of the early British abolitionist movement, then developed the idea of repatriating the "black poor of London" to West Africa. A first experiment of this kind in 1787 failed grandiosely. A second attempt a few years later, however – this time together with African-American remigrants from Nova Scotia – was successful. In 1792, 1131 black settlers reached Freetown in the West African country of *Sierra Leone* from Halifax on 15 ships.

Freetown, the "City of Freedom", was an explicitly Christian project from the beginning [see Map 10]. Upon arrival on the continent of their ancestors, the returnees sang the song "of Moses and the Lamb". Even before they embarked on the other side of the Atlantic, they had divided into groups, each with its own leader, mostly the preachers of their respective Christian communities. In Sierra Leone, Baptist, Methodist and other congregations thus quickly sprang up, each under African leadership. "In this way," says mission historian Andrew Walls, "the first Protestant church in tropical Africa was established in November 1792 ... It was a ready-made African church, with its own structures and leadership. This happened some 20 years before any [sc. European] missionary took effective responsibility there, and even then only temporarily; missionaries never controlled the whole."[3]

Subsequently, the Anglican 'Church Missionary Society' (CMS) in particular became active in Sierra Leone [Text 149]. As already mentioned, this society had a dual goal: the evangelization of the continent and the fight against the slave trade. Missionary and abolitionist interests went hand in hand. Leading figures in the Society, such as William Wilberforce [Text 145], were at the same time engaged as lobbyists in the campaigns against the slave trade. In 1807, their efforts were successful: the British Parliament banned the slave trade. Sierra Leone – elevated to the status of a British crown colony in 1808 – also became a base for the British navy, which now intercepted Portuguese slave ships on their way from Nigeria to Brazil [see Text 148]. The freed inmates were directed to Freetown, where many embraced Christianity. The growing influx of freed slaves from various regions of West Africa simultaneously changed the demographic profile of the colony-an important prerequisite for its later function as a bridgehead in the evangelization of other areas of West Africa.

A prominent example is Samuel Ajayi Crowther (c. 1806/08–1891), later the first black African bishop of modern times. Liberated by the British from an intercepted Portuguese slave ship in 1822, he became a Christian in Freetown and later engaged in missionary work in what is now Nigeria [Text 150; for details see. chapter. 14.5; Figure 34]. The ecclesiastical autonomy of the African congregations that developed in Sierra Leone remained intact for a long time. African Methodists there, for instance, sought egalitarian contact with the Methodists from Great Brittain. On the other hand, they also felt free to send back British preachers sent by the latter. The enormous significance of the Sierra Leone experiment lies primarily in its long-distance effects. Black Christians from Sierra Leone, multilingual and with roots in different regions, were to play a role in the further course of the Christianization of West Africa that could hardly be overestimated.

Liberia, also founded as a haven of "freedom", has a somewhat different history. In 1822, the state-supported U.S. Colonization Society had begun establishing settlements there for former slaves. In 1847, the Republic declared its independence, which was recognized by European powers even during the height of colonialism. Mass immigration from the United States led to conflicts with the local population. On the other hand, Liberia soon developed into a hub in the transatlantic networks of African intellectuals between the Caribbean and the rest of West Africa. Black missionaries and churches from the United States used the "Land of the Free" early on as a springboard for further activities on the continent [see Text 151]. Often ridiculed by European observers and conservative missionaries, Liberia was often perceived by African Christians as an emancipation project as well as proof of the "black race's" ability to govern itself.

Since the 1850s, the influx of Western missions to West Africa increased. In Ghana (Gold Coast), the Basel Mission had been active since 1832 and the Bremen Mission since 1847, from which the Presbyterian churches of the country later emerged. In present-day Nigeria, Methodists (1842), Presbyterians (1845) and Baptists (1850) soon worked alongside Anglicans. Catholics became more active again in the second half of the 19th century. For example, the 'Society for African Mission', founded in 1856, sent priests to Lagos for the first time in 1865.

A prominent feature of Protestant missionary activity in West Africa and other regions was the large number of *Bible translations* in different regional languages. Together with their African colleagues, Johann Christaller and Johannes Zimmermann of the Basel Mission translated parts of the Bible for the first time into Twi and Ga in Ghana, Jacob Friedrich Schön into Hausa and Igbo in today's Nigeria, Westlund into Kikongo, Johan Moffat into South African Tswana, and V. Eugene Johnson into Chinanga. Bible translations in themselves were by no means something new in mission history. In evangelical-awakened circles, however, they had a much higher significance and urgency than in earlier stages. They corresponded to the basic Protestant conviction that God's people should be given the Bible in their own language. Together with language studies (often connected with the introduction of a printing press), they were therefore repeatedly at the beginning of all missionary activities. At the same time, they had an enormous impact on traditional African societies, since in many cases writing only became widespread with the Bible translations. These were often the first (and for a long time the only) literature in the respective vernacular.

At the same time, they unfolded an emancipatory potential of which many of the – mostly rather conservative – European missionaries were often not even aware. This has been pointed out in particular by the West African-American historian Lamin Sanneh (1942–2019), who – himself born a Muslim in Gabon – taught at renowned universities in Europe and the USA. He emphasized that, precisely in the given colonial context, missionaries provided the emerging African communities with an instrument in the form of Bible translation that subsequently enabled them to develop independently – even entirely free of missionary control. Unlike in Islam, for example, where the Koran is valid authority only in Arabic, he identified this "translatability" – both linguistically and culturally – as one of the constitutive features of Christianity, which at the same time produced ever new forms of indigenous appropriation. Local believers could thus become self-appointed mediators of Christian faith and education in the course of African Christian history.

14.2 South Africa: Black Christians and White Settlers

Already from a purely climatic point of view, South Africa represented a different colonial and missionary context compared to West Africa. This was because it allowed for earlier and more intensive European settlement. Since 1652, the Dutch (together with their colonial church apparatus, the Dutch Reformed Church) had established themselves at the southern tip of the continent. In the 19th century, the Cape was then taken over by the British – first sporadically (since 1795) and permanently since 1806. In a series of border wars with the Bantu-speaking Xhosa, they continuously expanded the territory under their control. In 1834, slavery was banned throughout the British Empire. As a result, numerous Boers (settlers of Dutch origin) left the English-controlled Cape Colony between 1835 and 1848 in various waves of emigration – the so-called "Great Trek". This led later to the formation of two Boer republics on the territory of present-day South Africa (Transvaal, Orange Free State). In the process, they clashed with the expanding Zulu empire and other ethnic groups. By the end of the 19th century, southern Africa was an entity of disparate states (with two British and two Boer colonies; in between were some still independent territories under African rule) until 1910, when the Union of South Africa was formed (comprising Cape Colony, Natal, Transvaal and Orange Free State [see Map 16]). In 1884, Southwest Africa (Namibia) was declared a German "protectorate".

The Boer church, which had largely abstained from missionary activities, retained a privileged status for a long time, even under British rule. In the course of the 19th century, various splits occurred. In 1792, the Moravians resumed their work among the Khoikhoi (formerly called "Hottentots") of the Western Cape. In 1743, their first missionary, the German Georg Schmidt, had been expelled from the Dutch colony as a troublemaker. The small community he founded survived, however; and Magdalena, a Khoikhoi convert of the first hour, proudly showed the newcomers the Bible she had received from Schmidt fifty years earlier in 1792. British missionaries began arriving in the country in 1799. The 'London Missionary Society' (LMS), a non-denominational and abolitionist organization, was the first to arrive. Methodists, Presbyterians and (relatively late) Anglicans soon followed. Missions of other nationalities were also active in southern Africa. From Germany these were the 'Rhenish Mission' since 1829, the 'Berlin Mission' since 1834 and the 'Hermannsburg Mission' since 1854. Congregationalist missionaries arrived from the USA in 1835 and Lutheran missionaries from Norway in 1844. Especially the Lutherans established numerous stations in Natal and Transvaal. More missions followed in the second half of the century. The Catholics in particular now caught up significantly and became active in numerous areas (such as Lesotho). "Despite many setbacks, the missions were so successful that the number of Christian converts in southern Africa around 1860 can already be estimated at half a million."[4] Since the 1890s, South Africa became a hotspot of independent black churches, whose numbers grew by leaps and bounds until 1910 [see chap. 18.2]. However, splits from the white-dominated mission churches began as early as the 1870s.

In the tense field between European colonists and the African population, the various missions took different positions. The Boers (or "Afrikaan[d]ers," as they have called themselves since the 19th century) often sought to justify their claims as the "ruling race" with reference to Old Testament paradigms. They saw themselves as once Israel among the pagan peoples of Canaan. Evangelical and abolitionist Britons, on the other hand, emphasized the equality of all believers. Like the first LMS missionary John Philipp (1775–1851), they initially advocated the rights of blacks in the legislation of the Cape Colony with some success. Both sides argued in the language of Christian tradition, which, according to historian Elizabeth Elbourne, had "multiple meanings".[5] John Colenso, Anglican bishop of Natal from 1853 to 1883, supported the "civilizing" goals of British colonialism. However, the longer the more he became a harsh critic of its colonial practices. In Zulu culture he saw many parallels to elements of Christian faith and life. Thus, to the dismay of his conservative colleagues, he eventually accepted polygamists as converts. He also caused offence in questions of the interpretation of the Bible, whose verbal inspiration he doubted. Remarkably, this was partly a result of his intense discussions with his African parishioners. Eventually, a church trial was even opened against him on charges of "heresy," which was unsuccessful. This controversy received considerable international attention. Even Buddhist Bible critics from Sri Lanka invoked the Anglican bishop for their polemics in the 1870s.

In the emerging congregations, African Christians and European settlers were pastored together for a long time. In the second half of the 19th century, however, various missions increasingly introduced separate services for blacks and whites. As an intra-church step on the way to the later policy of "separate development," which led to the apartheid system in 1948, this change of course has been discussed intensively in recent times.

On the other hand, numerous mission stations – with their schools, printing presses and often extensive landholdings – developed into ethnic melting pots and places of intertribal balance. Their inhabitants often belonged to different ethnic groups. Many were refugees or social outsiders. By living together in the mission settlement, intermarrying and sharing common goals, they developed a new identity – Christian – and at the same time an awareness of a unifying African-ness. "Many no longer saw themselves as Sotho or Zulu, Qwabe or Cele, but simply as African Christians. Self-aware and prosperous communities with elite aspirations thus emerged from unsettled collections of disparate individuals."[6] As prosperity increased, so did the ability of these Kholwa communities (Kholwa = "believers," black Christians) to self-finance their education, evangelize independently, as well as challenge missionary authorities. The transregional flows of migrant workers triggered by the diamond and gold discoveries in Kimberley and the Transvaal since the 1870s also intensified the dissolution of traditional ethnic identities. At the same time, they repeatedly led to the spontaneous formation of black communities.

The first magazines published by black Christians themselves also appeared in the mission settlements. In Lovedale (Cape Province) in 1870, for example, the bilingual 'Kaffir Express'/'Isigidimi Sama-Xosa' celebrated the dawn of a new era for African Christians. Although nominally still published under missionary responsibility, the paper was de facto written primarily by members of the regional Xhosa elite. Similarly, the 'Inkanyiso yase Natal' ('Illuminator of Natal'), founded in Pietermaritzburg in 1889, prided itself on being "the first native journal in Natal and the second in South Africa". Initially published under a missionary umbrella, the paper soon became formally African owned. Its aim was to make the voice of Afrikaners heard in the colonial public sphere of Natal ("to give publicity to our thoughts"). The central point was the demand for "equality of all believers," which had once been promised by the missionaries but was now increasingly threatened by restrictive colonial legislation. In this context, the journal functioned as a mouthpiece for Natal's Christian African educated elite, which began to organize here – as elsewhere. They founded their own associations, such as the 'Natal Native Congress' in 1895, a regional forerunner of the 'African National Congress' (ANC), which was launched in 1912. In this process, black Christians in various capacities – such as John Dube, Solomon Kumalo, Martin Luthuli or J. T. Jabavu [see Text 166b] – took a leading role.

14.3 East and Central Africa: David Livingstone and Other European "Discoverers"

East and Central Africa became the target of Protestant missionary activities only late. Apart from the coastal regions, these areas were also largely unknown in Europe at that time. These were the famous (and very extensive) "white spots" on the map of geographical knowledge of that time. In their exploration, individual "pioneers" of the modern missionary movement played an important role. For example, the Swabians Johann Ludwig Krapf (1810–1881) and Johannes Rebmann (1820–1876), who – characteristic of the spirit of ecumenical cooperation in this early phase – were active in the service of the Anglican 'Church Missionary Society' and sought to establish a chain of mission stations inland from the Kenyan coast [Text 161]. In 1848/49, they became the first Europeans to set eyes on Mount Kilimanjaro and the Mount Kenya massif. They also made a name for themselves by translating the New Testament into Kiswahili for the first time and by studying East African languages.

Even more far-reaching were the consequences of the discoveries of the Scottish missionary *David Livingstone* (1813–1873). Between 1852 and 1856, he was the first European to cross the African continent from west (Angola) to east (Mozambique). His bestseller "Missionary Travels and Researches" (1857) and other publications not only enormously expanded Europe's knowledge of the interior of Africa. They also increased the prestige of the Protestant missionary movement among the previously mostly skeptical British public.

Livingstone was originally drawn to China. In 1841, however, he found himself in South Africa, which he soon left again – because it was "overpopulated by missionaries" – in order to do pioneering work in what is now Botswana in the service of the 'London Missionary Society' (LMS). Among the (few) converts from this time was the Bekuena chief named Setschele, who was baptized after long discussions. One of the curious aspects of this encounter is that Setschele – nowan "avid Bible reader" – soon became "corpulent" for lack of bodily movement. Among the tragic aspects – or rather, inevitable consequences of a constellation that repeatedly led to conflicts in the further course of African Christian history – are the impacts of the missionary commandment of monogamy in polygamous African societies: Setschele dismissed the multitude of his now "superfluous wives" after his baptism, which triggered a revolt against him [Text 162]. – Between 1852 and 1856, Livingstone made extensive exploratory trips to investigate the navigability of the Zambezi River. On this occasion, he discovered, among other things, the Victoria Falls in present-day Zimbabwe. Later voyages took him to Lakes Chilwa, Malawi, Tanganyika, Mweru and Bangweulu, among others. His last expedition started in 1866 from Zanzibar to find and map the headwaters of the Nile and the Congo River. In the process, he traversed areas of present-day Mozambique, Malawi, Zambia, Tanzania and Zaire. In 1873 he died, alone with his African helpers, in a remote village in what is now Zambia.

In 1857, Livingstone had left the LMS and continued his work in the service of the London 'Royal Geographical Society' and the British government. This change has occasionally been interpreted as an abandonment of his original missionary objective, but this is not the case. Livingstone was always both, missionary and explorer. His search for the course of Africa's great rivers and their use as transportation routes always also served the goal of promoting the spread of Christianity and combating the slave trade. *"Christianity, Civilization and Commerce"* was the decisive slogan in the debates of evangelical-abolitionist circles, to which Livingstone was also committed. He saw his task as enabling the peaceful penetration of Africa and replacing "illegitimate" trade (with slaves) with "legitimate" trade (with agricultural products). And the further he penetrated, the more he was filled with disgust for both the Arab and the Portuguese slave traders.

This concept had been shaped by theorists of the antislavery movement such as Thomas Fowell Buxton (1786–1845). In his 1839 work "The African Slave Trade and its Remedy," Buxton advocated a fundamental reform of West Africa's social and economic structures to free the continent's inhabitants from dependence on the slave trade. More missionaries and schoolmasters, spreading the Bible and the plow – that was his vision [Text 152a]. Instead of people,

Africa was to export agricultural products (such as palm oil, palm kernels or cotton), the demand for which was steadily increasing in Europe. This would – thus the assumption – lead to growing prosperity among the Africans and make the slave trade increasingly unattractive.

One of Livingstone's most bitter experiences was that by opening up intra-African traffic routes, he unintentionally opened up new routes for slave traders too. The fact that he de facto paved the way for the colonial advance of Great Britain is another aspect of his work. He saw himself primarily as a friend of the Africans and rejected white rule in Africa. Posterity remembers him as a person with many facets: as an exemplary Protestant missionary, a pioneering explorer, an icon of British imperialism, and – since the 1960s – also as a patron saint of African nationalism.[7] After his death, the Anglican cathedral was built in Zanzibar in 1873 over the remains of the old slave market, which had been closed only six months earlier. This was meant as a sign of the triumph of Christianity over slavery, which Livingstone had always striven for.

At least four new British missions in Africa with different denominational orientations owe their emergence to Livingstone. These include the Anglican 'Universities Mission to Central Africa' (UMCA), which became active in Zanzibar, on the Tanzanian mainland, as well as in Malawi and Zambia. On the Roman Catholic side, the activities of the Fathers of the Holy Spirit (since 1868) and White Fathers (since 1878) in the area of present-day Tanzania are noteworthy. With the colonial division of Africa in 1884/85, the overall picture changed. Thus, various German Lutheran missions (such as the Leipzig and Berlin [Berlin I] Missions) became active in German East Africa (Tanzania) from 1885. Among them was also a new foundation like the 'Evangelische Missionsgesellschaft für Deutsch-Ostafrika' (Berlin III), which was characterized by particular closeness to the colonial establishment.

The profile of the Christian communities that emerged in East Africa varied greatly from region to region, ethnically and socially. Migration movements also played a stimulating role here in many cases. In Kenya, for example, as in West Africa, it was remigrants (here, however, not from America but from India) who formed the core of the African Christian communities: In 1864, the first freed or ransomed African slaves returned from the Indian subcontinent. Later leaders were recruited from the ranks of these mostly educated and multilingual 'Bombay Africans'.[8] In general, the growth of the Christian communities owed much to African initiatives that find little or no mention in contemporary missionary journalism. For example, the commitment of the young Tongan evangelist David Kaunda, who in 1905 successfully worked among the Bemba tribe, which was considered particularly dangerous (and therefore avoided by the missionaries). His story only became known later, as he became the father of a more famous son – Kenneth Kaunda, the first president (1964–1991) of independent Zambia.[9]

14.4 African Christian Rulers: Madagascar, Uganda, Ethiopia

African rulers and kings were often among the fiercest opponents of the European missionaries. Others invited the Western messengers of the faith to their territories on their own initiative, albeit for quite different motives. These included the hoped-for access to Western technology (including firearms), medicine and modern education, or the services of missionaries as language teachers and interpreters. But equally attractive – in a world experienced as arbitrary – was their doctrine of a supreme God who is ethically consistent and who can be worshipped everywhere (and not just locally).

a. *Madagascar* – an independent country until 1895 – offers the example of different phases in the relationship of local rulers to Western missionaries. Here, the 'London Missionary Society' (LMS) had been active since the 1820s, at the express invitation of the king of the Merina Empire, Radama I, who saw himself as a modernizer. In a letter dated Oct. 29, 1820, he asked the LMS in London to "send to us as many missionaries as you are able" as well as various craftsmen "who are skilled in weaving, carpentry and joining and spinning" [Text 163a]. The latter came and at the same time acted in many cases as a kind of development worker and teacher for the young Merina aristocracy. They also introduced the printing press and thus disseminated the New Testament, now translated into Malagasy, as well as other Christian texts in leading circles such as the military. Then, with the death of King Radama I in 1835, an abrupt change in religious policy occurred. The new queen, Ranavalona I (r. 1835–1861), banned all missionary activity and decreed the death penalty for anyone who continued to pray to the Christian God [Text 163b]. The Bible was apparently understood in Madagascar more and more as a book that contained traditions about the ancestors of foreigners. Thus, it endangered loyalty to the Madegassian kingship. Prophetic movements increased the unrest. As a result, there were fierce persecutions of Christians. The number of martyrs was at least 200. Other believers hid in remote places or fled to neighboring islands. However, underground, the fledgling church – under local leadership only – experienced astonishing growth (from about 1,000 to 2,000 Christians in 1835 to about 7,000 to 10,000 in 1861). Even a son of the queen, Prince Rakotand/Radama, was secretly baptized in 1846.

With the death of the queen in 1861, British missionaries and Madegassian religious refugees returned to the island. The new ruler – Ranavalona II –

officially converted to Christianity in 1869 along with her prince consort. The baptism, performed by a local pastor, took place in public before the nobility and the grandees of Merina society. The Christian community subsequently experienced explosive growth. It was firmly anchored, especially in the palace. By 1869, there were reportedly 468 Congregationalist congregations, with 158 pastors, 935 preachers and about 153,000 believers, out of a Merina population of about 800,000.[10] Other Protestant missions followed. The Catholics came rather late – after earlier and ultimately unsuccessful advances by individual Jesuits and Lazarists in the 17th century – and became active primarily in the coastal region. Under French colonial rule (since 1895), their numbers increased significantly, although the new colonial administration increasingly adopted an aggressive anticlerical course.

b. *Uganda* also experienced enormous church growth from the end of the 19th century. Here, too, it was the ruler of the country – theor king of Buganda, the core area of what later became Uganda – who invited Christian missionaries in the 1870s. Here, too, there were soon setbacks and fierce persecution of Christians, and here, too again, the new religion set in motion a momentum of its own that led to a "Christian revolution"[11] among the country's aristocratic elite. Buganda, religiously and socially in a state of upheaval, was a prosperous and power-politically expansive state as well as open to outside influences. Arab Muslims from Zanzibar arrived in 1840, Anglican missionaries from the CMS in 1877 and the French Catholic White Fathers in 1879. In 1879, a religious debate between Catholic and Protestant missionaries took place at the royal court because the Kabaka, according to a contemporary account, "wanted to learn more about the differences between Protestant and Catholic" [Text 164a]. King Mutesa (r. 1856–1884) virtually organized a competition between the rival religions, which he, of course, always sought to place under his direct control. His sympathies were initially with Christianity as a technologically superior force. In 1875, the Muslims were persecuted. Ten years later, under his son and successor Mwanga (r. 1884–1897), Christians were persecuted, both Catholics and Protestants. The steadfastness and willingness to suffer of the Ugandan martyrs of 1885 [Text 164b] caused a sensation not only among the international missionary public. It also led, for example, to a solidarity campaign by Indian Christians, who organized a collection for their African "brothers in faith" and sent it, together with a letter of support, to Uganda via the CMS.

But Christianity had already taken deep roots in Buganda, especially in circles of young aristocrats at court, the future elite of the country, who soon set about spreading their new faith with the zeal of recent converts. In the process, a Protestant and a Catholic party formed, which increasingly challenged the power of traditional royalty and at the same time rivaled among themselves. In 1888, Protestants, Catholics and Muslims carried out a successful coup d'état in concerted action, replacing King Mwanga with a common candidate. Troubled times and a civil war with changing constellations followed. Finally, Mwanga succeeded in returning to power, now with the help of the Catholic party, and in 1889 a state treaty appointed a Protestant as first minister (*Katikiro*) and divided the most important state offices equally between Catholics and Protestants. Mwanga himself was also later baptized, and his son and successor Daudi Chwa became an avid Anglican. In 1894, Uganda became a British protectorate. However, mass conversions to Christianity had begun long before. Now they continued in a colonial context. As of 2014, about 82% of the population belongs to a Christian church. Not "as a reaction to [British] conquest, but as an incorporation of a 'modern' religion into the very fabric of its own political and social structures, a process controlled and directed by Baganda [Ugandan] themselves rather than by outsiders" since the 1880s, Christianity found its way into the East African country.[12]

c. Unlike the monarchs of Madagascar and Uganda who converted to Christianity, the rulers of *Ethiopia* were part of a long tradition of Christian princes that, according to their claims, even reached back to the biblical King Solomon. In the mid-19th century, Ethiopia's period of political disintegration and decay – lamented in biblical terminology as the "time of the judges" – came to an end. A new ruler – Tewodros (Theodore, *r.* 1855–1868) –eliminated rival regional princes, restored the central imperial power and had himself crowned king of kings. His program, as one foreign observer put it, was "to reform Abyssinia, restore the Christian faith and become master of the world." The latter even included the idea of a crusade from Ethiopia to liberate Jerusalem from Muslim rule. This idea was to recur again and again in the period that followed. Although Tewodros largely failed with his plans, he did initiate a turnaround that was reinforced under his successors. – Yohannes IV (*r.* 1871–1889) has often been described as one of the leading architects of modern Ethiopia. He, too, was constantly involved in struggles and sought to secure the unity of the empire as much as possible by eliminating European influence. At the same time, he modernized his army by acquiring European weapons and pursued a policy of territorial expansion. A side effect was the forced Christianization of pagan peoples such as the Galla – though in some cases in areas that had once been Christian. He sought to overcome internal divisions in the Orthodox state church by convening an Ethiopian council in Borumeda in 1878. The subject of the dispute was ancient dogmatic controversies over the two natures of Christ. The church was also strengthened by the sending of new Coptic bishops from Egypt.

The restoration of Ethiopia's Christian emperorship reached a climax under *Menelik II*, who ruled first as king of the Shoa region (1866–1889) and from 1889–1913 as ruler of the still expanding entire empire [see Map 17; Photo F13–16]. He was both a preserver of inherited ecclesiastical traditions and a modernizer of the country. Telegraph, telephone and railroad now took hold, and in 1892 Addis Ababa was declared the new capital. In 1895/96, the Italians attempted to conquer Ethiopia and were crushed at Adwa in 1896. Thus – at the height of European colonialism and imperialism – the ancient Christian empire was the only country in Africa (besides Liberia) to succeed in preserving its political independence. This victory was to further increase its fascination among the emerging black elite of the entire continent. Especially since this political independence went hand in hand with religious and ecclesiastical autonomy. Menelik maintained friendly contact with Western missionaries. He pointed out to them, however, that there was nothing to missionize in his country, since the Ethiopians were already Christians, and that he felt responsible for the evangelization of Africa. They could become active in Asia instead. Besides, they would still have enough to do at home – i.e. in Europe. This was the content of a letter from Menelik to a Protestant missionary, which was also printed in the black press of West Africa in 1896.[13] Documents like these reveal the growing influence of Ethiopia as a symbol of ecclesiastical and political independence on African Christians on both sides of the Atlantic.

14.5   S. A. J. Crowther, First Black African Bishop, and Controversies about the "Three Selves"

Samuel Ajayi Crowther (*ca.* 1806/08–1891; see Figure 34) was a formative figure in the debates among African Christians in the 19th century. As a "slave boy who became bishop", he quickly achieved international fame. Born around 1806/08 in Osogun in present-day Nigeria, he was captured – as already mentioned – together with his family by African slave hunters, taken away on a Portuguese slave ship, freed there by the British navy and taken to Sierra Leone in 1822. He fell into the care of missionaries of the Anglican CMS there, was baptized, and ordained a priest in 1843 [Text 150]. He quickly attained positions of influence and high responsibility. In 1864, he was finally consecrated by the Anglican Archbishop in Canterbury as the first black bishop of modern times, responsible for British Equatorial West Africa – a vast ecclesiastical territory. Queen Victoria was also impressed by him.

This was an event of historic significance and radiated far beyond the domestic church sphere. Crowther became a symbol of the aspirations of educated West Africans. His elevation to bishop was also seen as a visible confirmation of the 'Christianity-Civilization' concept (Christianity as a vehicle of civilizational advancement) and at the same time as vivid proof of the viability of the vision of an African church capable of self-government, self-support and self-propagation. The latter were the famous *"Three Selves"* as formulated in particular by Henry Venn (1796–1873) – protagonist and leading theorist of CMS. In a programmatic statement of 1851, he had described it as the goal of all missionary work to make itself superfluous as quickly as possible ("euthanasia of the mission") and to quickly place responsibility in the hands of a "native church." The background to this concept was, on the one hand, the emancipatory ideals of the early British missionary movement in particular, but also the high mortality rate of European missionaries in tropical Africa as the "grave of the white man." In Crowther – "chosen by God" to bring the gospel to his own people – this vision now visibly found its fulfillment.

The news of Crowther's episcopal consecration stimulated lively debates in other "mission fields" as well. Referring to his example, the demand for a "native bishop" was also voiced in India, Sri Lanka, New Zealand and East Africa. In India's colonial press, this demand sometimes led to heated controversy. Conversely, in South Africa, for example, the already mentioned 'Kaffir Express', one of the earliest examples of a black journal in the Cape Province, already referred in its first issue in 1870 to Crowther as an example of the progress that could be achieved through "Christianity and education". In this way, the paper countered the racism of white settlers who denied Africans the ability to be educated (and criticized corresponding efforts by missionaries).

In the 1880s – and thus in times of emerging high imperialism – the mood changed in many places in the colonial and ecclesiastical establishment. Crowther was increasingly cold-shouldered in West Africa. When, after his death in 1891, he was succeeded by a white (rather than an African) successor, this triggered violent protests in Lagos, Ghana and Liberia. This step was castigated as discrimination against "all Africans" in the black press of West Africa. One of the consequences was the emergence of independent African churches, which began in the 1890s and accelerated in the following period [see chap. 18.2].

Notes to Chapter 14

1. Hastings (1994), *Church in Africa*, 177.
2. Hastings (1994), *Church in Africa*, 176.
3. Walls (2002), *Sierra Leone*, 48 (emphasis KK).

4. Marx (2012), *Südafrika*, 71.
5. Elbourne (2002), *Blood Ground*, 5; cf. Ward (2017), *Late 18th Century to 1914*, 230-235.
6. Etherington (1970), *Melting Pots*, 600; Elphick (1997), *Equality of Believers*, 98; Hastings (1994), *Church in Africa*, 359 ff.
7. Ross (2002), *David Livingstone*, 239 (ff).
8. Hock (2005), *Christentum in Afrika*, 105; Isichei (1995), *Christianity in Africa*, 136 f.
9. Isichei (1995), *Christianity in Africa*, 141.
10. Sundkler/Steed (2000), *Church in Africa*, 497.
11. Ward (1998), *Ugandan Identities*, 161.
12. Ward (1998), *Ugandan Identities*, 169.
13. Koschorke et al. (2016), *Discourses of Indigenous Christian Elites*, 325.

Further Reading for Chapter 14

14.1 (*West Africa: Slave Emancipation and Transatlantic Resettlement Projects*)

Ward (2017), *Late 18th Century to 1914*, 121–144; Hastings (1994), *Church in Africa*, 173–196; Walls (2002), *Sierra Leone*, 45–56; Sanneh (1999), *Abolitionists Abroad*, 1–181; Hanciles (2014), *Black Atlantic*; 29–50; Hanciles (2005), *Back to Africa*, 191–216; Campbell (2024), *Origins of the Back-To-Africa Movement*; Burlacioiu (2024), *Sierra Leone*; Koschorke (2024), *Transatlantic Ethiopianism*; Isichei (1995), *Christianity in Africa*, 153–183; Sundkler/ Steed (2000), *Church in Africa*, 169–277; Baur (1994), *Christianity in Africa*, 110–153; Campbell (1998), *Songs of Zion*; Walvin (1998), *Olaudah Equiano*; Drescher, S. (2009), *Slavery and antislavery*; Stanley (2005), *Christian missions (and) antislavery;* Jakobbson (1972), *Am I not a Man;* Fountain (2010), *African American slaves and Christianity*; Martin (2002), *African Mission Movement*, 57–72.

14.2 (*South Africa: Black Christians and White Settlers*)

Ward (2017), *Late 18th Century to 1914*, 230–235; Hastings (1994), *Church in Africa*, 197–208; Elphick/ Davenport (1997), *Christianity in South Africa*; Pillay/ Hofmeyr (1991), *Perspectives*; De Gruchy (2009), *South Africa II*, 1–51; Hock (2005), *Christentum in Afrika*, 87–103; Ilife (2017), *Africans*, 103ff. 130ff. 267ff: Villa-Vicensio/ Grassow (2009), *Colonisation of South Africa I*; Marx (2012), *Südafrika*; Lessing (2012), *German Protestant Church;* Elbourne (2002), *Blood Ground*; Elphick (2012), *Equality of Believers*.

14.3 (*East and Central Africa: David Livingstone and Other European "Discoverers"*)

Ward (2017), *Late 18th Century to 1914*, 223ff. 235ff; Hastings (1994), *Church in Africa*, 250–305; Hock (2005), *Christentum in Afrika*, 104–113; Isichei (1995), *Christianity in Africa*, 128–152; Sundkler/Steed (2000), *Church in Africa*, 445–487. 510–562; Walls (1993), *Livingstone*, 140–152; Ross (2002), *David Livingstone*.

14.4 (*African Christian Rulers: Madagascar, Uganda, Ethiopia*)

(Madagascar:) Sundkler/Steed (2000), *Church in Africa*, 487–509; Raison-Jourde (1995), *Madagascan Churches*, 292–301. – (Uganda:) Ward (1998), *Ugandan Identities*, 158–170; Hastings (1994), *Church in Africa*, 371–384.464–475; Hock (2005), *Christentum in Afrika*, 105–109; Gründer (1992), *Welteroberung*, 536–550; Koschorke (2019), ‚*Christian Patriot*', 169–172 (links India – Uganda). – (Ethiopia:) Marcus (1995), *Menelik II*; Hastings (1994), *Church in Africa*, 222–241; Hock (2005), *Christentum in Afrika*, 110–114.

14.5 (*S.A.J. Crowther, First Black African Bishop*)

Hastings (1994), *Church in Africa*, 293–298.343–357; Sanneh (1999), *Crowther and the Opening of Nigeria*, 173–197; Hock (2005), *Christentum in Afrika*, 72–80; Ajayi (1965), *Making of a New Elite*; Koschorke (2011), *Bischof Samuel Ajayi Crowther*, 315–324.

CHAPTER 15

Latin America

15.1 Independence Struggle and the Church (1804–1830)

Between 1810 and 1825, the Iberian powers lost all their colonial possessions in the Americas. In Hispano-America, the Creole upper class had become increasingly alienated from the Spanish motherland, as discussed earlier [see chap. 9.4]. Ideas of the European Enlightenment, the example of the French (and North American) Revolution, growing resistance to forced centralization efforts by the crown, and a new self-image as "Americans" accelerated this development. When French troops occupied the Spanish motherland in 1808, the colonies considered themselves sovereign with the right to govern themselves. The Indian population was not a factor in the outbreak of revolution. In 1810, the Creoles in Venezuela, Buenos Aires, Bogotá, and Chile took over regional government using Spanish institutions and declared independence. In 1810, the struggle for freedom also began in Mexico. Subsequently, the uprising against Spain developed into a multiply confused movement without a guiding center or unified goals. New partial states emerged and dissolved again. The Battle of Ayacucho (in Peru) in 1824 sealed Spain's military defeat. Until the end of the 19th century, remnants of Spanish rule existed only on the periphery, on the islands of the Caribbean (Cuba, Puerto Rico) and in the Pacific (Philippines, Guam).

The development in Portuguese America was different. Here, it was the Portuguese royal family that moved to Rio de Janeiro in 1808, fleeing from Napoleon's troops. After the fall of Napoleon, King John VI returned to Lisbon in 1821, leaving the government of Brazil to his son Peter I. The latter declared independence in 1822. The latter declared the country's independence from Portugal in 1822 and had himself crowned emperor. The Brazilian Empire, which was much more stable than the neighboring regions formerly ruled by Spain, lasted until 1889. But the first Latin American country to declare its independence from European rule was the French colony of Haiti. Supported by an uprising of slaves, a black republic was proclaimed here for the first time in 1804.

In the emancipation process of Spanish America, the Catholic Church did not take a uniform position. The high clergy and the bishops, who came from Spain, remained loyal to the crown, while the lower clergy – mostly made up of Creoles, mestizos and occasionally Indians – supported the cause of the revolution. Priests became spokesmen for the movement in many places and also led the armed struggle. In Mexico, for example, the clerics Miguel Hidalgo [see Figure 32] and José María Morelos were executed as rebels in 1811 and 1815, respectively [Text 264a + b]. In what is now Colombia, the community priest Fernández de Soto Mayor wrote a political catechism declaring the struggle for independence "just and holy" [Text 266]. Plans to erect a monument to Las Casas, hailed as the first to "fight against the horrors of the Conquista", were discussed [Text 265]. The Virgin Mary – according to the sermons and writings of numerous clerics – was also on the side of her "American children." Other revolutionaries, such as the "liberator of Venezuela" Simón Bolívar (1783–1830), were liberal Freemasons. But they too knew how to use the symbols of religion in the struggle for independence [Text 264c].

At the end of the revolutionary period, the Church was largely destroyed. Many bishoprics were vacant, as bishops loyal to the king had returned to Spain. New appointments were blocked. In Brazil, out of six bishoprics, only two were still occupied in 1825. In Spanish-speaking America, the number of vacancies reached a peak in 1829. During the years of warlike conflict, both parties to the conflict had made the church pay heavily. This plunged them into considerable financial difficulties. "Religious orders", according to the 1825 report of the papal envoy Giovanni Muzi on the situation in Chile and Argentina, "are non-existent in many places. Where they still exist, the members are generally beyond all observation of the rule." Also to be deplored, according to the same report, was the ecclesiastical loss of control in the public sphere. For, as a result of freedom of the press, many pernicious writings were now in circulation "which the ordinary church leader cannot prevent" [Text 269]. The massive exodus of religious priests also resulted in the end of missionary activities in many places. In numerous dioceses, the training of a new generation of priests also came to a standstill for years.

However, the collapse of colonial church structures did not lead to a new independence of the church. Rather, the new Creole masters needed the church as much as the old ones as an instrument of rule. After a phase of partly anarchic conditions, the patronage rights previously exercised by the Iberian crowns finally passed to the governments of the new nation states.

15.2   The Catholic Church and the New States (1830–1890)

Rome refused to recognize the new nation-states of Latin America for a long time. As late as 1824, Pope Leo XII issued an encyclical calling Hispano-Americans to obey Spanish King Ferdinand VII, who was vainly trying to restore his authority over the "rebellious" colonies. As a result, in Mexico (and other regions) there was a demand for a national church independent of Rome. A change in curial policy occurred under Pope Pius VIII, who established a nunciature in Brazil in 1830. His successor, Gregory XVI (1831–1846), began to recognize the independence of Latin American countries. During the first five years of his pontificate, he simultaneously reorganized the ecclesiastical hierarchy in Mexico, Argentina, Chile, Uruguay and Peru. Under Pius IX (1846–1878), the Curia then succeeded in concluding concordats with various countries (Bolivia in 1851, Guatemala and Costa Rica in 1852, Haiti in 1860, Nicaragua and Honduras in 1861, El Salvador, Venezuela, and Ecuador in 1862) [see Text 270]. The concordat with Ecuador, for example, provided for the recognition of Catholicism as "the religion of the Republic of Ecuador," to the exclusion of all non-Catholic cults and otherwise "a society condemned by the Church." Bishops and priests were henceforth to be able to communicate freely with Rome, and the "instruction of youth in the universities, colleges, public and private schools will conform in all things to the doctrine of the Catholic Religion" [Text 270].

The conclusion of a concordat depended, of course, on whether a conservative (and more church-friendly) or liberal (and anti-clerical) regime was in power in the country in question. Governments changed frequently. Liberal and conservative forces were in constant conflict in 19th-century Latin America. In Mexico, for example, liberal reforms under Gómez Farías in 1833/34 led to the dissolution of all missions run by religious orders, the abolition of "perpetual vows" (for nuns and monks) and the abolition of obligatory tithes to the church. At the same time, however, the patronage rights of the (now national instead of colonial) government over the Catholic Church were restored. For ecclesiastical self-determination was seen as a threat to the newly won state sovereignty. In 1852, Mexico saw a conservative revolt, for the first time in joint action by the military and the clergy, and in 1855, conversely, a bloody liberal revolution, now with the goal of complete separation of church and state. In the ensuing civil war, both parties in this conflict sought foreign support. With the help of exiled conservatives, the French intervened in 1861/62. They installed the Austrian Archduke Maximilian as monarch, who – crowned Emperor of Mexico in 1864 – was executed by the victorious Republicans in 1867. After his overthrow, the liberal constitution of 1857 was reinstated. With its strictly anticlerical articles, it remained in force until 1910/11 (or 1917).

The Empire of *Brazil* existed until 1889, combining a monarchical form of government with a moderately liberal religious policy. Roman Catholicism remained the state religion. Non-Catholic cults, however, were allowed to be practiced in buildings that were not recognizable as churches from the outside

[Text 276b]. The religious orders experienced a qualitative as well as quantitative low. Individual convents were dissolved for lack of new blood, and the property subsequently fell to the state. "State legislation increasingly aimed at the extinction of the orders. Foreign monks were no longer admitted to the traditional orders." Finally, in 1855, the admission of novices was forbidden until a new regulation by a reform of the orders which, however, never came about. The decline of the secular clergy was also dramatic, especially in relation to the exploding population. By 1889, the population had risen to about 12–14 million and thus quadrupled within a century. Whereas at the end of the 18th century there was one priest for every 1,000 inhabitants, by the end of the empire (1889) the ratio was about 1 to 17,000–20,000. Parallel to the advance of scientific and positivistic ideas, the church also lost its public reputation. "The upper classes regarded their unbelief almost as a privilege, as a sign of their cultural superiority".[1] At the same time, the decline of the school system once supported by the religious orders deprived the church of its intellectual leadership.

Despite the rise of aggressive liberalism in the second half of the 19th century, parallel to the advance of capitalist economies, a modus vivendi between church and state developed in most Latin American countries. Liberal ideology as such was limited to a small elite. The broad mass of the people mostly continued to live in traditional forms of Catholic piety, largely independent of church institutions and interspersed with numerous syncretic practices. In the countryside, everyday life had mostly changed little with independence. Despite a massive shortage of priests and weakened economically (by the loss of its land holdings), the church largely survived in the post-colonial era in outdated structures, but without any significant missionary or social impact. The central socio-ethical problem in Brazil, for example, was African-American slavery. It was maintained here until 1888 – longer than in any other state on the continent. The abolition movement was supported by liberals, Freemasons and individual humanists, but hardly by church actors. Individual religious orders and bishops did free their slaves in the 1870s and 1880s. However, there was no fundamental condemnation of slavery as an unjust institution by the church hierarchy.

15.3 Romanization of Latin American Catholicism

The German Franciscan priest Wilhelm Schürmann, who had been working in now republican Brazil in the state of St. Catherine since 1894, aimed to "bring help to Brazil's decaying Catholicism, which was heading for ruin."[2] He expected help in particular from the increased influx of European religious.

His description of the religious conditions on the ground was hardly less critical than that of the first Protestant missionaries from the USA. In Latin American Catholicism, they could often identify little more than a paganism whitewashed by Christianity.

The chaotic conditions in many places at the end of the revolutionary epoch became the trigger for a countermovement that has been called the Romanization of Latin American Catholicism. For the ecclesiastical restoration that began in the 1830s was closely linked to the growing influence of Rome. Through the now gradually expanded system of nunciatures, Rome was much more directly represented on the subcontinent than had been possible in the days of Iberian colonial rule. In a series of concordats since 1851, Rome had granted various national governments the right of patronage, but reserved the final decision in filling bishop's chairs. Unpopular liberal candidates were subsequently refused approval. At least since the encyclical 'Quanta cura' and the 'Syllabus errorum' of 1864, Pope Pius IX (1846–1878) had dedicated himself to the fight against all "errors" of modern liberalism, such as the demand for freedom of religion and opinion, secular education or against the principle of popular sovereignty. This proclamation aroused great excitement not only in liberal circles in Europe but also in Latin America. Conversely, however, there was a rise in the number of churchmen there who saw in a close – "ultramontane" – connection to the papacy the only alternative to the church's dependence on the oligarchic state. In colonial times, the pope had been an important symbol, but distant. Now he became the direct point of reference for the church's own "struggle" against liberal anticlerical governments.

As early as 1859, the Collegium Pio Latinoamericanum had been founded in Rome. Here whole generations of priests were trained who later assumed leadership positions as bishops in the churches of the subcontinent. The Romanization of the Church, theology, and devotional practice was reinforced by the swelling influx of priests and congregations from Italy and France beginning in the mid-19th century. The First Vatican Council of 1869/70, a global gathering of ultramontane Catholicism, also included (out of a total of 770 council fathers) 30 bishops from Latin America. This is a significant difference as compared to the Council of Trent of 1545–1563, where not a single representative of the Church from the New World was present. The ultramontane element in Latin America was also strengthened by the influx of numerous Jesuits and other religious orders, especially female communities, expelled in the European culture wars of the 1870s. Like other European priests now increasingly active there, they often had little understanding for the popular Catholicism they encountered locally, which they often saw as mere "superstition" [Text 283f]. In the 1870s, moreover, the influx of European immigrants also from non-Iberian Catholic countries (including Italians, Poles, Germans) increased. Latin American Catholicism became both more European and more Roman.

This development reached a symbolic climax with the *Latin American Plenary Council of 1899 in Rome*. Attended by 53 of the 104 Latin American hierarchs at the time, the council became a showcase for Latin American Catholicism. The goal was the religious revival of the continent and the "Latin race" (sic) living there. Among other things, new initiatives were discussed for the mission among indigenous people, for the establishment of Catholic universities, and for dealing with Protestant "heretics" [Text 282]. The clericalization of religious life was promoted.[3] At the same time, national and supra-regional cooperation within the Roman Church of Latin America was strengthened. Significantly, the place of preparation and meeting was the Vatican.

15.4 Forms of Protestant Presence in Latin America

During the colonial period, Protestants had been denied access to the Spanish and Portuguese possessions in America [see Map 7]. Individual invaders (such as Western European corsairs) or stranded sailors were persecuted by the Inquisition. The first Protestants to reside legally in Latin America at the beginning of the 19th century were so-called residents, i.e. foreign merchants, ship crews or technicians who worked there temporarily and practiced the religion of their country of origin in so-called foreign congregations. In 1819, the first Anglican church in South America was established in Rio de Janeiro. Previously, Anglican services there had taken place only sporadically aboard British ships off the coast [Text 276a]. After Brazil's independence in 1822, there was a large-scale immigration of Protestant settlers, initially mainly from German-speaking countries. Promoted by the government – which wanted to create small-scale agriculture and at the same time "whiten" (sic!) its own Brazilian population – in some cases entire village communities, together with their pastor, arrived in Southern Brazil since 1824 from various German regions hit by famine crises [Text 277]. Immigrant congregations thus emerged, in many cases characterized by the close connection of national (here: German) and confessional (here: especially Lutheran) identity. Later, the first congregations of Scottish and North American Presbyterians and Methodists were also formed.

An early stage of Protestant presence in Latin America is marked by the interdenominational activities of *Bible colporteurs*. The Bible in the vernacular had been a largely unknown book there since its prohibition by the Tridentine colonial church [cf. chap. 7.2.], and its dissemination in the 19th century had been a Protestant enterprise throughout. Even before the official representatives of the British and American Bible societies, it was often laymen (merchants, doctors, members of the navy) who distributed the Bibles in various regions with great commitment (and repeatedly also personal risk). Liberal clerics and officials could certainly welcome such actions as a contribution to the literacy and modernization of the country. The people were often curious to "get to know what had been withheld from them for so long" [Text 278].

Even where tolerated (and sometimes even encouraged) by the state, Protestants often had a difficult time in civil life. Mixed-denominational marriages were taboo. Even in liberal Mexico, marriages across denominations were often possible only at the price of humiliating rituals. This was the case of the German merchant August Haas, who in 1843 was only allowed to marry his beloved from a leading family after completing his conversion.

> He first had to take lessons on the duties and rules from the *cura* [priest]. He had to knock on the closed church door, dressed in penitent garments, and while standing outside, answer the question given from inside: 'A poor lost sinner asking to be accepted into the arms of the only true religion' and so on". Before the wedding, "poor Haas had to walk in the streets with a candle and had present a general confession as well as give his solemn promise to fulfill all duties that the Church stipulates for married couples. [Text 281]

Since the 1870s, there has been increased European immigration not only to the USA, but also to Latin America. It was mainly the so-called ABC countries (Argentina, Brazil, Chile) that attracted migrants from the Old World. Most of them came from traditionally Catholic countries (such as Italy and Spain), but a considerable number also came from Protestant regions. Also since the 1870s, there has been a rapid advance of Anglo-Saxon missionary Protestantism in South America. Its goal was to "spread the blessings of education and Christianity and to establish and maintain mission schools and Christian mission stations" (according to the U.S. Methodists in 1873). It led to the establishment of separate denominational congregations among the formerly Catholic population (as in Rio de Janeiro in 1861 [Text 279]) and, beginning around 1880, increasingly to the founding of a network of schools, high schools, orphanages, and clinics in the most important cities. Initially, the main sponsors were the classical U.S. denominations (Presbyterians, Methodists, Episcopalians). After the American War of Secession, various free-church groups joined in. The Presbyterians, for example, became active in Colombia beginning in 1856, Brazil in 1859, Mexico in 1872, and Guatemala in 1882. The Methodists went to Mexico in 1873, Brazil in 1886, the Antilles in 1890, and Costa Rica, Panama, and Bolivia toward the end of the century. Despite its sporadic spread, Protestantism initially remained marginal in 19th-century Latin American societies. However, as a "civilizing Protestantism" and bearer of a democratic model of society, it had considerable long-term effects.

Notes to Chapter 15

1. Prien (1978), *Geschichte*, 427.
2. Meier (1993), *„Katholizismus Brasiliens Hülfe bringen"*, 3–24 (quotation on p. 12).
3. Thus Dussel (1992), *Church in Latin America*, 195.
4. Bastian (1995), *Protestantismus*, 135.

Further Reading for Chapter 15

15.1 (*Independence Struggle and the Church [1804–1830]*)

González/ González (2008), *Christianity in Latin America*, 131–159; Prien (2013), *Latin America*, 271–285; Dussel (1992), *Church in Latin America*, 81–104; Bakewell (²2004), *History of Latin America*, 382–442; Garrard-Burnett/ Freston/ Dove (2016), *Religion in Latin America*, 231–250 (by J. Klaiber); Buisson/ Schottelius (1980), *Unabhängigkeitsbewegungen*; Goodpasture (1989), *Cross and Sword*, 107–119 (documents); Keen (1996), *Latin America*, 160–179; Dreher (2017), *Latin America*, 208–218.

15.2 (*The Catholic Church and the New States [1830–1890]*)

Prien (2013), *Latin America*, 285–314; González/González (2008), *Christianity in Latin America*, 131–159; Garrard-Burnett/ Freston/ Dove (2016), *Religion in Latin America*, 251–268 (by M. Butler); Dussel (1992), *Church in Latin America*, 105–115; Dreher (2017), *Latin America*, 218ff; Klaiber (1992), *Peru*, 1–58.

15.3 (*Romanization of Latin American Catholicism*)

Prien (2013), *Latin America*, 314–360; Prien (1978), *Geschichte*, 368–400; Dussel (1992), *Church in Latin America*, 105–116; Dreher (2017), *Latin America*, 218–222; Goodpasture (1989), *Cross and Sword*, 120–147. 160–182 (documents); Klaiber (1988), *Peru*, 45–47.68 ff; Meier (2018), *Studien*, 190–217.

15.4 (*Forms of Protestant Presence in Latin America*)

Prien (2013), *Latin America*, 361–365. 374–386. 160–164. 199ff; González/ González (2008), *Christianity in Latin America*, 184–205; Dussel (1992), *Church in Latin America*, 313–350; Garrard-Burnett/ Freston/ Dove (2016), *Religion in Latin America*, 286–303 (by S.C. Dove). 304–318 (by M. Dreher); Goodpasture (1989), *Cross and Sword*, 148–159. 183–198 (documents); Dreher (2017), *Latin America*, 205–222; Dreher (1978), *Kirche und Deutschtum*; Bastian (1995), *Protestantismus*, 103–157; Spliesgart (2006), „*Verbrasilianerung*".

Illustrations for Part 3

FIGURE 26
China: Robert Morrison (1782–1834), first protestant missionary to China (and the Chinese diaspora) and his team (Li Shigong, Chaen Laoyi) translating the Bible into Chinese (image from ca. 1828).

FIGURE 27
Liang Fa (1789–1855), first Chinese protestant minister and evangelist, who was instrumental in printing and disseminating Morrison's translation of the Bible. His own Bible tracts influenced the later leader of the Taiping movement Hong Xiuquan (see fig. 28).

ILLUSTRATIONS FOR PART 3

FIGURE 28
Hong Xiuquan (1814–1864), leader and "Heavenly King" of the Christian-inspired Taiping mass social revolutionary movement (1850–1864).

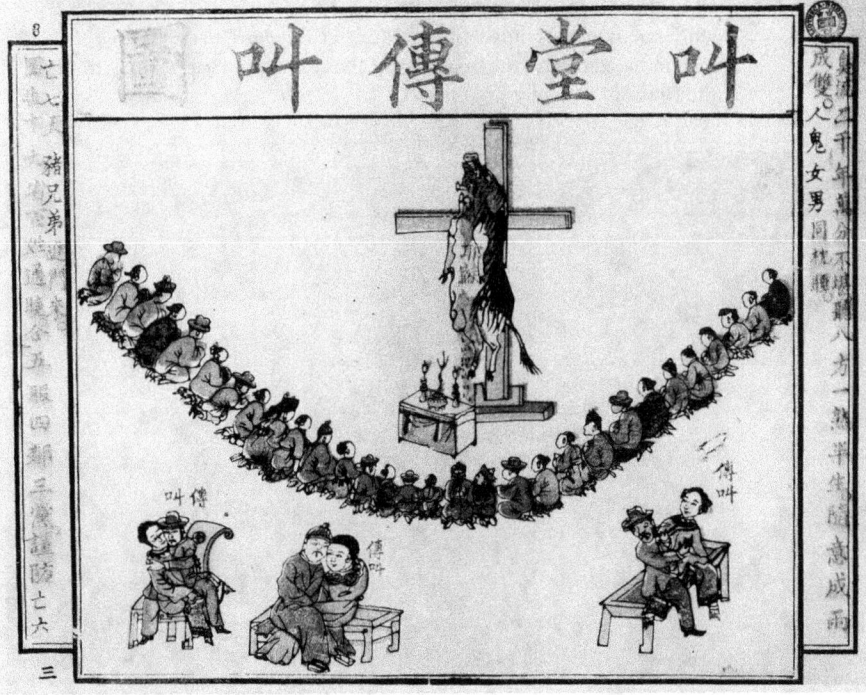

FIGURE 29   China: Anti-Christian cartoon (before 1891) showing the worship of a crucified pig and immorality of Europeans.

FIGURE 30 Japan/Nagasaki: First contact of the "Hidden Christians" in 1865 with a French missionary after the "opening" of the country in 1854 (relief in front of the Urakami Cathedral) [= photo C17].

FIGURE 31 Japan: entrance to Doshisha University, founded in 1875 as an English school by Protestant educator Niijima Jo (Joseph Hardy Neesima; 1843–1890) [= photo C15].

ILLUSTRATIONS FOR PART 3

FIGURE 32
Miguel Hidalgo (1753–1811), Mexican priest, scholar, and one of the pioneers of Mexican independence.

FIGURE 33
Official medallion of the British Anti-Slavery Society (since the end of the 18th century), which was strongly supported by evangelical forces within the missionary movement. The medallion was designed by Josia Wedwood in 1795.

FIGURE 34
Samuel Ajayi Crowther (c. 1806/08–1891), first black African bishop of modern times (in British-colonial West Africa) and symbol of the upward aspirations of modern African elites across the continent.

FIGURE 35 Ethiopia: The Ethiopian victory at Adwa in 1896 over an Italian invasion force was an event of pan-African significance and fueled emancipation efforts by black Christians on both sides of the Atlantic [= photo F16].

FIGURE 36
South Africa: Mangena Maake Mokone (1851–1931), formerly a Methodist preacher, founded the 'Ethiopian Church' in 1892, one of the first and most successful independent African churches in southern Africa.

FIGURE 37 Black transatlantic church fellowship (1896): Bishop Henry Turner (of the North American 'African Methodist Epicopal Church' [AME]) welcomes James Dwane (Pretoria) as representative of the "Ethiopian Church" of South Africa and its acceptance into the AME fellowship.

PART 4
1890–1945

CHAPTER 16

Churches and Missions in the Age of High Imperialism

16.1 Growing Colonial Rivalries

Toward the end of the 19th century, the pace of colonial acquisitions in Africa and Asia accelerated dramatically. European powers acquired (or subjugated) larger overseas territories between 1884 and 1914 than in the previous 75 years. Sub-Saharan *Africa* – still largely unknown to Europeans in its interior at the beginning of the 19th century – was de facto partitioned at the Berlin Congo Conference in 1884/85. The rival colonial powers staked out their claims, some of which were drawn on the map with a ruler. The effective seizure of the continent was largely completed by 1900 [Map 16]. Only two countries remained free of European colonial rule: the Christian empire of Ethiopia, which had successfully expelled Italian invaders in 1896, and the independent Republic of Liberia, founded in 1847 as a home for African-American returnees from the United States.

In *Asia*, the European powers rounded out their respective colonial possessions. Great Britain also annexed Upper Burma in 1885, rounding out its holdings on the subcontinent. Also in the 1880s, France formed its 'Indochinese Union', consisting of present-day Laos, Cambodia and Vietnam. In Indonesia, the Netherlands gradually extended its rule over the entire island kingdom (where previously it often had controlled only the coastal regions). Between these colonial blocs, buffer zones formed with nominally independent countries, but de facto subject to strong restrictions on sovereignty. Thus Siam (Thailand) between British India and French Indochina, and Persia (Iran) between the British Empire and Russia, which was expanding in Central Asia. China remained nominally independent and undivided. Since the 1890s, however, Western powers had been staking out their own spheres of influence and zones of economic exploitation there in a system of unequal treaties. In 1900, a total of eight nations took part in a "punitive expedition" after the so-called Boxer Rebellion: in addition to England and France, this was Germany, Italy, Austria-Hungary, Russia, the United States and (as an emerging Asian power) Japan.

In *Latin America*, which was not under formal colonial control, the economic influence of the USA increased steadily toward the end of the

19th century. In the 1840s, they had already annexed large parts of Mexico. In the American-Spanish War of 1898, the U.S. expelled the Spanish from their last possessions in the Caribbean (Cuba, Puerto Rico) and the Pacific (Philippines, Guam) and now entered the circle of colonial powers themselves. But Latin America also became the target of renewed European desires. The German colonial ideologist Ferdinand Fabri, for example, advocated in the 1880s not only (successfully) the establishment of German colonies in Africa, but also (unsuccessfully) in Brazil (with the German settlers living there as the imperial vanguard). The French failed with their short-lived attempt to install a European governor in Mexico in the form of the Habsburg Archduke Maximilian as Mexican emperor. The latter was captured by the legitimate government of the country and executed in 1867.

New colonial powers appeared on the scene. In the Caribbean and the Pacific, these were, as mentioned, the USA, and in Africa, among others, Belgium. The Belgian 'Congo Free State', however, was not a state colony, but from 1885 to 1908 "private property" of King Leopold II, with a highly effective – and even by the standards of the time unusually cruel – system of forced labor and exploitation. Germany and Italy were latecomers to the colonial business. Italy was driven out of Ethiopia in 1896, but established a foothold in Libya as well as in East African Eritrea and Somaliland. Germany acquired (or forced the cession of) possessions in West Africa (Togo, Cameroon), East Africa (especially in the territory of present-day Tanzania), Southwest Africa (Namibia), China (the "leased territory" of Kiautschou), and individual territories and islands in the South Seas (such as New Guinea, Samoa). The German colonial period was fortunately only short (1884–1919), but all the more fatal due to the genocide of the Herero and Nama (1904–1908) in what is now Namibia.

This new phase of European-Western dominance has been called *high imperialism*. Different definitions of this term emphasize different features. These include the transition from informal to formal rule overseas; growing technological superiority of Europeans as a result of advanced industrialization; the search for overseas sources of raw materials, sales markets and settlement areas; escalation of international rivalries, compensation principle (balancing of interests at the expense of powerless third parties), colonial possessions as a bargaining chip. For example, Germany "ceded" the free Sultanate of Zanzibar to England in 1890 (in exchange for Helgoland). Many territories in Asia or Africa were occupied (or reclaimed) only to deny access to colonial rivals there. Overall, the last decades of the 19th century thus saw the transition from the previous (British-dominated) free trade imperialism to (multinational) colonial competition.

Europe's colonial expansion was accompanied in many places by rising *racism and social Darwinism*. In the 16th and 17th centuries, for example, the Chinese were still considered "white" in the eyes of many European visitors. It was not until the 18th century, and then at an accelerated rate in the 19th century, that they came to be regarded as "yellow," as the historian Walter Demel ("How the Chinese Became Yellow") has shown. At the same time they were sorted into a hierarchy of "races" of different value (white – yellow – brown – red – black etc.), which at the same time served to legitimize colonial raids. A determined champion of British imperialism was, for example, the English capitalist Cecil Rhodes, after whom today's Zimbabwe was named "(Southern) Rhodesia" until independence in 1980. God, Rhodes said, had "evidently fashioned the English-speaking race into His chosen instrument." "I maintain that we are the first race in the world and that the larger parts of the world we inhabit, the better it is for mankind" [Text 167a].

16.2 New Missionary Actors

In the last quarter of the 19th century, the number of Protestant and Catholic missionaries in the global South grew by leaps and bounds. The number of German Protestant missionaries alone tripled from the mid-1870s to the end of the century. In 1900, the (third) World Missionary Conference in New York gave the total number of Protestant missionaries worldwide as 15,460, which included both "ordained and lay" as well as members of "both sexes." The latter figure is particularly noteworthy. For separate societies for female missionary personnel with specific tasks (especially in teaching native women in India or China, for example) were among the characteristics of the American missionary movement in particular. The increase of Catholic missionary activities at the end of the 19th century in various continents was also enormous [cf. Text 175–180]. In Africa alone, for example, there were probably about 10,000 Western missionaries and religious active around 1910, of whom more than 4,000 were Protestants and about 6,000 Catholics.

In addition to the traditional ones, numerous *new mission societies and congregations* became active overseas, including those that had only been founded as a result of the changed colonial situation. In Germany, for example – which had entered the circle of colonial powers in 1884 – ten new smaller missions such as the 'Deutsch-Ostafrikanische Evangelische Missionsgesellschaft' (German East African Protestant Mission Society) in Berlin (1886) were established between 1886 and 1896. Unlike the earlier Protestant missionary movement, which – such as the German-Swiss 'Basel Mission' and the British 'Church Missionary Society' (CMS) – had cooperated closely across denominational and national boundaries, these propagandists of a German colonial mission followed the principle of 'German men to German colonies'. This earned them the reproach of 'furor teutonicus' from ecumenically minded traditionalists like Gustav Warneck (1834–1910), the spiritus rector of the German mission. Lively controversies about the "national" or "international" character of the mission" followed. The latter was affirmed by the majority of Protestant mission representatives at the German Mission Conference in 1885.[1] Similar debates between colonial missionary start-ups and ecumenically oriented societies occurred in other contexts as well.

"Why is the 19th century a missionary century?" was the title of a paper published by the afore-mentioned Gustav Warneck in 1880, in the period before the high-imperialistic phase of European colonialism. He refers, among other things, to the increased missionary enthusiasm on the home front, the "geographical discoveries" of the 19th century, the "colonial possessions of the Protestant states," the Protestant-inspired "anti-slavery" movement of the early 19th century, and "the facilitation of world traffic through the invention of the *new means of communication*." Indeed, this category of "world traffic" – in 19th century terminology the equivalent of today's term "globalization" – is a crucial factor also in analyzing religious dynamics of the period. For a wealth of technological innovations – such as railroads, steamships, telegraphy and tropical medicine – or the opening of the Suez Canal in 1869 had drastically shortened the exchange of news as well as travel times between different parts of the world. At the same time, they massively facilitated missionaries' access to regions that had once been difficult to reach.

Conversely, however, the increased mobility since the 1890s also increasingly changed the profile of missionary work overseas. Previously, missionaries who had been active in a particular region for many years were usually very familiar with the local conditions and had often become part of the local milieu. Now, however, a new generation of missionary newcomers arrived in colonial port cities in rapid succession. They went – often before visiting their congregations – first to the clubs of the Europeans, where they were then informed about the "unreliability" of the "natives". At the same time, the improved means of communication made it possible for the respective colonial or missionary headquarters to exert greater influence on developments overseas. Thus, the scope for local experiments became narrower. Conversely, however, communication was always a two-way process. News from the so-called "mission fields" and the emerging churches overseas increasingly reached Europe and the United States. They triggered sometimes controversial debates there.

The climax of the Protestant missionary movement of the 19th century was the (fourth) *World Missionary Conference in Edinburgh in 1910*. With its 1,215 delegates from numerous Western countries and overseas mission territories, it became an army show of worldwide Protestantism. At the same time, it marked a new stage in Christian globalization. For the first time, it united numerous churches and missions that had previously been separated both denominationally and geographically (and in some cases came into contact with each other for the first time on the "mission fields"). The optimism of the Edinburgh conference – which aimed at the "evangelization of the world in one generation" – has often been interpreted as an expression of Christian triumphalism. At the same time, however, the discussions were determined by the "awakening of great nations" in Asia (and Africa). In the eyes of the conference it seemed open whether they would follow a path *with* or *without* Christ [Text 70]. In a completely new way, churches and missions of the West thus faced unifying challenges from developments in the world beyond Europe.

16.3 Indigenous Counter-Movements

In numerous regions of Asia and Africa, resistance to European rule began to arise in the 1880s and 1890s. Initially largely independent of each other, the beginnings of nationalist movements formed in different colonial contexts. In India, for example, the 'Indian National Congress' (INC) was founded in 1885, initially more an assembly of notables than the national revolutionary movement of later years. The "blessings" of British rule were welcomed, but increased participation of native elites was urged [Text 63b]. From 1905 onward, the tone became more strident. Now the demand for 'swaraj' (self-government) was on the agenda. The victory of Japan over Russia in 1904/05 – that is, of an "Oriental" nation over a major European power, and this at the height of Western imperialism – spurred nationalist (and increasingly pan-Asian) aspirations across the continent [Text 65].

In many places, this *"national awakening"* was accompanied by a revival of traditional religions. In most cases, religious nationalism preceded political nationalism. "The whole character of Buddhism," reported a missionary observer from southern Sri Lanka around 1899, "has changed in recent years. Whereas some time ago the mass of the people knew nothing about Buddhism ... the present Buddhism is a widespread force opposed to Christianity" [Text 64b]. In the same year, the magazine 'The Hindu Organ', published in Jaffna, northern Sri Lanka, described this revival as an all-Asian phenomenon:

> Everywhere throughout the East there is a revival of [Asian] learning and literature, and the work of rescuing the glory of the Oriental religions from the forgotten past is going on apace. In India, Burma, Siam [Thailand], Annam [Vietnam], Japan, and even in China, ... the need for religious and moral education is largely felt. [Text 62]

The resurgence of the old religions was associated with a close intertwining of religious and national identity. Among the Sinhalese in colonial Sri Lanka, for example, being a Buddhist was now considered a sign of "patriotism". An Indian nationalist had to be Hindu at the same time, etc. Conversely, missionary Christianity (and membership in a missionary church) was now increasingly criticized as "denationalizing." And it was in response to this challenge that debates began among Asian Christians from different missionary (or cultural) contexts about a "national form" and "native shape" of the Christianity introduced by the Western missionaries.

Since the end of the 19th century, corresponding *indigenization efforts* – initially spontaneous and not very coordinated – have accumulated in various regions of Asia. They were directed at different features of church and religious life. "Indigenous leadership," i.e., the demand of local Christians for church leadership positions, had been lively discussed in the Protestant mission churches of the continent for some time. In the Anglican context, this was reflected, among other things, in the controversies about a "native bishop". Quite early, Indian Christians, for example, also referred to examples from Africa (such as the black Bishop Samuel A. Crowther), which was considered a model in this respect. Different experiments of a cultural indigenization of missionary Christianity (in liturgy, music, architecture, naming, etc., later also with first Christian ashrams) intensified since 1900. Very early criticism was voiced against the denominationalism (respectively the imported "sectarianism") of the missionaries, with the result of various local ecumenical initiatives and national church experiments [Text 66–69]. In Madras (now Chennai), for example, a 'National Church of India' was founded in 1886. It pursued the goal of gradually uniting all Indian Christians, irrespective of their denominational affiliation, in *one* national church under indigenous leadership [Text 77; for details see chap. 17.2]. In Japan, Kanzi Uchimura founded the 'Non-Church' movement in 1901, which still exists today and saw itself as a Christian alternative to Western church models [Text 78; cf. Figure 41]. Initiatives for a Rome-independent Church, too, intensified in Catholic Asia.

The most important example is the 'Iglesia Filipina Independiente' proclaimed in the Philippines in 1902, to which initially about 20% to 25% of the island's population belonged.

In Africa, the emancipatory aspirations of black Christians were articulated primarily through the establishment of *mission-independent churches* under African leadership. The early 1890s saw a whole wave of the establishment of such 'African Independent Churches' (AIC's) simultaneously, but independently, in the west and south of the continent. Some were short-lived, others enjoyed long duration [Text 170–171; see chap. 18.2 for more details]. They also gained enormous importance, especially as a precursor to the later explosive church growth in sub-Saharan Africa in the post-colonial era. In a first phase, these AICs were still strongly oriented to the liturgical or confessional traditions of their respective missionary mother churches (e.g. Anglicans, Methodists or Baptists), from which they had separated. In a second wave, diverse local prophetic movements formed under the leadership of charismatic leaders [Text 172–173]. Founders of African churches such as Mojola Agbebi (1860–1917) in present-day Nigeria are considered pioneers of African nationalism [Text 170d].

Independentist and national church aspirations also existed among Latin American Protestants, as the Panama Conference of 1916, discussed in more detail below, records. "Probably in no other area except Japan," it said in a report there, "have [U.S.] missionaries encountered such a strong nationalistic sentiment as in some Latin American countries." This was especially true, it said, of "evangelical churches founded by North Americans in Brazil, Chile, Puerto Rico, and Mexico." Separatist communities – such as the 'Iglesia Presbiteriana Independiente' founded in Brazil in 1903 or the 'Iglesia Evangélica Independiente' formed in Mexico in 1897 – enjoyed great popularity. Especially in Mexico, the goal of an interdenominational national church, free from North American influence, enjoyed great sympathy [Text 287].

16.4 Multiplicity of Transregional and Transcontinental Networks

Edinburgh 1910 was not only the culmination of the Protestant missionary movement of the 19th century. It also gave birth to the modern ecumenical movement of the 20th century in the Protestant churches of the Western world. It became the direct or indirect starting point of various strands of organized ecumenism (such as the 'International Missionary Council' or the 'Faith and Order' movement), which finally led to the establishment (and further developement) of the World Council of Churches in Amsterdam in 1948.

Edinburgh established a communicative network that was used for a variety of purposes. After the outbreak of World War I, for example, it was the international participants in this assembly to whom leading German theologians and church representatives addressed their declaration on the war guilt question in 1914.

In previous research, far too little attention has been paid to the extent to which Edinburgh responded to developments and controversies in the emerging overseas churches. It was, after all, the "awakening of great nations" in Asia [and Africa] that made united action by all Christendom ("the church [singular!] in Christian lands") so exceedingly urgent in the eyes of the conference [Text 70b + a]. The detailed reports from overseas - both from missionaries and local church leaders – played a significant role in the deliberations. "I have heard said it again and again", reported the Anglican bishop from Bombay, for example, "that it is only we foreign missionaries who keep the Indian Christians from [church] unity" [Text 69b]. And Chinese delegate Cheng Ching Yi told the assembly: Your denominationalism does not interest us. We Chinese Christians "love unity and national life".[2] The issue of church unity and the development of national (rather than denominational) organizational structures therefore played a defining role both in Edinburgh itself and especially in its Asian Continuation Conferences of 1912/13 [Text 71]. These triggered an indigenization push in the Protestant mission churches of the continent and initiated a dynamic phase of the Asian ecumenical movement.

In addition to (and outside of) the various missionary communication channels in the environment of the Edinburgh ecumenism, a multitude of supra-regional (and partly transcontinental) *indigenous Christian networks* also played a significant role. They add considerably to our understanding of Christian internationalisms at the beginning of the 20th century. In 1906, for example, a delegation of Japanese Christians visited India "at the special request and invitation" of their Indian coreligionists. This resulted in a multitude of mutual contacts and the beginnings of a Christian Pan-Asianism. At the same time, Indian Christians' were connected through a network of their own associations with the Indian Christian diaspora in South Asia, South Africa, Great Britain and the USA. Not only through the missionary press, but increasingly also through their own journals, Asian and African Christians, for example, were in contact with each other. This led to increased exchange of information and influenced local discussions. Ethnic diasporas or voluntary migration (or migration forced by economic hardship) was also a major factor in the non-missionary spread of Christianity in different regions of the colonial world at the turn of the 19th and 20th centuries.

A special phenomenon in Christian Asia around 1900 was the emergence of *indigenous missionary societies*. In 1905, for example, a 'National Missionary Society' of Indian Christians was founded in Serampore. It followed the motto "Indian men, Indian money, Indian leadership" and became active inside and outside the country. That Asia could only be evangelized "through her own sons" (and daughters) – China through Chinese, Japan through Japanese, India through Indians, etc. – was the conviction of a major conference in Tokyo in 1907. This, by the way, was the first ecumenical assembly in Asia with a majority of Asian delegates. The debates there were also related to the discussions about the goal of the "Three Selves" [see chapter 17.2]. In the process of emancipation of Asian churches, the goal of "self-propagation" seemed to be the most quickly attainable.

An autonomous (not Western missionary) spread of the gospel was also the goal of that broad movement of black Christians on both sides of the Atlantic, commonly called *Ethiopianism* [for details see chapter 18.2]. In many cases it was associated with the beginnings of a Christian Pan-Africanism. Ethiopiopianism has a longer history going back to the end of the 18th century and reached its peak at the beginning of the 20th century. Besides biblical promises (such as Ps 68:31 or Acts 8), non-colonized Christian Ethiopia – symbol of ecclesiastical and political independence – increasingly served as a reference point. This movement led not only to the sending of African-American missionaries to Africa in the course of the 19th century, but also to intra-African missionary activities. Since the 1890s, there has also been a proliferation of transcontinental black church formations in the so-called 'Black Atlantic'. The most prominent example has been the African Methodist Episcopal Church (AME) mentioned earlier. Founded in 1816 in Philadelphia (USA), it merged in 1896 in South Africa with the 'Ethiopian Church' of the former Methodist preacher Mangena Mokone, which had been established there only shortly before [see Figure 36 + 37; Photo H09–12] Another instructive paradigm is the 'African Orthodox Church'. Founded in 1921 as one of many black churches in New York, it already had offshoots in South Africa three years later (1924) and soon after (since 1929) also in East Africa [see Text 174]. Incidentally, these transatlantic connections came about initially through the African-American press.[3]

1906 is usually considered the starting date of North American Pentecostalism (Azusa Street Revival, initiated by African American preacher William Seymour). The *early Pentecostal movement* quickly became a transnational phenomenon. At the same time, however (and in some cases even earlier), intra-Christian revivals also occurred in other regions – such as Korea, India, South Africa, Chile or Brazil. This happened partly in loose connection with the Azusa movement, but partly completely independent of it. Pentecostal migrants and missionaries established links between the movements in different parts of the world.

The importance of the *Latin American Plenary Council* in Rome in 1899 for Latin American Catholicism has already been highlighted [see chapter 15.3]. It not only accelerated the so-called Romanization, but also strengthened the national and supra-regional cooperation within the Roman Church of Central and South America. Protestant counterpart – and at the same time counterpart to the Edinburgh Conference of 1910 – was in a certain sense the "Congress on Christian Work in Latin America" in Panamá in 1916. It sought to coordinate cooperation between the Protestant denominations (especially of U.S. origin) active there. Latin America, with its then 80 million inhabitants, was declared an open mission territory despite its nominally Catholic population. The focus of the consultations was on issues of social work and on the propagation of a Protestant ethic [see Text 287].

16.5 The First World War as a Caesura and the End of the 'Christianity-Civilization' Model

The hopes of the missionary community on the eve of World War I were high. The Edinburgh World Missionary Conference of 1910 saw itself, as mentioned, at a "turning point" in human history [Text 70b]. It expected the evangelization of the world still "in our generation". This expectation seemed by no means as completely unrealistic as it appears in retrospect. In 1911, for example, in China the Ching dynasty was overthrown, which had ruled the empire for centuries; and the first (provisional) president of the new republic – Sun-Yatsen – was a baptized Christian.

But then came the First World War (1914–1918) and with it the moral catastrophe of Western Christianity. The "Great War" – as it was called in the English-speaking world for a long time – by no means took place only on the battlefields in Europe or the Middle East. The colonies and other countries in the global South were also directly affected. Asians and Africans were used as soldiers on the battlegrounds of Europe or were forcibly recruited in their hundreds of thousands as laborers. India alone provided approximately 1.5 million troops and laborers. When the British and French conquered the German colonies in Africa, African colonial troops fought on both sides. News of the horror events in faraway Europe – the battle of Verdun alone claimed some 275,000 lives on the French side and 250,000 on the German side in 1916 – quickly reached an irritated public in Asia or Africa. In a very different way from earlier European conflicts, the First World War was also a media event overseas.

"Isn't Germany a Christian country?" asked in 1915, appalledly, African Christians in what is now Malawi. "Have the evil spirits got into the hearts of the [sc. European] kings?" From Sri Lanka in 1916, a Catholic priest recounted a bus trip in which a Buddhist monk asked him, to derisive applause from bystanders, "If all Europeans are Christians, why are they fighting each other?" In other ways, too, the war was a constant theme of Buddhist propaganda in the country – as proof of the "complete failure of Christianity in Europe" (Anagarika Dharmapala). Also in Sri Lanka, we learn in 1916, conversely, of a fundraising campaign by Sinhalese Catholics for their co-religionists in faraway Belgium, who had been victims of the "German atrocities". In the past, such donations went from Europe to overseas. Now they flowed in the opposite direction.[4]

Among the immediate effects of the war was a drastic reduction in missionary presence. German missionaries working in British or French colonies were immediately interned. In general, missionary activity was severely limited by the reduced supply of human and material resources. Native communities were now often left to fend for themselves. On the one hand, this accelerated the tendency toward local autonomy, which had already increased since Edinburgh. At the same time, mission-independent movements experienced rapid growth in many places. These included groups such as the 'True Jesus Church' (Zhen Yesu jiaohui), founded in China in 1917 in the midst of the turmoil of war (and expanding rapidly), which distinguished itself almost xenophobically from missionary Christianity. African Christian prophets such as William Wade Harris (Liberia) and Garrick Sokari Braide (West Africa) declared the war to be God's judgment for the sins of Europeans [cf. Text 173]. Individual clerics went into armed resistance against colonial rule. One prominent example has been provided, in 1914 in what is now Malawi, by John Chilembwe (c. 1870–1915), black Baptist minister, African nationalist, and later revered as one of the country's founding fathers [Text 172c].

In numerous colonies and regions of Asia and Africa, nationalist movements took off. For the period after the war, a higher degree of political participation was demanded – for example in British India or French Indochina. These hopes were spurred on by the 'Fourteen Points' of American President Woodrow Wilson, who in 1918 had declared the right of self-determination of peoples to be the cornerstone of a just post-war order. That this principle was now denied to the colonized peoples of the non-European world at the Versailles peace negotiations in 1919 was another serious disillusionment. Many Asian nationalists now turned away from the model of Western – and "Christian" – democracy toward socialist alternatives. So, for example, the Vietnamese Nguyen Ai Quoc, later known as Ho Chi Minh. Since the Russian October Revolution of 1917 – which had led to the destruction of the Russian Orthodox Church and the persecution of hundreds of thousands of believers – a social alternative was now on the horizon. In many regions of Asia, the Soviet revolution became the model for the future.

The war also had devastating effects particularly in the disintegrating Ottoman Empire. Here, the genocide of Armenian Christians occurred, which claimed at least one million lives between 1914 and 1918 (and still is being denied by Turkey up to the time of writing). The members of other Christian communities were also affected, especially in the border region with Russia. These included members of the Assyrian ("Nestorian"), Chaldean and Syrian Orthodox Churches ("Jacobite") along with their Uniate members.

In 1916, in Sierra Leone, West Africa, the commentator of a black journal spoke of an "extremely thin" civilizational crust of European Christianity ("exceeding thinness of ... European Christendom") in view of the experiences of the "European war".[5] This is an analysis quite similar to that of the Swiss pastor Karl Barth, who at the same time – and thousands of miles away – had distanced himself from the cultural optimism and war enthusiasm of his liberal theological teachers. In the context of the history of Christianity in Africa and Asia, the end of the 'Christianity-Civilization' model had far-reaching consequences. After all, the perception of Christianity as an emancipatory force and a "ladder of ascent to civilization" – capable of bridging cultural differences and opening the way to participation and equality for ethnic groups at different stages of development – had been one of the decisive reasons for the attractiveness of the missionary message in times of colonial dominance. This foundation was now decisively weakened. At the same time, the insight to distinguish the preaching of the gospel from its Western-European form was also growing in missionary circles.

Notes to Chapter 16

1. Raupp (1910), *Mission in Quellentexten*, 418 ff. 412–435.
2. Document 108 in: Koschorke et al. (2016), *Discourses of Indigenous Christian Elites*, 124.
3. Burlacioiu (2015), „*Within three years*".
4. Koschorke (2019), *Erste Weltkrieg als moralische Katastrophe*, 123–142 (with detailed references); cf. Ludwig (2020), *First World War as a Turning Point*; Liebau (2010), *World in World Wars*.
5. Document 264 in: Koschorke et al. (2016), *Discourses of Indigenous Christian Elites*, 289.

Further Reading for Chapter 16

16.1 (Growing Colonial Rivalries)
Porter (2016), *European Imperialism;* Abernethy (2000), *European Overseas Empires*, 81ff. 87–103; Pakenham (1998), *Scramble for Africa;* Osterhammel (1997), *Colonialism*, 21ff; Iliffe (³2017), *Africans*, 201–227; Gründer (2003), *Expansion*, 154–177; Reinhard (1990), *Expansion* IV, 36–85; Reinhard (1996), *Kolonialismus*, 213 ff. 229–279; Fieldhouse (1965), *Kolonialreiche* 175 ff; Demel (1993), *Rassentheorien;* Van Laak (2005), *Über alles in der Welt;* Von Albertini (²1985), *Kolonialherrschaft;* Gründer/ Hiery (³2022), *Kolonien* (German colonialism).

16.2 (New Missionary Actors)
Ward (2017), *Missionary Movement*, 137ff; Cox (2008), *British Missionary Enterprise*, 169–212; Robert (2011), *Christian Mission;* Latourette (ᴿ1980), *Expansion of Christianity*. Vol. IV + V; Porter (2003), *Imperial Horizons;* Etherington (2009), *Missions and Empire;* Stanley (1990), *Bible and the Flag;* Gensichen (1976), *Missionsgeschichte*, 42 ff; Raupp (1990), *Mission in Quellentexten*, 412–434; Warneck (1880), *Missionsjahrhundert;* Gründer (1982), *Deutscher Imperialismus;* Gründer (1992), *Welteroberung*, 368 ff. 387 ff.519–567; Lessing et al. (2012), *German Protestant Church;* Tyrell (2004), *Weltmission*, 13–136; Stanley (2009), *Edinburgh 1910*.

16.3 + 4 (Indigenous Counter Movements, Multiplicity of Transregional and Transcontinental Networks)
Kalu (2005), *African Christianity*, 258–277. 309–332; Ludwig (2002), *African Independent Churches*, 259–272; Elphick (2012), *Equality of Believers;* Koschorke (2002), *Rise of National Church Movements*, 203–217; Koschorke (2018), *Dialectics of the Three Selves;* Koschorke (2018), *Christliche Internationalismen um 1910*, 261–282; Thomas (1979), *Christian Indians and Indian Nationalism*, 78 ff.146 ff; Ahn (2014), *Korea as an Early Missionary Center*, 99–110; Weber (1966), *Asia and the Ecumenical Movement;* Stanley (2009); *Edinburgh 1910;* Robert (2009), *Christian Mission*, 53–80; Lindenfeld (2021), *Indigenous Experience*, 106–116. 192–206; 230–244; Ludwig (2000), *Tambaram;* Prien (2013), *Latin America*, 374–386; Prien (1978), *Geschichte*, 798 ff (Panama-Congress 1916); Campbell (1998), *Songs of Zion;* Martin (1989), *Black Baptist and African Missions;* Engel (2015), *African American Missionaries;* Burlacioiu (2015), „*Within three years*" (on the ‚African Orthodox Church').

16.5 (The First World War as a Caesura and Moral Catastrophe)
Ludwig (2020), *First World War as a Turning Point;* Greschat (2014), *Erste Weltkrieg und die Christenheit*; Koschorke (2019), *Erste Weltkrieg als moralische Katastrophe*, 123–142; Schjørring (2018), *First World War,* 19–40; Negel/ Pinggéra (2016), *Urkatastrophe*; Hofmann (2006), *Armenien*; Hovannisian (2007), *Armenian genocide*; Liebau (2010), *World in World Wars*.

CHAPTER 17

Asia

17.1 Religious Nationalisms and Indigenization Experiments

Toward the end of the 19th century, Asia experienced a revival of the continent's traditional religions. In colonial Ceylon (Sri Lanka), for example, Buddhism had entered a phase of seemingly inexorable decline around the middle of the 19th century. Prominent followers even expected its extinction in the near future. A revitalization came about, among other reasons, through a series of Christian-Buddhist disputes in the 1870s [Text 52]. The revival was accelerated by the public conversion of the American theosophist H. S. Olcott in Colombo in 1880. Subsequently, what has been labelled in religio-sociological discourse as *'Protestant Buddhism'* developed – as a "modern" form of Buddhism, in *protest against* and, at the same time, in *imitation of* the forms and contents of missionary Protestantism. The rational elements of Buddhist teaching were now emphasized, the lay element strengthened, a Buddhist 'catechism' propagated, and 'Young Men Buddhist Associations' (YMBA's, instead of YMCA's) organized. Even 'Buddhist Sunday Schools' were established [see Text 64].

The situation in India was analogous. According to a missionary observer at the beginning of the 20th century, the most striking feature of the recent development was "the steady advance of the ancient faiths. ... Hinduism, Islam, Buddhism, Jainism and Zoroastrianism each leaped up into new vigorous activity, every prominent sect experiencing a mysterious awakening". Their propaganda techniques were "almost without exception ... borrowed from [the Christian] missions." Everything "Oriental" was now glorified and everything "Western" rejected [Text 63c]. Comparable observations were also made in other Asian countries, such as Burma, Thailand, Vietnam, Japan and China [Text 62]. This development was accelerated by the Russo-Japanese War of 1904/05, which was closely followed even by "remote villagers" in the far corners of Bengal [Text 65]. It was perceived as the victory of an "Oriental" nation over the "Christian" Tsarist Empire (and its religion). It spurred nationalist and pan-Asian movements across the continent. "Asia is one" was the battle cry that could now be heard in numerous regions.

In many regions, religious and national identity became closely intertwined. For many educated Indians, being a Hindu was now seen as a sign of patriotism, and nationally minded Sinhalese (or Chinese) were emphatically identified as followers of Buddhism (or Confucianism). Conversely, the accusation of "denationalization" was now leveled with increasing severity against the mission churches (and especially their indigenous members). Thus, for the first time, Christian communities – geographically dispersed and denominationally fragmented – in different cultural contexts in Asia were confronted with a common challenge. Since the turn of the century, this triggered manifold debates and the search for a "native form" and "national shape" of Christianity.

In detail, this Christian indigenization movement, which could be observed simultaneously or with a time lag in different regions, was characterized by various features. These included, first and foremost, cultural forms of expression (such as experiments in liturgy, church music and architecture, language, clothing, naming, etc.); references to an "Oriental Christ" to be regained from the West (who had "stolen" him); or – in the Indian context – early precursors of the Christian ashram movement [text 66–67]. Remarkable there was also the changed perception of the St. Thomas Christians. Previously often ridiculed as backward, they were now increasingly idealized as representatives of an original, pre-colonial and "native" Christianity.

One particular point of contention early on was the question of indigenous leadership and, in particular, the issue of a *native episcopate*. "It was acknowledged by all", was the complaint of an Indian Christian journal in 1899, "that India is sadly behind-hand as regards the Episcopate. No Native of the soil ... has yet been consecrated [sc. in the Anglican Church] bishop" [Text 67]. Yet, there existed alternative role models, as for example a look at West Africa and the black (assistant) bishops already working there demonstrated. "When is India to have her own native bishops?", another Indian-Christian journal (the 'Christian Patriot' published in Madras/Chennai) commented in 1898 on corresponding newspaper reports. Such demands had already been discussed since the 1870s, in the context of the debates about the "Three Selves". This was originally a missionary concept aimed at the establishment of a 'self-governing, self-financing and self-expanding' 'native church' as the final goal of all missionary work. Towards the end of the 19th century, these demands were increasingly delayed by conservative missionaries ("The time is not yet ripe"). Now, however, they gained renewed urgency through the reference to the African example. And conversely, when in 1912 with V.S. Azariah (1874–1945; Figure 39) – one of the Indian delegates at the World Missionary Conference Edinburgh 1910 – the first Asian Christian was consecrated bishop in the Anglican Church, the just mentioned 'Christian Patriot' put him in a row with "his great African predecessor Bishop [S.A.] Crowther" [see Figure 34].

17.2 Ecumenism as a Protest Movement, National Church Aspirations

The area where the "foreign", alien character of Protestant missionary Christianity was most directly visible was its denominational fragmentation. Especially in the large cities, there was an increasing number of competing mission churches, some of which already carried the indication of their foreign origin in their names. For why should an "Indian" Christian belong to the (Anglican) 'Church of England' or the (Lutheran) 'Danish Mission'? In 1813 only British missions, and since 1833 also the societies of other countries, had been allowed to work in colonial India. Thus, not only in certain regions, but sometimes even within Christian families, the broad denominational spectrum of mission Protestantism – Anglican, Presbyterian, Methodist, Lutheran, etc. – was to be encountered, and this partly even in its multiple national variants (such as British or American Methodists). Thus on Sundays, as one Indian Christian complained at a mission conference, his family members had to go to different churches.

"We hope for a time," said an Indian Christian journal in 1897, "when the deplorable sectarian differences which characterize our Western Christianity" shall be superseded by a freer and fuller growth of Christian doctrine and spiritual life [sc. in India] … We warn … not only against the English [Anglican] and Roman [Catholic], but also against the Scotch, German and American missions" [Text 69a]. From this attitude sprang a variety of initiatives aimed at developing an "Indian" Christianity in a "national" context (rather than denominational separation). The 'National Church of India' founded in Madras (Chennai) in 1886 by members of the South Indian Protestant elite has already been mentioned. It was not the first independent church foundation in Protestant India [cf. chapter 13.1.4], but it was the first with a "national" claim. Therefore, it sought to gradually unite "all" Indian Christians regardless of their denomination [Text 77]. Even if it did not achieve this goal, many initiatives with similar aims followed. So for example, the 'National Missionary Society of India' (NMS), founded in 1905 at a historical place (Serampore). As an interdenominational association of Indian Christians from different parts of the country and as an emancipatory act, it was of great importance – in addition to its evangelistic activities inside and outside India. Such undertakings also strengthened the urgency of trans-denominational cooperation within the Protestant mission churches.

Analogous efforts and national church movements also existed in other Asian countries. In China, after the so-called Boxer Rebellion in 1899/1900, Chinese Christians intensified their search for forms of church life outside missionary control. In 1906, a federation of mission-independent churches was formed under the name 'Chinese Christian Independent Church' (*Zhongguo Jidujiao zilihui*)- It grew to 330 member congregations in various parts of the country by 1924. In Japan, the rapid growth of the Protestant community since the 1880s was in any case largely due to the involvement of educated lay activists (mostly with samurai backgrounds). Kanzo Uchimura's 'Non-Church' movement (*Mukyôkai*), founded in 1901 (and still in existence today), was an expression of the desire not to belong as a Christian to any mission-led and denominationally determined church organization [Text 78; Figure 41]. Mission-independent efforts also formed in Burma, early on in colonial Sri Lanka [Text 76], and in other countries. The most prominent example in Catholic Asia has been the 'Iglesia Filipina Independiente'. Founded in 1902, in the aftermath of the Philippines' anti-Spanish liberation struggle, it temporarily comprised up to 25% of the archipelago's population. It remains the largest non-Roman Catholic church in the country [Text 79].

One of the most astonishing phenomena in Christian Asia at the beginning of the 20th century has been the multitude of *indigenous missionary initiatives*. They were mostly related to debates about the "Three Selves," that is, the goal of a self-governing, self-financing, and self-expanding "Native church". Originally a missionary concept (formulated by pioneers such as the Briton Henry Venn [1796–1873] and the U.S. American Rufus Anderson [1796–1880]), the formula – in the face of missionary reluctance to grant participation – increasingly mutated into an emancipatory slogan of indigenous Christian elites at the end of the 19th century. The field of action where this formula could be implemented most quickly was the postulate of "self-propagation". For India, the example of the 'National Missionary Society', founded in 1905, has already been mentioned. This in turn was inspired by the example of the 'Jaffna Student Foreign Missionary Society', founded in 1900 by Sri Lankan Christians, which soon sent missionaries of its own to Tamils in South India and South Africa. At the 1907 Tokyo conference of the 'Student World Christian Federation' (the first Christian conference in Asia with a majority of Asian delegates), Japanese representatives emphasized the "commitment of Japanese Christians to the evangelization of Formosa [Taiwan], Korea, Manchuria, and North China."[1] The Protestant churches of Korea, which had been founded only a short time before, were already sending their own evangelists to compatriots in the Korean diaspora in Siberia, Manchuria, Japan, Hawaii, California, and Mexico in 1910. At the same time, direct contacts between the Asian churches also increased. In 1906, for example, a Japanese delegation visited India at Indian invitation. It attracted great attention and strengthened the "fraternal bonds" between the Christians of both nations.

The enormous importance of the Edinburgh World Missionary Conference of 1910 – both as the peak of the Protestant missionary movement of the 19th century and as the starting point of the Western ecumenical movement of the 20th century – has already been mentioned [see chapter 16.4]. It reacted in a hitherto singular way to developments and controversies in the overseas churches as well as to the "awakening of great nations" in Asia (and Africa) [Text 70b]. The number of Asian delegates in Edinburgh was admittedly very limited (18). However, they were given prominent places in the conference program. Later, they occupied important leadership positions in their home churches – for example, V. S. Azariah (1974–1945) in India, Cheng Jingyi (1881–1939) in China, and Harada Tasuku (1863–1940) in Japan.

Impulses from the emerging Asian ecumenical movement were taken up in Edinburgh and returned to Asia in increased form. Initially, this happened mainly in the series of the 21 Continuation Conferences that took place in seven Asian countries in 1912/13. Topics were – so at the National China Conference in Shanghai in March 1913 – the promotion of the "unity of the Church of Christ in China", the development of the "indigenous character" of the churches, self-administration of the congregations as well as the promotion of "Chinese Christian leadership". Emphasis was placed on the necessary "freedom of development in form and organization" in order to "develop natural expressions of the spiritual instincts of Chinese Christians" [Text 71].

A concrete consequence of the Asian Continuation Conferences was the formation of 'National Missionary Councils' (now in a national instead of denominational framework), which later (since 1923) were transformed into 'National Christian Councils' (NCC). In India, for example, this was combined with the provision that half of the seats in the NCC were to be reserved for indigenous members. This laid the foundations for a cross-denominational self-organization of the Asian churches. After the Second World War, this self-organization reached its first peak with the founding of the Church of South India (CSI) in 1947. All in all, the Asian ecumenical movement achieved a disproportionately higher dynamic compared to that of the Western world. Unlike for the churches of Europe – according to one prominent representative –, church union was regarded a "necessity for survival" by Asian Christians.

17.3 Developments in Catholic Asia

While Edinburgh in 1910 marked a first high point of intra-Protestant globalization, and accelerated cooperation among related churches in Asia (through the network of 'National Missionary [or National Christian] Councils' that had been established since 1913 respectively 1923), important centralization processes in Catholic Asia took place during the pontificate of Pope Leo XIII (1878–1903). In 1886, a unified ecclesiastical hierarchy was established in India for the first time, including the archdiocese of Goa, which remained under the Portuguese Patroado. In addition, six new archdioceses were created, as well as other dioceses that were now directly subordinated to the 'Propaganda Fide' in Rome [Text 73]. Thus the decades-long so-called Propaganda-Padroado conflict – between the Roman curia and Portugal, which insisted on its traditional patronage rights [see Text 8] – was in principle ended and the resulting local schisms defused. In Japan, a proper ecclesiastical hierarchy was established in 1891, with a metropolitan in Tokyo and three suffragan bishops. Korea was initially assigned to the Japanese province, but was then separated in 1894 and assigned to the Chinese region. In China, five regional synods were held for the first time in 1880. Since 1891, a representative of the Apostolic See resided in Beijing.

In 1919, Pope Benedict XV (1914–1922) issued the missionary encyclical 'Maximum Illud'. As a consequence of the sad experiences of the First World War, he emphasized the "absolute necessity" of the formation of an indigenous clergy and the establishment of an indigenous episcopate. The first steps were taken under his successor Pius XI (1922–1939). He consecrated six Chinese priests as bishops in St. Peter's Basilica in 1926 [Text 74]. By 1940 there were already twenty native bishops in China. 1927 also saw the consecration of the first Japanese bishop. Already in 1924 the first (and so far last) Chinese National Council had been held in Shanghai. Such a plenary council for China had been discussed again and again since the 1890s. So far, however, it had failed due to the opposition of France, which invoked its mission protectorate acquired as part of the "unequal treaties" in the mid-19th century. The independence of the mission in the face of quasi-colonial dependence, the relationship between native and foreign priests, and the gradual transfer of leadership positions into Chinese hands were important topics of the National Council, which at the same time was still strongly influenced by European dominance.

However, another important question was deliberately left out of the council deliberations; "like a wasp's nest": the old controversy about the "Chinese rites". The ban of these rites by Pope Benedict XIV in 1742 [Text 28] had significantly hindered the development of a culturally adapted Chinese Catholicism. It is true that the so-called Oath of Rites decreed by the Pope at that time for missionaries (and since 1895 also obligatory for native priests) was again formally confirmed in Shanghai in 1924. In 1939, however, it was officially revoked by Rome. Because, according to the reasons given by the 'Propaganda Fide' in its instruction 'Plane compertum est' of December 8, 1939 addressed to the Chinese church: "With the changes in customs and thinking over the course of centuries [these ceremonies] retained merely a civil [sc. and no religious] significance (civilem tantum significationem) of piety towards the ancestors or of love of the fatherland or of courtesy towards one's neighbor" [Text 75]. A 300-year series of ecclesiastical pronouncements on the question of Chinese rites thus came to a close – amid the turmoil of the undeclared Japanese-Chinese War. This statement was preceded in 1936 and 1935 by similar declarations relating to Japan and Manchuria, which also emphasized the civil character of Confucius and ancestor worship.

17.4 Between World War I and World War II

The change of mood that the First World War triggered in the Asian public as a moral catastrophe of Europe and European Christianity has already been discussed. The loss of prestige of the West was aggravated by the disappointment over the 'Fourteen Points' of the American President Woodrow Wilson of 1918. For the right of self-determination of the peoples promised there as a principle of a just post-war order was denied to the colonized nations of Asia and Africa. Especially in *China*, there were fierce protests against the 1919 Treaty of Versailles, which were increasingly also directed against the missionaries as "agents of imperialism and capitalism". This so-called "Anti-Christian movement" gained popularity, especially among students and intellectuals [Text 81]. It proceeded in various waves and reached a peak in 1924/1925 (and then again in 1927). Points of contention included the extraterritoriality of missionary institutions and Chinese control of missionary schools. This mainly affected Protestant educational institutions in the cities. The Catholics, on the other hand, were more present in the countryside.

The situation in *Korea* was quite different. Here, the rapidly expanding Protestant community developed early into a bearer of a Korean national consciousness. Korea had been a Japanese protectorate since 1905 and was formally occupied by Japan in 1910. Christian groups played a defining role in the country's independence movement from the beginning. On March 1, 1919, a declaration of independence by the Korean people was read in Seoul, accompanied by nationwide demonstrations. Of the 33 signatories, 16 were Korean church leaders. At the same time, large protest meetings were also held in Pyongyang on church property, led by Presbyterian and Methodist ministers [Text 80a]. Earlier, in February 1919, the Korean YMCA in Tokyo had proclaimed the country's independence. Through Christian networks, the movement spread rapidly. Korean Protestants also used their international connections, for example, to win over the American public to the national cause.

The Japanese occupiers cruelly crushed the independence movement. In the village of Cheamri, for example, "all adult male Christians" and other activists were rounded up in the village church on April 15, 1919. The soldiers then set fire to the church [Text 80b; Figure 43; Photo D15–17]. Phases of less brutal colonial and "cultural" policies followed, which in turn were later replaced by increased repression, especially after the introduction of compulsory Shinto ceremonies in 1925 and 1937, respectively. Many Christian patriots fled abroad. Rhee Syng-man, a Protestant, became president of the provisional government-in-exile. In any case, the Christian movement in Korea, unlike in China, for example, was perceived as an ally (rather than an opponent) of national aspirations. At the same time, this may have become a major factor in its later explosive growth.

In *Japan* itself, the churches counted only a small number of baptized members in the 1920s. The circle of sympathizers was incomparably larger. In politics and society, militaristic tendencies intensified from the end of the 1920s, with growing pressure on the Christian community to adapt. A decisive voice of protest from a Christian perspective came from Toyohiko Kagawa (1888–1960), prominent as a social activist, evangelist and pacifist. In 1928 he was among the co-founders of the 'National Anti-War League'. In 1940 he was arrested for apologizing in China for the Japanese invasion. Evangelism and social reform belonged closely together for him. Because only a large number of believers, , he was convinced, could initiate a moral, social and political transformation of national life. With Japan's entry into the war (against China in 1937 and against the United States and its allies in 1941), the government also tightened its control of religious organizations. Thus, under pressure, 34 Protestant denominations joined together in 1941 to form the 'United Church of Christ in Japan' (*Nihon Kirisuto Kyôdan*) [Text 84]. It had to conform to national laws in other ways as well. After 1945, the Kyôdan continued to exist, albeit in a modified form.

In the territories occupied by Japan, the Christian communities were subjected to severe persecution in some cases. This was the case in *Taiwan*, which had already been annexed in 1895, [Text 85] or in the Philippines and Indonesia, where the Japanese had been advancing since 1941/42. Elsewhere, native Christians were forced to collaborate. Japanese clerics were used in "civilizing" missions. In the *Philippines* – the Asian nation with the highest number of Catholics – the gradual transition from American colonial rule to political independence had already begun in 1935. In the majority Protestant churches of *Indonesia*, ties with the Dutch colonial administration were loosened in the

1930s and the establishment of autonomous regional churches was pushed forward.

In 1938, a large international mission conference took place in *Tambaram* (near Madras/Chennai) in southern India – so to say a Christian Mini-UNO on the eve of the Second World War [see Figure 44]. It was not only the choice of the conference venue that indicated the growing importance of Asia in the global Protestant ecumenism. Also, for the first time, a slight majority of the delegates came from the so-called 'young churches' of the Global South, which sought to introduce their own issues and perspectives into the debates. Already in the run-up to the conference, a group of critical Indian Christians spoke out energetically on the conference theme – the relationship between Christianity and culture [Text 83a]. Africans sought to put specifically African concerns (such as the biblical right of polygamy) on the agenda. At the same time, they used the conference for direct contacts with Asian church leaders [Text 185] and – so for example the South African pastor S. S. Tema – also for discussions with Mahatma Gandhi. Such experiences at the same time changed the perception of their own home churches. The South African women's representative Mina Soga and the later ANC politician Albert Luthuli [see Figure 51], for example, returned from India as resolute critics of the conditions in their home country.

The Indian bishop V. S. Azariah (1874–1945; Figure 39) was exceptionally impressed above all "by the ecumenical character of the assembly." "The fellowship in Christ which leapt over barriers of race, language, and denomination was most inspiring. At the Christmas celebration, I noticed the South African White and the South African Bantu and Negro, the Chinese and the Japanese, the Burmese and the Indian, the French and German delegates kneeling side by side before the symbols of our redemption. Where would such a thing be possible except at the foot of the cross?" [Text 83b].

Footnote to Chapter 17

1. See Koschorke (2014), *Polycentric Structures*, 15–28 (quotation on p. 25).

Further Reading for Chapter 17

17.1 (Religious Nationalisms and Indigenization Experiments)
Gombrich/ Obeyesekere (1988), *Buddhism Transformed*, 202–241 („Protestant Buddhism"); Beckerlegge (2008), *Religious Reform Movements*; Kopf (1979),

Brahmo Samaj; Thomas (1979), *Christian Indians and Indian Nationalism,* 85ff. 159ff; Lindenfeld (2021), *Indigenous Experience,* 192–199; Koschorke (2019), „*Christian Patriot",* 96–112;

17.2 (*Ecumenism as a Protest Movement, National Church Movements*)

Weber (1966), *Asia and the Ecumenical Movement*; Thomas (1979), *Christian Indians and Indian Nationalism,* 66 ff.78 ff.146 ff; Stanley (2009), *Edinburgh 1910,* 91–166; 303 ff; Koschorke (2002), *Rise of National Church Movements,* 203–217; Koschorke (2019), „*Christian Patriot",* 211–249; Sonntag (2018), *Christian Patriotism and Japanese Expansionism,* 285–298.

17.3 (*Developments in Catholic Asia*)

Phan (2018), *Asia in the 20th Century,* 396–421; Metzler (1980), *Synoden in China, Japan und Korea,* 181–225; Minamiki (1985), *Chinese Rites Controversy,* 183–204; Frykenberg (2008), *Christianity in India,* 350–379.

17.4 (*Between World War I and World War II*)

Harper (2000), *Bishop V. S. Azariah,* 138–366; Bays (2012), *New History,* 107–112; Bays (1996), *Christianity in China,* 307–337; Kim/Kim (2015), *Korean Christianity,* 107–156; Iglehart (1960), *Japan,* 164–257; Drummond (1971), *Christianity in Japan,* 220–269.320–326.352–359; Sonntag (2018), *Christian Patriotism and Japanese Expansionism,* 285–298; Aritonang/ Steenbrink (2008), *Christianity in Indonesia,* 175 ff; Ludwig (2000), *Tambaram,* 26–78. 86–196.311 ff.; Ellsberg (1991), *Gandhi on Christianity.*

CHAPTER 18

Africa

18.1 The Christian Missions and the "Scramble for Africa"

In the last quarter of the 19th century, the race of rival European powers to Africa ("scramble for Africa") intensified. At the Berlin Conference on the Congo in 1884/85, the colonial powers agreed on principles for the division of the continent. This was effectively completed by about 1900. Instead of a multitude of African small states or settlement areas, henceforth only seven colors – those of the colonial British, French, Portuguese, Spanish, and newly also the Germans, Italians and Belgians – determined the political map of Africa. "White" (and thus free from European colonial rule) remained only the Christian empire of Ethiopia as well as the Republic of Liberia, founded by African-American remigrants [see Map 16]. In Germany, colonial propagandists such as Friedrich Fabri had already called for English-style imperial expansion and "a new India" under German rule in Africa in the late 1870s [Text 167c]. With the establishment of its "protectorates" in Togo, Cameroon, German Southwest Africa (Namibia), and German East Africa (in the area of present-day Tanzania, Rwanda, and Burundi) since 1884, the German Empire, proclaimed in 1871, now also attained its "place under the sun" of colonialism.

The mostly arbitrary drawing of colonial borders created new territorial units, the cause of numerous conflicts even decades later in post-colonial times. Existing settlements were often torn apart, different ethnic groups amalgamated into peoples, and tribal affiliations were arbitrarily determined by the colonial administration. In many cases, colonial rule was not exercised directly, but rather through a system of "indirect rule", if only to save costs. This was the case in British-controlled Nigeria, where local government was largely left to native authorities – both traditional and invented ones. In the north of the country, for example, this led to the rise of Muslim emirs (local rulers) to power over previously non-Islamic ethnic groups.

With the acquisition of its own colonies, a new type of colonial mission emerged in the German Empire. For example, the 'Deutsch-Ostafrikanische Evangelische Missionsgesellschaft' (Berlin III) was established in Berlin in 1886. It sought to offer the "German missionary" the opportunity "to work where his fatherland was beginning to lay down new roots. No longer will a foreign country, hostile to all German efforts, reap what German diligence and German labor have sown" [Text 167d]. The majority of German Protestant societies, on the other hand, emphasized the "international character of the mission" as in the decades before [Text 167e]. In general, the various colonial powers had committed themselves in the Congo Act of 1885 to admit missionaries of other nationalities to their territories.

At the same time, however, missions from their own country continued to be regarded in many cases as useful helpers in establishing and consolidating colonial rule. They often behaved accordingly. This was especially true where confessional and national identities were closely intertwined. For example, the tricolor flew above every French mission station in what is now Congo-Brazzaville. The goal was to spread "the cross", i.e. the Catholic faith, "and the name of France". Until the French government officially took possession, "the honor of the French flag" was to be maintained. At the same time, the aim was to keep Protestants (and British colonial rivals) out in the race of the missions.[1] Elsewhere, it was Protestant actors who received support from the respective colonial power. In Portuguese territories (such as Mozambique), Catholic missions were granted the "character of national institutions" [Text 167g]. At the same time, they were massively privileged compared to Protestant ventures.

In detail, the relationship of the various missions to the colonial authorities varied greatly. They ranged from servile submissiveness to mistrust and open opposition. A crucial difference lay in whether or not the mission in question had been active in the country for any length of time before colonial rule began. Where it had already established a deeper connection with the local population, it could become – as in the case of the Scottish Blantyre Mission in present-day Malawi – a fierce critic of colonial exploitation. In other cases, missions limited themselves to a protest against individual grievances (such as the brandy trade, fraudulent lending, coercive measures, etc.), which, however, did not call into question the fundamental welcoming of the "blessings" of European rule. The call for colonial state intervention could be motivated by missionary self-interest as well as humanitarian motives – for example, to protect local ethnic groups from the uncontrolled intrusion of European adventurers (as in Uganda). An important factor was also the change in colonial state religious policy. France's intensified anticlerical course since 1905, for example, significantly restricted the activities of Catholic orders in French territories (such as Madagascar).

The motives and objectives of missionary actors were as varied as their relationship to the colonial state. Both the British and the French liked to use the civilization paradigm. This could have quite opposite effects. On the one hand, it often served only to legitimize colonial occupation and the suppression of indigenous resistance. On the other hand, however, it contained an emancipatory aspect – in contrast to the rampant Social Darwinism of numerous

European settlers who, for example, declared missionary educational efforts for blacks in South Africa to be superfluous. For it opened up the prospect of "climbing up the ladder" of civilizational progress. It was precisely this perspective of advancement – later often denied to them – that African educated elites were to refer to vehemently in the period that followed. "That the African is capable", said the head of the Anglican 'Church Missionary Society' in 1890, "of adopting Christianity and taking his place among the first peoples, I consider an indisputable fact. We have only to think of what Europe was at the beginning of our era," that is, in times of pre-Christian paganism and horrendous barbarism. "The task to be solved and the preconditions of the same were [then] quite the same in Europe as we find today in Africa" [Text 167b]. Overcoming civilizational differences among the peoples of the southern hemisphere was thus also considered a central goal of missionary work.

German colonial rule was short-lived (from 1884 to 1914/19). Its effects, however, were highly fatal. In 1904/07, what has been called the first genocide of the 20th century took place in German Southwest Africa (today Namibia): the suppression of the Herero and Nama uprising, which was carried out with the aim of "extermination". It claimed about 50,000 to 70,000 lives. Previously, Rhenish missionaries working there had supported the establishment of German rule. On the other hand, they referred to the social and economic background of the uprising, which is why they were attacked in the colonial press as "enemies" of the German colonists: "The mission has become black and stands against the whites in the protectorate" [Text 168a]. After the suppression of the uprising in 1907, there were mass defections of socially uprooted and culturally disoriented Africans to the mission churches. These often offered the only social framework that kept certain possibilities of social reorganization open to them.

18.2 The Emergence of African Independent Churches

Since the 1890s, mission-independent churches under black leadership began to form – initially spontaneously and independently of each other – in western and southern Africa. This happened in reaction to the growing paternalism (and increasingly racism) in parts of the missionary community and changed the profile of African Christianity in the long run. The formation of these 'African Independent (or Initiated) Churches' (AIC's) occurred in waves. While the black churches of the first wave were distinguished from the former white mother churches primarily by their African leadership, but otherwise often still largely retained their confessional and liturgical traditions, a second wave – beginning around 1910 – was carried primarily by charismatic personalities who moved through the country, baptizing and gathering a growing following. In this second phase, elements of traditional African religiosity – such as visions, prayer healings or dance – were also much more strongly incorporated. At the same time, fetishes were burned and the Bible was taught.

The *first wave* in West Africa was triggered by the controversies surrounding the deposition of S.A. Crowther (c. 1806/08–1891). The first black bishop in modern times – symbol of the hopes for advancement of Western-educated elites throughout the continent – had, as already mentioned, not been formally deposed toward the end of his ministry, but his powers had been increasingly restricted [see chap. 14.5; Text 150.160]. Most importantly, he was given a white successor instead of a black one in 1891, a fact that provoked strong protests in the British possessions along the West African coast. Crowther's ouster was understood as an attack on the rights of "all Africans" – such was the angry reaction in the black press of West Africa, the majority of which was in the hands of native Christians. As a result, a variety of mission-independent churches (such as Mojola Agbebi's [1860–1917] 'African Church' [Text 170d] in 1901) were formed, which soon also networked or – such as the 'African Communion of Independent Churches' in 1913 – formed supra-regional structures.

At the same time, there was a split within the Methodist mission church in South Africa. The reason was the discrimination of native clergy like Mangena Mokone (1851–1931), who founded the 'Ethiopian Church' in Pretoria in 1892 [Figure 36]. This was by no means the first black church in South Africa, but it was the first to call itself 'Ethiopian'. In this it became the model for numerous other mission-independent church foundations. In the years that followed, South Africa developed into a hotspot of *Ethiopianism* – viewed with suspicion by missionaries and colonial authorities. "They go about preaching the doctrine of equality" [Text 171c]. They found followers among Western-educated Africans as well as migrant workers who flocked from far and wide to the country's mining fields and nascent industrial centers. In 1896, Mokone's 'Ethiopian Church' joined the African-American 'African Methodist Episcopal Church' (AME), founded in Philadelphia in 1816, making it even more of a transatlantic movement than before [Figure 37]. Other transatlantic church foundations by black Christians (such as the 'African Orthodox Church' in 1921ff) followed [cf. Text 174].

The reference to Ethiopia as a symbol of redemption for black people has a long history. It can already be found at the end of the 18th century in the African-American communities of the Caribbean and southern USA and goes back, among other things, to certain biblical passages. The promise in Psalm 68:32 ("Ethiopia will stretch out her hands to God," according to the English King James Bible) has been particularly significant. Since the 1880s, this "Ethiopian discourse" also played an increasingly important role in the emancipatory debates of African Christians [Text 171b]. It intensified again massively after 1896, when Christian Ethiopia repulsed the Italian invaders at the height of European colonialism [Figure 35; Photo F15/16; Map 16 + 17]. Ethiopia – black, Christian, free – was henceforth regarded as a symbol both of ecclesiastical and political independence. In the ears of African Christians, the name often had the same magical sound as "Jerusalem". Ethiopianists increasingly articulated political demands ("Africa for the Africans"), supported independent evangelistic activities – both intra-African as well as transatlantic – [cf. Text 170a] and were closely connected with the beginnings of a Christian Pan-Africanism. Ethiopianist ideas, however, became popular also within the established mission churches.

The *second wave* of African independentism emerged from a charismatic renewal. At its center were often personalities who enjoyed a reputation as prophets. In addition to visions, healing of the sick through prayer also played an important role. The movement was very heterogeneous in itself, but in many places it spread much faster than the mission churches. At the same time, the founding of churches of their own was often not the result of deliberate planning and took place only in a later phase or in areas without a Western missionary presence.

William Wadé Harris (1865–1929) from Liberia, for example – raised by a Methodist minister and for a time a teacher in an Anglican school – is considered probably the most successful evangelist in West Africa in this period. In 1910, while in prison, he experienced a "calling" to be a prophet by the archangel Gabriel. After his release, he discarded European clothing and roamed the Ivory Coast and parts of Ghana in white robes as a preacher of repentance. Crowds flocked to him because of his reputation as a miracle worker. Between 1912 and 1914, he is said to have baptized between 100,000 and 120,000 people within a few months. He preached the Ten Commandments to his hearers, inculcated Sunday sanctification, and called for the destruction of idols. Other traditional lifestyles, however, such as polygamy, were not condemned. The newly baptized were exhorted to join the mission churches of their respective homelands (which caused a considerable influx among both Catholics and Methodists). In other regions, however, separate "Harris" congregations were quickly formed and subsequently experienced tremendous growth.

In Nigeria, it was *Garrick Sokari Braide* (c. 1885–1918) who triggered mass conversions from c. 1912 [Text 173]. Active as an Anglican evangelist, he soon gained a reputation as a gifted miracle worker and prophet. He fought traditional religion, had its cult objects burned, and challenged the traditional "rain doctors" to a contest, which he defeated by invoking the Christian God.

His followers therefore celebrated him as the "second Eliah". Around 1915, he broke with the Anglican missionary church. Numerous congregations in the Niger Delta followed Braide. The British colonial authorities also took action against him. One of the accusations related to the decline in taxes on imported alcohol, which he had campaigned against. Followers of Braide founded the 'Christ Army Church' in 1916, a new denomination that, among other things, approved polygamy. Later, his movement disintegrated into various factions that persist to this day in southeastern Nigeria (as well as an internationalized community).

In South Africa, *Isaiah Shembe* (ca. 1865–1935) became the founder of the *Ibandla lamaNazaretha*, the largest African-initiated church of its time. Shembe – who had been baptized in the 'African Native Baptist Church' in 1906 – started his religious career around 1910 as an itinerant evangelist and so-called faith healer [Text 172]. Within ten years he gathered a large following in Natal, with dozens of congregations scattered throughout the province. The center became the 'holy' city of eKuphakemeni in an area free from white control. The 'Shembe Church' eventually reached a membership of over one million before disintegrating into rival groups in the 1980s.

Singular in various respects is the history of the Kimbanguist Church in Belgian Congo (Zaire). It goes back to the public activity of *Simon Kimbangu* (1899–1951), which lasted only one year. Through a spiritual vocation experience, he knew himself commissioned by Jesus Christ personally to continue his work. For "disturbing public order" and endangering the colonial economy, he was sentenced to death by a Belgian military court on October 3, 1921, but was subsequently "pardoned" to life imprisonment. His movement continued to live underground and, during periods of persecution (which did not officially end until 1958), spread not only throughout Belgian Congo territory but also to various neighboring countries. From about 100,000 in 1959, the number of members currently grew to several million. Here, too, various splits occurred after Kimbangu's death in 1951. As the first African-independent church, the 'Église des Jésus Christ sur la terre par le prophète Simon Kimbangu' was admitted to the World Council of Churches in 1959. In the early 2000s, however, its membership was suspended (and definitely terminated in 2021).

Of particular importance were also the so-called *Aladura churches*, which were established from the 1920s. *Aladura* is a Yoruba word meaning prayer. The prayer groups and churches designated by this collective term (such as the 'Christ Apostolic Church', which split off from the Anglicans in the 1920s) first spread in Nigeria and, since the 1970s, increasingly in the international African diaspora. There were also various contacts with the contemporary U.S.

Pentecostal movement. African historians emphasize the independent roots of these early African churches.

18.3 Themes of the Twenties and Thirties

The end of World War I did not bring an end to European colonial rule in Africa. Rather, it continued under a different name and the aegis of the 'League of Nations' founded in 1919 – as so-called (A,) B and C mandates. However, certain minimum standards for 'acceptable rule' were now established. The former German colonies were divided up and went partly to France and England (Cameroon, Togo, Tanganyika) or to Belgium (Rwanda, Burundi). Namibia, the former German Southwest Africa, was declared a mandate territory of South Africa. This country had attained semi-autonomous status within the British Empire in 1910 as the Union of South Africa.

In terms of mission history, the 1920s and 1930s were characterized for the first time by a new Catholic dominance ("Catholic breakthrough").[2] The Protestant missions – weakened by the economic consequences of World War I, dwindling support from the home countries and the growth of independentist movements within the established mission churches – lost the dominant position they had attained as pioneers of evangelization on the continent in the 19th century. Conversely, the new missionary policy of the popes (Benedict XV [1914–1922] and Pius XI [1922–1939]; s. ch. 17.3) had a beneficial effect in Africa as in Asia. A growing number of Catholic missionaries flocked to the continent. This happened both through the sending of new congregations and orders – not previously active in Africa – and through increased activities of the societies already established there (such as the Capuchins, Jesuits or White Fathers). Increased efforts were now also made within Catholicism to form an indigenous clergy. In 1931, for example, the first ordination of an African to priesthood took place in Basutoland [Text 179]. In 1939, Joseph Kiwanuka, the first Catholic African bishop of modern times, was consecrated in Uganda (he served until 1966, finally as Archbishop of Rubaga). This happened three quarters of a century after the consecration of the Anglican S.A. Crowther in 1864 as Africa's first black bishop in modern times.

An important factor in Catholic success was the new commitment to *education*. Protestants continued to set the tone in higher education, with institutions such as Lovedale in South Africa, the Hope Waddel Institute in Nigeria, and Achimota College in Ghana [Text 181c and 186; Photo G18]. In elementary and secondary education, however, Catholics gradually caught up with Protestant competitors, laying the groundwork for later growth. Earlier plain "bush schools" (usually run by a catechist) were increasingly transformed into elementary schools with a teacher in the 1920s, and former training centers for catechists were transformed into teacher seminaries [cf. Text 179]. After the elementary schools were established, middle schools then began to be established, usually with colonial government support. A first Catholic university was established in Lesotho in 1945, and another in Kinshasa (Congo) in 1949. From the beginning of the century, there were also the first examples of modern schools founded by Africans. In 1900, for example, the Ohlange High School in Durban was founded by John Dube (1871–1946), a pastor's son and later president of the (South) African National Congress. It was inspired by the model of Tuskegee College in the U.S., an African-American initiative where students were educated in a Christian spirit and an ethic of hard work.

In 1912, the forerunner of the later African National Congress (ANC) was founded in South Africa. It was largely supported by the country's black Christian educated elite. Among the ANC's lesser-known activities were intermittent efforts to establish an interdenominational national church in South Africa. Overcoming the denominational boundaries imported by the missionaries was also otherwise the subject of various local grassroots initiatives in the 1920s. In 1920, for example, a conference of South African Christians demanded "that all natives should unite and form a national native church" [Text 182].

It was not only the various mission churches that experienced considerable growth in the interwar years. For example, there were about 10 million Christians in Africa in 1910, about 16 million in 1930 and about 34 million in 1950.[3] Islam also continued to spread under European colonial rule in the interior of the continent – in part directly promoted by the system of 'indirect rule', which gave local chiefs far-reaching rights. In French territories, moreover, it was often the anti-clerical attitudes of local colonial officials that encouraged the further advance of the Prophet's religion. So-called traditional African religions and cults were in retreat in many places. At the same time, a dispute often flared up in the missionary communities over the – Christian – validity of certain traditions that had been rejected by earlier missionaries as pagan or inhumane but were defended by African Christians as part of their cultural heritage. These included certain initiation rites, practices such as the cultic drinking of beer, the bride price, or – according to a controversy bitterly fought in colonial Kenya in the 1920s/30s – the widespread custom of female circumcision (or genital mutilation). This debate also led to secessions from the Anglican Church.

Another tradition disputed between missionaries and African Christians was that of *polygamy*. Rejected by the early missionaries as contradicting the will of God revealed in the New Testament, it was later defended by African

Christians in many new ways. This was after reading the Old Testament (now also translated by the missionaries and their "helpers"), which speaks of anointed kings like David or Solomon, who led a life pleasing to God and yet had many wives. Biblical tradition thus supported the African – polygamous – order of life, while monogamy increasingly came under suspicion of being "only the white man's custom." Numerous foundations of independent churches were based precisely on two issues: the question of African leadership and the validity of polygamy. That this problem was also virulent in established circles is shown by the history of the 1938 World Missionary Conference in Tambaram, South India, which was also attended by a delegation of West African Christians [see chap. 17.4]. The leading figure was the Presbyterian minister Christian Goncalves Kwami Baëta (1908–1994) from present-day Ghana [see Figure 53]. He traveled to Tambaram with the intention of presenting this very question – about the biblical right of polygamy – to the ecumenical assembly there. Prior to that, he had coordinated with representatives of other Christian communities in a tour along the Gold Coast that lasted several weeks. To be sure, the West African delegation's push in Tambaram on the marriage issue was unsuccessful. As an early African initiative in global ecumenism, however, it remains highly remarkable.[4]

In 1935, fascist Italy invaded Ethiopia again – after the ignominious defeat in 1896. The Italian occupiers proceeded with extreme brutality, but could not effectively suppress the resistance of local guerrillas. The invasion triggered a wave of international solidarity with Ethiopia, not only on the African continent but also in India and other Asian countries. In the United States, African-American dockworkers refused to unload Italian ships. Pope Pius XI – who refrained from any moral condemnation during the fighting – experienced sharp criticism for this in the West African press [Text 183]. In 1941, British troops and native resistance drove the Italians out of the country – a foretaste of the process of decolonization in Africa in the 1960s.

18.4 Christian Elites and the Political Independence Movements

"The Second World War," according to Africa historian Christoph Marx, "completed what the First had begun: the delegitimization of colonial rule."[5] In the political emancipation processes that followed, Christian educated elites often played a leading role, especially in the British-controlled territories of Equatorial Africa.

In South Africa, however, forms of modern self-organization were used early on, especially by educated African Christians. For example, the 'Natal Native

Congress', founded in 1900, or the forerunner of the later so named 'African National Congress (ANC), established in 1912. Among the pioneers and leaders of the ANC were, for example, from 1912 to 1917 the already mentioned John Dube, founding member and son of a Congregationalist pastor, or later Albert Luthuli (1898–1967), son of a Methodist lay preacher, South African participant in the 1938 Tambaram World Missionary Conference and from 1952–1967 president of the ANC [see Figure 51]. In Nyasaland (now Malawi), it was a Baptist preacher, John Chilembwe (1871–1915), who became the leader of a (suppressed) first anti-colonial uprising in 1915. He is still honored in Malawi today with an annual memorial day as a "Hero of Independence." With a view to West Africa, the Nigerian historian E.A. Ayandele noted as early as 1966 that the church and the black press had already become the "cradle" of a rapidly developing national consciousness in educated circles by the end of the 19th century.[6] Herbert Macaulay (1864–1967), for example, can be considered the most influential representative of Nigerian nationalism in the 1920s and early 1930s: He was a graduate of a missionary school, grandson of the famous black bishop S.A. Crowther, and brother of the co-founder of a mission-independent black church.

It was, among others, the modern historian Horst Gründer who pointed out the formative relevance of mission schools in the formation of an anti-colonial elite, which then led African countries to independence in the 1950s (Ghana in 1957) and especially in the 1960s. Personalities such as Nmamdi Azikiwe (1904–96), first president of Nigeria (r. 1963–1966), Kwame Nkruhmah (1909–1972), leader of independent Ghana (r. 1957–1966), Julius K. Nyere (1922–1999), first president of Tanzania (r. 1964–1985), or Hastings Kamazu Banda (c. 1898/1907–1997), first prime minister and then president of Malawi from 1964 to1994, were each graduates of (or teachers at) Protestant or Catholic mission schools or other Christian educational institutions. The missionaries of the pre-war and post-war periods were mostly conservative and warned against premature independence. But what Gründer called the "dialectic of Christianization" was now at work.

> Central institution in this process of political-social change was the missionary school ... Against the expressed will of many missionaries and missionary leaderships, who rejected too early emancipation, missionary schools ultimately became catalysts of national emancipation and social progress" ... "The teaching of Christianity and missionary school education possessed not only a system-immanent significance in that they proved useful for personal advancement ... but at the same time a system-transcending function in that they provided the conditions for the national struggle for emancipation For the opposition of the colonized peoples and the burgeoning national protest were first articulated among

Christians and resulted from the teachings of the Christian message." "Christianity, or rather the mission, thus created quite essential conditions for an intertribal, politically unifying racial self-awareness. ... Above all, it was the teaching of the Bible that created an important prerequisite for the justification of the replacement of colonialism. The Bible served as a 'manual' or Christian doctrine as a legitimizing framework for the struggle for independence. ... The Bible, which contained not only something about 'obedience to authority' but also something about brotherhood, humanity, and social justice, became a spiritual weapon in the hands of those on whom its white interpreters had wanted to impose political obedience and social conformity.[7]

African Christians also played a prominent role in the Pan-African movement that began in the early 20th century. The First Pan-African Congress in London in 1900, for example, was opened by African-American AME Bishop Alexander Walters. Among his African participants was Anglican (assistant) bishop James Johnson of Nigeria. Christian activists from Nigeria also played a leading role in the 'First Universal Races Congress' in London in 1911.[8] The development of a political Pan-Africanism ran in part parallel to the formation of a "black ecumenism" through the cooperation of newly emerged African and African American churches.

Notes to Chapter 18

1. Gründer (1992), *Welteroberung*, 527 f.
2. Hastings (1994), *Church in Africa*, 559.
3. Iliffe (1997), *Geschichte Afrikas*, 303.
4. Ludwig (2000), *Tambaram*, 26 ff.31 ff.
5. Marx (2004), *Geschichte Afrikas*, 248.
6. Ayandele (1966), *Missionary Impact*, 175; cf. Ajayi (1965), *Making of a New Elite*.
7. Gründer (1992), *Welteroberung*, 580.582.584 f.
8. Langley (1973), *Pan-Africanism*, 27–40.

Further Reading for Chapter 18

18.1 (Christian Missions and the "Scramble for Africa")

Iliffe (^{3}2017), *Africans*, 201–227; Pakenham 1998), *Scramble for Africa;* Boahen (1985), *Africa under Colonial Domination*, 1–86. 114–282; Benjamin (2006),

Western Colonialism 1,166f. III,996–998; Reinhard (1990), *Expansion* IV, 36–77; Gründer (1992), *Welteroberung*, 519–550; Hastings (1994), *Church in Africa*, 397–492; Ward (2017), *Late 18th Century to 1914*, 137–144; Blakely et al. (1994), *Religion in Africa*, 21–88; Hock (2005), *Christentum in Afrika*, 126–132; Lessing et al. (2012), *German Protestant Church in colonial Southern Africa*.

18.2 (*The Emergence of African Independent Churches*)
Hastings (1994), *Church in Africa*, 505 ff. 513 ff.527–31.534–539; Kalu (2005), *African Christianity*, 280 ff; Kitzhoff (1996), *African Independent Churches*; Hock (2005), *Christentum in Afrika*, 145–47. 165 f. 168; Ludwig (1992), *Kirche im kolonialen Kontext*; Ludwig (1993), *Elijah II*, 296–317; Simon (2022), *Kimbanguismus*; Blakely et al. (1994), *Religion in Africa*, 22–45. 72–88. 240–341; Koschorke (2024), *Transatlantic Ethiopianism*; Campbell (1998), *Songs of Zion*; Engel (2015), *African American Missionaries*.

18.3 (*Themes of the Twenties and Thirties*)
Hastings (1994), *Church in Africa*, 540 ff.559 ff; Kalu (2005), *African Christianity*, 309–332. 333–360; Sundkler/ Steed (2000), *Africa*, 608–900; Iliffe (^{3}2017), *Africans*, 228 ff; Boahen (1985), *Africa under Colonial Domination*, 508–539. 565–745; Hock (2005), *Christentum in Afrika*, 132–140. 151 ff.187 f; Ludwig (2000), *Tambaram*, 36–46.52–69; Ntageli/ Hodgetts (2011), *More than one Wife*.

18.4 (*Christian Elites and National Independence Movements*)
Elphick (2012), *Equality of Believers;* Koschorke (2018), *Dialectics of the Three Selves*, 127–142; Gründer (1992), *Welteroberung*, 568–594; Grohs (1967), *Stufen afrikanischer Emanzipation;* Hastings (1994), *Church in Africa*, 540–559; Ward (2018), *20th Century,* 361ff; Langley (1973), *Pan-Africanism;* Dictionary of African Christian Biography (Boston; online), s.v. Kwame Nkruhmah, Nmamdi Azikiwe, Julius K. Nyere, Hastings Kamazi Banda etc.

CHAPTER 19

Latin America

19.1 The Situation around 1900

The year 1900 saw a new Latin America that had little to do with the republics in the initial phase of independence. On the whole, the liberal elites (or national oligarchies) had prevailed with their demands – such as the separation of church and state, religious freedom, a laicist education system, etc. – and the new Latin America was no exception. Slogans such as those of "progress" and "scientificity" dominated the debates. The Roman Catholic Church found itself on the defensive, fighting retreat battles to preserve former privileges. At the same time, it was strongly concerned with itself and anxious to determine its position in the new political and social order.

At the same time, the existing – and rapidly changing – social conditions were hardly questioned. In the last third of the 19th century and early 20th century, several Latin American nations had moved to export-oriented economies. Many governments considered the easiest and fastest way to the prosperity of their nations to be the exploitation and export of mineral and natural resources. The emphasis in each case was usually on specific trade goods. Argentina exported beef, Central America bananas, Cuba sugar, Chile copper and nitrates, Brazil rubber and coffee, Bolivia tin. In the short term, this led to a limited economic upswing, from which the ruling oligarchies (mostly landowners) profited most. At the same time, it increased neocolonial dependence on the world market and the most important foreign trading partners. Initially, these came primarily from Western Europe (and especially Great Britain), and later increasingly from the United States.

The system of export-oriented economies worked until the Great Depression of 1929/30, when the Great Crash had a devastating impact on Latin America, with effects that varied from country to country. It triggered political instability, military coups and social unrest. At the same time, it initiated, to varying degrees, a process of industrialization to produce previously imported goods. Even before this industrialization push, there had been a dramatic increase in population in many places, which exacerbated social problems. Whereas Latin America had a population of about 50 million around 1880, by 1930 this figure had probably risen to almost 100 million. Increased immigration and urbanization accompanied this development. The population of Buenos Aires, for example, grew from 300,000 to 1.2 million between 1880 and 1910. Overall, social change in the countryside and in the cities was very different.

Around 1930, the relationship between church and state changed in many places. "The Church, after decades of opposition to, and persecution by, liberal states, could now establish relationships of alliance, harmony, or at least toleration (with perhaps the sole exception of a 15-year period in Mexico) with populist states."[1]

19.2 Regional Profiles: Brazil, Mexico, Cuba

A military coup took place in *Brazil* in 1889. Emperor Pedro II (r. 1840–1889) was overthrown and the republic was proclaimed. This was supported by an alliance of liberals, freemasons and positivists. The new constitution of 1891 provided for separation of church and state, introduction of civil marriage, secularization of cemeteries, and a series of anticlerical measures. Protestants welcomed the newfound freedoms. The Catholic bishops protested against the loss of previous prerogatives.

The following development was characterized by manifold attempts of the Catholic episcopate not to resume its lost status as a privileged state church, but to gain influence and visibility in the public sphere in a new way. This goal was served by various activities in education (such as the founding of a Catholic university), the establishment of seminaries loyal to the line, the founding of newspapers, mass events (such as Eucharistic congresses or national pilgrimages), and a strong expansion of the church infrastructure. The number of bishoprics, for example, was increased from 12 to 58 between 1891 and 1920, and churches and convents closed in the 19th century were reopened. In this process, ultramontane Restoration Catholicism was increasingly combined with a Brazilian patriotism that had grown during World War I. According to Cardinal Dom Leme, one of the defining figures of the 1920s and 1930s, Brazil was the "greatest Catholic nation in the world" and "essentially" Catholic. The Catholic Church, not as the state church, but as the "national church" of the Brazilians, therefore deserved a prominent position. In 1931, the Virgin of Aparecida was proclaimed patron saint of Brazil. The erection of the famous statue of Christ, Cristo Redentor, on the summit of Corcovado in Rio de Janeiro also took place in this year.

Structural deficits, such as the massive shortage of priests, changed little. European religious, who began streaming into the country again in the 1890s, often lacked sensitivity for local Christian traditions and forms of piety [see Text 284]. A military coup in 1930 ended the so-called First (or Old) Brazilian

Republic (1889–1930). The following presidency and dictatorship of Getúlio Vargas (r. 1930–1945 as well as 1950–1954) saw a new alliance of Catholic Church and state under the sign of an anti-communist nationalism. This alliance has been compared by Latin American historians to a second "colonial pact" or described as a renewal of the colonial "Cristendom" model – characterized by the close intertwining of church and state power.

The sharpest confrontation between the Catholic Church and liberal-revolutionary forces occurred in *Mexico*. Since 1914, the Mexican Revolution of 1910–1920 also led to a campaign against "religion" as a stronghold of "ignorance". In the name of the "light of science" Catholicism was fought in order to save "the representatives of the Mayan race from darkness and corruption". This campaign was accompanied by acts of fanatical violence such as the murder of priests, desecration of churches, rape of nuns and looting. In 1917, a new constitution was adopted that further strengthened earlier anti-clerical articles. It provided for the nationalization of all ecclesiastical properties, prohibition of religious orders and vows, abolition of the clergy's right to vote, limitation of the number of priests (one per 15,000 inhabitants), exclusion of foreign clergy, laicalization of the school system, and a ban on appeals to Rome.

In view of popular resistance, the anti-clerical measures were temporarily relaxed. But in 1926 they were drastically tightened again. This triggered the uprising of the *Cristeros* ("Christ fighters") with numerous victims, which lasted until 1929 and could not be ended by the government troops for a long time despite their oppressive superiority. The Cristeros were Catholic peasant militias in the central and western highlands, which included former followers of the social revolutionary Emiliano Zapata (1879–1919). An important motive was disappointment with the slow pace of agrarian reform and the central government's interference in communal affairs. At the same time, however, the Cristeros fought in the name of the Virgin of Guadelupe and the Catholic religion. These men, according to the report of one of the participants in the uprising,

> did not pay attention to the fact that the government had many soldiers, many arms, a lot of money to make war on them ... But what they saw was the need to defend their God, their religion, the Holy Church their mother ... These men ... went to the battlefields in search of God, Our Lord. The valleys, the mountains, the forests, the hills are witnesses that these men spoke to the Lord our God, under the holy name 'Viva Cristo Rey', but also 'Viva la Santísima Virgen de Guadalupe', 'Viva México' ... [Text 291b]

In 1929, masses were celebrated again for the first time. Within the Mexican church, however, tensions arose between representatives of the hierarchy and former *cristeros* who felt betrayed by the tactical behavior of the bishops and the Vatican. In 1934–1937, the church struggle flared up again. It was triggered by the introduction of anti-religious socialist education in schools. Beginning in 1938, a modus vivendi developed. In essence, the state renounced application of the 1917 provisions and the church renounced political influence. This compromise lasted until 1992, when a comprehensive constitutional reform redefined the relationship between church and state. As a result, the Vatican and Mexico established diplomatic relations.

Cuba differs from other Latin American countries in that it was a Spanish colony until 1898. Liberation from Spanish rule, however, meant only extradition to North American imperialism, even though the country became nominally independent as a republic in 1902. Along with the old colonial masters, numerous Catholic clergymen also left the country in 1898. Since the Catholic Church was considered a bulwark of royalism and conservatism, anti-clerical sentiment had spread widely among Cubans. The new constitution of 1901 established the separation of church and state. The first president of republican Cuba was Tomás Estrada Palma (r. 1902–1906), a Protestant. Previously, a Protestant diaspora had formed in the United States among emigrant Cubans. In 1866, the 'Iglesia de Santiago Apóstol' was founded in New York, as well as other Cuban Protestant congregations, especially in Florida. During the Cuban struggle for independence from 1868 to 1898, their members were characterized by strong patriotism. With Cuba's independence, a return of emigrants to their homeland began. Protestants now formed cells from which Protestantism spread to Cuba [Text 285]. After the exodus of Spanish clerics in 1898, Cuban Catholicism suffered from a massive shortage of priests. An upswing began here, as in other Latin American countries, with the 'Catholic Action' founded in 1928.

19.3 World Economic Crisis and Social Question

For Latin America's export economies, the world economic crisis of the early 1930s spelled disaster. Commodity prices collapsed worldwide (in Brazil, for example, the price of coffee fell by 50%). Costs for imported industrial products rose inversely. Unemployment and social tensions worsened. In this situation, a slow opening of the Catholic Church to social issues can be observed. Previously, Pope Leo XIII's 1891 social encyclical *Rerum Novarum* – which formulated a third way between liberalism and socialism – had received little attention in Latin American Catholicism for decades. Instead, individual socially sensitive bishops found themselves exposed to the repression of national oligarchies.

In the hesitant beginnings of a Latin American social Catholicism in the 1930s, the 'Catholic Action' (Acción Católica) played an important role. This was an organization of Catholic laity whose task was to work closely with the bishops to build a society oriented toward Catholic social principles. By training and activating lay people loyal to the church, the church wanted to alleviate the shortage of priests. At the same time, it sought to influence different social groups (instead of cooperating only with the aristocratic elites). Linked to this were efforts to form Catholic trade unions, cooperatives, youth groups and welfare institutions. In this regard, the development in the individual countries was very different. Whereas in Brazil, Mexico and Argentina, for example, Catholic Action occasionally grew into a mass organization, in other countries it did not become a widespread movement.

The 'Catholic Action' also gained importance through the fact that later leading representatives of Latin American liberation theology gained first experiences here. These include Dom Hélder Câmara (1909–1999), later archbishop of Olinda and Recife (Brazil); the Peruvian priest Gustavo Gutíerrez (*1928), often called the "father of liberation theology"; or the influential Chilean Jesuit Alberto Hurtado (1901–1952). The latter, in a 1947 memorandum presented to Pope Pius XII, emphasized the need to confront the realities of industrialization, urbanization, immigration, and proletarianization of the workforce. The rampant social unrest, he said, was not simply due to communist agitation or the effect of Protestant propaganda. Rather, he said, the Latin American church – and especially its leadership – must be shaken out of its conservatism. "There has been no effort to put into practice the teachings of the social encyclical [of 1891]; even the dissemination of its teachings is carried out with extreme 'caution' in order not to alienate the ruling classes." Protestants, for example, are different. "Where priests are lacking, Protestants go from house to house, preaching the Gospel and practicing charity" [Text 295].

19.4 Denominational Pluralization, New Religions

By 1920, Protestantism had succeeded in establishing itself firmly on the continent, albeit as a small minority. The development of regional and supraregional organizational structures had already begun. In areas of European immigration, synodal unions of immigrant congregations were established. In Brazil, for example, four regional synods of German Protestant immigrant congregations were formed between 1886 and 1912. In Chile, a national synod was established in 1906, and in the La Plata region a supra-national synod was established in 1899/1900 with the founding of the 'German Evangelical La Plata Synod' (for Argentina, Uruguay and Paraguay). The various denominations (such as Methodists, Presbyterians or Baptists) that had emerged from the activities of North American missionary Protestantism also had their annual conferences, synods, conventions and regular meetings. They were especially active in education, where in many places they presented themselves as a progressive alternative to both Roman Catholic and liberal-positivist educational institutions. Social change, they stressed. was to be achieved through renewal of the individual. At the same time, the *Panama Congress of 1916* strengthened approaches to the formation of continental forms of organization and the development of an all-Latino Protestant consciousness. German immigrant congregations, on the other hand, in many cases continued to maintain a close symbiosis of Protestant identity and Germanness. In the process, they did not remain unaffected by the emerging church struggle in their country of origin. In 1934, for example, a National Socialist wing was formed among the local pastors in southern Brazil [Text 289].

The *Pentecostal churches* became a rapidly growing force within the Protestant spectrum. Their rapid expansion since 1930 may also be seen as a reaction to the world economic crisis. Their polycentric beginnings go back to early 20th century, first in Chile (1909) and Brazil (1911) [Text 286]. This happened partly in loose connection with, but partly also completely independently of the Azusa revival of 1906 in the USA. The first congregations were mostly formed by splits within the "historic" Protestant churches (such as Methodists, Baptists or Congregationalists). The early Pentecostal movement was carried mainly by the lower – impoverished and poorly educated – classes in smaller towns and rural areas. After two or three generations, it increasingly found its way into the middle class as well. It was characterized by emotional worship services, the experience of baptism in the Spirit, sometimes glossolalia ("speaking in tongues"), leadership by lay people and, in many cases, a prominent role for women in the founding of new congregations. Migration and high mobility were defining characteristics, as was the urge to pass on the faith. A bewildering array of independent congregations soon formed.

The traditional religious monopoly of Catholicism was increasingly challenged not only by the advance of Protestantism. At the end of the 19th century, the increasing migration flows from different regions of the world (also outside Europe) brought different religious traditions to the continent. Along with Chinese "coolies" and Japanese immigrants came Buddhists, Confucians and Shintoists. Muslims and Indian Hindus arrived in the Caribbean from the

British colonies in Asia. From the Ottoman Empire, Oriental Christians and Muslims sought a new home in South America.

But of course it was above all also the diverse hybrid forms between popular Catholicism and the African heritage of the former black slaves that determined the picture of *growing religious pluralization*. In Brazil, for example, it was the Afro-Brazilian religion of Candomblé, or in Cuba the cult of Santería ("Way of the Saints"), which combined Catholic popular piety with traditional African religiosity (such as that of the Yoruba from present-day Nigeria). Elements of both religions – such as the Catholic saints and the deities (*orishas*) of the Yoruba pantheon – were able to enrich each other without simply merging. They widely coexisted in parallel and intertwined forms [see Photo K02–06]. – In addition to such mixed forms, which had developed over a longer period of time, there were also syncretistic new foundations in the 1920s. In Brazil, for example, the "new" religion of Umbanda was initially founded by and for members of the white urban middle class. Later, it gained followers in all population groups. Umbanda combines elements of (white) spiritualism (in the tradition of Alan Kardec), (black) Afro-Brazilian cults (Candomblé, Macumba), American Indian religiosity and Christianity. At the center is the belief in a world of spiritual beings: Deities, mythical figures as well as the souls of the deceased. These incarnate in the cult in initiated mediums and thus enable communication with the human world. The Umbanda religion was initially practiced under the guise of spiritism, and was not permitted by law until 1934. With its merger into the federation of the "União Espírita da Umbanda do Brasil" in 1939, the new religion was finally established [Text 288].

Elsewhere, for example, in circles of black 'brotherhoods' a festive culture of its own was able to develop from individual elements of Catholic liturgy and practice. In 1941, a European visitor to the Brazilian city of Salvador Bahia described the ceremony of "washing the church" (lavagem do Senhor de Bomfim), celebrated with great pomp. This had originally perhaps been a simple cleaning event, which had since turned into a popular festival with impressive processions. The black Christians, a priest explained to the European visitor, "are very pious here. But they do it in their own way" [Text 293].

In Jamaica, an Old Testament-inspired religious and social movement formed among the black population in the 1930s with the *Rastafari*. It is in the broader context of the so-called Ethiopianism – which looked at Ethiopia as a symbol of political and religious liberation – and recognized Ethiopian ruler Haile Selassie as the returned Messiah. A 1966 visit to Jamaica by the Ethiopian emperor led to a stampede of thousands of supporters to the airport. Many Rastafari expected liberation from "Babylon" – the corrupt Western system of oppression – and return to Africa [see Photo L06–15].

Footnote to Chapter 19

1. Dussel (1992), *Church in Latin America*, 150.

Further Reading for Chapter 19

19.1 (*The Situation around 1900*)

Bakewell (^{2}2004), *History of Latin America*, 443–496; Strassner (2018), *Latin America*, 298–307; Dussel (1992), *Church in Latin America*, 117–138. 139–152; González/González (2008), *Christianity in Latin America*, 160 ff; Tobler/ Bernecker (1996), *Handbuch* III, 8 ff.87 ff.265 ff.487 ff. 1059 ff; Garrard-Burnett/ Freston/ Dove (2016), *Religion in Latin America*, 346–358 (by B.L.H. Sandoval).

19.2 (*Regional Profiles: Brazil, Mexico, Cuba*)

Prien (2013), *Latin America*, 337–343. 432–438 (Mexico). 343–356 (Brazil). 377f (Cuba); Tobler/ Bernecker (1996), *Handbuch* III, 257–315 (Mexico). 483–503 (Cuba). 1049–1096 (Brazil); Strassner (2018), *Latin America*, 298–342; Dussel (1992), *Church in Latin America*, 222 ff. ('Christero'-Movement); Meyer (2013), *La Cristiada*; Garrard-Burnett/ Freston/ Dove (2016), *Religion in Latin America*, 269–285 (Messianic Movements, by S. Sullivan-González).

19.3 (*World Economic Crisis and Social Question*)

Dussel (1992), *Church in Latin America*, 139–152; Strassner (2018), *Latin America*, 304ff; Tobler/ Bernecker (1996), *Handbuch III*, 8–73. 291–309.1073–1088, Goodpasture (1989), *Cross and Sword*, 200–221 (documents); Garrard-Burnett/ Freston/ Dove (2016), *Religion in Latin America*, 346–358 (by B.L. Hernández Sandoval).

19.4 (*Denominational Pluralization, New Religions*)

(a) Protestantism: Prien (2013), *Latin America*, 443–558; Bastian (1995), *Protestantismus*, 130–205; Garrard-Burnett/ Freston/ Dove (2016), *Religion in Latin America*, 286–318; Dreher (1978), *Kirche und Deutschtum*, 84–102. – (b) Pentecostalism: González/González (2008), *Christianity in Latin America*, 270–296; Bastian (1995), *Protestantismus*, 160 ff; Freston, P. (1995), *Pentecostalism in Brazil*, 119 ff; Rivera-Pagán (2008), *Pentecostal Transformation*, 190–210; Anderson (2004), *Pentecostalism*, 63 ff; Garrard-Burnett/ Freston/ Dove (2016), *Religion in Latin America*, 414–450. – (c) New Religions: González/ González (2008), *Christianity in Latin America*, 180 ff; Scharf da Silva (2017), *Umbanda*; Barsch (2003), *Rastafa*ri; Garrard-Burnett/ Freston/ Dove (2016), *Religion in Latin America*, 603–665. 723–728; Blakely et al. (1994), *Religion in Africa*, 135–159 (Candomblé).

Illustrations for Part 4

FIGURE 38
Pandita Ramabai (Saravasti) (1858–1922), Indian social reformer, Christian education activist, and founder of the Pandita Rambai Mukti Mission (image on Indian postage stamp from 1989).

FIGURE 39
India: V. S. Azariah (1874–1945), evangelist, first Indian bishop in the Anglican Church, pioneer of the Asian ecumenical movement.

FIGURE 40
Lilivathi Singh (1868–1909), publicist, college professor, and Christian education pioneer who worked primarily for the rights of Indian women to education.

FIGURE 41
Japan: Kanzo Uchimura (1861–1930), author, Christian evangelist, and founder of the 'Non-Church Movement' (Mukyokai) in Meiji and Taisho period Japan.

FIGURE 42 China: Tsinghua University in Beijing, founded in 1911 by U.S. missionaries, today one of China's leading universities [= photo B16].

FIGURE 43 Korea: The Cheamri Massacre of 1919, committed by Japanese soldiers against Christian villagers [= photo D15].

ILLUSTRATIONS FOR PART 4

FIGURE 44   Group photo of the 1938 world missionary conference in Tambaram, India (near Madras/ Chennai). This was the first ecumenical assembly with a majority of delegates from Asia, Africa and Latin America.

PART 5

1945–1990

CHAPTER 20

Postcolonial Order and Ecclesial Emancipation Movements

20.1 End of the Second World War, Waves of Decolonization

World War II ended with the surrender of Germany on May 8, 1945, and of Japan on September 2, 1945. It had claimed an enormous number of victims – between 50 and 70 million people, even more among the civilian population than among the soldiers. The scale of destruction was unprecedented in modern history. In Europe, the victims included six million systematically murdered Jews. Some 60 states around the world were directly or indirectly involved in the fighting. These included the Western colonies in Asia and Africa, affected by sending contingents of troops to the battlefields of Europe. The experience of the war strengthened independence efforts there [cf. Text 192]. In East Asia and the Pacific, the Japanese had occupied or taken control of large areas of the French (Vietnam, Laos, Cambodia), English (Hong Kong, Singapore, Burma, Malaya), Dutch (Indonesia), Australian (New Guinea), and American (Philippines) colonial empires since 1941, in addition to parts of China (since 1931 or 1937) and Korea, which had already been occupied in 1910 – with varying consequences for the Christian communities there. In many places, they were suspected by the Japanese as fifth column of the West and subjected to harsh repression [Text 85]. Numerous Latin American states that had remained neutral during World War I now declared war on Germany (or the allied Axis powers). In the Soviet Union, the "great patriotic war" against the German aggressors gave respite to the Russian Orthodox Church, which had previously been most brutally persecuted. After 1945, however, repression against Christians and churches in the Soviet sphere of power intensified again, now also in Eastern Europe. Harsh persecution also hit believers (and monks) in other religious contexts under communist rule, such as in Buddhist-majority Mongolia.

As a direct result of World War II, the political map of the world changed. Between 1945 and 1975, Western colonial rule dissolved in almost all areas of the global South. One of the salient features of the history of Christianity in the 20th century lies in the fact that the disappearance of the European colonial masters from large parts of Asia and Africa did not at the same time mean the end of the churches that had emerged there from the Western mission. Quite the contrary: in quite a number of casesChristian communities even experienced

© KLAUS KOSCHORKE, 2025 | DOI:10.1163/9789004699830_021
This is an open access chapter distributed under the terms of the CC BY-NC-ND 4.0 license.

explosive growth in the subsequent period. The process of decolonization took place in waves. At first, Asia was at the center of the action. In 1946 the Philippines became independent (from the USA), in 1947 India and Pakistan (from Great Britain), as did Ceylon (Sri Lanka) and Burma (Myanmar) in 1948, and then Indonesia in 1949. Although Indonesia's independence had already been declared in 1945, it was not recognized by the Dutch colonial power until 1949. The situation was similar in Vietnam, where the former French colonial rulers were forcibly expelled in 1954, resulting in the division of the country. In Laos and Cambodia, French rule had already ended in 1953. With the independence of Malaya (the core territory of what later became Malaysia) in 1957, the process of political decolonization in Asia was essentially completed.

1960 then became the "Year of Africa." In that year, twelve French colonies in sub-Saharan Africa gained independence, as did the giants Nigeria (previously British-controlled) and the Belgian Congo. Subsequently, this development continued at a rapid pace. By the end of the 1960s, the continent was essentially free of Western colonial rule – apart from the Portuguese possessions (mainly Angola and Mozambique), which gained independence only in 1975. In Southern Rhodesia (Zimbabwe) white minority rule continued until 1980, and in South Africa until 1990 (end of apartheid system) respectively 1994 (free elections).

The states of Central and South America on the mainland had already gained political independence from Spain and Portugal in the 1820s. At the end of the 19th century, the last remnants of Spanish colonial presence disappeared from the insular peripheral zones (Cuba, Puerto Rico). At the same time, however, the new nations of the continent were exposed to growing economic, political (and in some cases military) pressure from the United States. In the post-World War II era, the Cuban Revolution of 1959, widely perceived as a beacon, marked an important turning point. With the victory of the Sandinistas in Nicaragua in 1979, a revolutionary regime was established for the first time on the Latin American mainland. Fierce confrontations between conservative and social-revolutionary forces defined the situation in Latin America in the 1970s and 1980s.

20.2 New Alliances, Movement of "Third World"-Countries

In the aftermath of World War II, new power blocs and structures of a bipolar world order were formed, which were to determine the postwar period until the watershed year 1989/90. On the one hand, there was the – later so-called – "First World" as a community of liberal-capitalist states under the leadership of the USA. It comprised the members of NATO, founded in 1949 (in Europe and the North Atlantic), various countries in Asia and the Pacific with a U.S. military presence (such as Japan, South Korea, Taiwan, Thailand and the Philippines), and other allied states (such as Australia). On the other side stood – as "Second World" – the camp of socialist-ruled countries led by the Soviet Union, united in the 'Warsaw Pact' founded in 1955. In East Asia, Outer Mongolia and China, where the communists took over in 1949, were temporarily part of this alliance until China's break with the Soviet Union in the 1960s.

A third group consisted of the new states of Asia and Africa, which had just freed themselves from colonial foreign rule and, as "non-aligned states," sought to forge a third path between the rival power blocs. At the same time, however, they always had to position themselves in this field of tension. An important first step in this process was the Non-Aligned Conference in Bandung, Indonesia, in 1955. It was attended by 29 Asian and African nations. As the process of decolonization progressed in the 1960s, the self-designation "Third World" spread as a collective term for politically, economically and culturally heterogeneous states. In detail, this term has subsequently experienced very different definitions. Characteristic features were the reference to the common colonial past; the struggle against "neocolonial" dependencies and imperialist exploitation; poverty, economic backwardness or – in dependency theory terms – "underdevelopment" produced by the centers of the capitalist world; and pride in their own cultural heritage. "Never again," historian Jürgen Osterhammel wrote in 1995, "has the 'South' challenged the 'West' with such depth and broad impact as in the now-classic anti-imperialist teachings and polemics" of this period, referring to Gandhi, Nehru, Mao Zedong. Ho Chi Minh, Frantz Fanon, Kwame Nkrumah, and Leopold S. Senghor. The "sole exception" that Osterhammel mentions in this regard – apart from the "economy of 'dependency'" – has been, quite remarkably, the "theology of liberation" formulated in Latin America in the 1970s and 1980s.[1] In any case, the reference to the category 'Third World' has also played a determining role in the self-understanding and debates of Latin American, Asian and African theologians since the 1970s. In 1976 the Ecumenical Association of Third World Theologians (EATWOT) was founded in Dar es Salaam as a transcontinental and interdenominational platform of critical Christians from the global South. For its part, it triggered partly intense debates in church and academic circles in Europe.[2]

20.3 Forms of Ecclesiastical and Theological Emancipation

The process of political decolonization also strengthened emancipation efforts in the so-called "historical" churches in the Global South that had emerged from Western missions, although some of these efforts had begun much earlier. Reference should be made to the ecclesiastical independentism in Africa in the early 20th century as well as to National church movements in Asia at the same time [see chapters 17.2 and 18.2]. It is no coincidence that the Asian ecumenical movement experienced a new high point in 1947 – the year of India's political independence – with the founding of the Church of South India (CSI). As the first union worldwide of churches of the episcopal, presbyterial and congregationalist tradition (and thus as a sign of overcoming imported Western denominationalism), the CSI attracted great attention in the global ecumenical community. Moreover, this happened already one year before the founding of the Ecumenical Council or World Council of Churches in Amsterdam in 1948. With Cherakarottu Korula Jacob as its first moderator, an Indian was at the head of the CSI.

In neighboring Sri Lanka, Lakdasa de Mel (1902–1976) was the first native priest to be ordained as an Anglican bishop in 1948 – in the year of the country's independence. As bishop of the newly established diocese of Kurunagala in the Sinhalese heartland (since 1950) and later as Anglican 'Metropolitan of India, Pakistan, Burma and Ceylon' (since 1962), he was one of the most distinguished Christian leaders in post-war Asia. The new cathedral at Kurunagala was built in 1956, incorporating Sinhalese architectural styles. It was inspired by earlier examples of indigenous sacred architecture in Sri Lanka. It then in turn served as a model for ecclesiastical buildings such as the Anglican cathedral in Colombo [see Figs. 48 + 47; Photo E-22/23] in the following years.

Specifically, the *transfer of leadership* positions to indigenous Christians proceeded at different paces in the various mission churches. Parallel to the political emancipation process, numerous African churches gained full autonomy in the early 1960s. At the same time, overarching national organizational structures were formed (or strengthened) in various countries, in the form of the National Christian Councils, some of which had existed since the 1920s. Since the 1960s, there have also been more continental mergers. In 1959, for example, the forerunner organization of the Christian Conference of Asia (CCA) was founded in Kuala Lumpur (Malaysia). At the same time, it influenced the formation of the All Africa Conference of Churches (CCAA) in Africa in 1963. About 100 churches from 42 countries – mostly Protestant, as well as Orthodox, Catholic and also independent ones – were represented at the founding event in Kampala (Uganda) [Text 197]. The conference called on the churches of the continent to "participate wholeheartedly in the building of the African nation." The formation of the Pacific Conference of Churches followed in 1966, of the Middle East Council of Churches (MECC) in 1973, and of the Caribbean Conference of Churches (CCC) in the same year. Since 1982, the

Latin American Council of Churches (CLAI) worked in close cooperation with the respective Catholic churches in the region. Initially, the Roman Catholic Church had participated at best sporadically in projects of interconfessional cooperation. But with the Second Vatican Council (1962–1965), the ecumenical climate improved considerably also overseas.

Protest against the dominance of Western academic theology and the development of specific own models of theology – related to the Asian, African or Latin American context – are another overarching feature of multifaceted developments in the phase of decolonization after 1945. These approaches, which were very heterogeneous in detail, were for a long time primarily oriented toward the *"indigenization" or "inculturation" paradigm*. In other words, the aim was to combine the respective cultural heritage with the gospel, which, according to Southern critics, had been transmitted by the missionaries only in a "Western" form. Theologians in Africa discussed approaches to an "African theology" [see Text 206–211]. They sought (and still seek), for example, to relate the centrality of ancestor veneration in African tradition to the biblical faith in God. A new stage was marked by the development of *"contextual" theology* models since the early 1970s. It was based on the insight that the reference to traditional cultures (such as Confucianism) had become largely irrelevant, for example in revolutionary China or the modern transformation societies of East Asia. Therefore, in addition to cultural elements, socioeconomic factors, technological developments, and processes of secularization had to be taken into account as well (or even more so) in the analysis of the "context." That is the concept of "contextualization" formulated in 1972 by the Taiwanese educationlist Shoki Coe. It was widely disseminated especially as a guiding principle of 'Theological education in the Third World' by the World Council of Churches [Text 100].

Finally, Latin American *liberation theology* of the 1970s and 1980s sought to combine a sociological analysis of structures of oppression with a call to committed action and a preferential "option for the poor" [Text 303–305; see chapter 23.3]. Although intensively received both within and outside Latin America, it was by no means the only model of liberation theological reflection. In Korea, for example, the 'Minjung theology' developed in the 1970s during the period of dictatorial military rule as a very independent model of theology. Nonetheless, it was oriented toward liberating action [Text 101]. Other Asian voices (such as the Sri Lankan Jesuit Aloysius Pieris) emphasized – like Latin American liberation theology – the need for social engagement. But they strongly criticized its insufficient consideration of the religious element or the "liberatingdimension" (besides enslaving features) of different (also non-Christian) religious traditions [Text 102].

Emancipatory efforts were also expressed in various approaches to a *new historiography*. Instead of the traditional history of missions, which usually focused on the initiatives and activities of Western missionaries, a variety of projects emerged to describe the genesis and formation of non-European Christianities in the context of their respective societies and cultures. Special attention was paid to the initiatives of indigenous actors. In India, for example, a pioneering study by Kaj Baago in 1969 on the "Pioneers of Indigenous Christianity" in the 19th century stimulated the development of a corresponding infrastructure and archives. The 'Latin American Church History Commission' (Comisión de Estudios de Historia de la Iglesia de América Latina/ CEHILA), founded in 1972, pursued analogous goals. This it did together with a strongly liberation-theological approach and on a pan-continental level. And the aforementioned EATWOT established a 'History Group' in 1983 with the mandate to write studies on the "history of the churches in the Third World" from the perspective of colonized peoples and marginalized groups. At the same time, the aim was to promote "mutual understanding among the churches in the countries of the Third World."[3] This project, in turn, also provided impulses for the "World Christianity Studies" that had been established since the 1990s, initially primarily in the Anglophone language area.

Here, too, it should be remembered that there had already existed quite remarkable approaches to an indigenous Christian historiography long before the end of the colonial era. At the end of the 19th century, for example, two West African pastors – Carl Reindorf (1834–1917) from what is now Ghana and Samuel Johnson (1846–1901) from what is now Nigeria – wrote detailed histories of their respective homelands, written from the perspective of indigenous people and making extensive use of oral sources.[4] In early 17th-century Peru, Guamán Poma de Ayala, mentioned elsewhere, was the author of a world chronicle that paralleled the history of Western Christianity and the Inca rulers of Peru until the arrival of the Spanish. He then described in detail and with rich illustration early colonial society – sharply criticizing colonial church reality, while at the same time paying tribute to American-Indian Christianity [chap. 9.2; Text 249; Figs. 10/11].

20.4 Growing Importance of the Southern Churches in the Global Ecumenical Movement

The 1938 World Missionary Conference in *Tambaram*, India, had already seen – for the first time at an ecumenical gathering – a majority of delegates from the global South [Text 83.185]. When in 1948 in Amsterdam the 'World Council of

Churches' (WCC) – already planned before the war – was founded as a global union of (at first) 145 Protestant and Orthodox churches from 44 countries, 27 Asian churches were also among the founding members. Some of their delegates – such as the Chinese T. C. Chao, who was elected one of the six presidents of the WCC – took prominent positions. Nevertheless, they expressed frustration with the slow pace of union efforts among Western churches. The South Indian Church Union (CSI) [Text 87a], which had been completed a year earlier, had generated a disproportionately greater momentum.

In 1961, the third General Assembly of the WCC was held in *New Delhi*, India. This was the first time a non-Western country served as host. In addition to newcomers from the Eastern bloc (such as the Russian Orthodox Church), the event saw considerable growth from the new independent nations of the South. Of the 23 new member churches, 18 came from countries in what was now officially called the 'Third World': eleven from Africa, five from Asia, and two Pentecostal churches from Latin America (Chile). The theme of the conference was also largely determined by the revolutionary spirit of the time and the problems of "rapid technical and social upheaval". In addition, especially in an Asian environment, questions of interreligious dialogue gained new importance.Christ: *the* light or just *one* "light of the world" (among others)? – a controversially and intensively discussed question.

Third World issues increasingly dominated the agenda of the WCC in other ways as well. In 1966, a "World Conference on Church and Society" was convened in Geneva. Issues of a "theology of revolution" and the problem of a right of resistance or possible violence against systems of injustice were controversially discussed. In 1968, the WCC opened a study process on "The Church and the Poor," focusing on its global socio-economic context. The theme of the WCC's fourth assembly in Uppsala in 1968 was "Behold, I make all things new." Issues of church unity were thereby related to the renewal or unity of global human society. The church, the conference claimed, "dares to speak of itself as the sign of the future unity of humanity." Evangelical critics saw this as a "horizontalization of the gospel." This criticism was one of the starting points of the subsequently intensifying conflict between "ecumenists" and evangelical voices within global Protestantism.

In the Catholic world, the *Second Vatican Council* (1962–1965) marked a profound caesura. It was the "most universal" of all councils in the history of the Catholic Church or, according to the Brazilian theologian Oscar Beozzo, the "first council that can be called universal because of the composition of its members, since it brought together representatives of the churches of all five continents.[5] The European episcopate made up barely half of all participants. There were 956 bishops from both Americas (601 of them from Latin America and 243 from Brazil), more than 300 from Asia, and almost 279 from Africa. In its preparation, the Council had been still almost exclusively a European undertaking. In the process of its reception, however, it set in motion manifold dramatic changes. In Latin America, for example, it fueled discussions about liberation theology and the social commitment of the church [which are discussed in more detail in chapter 23.3]. In Africa, the liturgical reform adopted by the council (with greater attention to the respective mother tongues) met the thirst of the new states for cultural Africanization. In Asia, it spurred numerous experiments in interreligious (and interconfessional) cooperation and new forms of communal life and worship.

In 1969/70, the WCC had launched an *anti-racism program* as a sign of solidarity between churches in North and South. It established a fund to support African Christians (especially in apartheid South Africa) in their struggle for economic, social and political justice. This move sparked fierce debates in the churches of Central Europe, including threats of withdrawal from the WCC. In general, it is a feature of the 1960s and subsequent decades that developments in the global South increasingly had repercussions for the churches of Europe – and vice versa. In 1973, at the Bangkok World Mission Conference, African churches proposed a "moratorium" (temporary suspension) on the transfer of money and the sending of missionaries from the North to the South. As a result, the structures of many European mission societies changed. Some, and they – such as the 'Vereinigte Evangelische Mission' (VEM/UEM; previously Rhenish Mission, in Wuppertal/Germany) or the Basle Mission (Basel/Switzerland) – closed their mission seminaries. Instead, they now transformed themselves, along with their earlier mission foundations, into partnership organizations.

Latin American *liberation theology*, as already mentioned, attracted enormous interest in Christian circles and among social activists on other continents as well, including – across denominational lines – in Western Europe. Their journalism was translated many times and found a wide audience. In the 1980s, for example, the number of church houses named after the liberation theologian and archbishop of San Salvador (in El Salvador) Óscar Romero (1917–1980) skyrocketed in various Central European countries. The latter had been murdered in 1980 by henchmen of the military dictatorship there while he was celebrating Mass at the altar [see Figure 55]. Conversely, representatives of the ecclesiastical and political resistance in Europe gained new significance and relevance overseas as well. Thus Dietrich Bonhoeffer (1906–1945), long frowned upon as a "traitor to the fatherland" even in conservative church circles in his home country, inspired the resistance of Christian activists in Asia (in particular in Korea) and especially in countries such as South Africa or Brazil, whose dictatorial regimes sought to legitimize themselves in Christian terms. Both Romero and Bonhoeffer are united in a gallery of *"martyrs of the 20th century"* erected in 1998 at the west portal of Westminster Abbey in London. Other "blood witnesses" honored there include Martin Luther King (†1968, from the U.S.), Father Maximilian Kolbe (†1941, from Nazi Germany), and Chinese Christian Wang Zhiming, who was a victim of persecution in the Chinese "Cultural Revolution" in 1973. These names from the global ecumenical community stand for a transcontinental culture of remembrance in the Christian world, the development of which has accelerated since the 1970s.

20.5 New Actors and Movements

A new player on the stage of world Christianity in the post–war period was the *Pentecostal movement,* which was very diverse in itself. Still a marginal phenomenon in many places in the 1950s, it subsequently underwent a dynamic development. Since the 1970s it has gained in importance by leaps and bounds, especially in Latin America and Africa. In Brazil, for example, it has become since the 1980s the strongest force in the Protestant camp [see chapter 23.4]. Globally, the enormous growth of Pentecostal and Neo-Pentecostal groups and communities took place primarily in the South. In the 1990s, they increasingly formed transnational networks as well. The polycentric beginnings of the Pentecostal movement go back to the first decade of the 20th century. They were partly connected with North American centers (such as the Azusa Street Revival in 1906 in a black church in Los Angeles) or originated quite independently of them (for example in India, Korea or Chile). The subsequent growth varied greatly from region to region. The intensity of interaction with other independentist groups (such as the older African Independent Churches in Africa) or the incorporation of elements of Catholic popular religiosity – as in Latin America – also differed from region to region.

Within the Protestant spectrum, there have always been voices critical of ecumenism. In Latin America, various fundamentalist churches of North American origin refused to join the WCC, which was founded in 1948. In the 1960s, opposition from conservative evangelical circles to the World Council of Churches' commitment to human rights, which was deplored as "politicization," intensified. This was one of the factors that led to the founding of the *'Lausanne Movement'* as a worldwide federation of evangelical groups at the 'International Congress for World Evangelization' in Lausanne in 1974. Participants included also representatives from many countries of the global

South. The core demand was to give priority to world mission (instead of sociopolitical activities). At the second world congress of the movement in 1989 in Manila, however, the social obligation of Christians was emphasized together with the task of evangelization.

Notes to Chapter 20

1. Osterhammel (1995), *Colonialism*, 115.
2. Collet (1990), EATWOT, 315–334 (Reception of EATWOT-Theology in Europe).
3. Baago (1969), *Pioneers of Indigenous Christianity*; RGG4 II, 989–995 („Dritte Welt": W. Gern/ G. Collet)/ RGG⁴ II, 84 f („CEHILA": E. Dussel); Vischer (1983), *History of the Church in the Third World*, 131 f.
4. Jenkins (1998), *African Pastors*.
5. Beozzo (2002), *Zweites Vatikanische Konzil*, 219.

Further Reading for Chapter 20

20.1 (*End of World War II, Waves of Decolonization*)

Jansen/ Osterhammel (2017), *Decolonisation;* Rothermund (2006), *Companion to Decolonization,* passim, esp. 5–52 (context). 53–102 (Asia). 127–195 (Subsaharan Africa); Holland (1985), *Decolonization;* Reinhard (1988), *Expansion* III, 187–204; Ansprenger (⁴1981), *Auflösung der Kolonialreiche;* Wendt (2007), *Globalisierung*, 315–388; Iriye/ Osterhammel (2013), *Geschichte der Welt* VII, 101–107; Osterhammel (1997), *Colonialism*, 113ff; Abernethy (2000), *European Overseas Empires*, 325–362; Lloyd (1996), *British Empire*, 321–346.

20.2+3 (*New Alliances, Cooperation of "Third World"-Countries, Forms of Ecclesial and Theological Emancipation*)

Collet (1990), EATWOT; Vischer (1983), *History of the Church in the Third World*; EATWOT (Ed.) (1978–2007), *Voices from the Third World*; Frieling (1992), Ökumenischer Gedanke, 71–117; Parratt (2004), *Third World theologies*; Rowland (²2007), *Companion to Liberation Theology;* Dussel (1992), *Latin America*, 153–184; Büschges, et al. (2021), *Liberation theology;* Kalu (2005), *African Christianity*, 333–360; Hastings (1979), *African Christianity*; Dickson (1984), *Theology in Africa*; England (1981), *Living Theology in Asia;* Barron (2023), *African Christian Theology*.

20.4 (Growing Importance of Southern Churches in Global Ecumenism)

Weber (1966), *Asia and the Ecumenical Movement*, 179–187.220–248; Fey (^{3}1993), *Ecumenical Movement* II, 1–26.93 ff.171ff. 373ff. 411ff; Briggs/ Oduyoye/ Tsetis (2004), *Ecumenical Movement* III; Frieling (1992), Ökumenischer Gedanke, 78–99; Phan (2002), *Vatican II in Asia*, 243–258; Beozzo (2002), *Zweites Vatikanische Konzil*, 203–218; Meyer-Herwartz (1979), *Rezeption des Antirassismus-Programms*; Besier/ Boyens/ Lindemann (1999), Ökumenische *Bewegung*, 155–185; Duguid-May (2018), *Ecumenical Movement*, 147–182; Thomas (1990), *My Ecumenical Journey*.

20.5 (New Actors and Movements)

Robert (2011), *Christian Mission*; Cox (2008), *British Missionary Enterprise*, 241–262; Hollenweger (1997), *Pentecostalism;* Anderson (2004), *Pentecostalism*; Miller/ Yamori (2007), *Global Pentecostalism*; Haustein/ Maltese (2014), *Handbuch;* Suarsana (2010), *Christentum 2.0?*; Corten/ Marshall-Fratani (2001), *Between Babel and Pentecost*; Kalu (2005), *African Christianity*, 388–409; Garrard-Burnett/ Freston/ Dove (2016), *Religion in Latin America*, 414–450.

CHAPTER 21

Asia: the 1950s

21.1 Christians as a Minority in the Process of Nation Building

By the end of the 1950s, almost all Asian countries had gained independence from Western colonial rule [see chap. 20.1]. Central on the agenda now was the reconstruction of the new nations. The Christian communities of the continent found themselves challenged to redefine their role as religious minorities in this process of 'nation building'. This happened in detail under very different conditions.

In 1947, the *Indian subcontinent* was forcibly divided into India (with a Hindu majority) and Pakistan (with a predominantly Muslim population). While Pakistan proclaimed itself the world's first Islamic republic in 1956 and declared Islam the state religion, India defined itself as a secular state and established the principle of religious freedom in its 1950 constitution. At the same time, however, the country's Christian community faced increasing reprisals and restrictions on its missionary activities and ecumenical contacts in the face of a strengthening Hindu nationalism [Text 87b+c]. The abovementioned South Indian Church Union (CSI) of 1947 [Text 87a], which sought to overcome imported Western denominationalism, saw itself as an expression of a new form of Christianity in independent India. It inspired analogous union projects in northern India and other Asian countries as well. – Neighboring *Sri Lanka* (Ceylon), in turn, which became independent in 1948, experienced a swell of Buddhist nationalism beginning in 1956 (and intensifying during the 1960s). Political emancipation, according to its supporters, was now to be followed by cultural liberation from Western dominance, and Buddhism was to be given "a prominent place" in the national life of the Sinhalese majority. As a result, Sinhalese was declared in 1956 the only official language (the starting point for later bloody conflicts with the Tamil minority). Private schools, which were mainly Catholic, were nationalized without compensation in 1960–61, and the traditional lunar calendar (with the Poya festival as a holiday) was temporarily reintroduced in 1967 replacing the Western seven-day week.

In *Indonesia*, the state philosophy of the Pancasila constitutionally offered the Christian churches their own living space. First formulated in 1945 by the later President Sukarno and subsequently enshrined in the constitution, these "five pillars" named as basic principles of national coexistence: faith in one God, humanism, unity of the country, popular sovereignty; and social justice [Text 88]. With the principle of the "All-One Divine Rule," five religions (Islam, Protestantism, Catholicism, Hinduism, Buddhism) thus enjoyed official recognition in the predominantly Islamic republic. Faiths without written traditions or non-religious beliefs, on the other hand, were denied this recognition. In 1950, most Protestant churches, which – concentrated in different regions – represented about 7 % of the total population (Catholics *ca.* 3%), joined together to form the 'Council of Churches in Indonesia' (DGI). Integrated into the Pancasila system, they gained an Indonesian face more clearly than before since the country's independence. At the same time, their positions on social issues were often characterized by a desire for loyalty to the government and majority society. In 1965, an attempted coup by leftist military forces was quickly crushed. As a result, the Communist Party was dissolved and thousands of its members were arrested. In the ideological vacuum that followed the coup, there was mass influx to Christian churches [Text 97].

In *Japan,* the country's defeat in 1945 resulted in the collapse of the old system. The tenno (emperor) was demythologized, the separation of religion and state was proclaimed, and a democratic constitution was enacted. The immediate consequence, according to the Japanese theologian Yagi Seiichi, was "a negative evaluation of everything traditional and an almost unreserved devotion to Western culture, including Christianity ... The number of Christians and the influence of Christians on spiritual life in Japan increased remarkably".[1] Then, at the end of the 1960s, there was a counter-movement and various efforts to "free" Japanese Protestantism again from the "captivity of German theology." – In 1946, Japanese Christians spoke of Japan's "responsibility" for the events of the Second World War much earlier than other social or political forces in the country. It was assumed now necessary to "build a new Japan based on the cross of Christ" [Text 89]. In 1967, the 'United Church of Christ' in Japan adopted a declaration that has often been described as analogous to the "Stuttgart Confession of Guilt" of the German Protestant Church in 1945.

In *Korea,* World War II also ended the long period of Japanese occupation (since 1910). Christians in the South welcomed the new religious freedom and dreamed of transforming the country into a Christian nation. Although initially only a small minority nationwide (of about 2–3%), they were strongly represented among educated Koreans. For example, the leaders of the transitional government in the South (around Rhee Syng-man, later president of South Korea) were all Christians. The center of Korean Christianity (with about 18% of the population) was, however, in the North, which had been occupied by the Soviets since 1945. Even before the country was divided in 1948, a massive exodus of Korean Christians from the north to the south began, which decisively changed the profile of Christian presence there. The Korean War of 1950–1953 led to renewed devastation and strengthened the anti-communist attitude of the churches in the South. Then, in the 1960s, a period of unprecedented church growth began. The number of Christians rose from about 600,000 in 1950 and 1,140,000 (1960) to 2,200,000 (1970) and 7,180,627 (1980; according to government figures available for this year for the first time) [cf. Text 96]. The accelerated industrialization since the 1960s led to growing social tensions. At the same time, it increased social involvement of South Korean Christians. In the 1970s, a specifically Korean form of liberation theology emerged in the form of Minjung theology [Text 101; see chapter 21.4].

The *Philippines*, the Asian nation with the highest percentage of Catholics (approx. 84% in 2000), gained independence from the USA in 1946. Heavily devastated in the Second World War as a battlefield between the Japanese and the Americans, the efforts of the young republic initially focused on rebuilding the country and its infrastructure. The Catholic majority and the older ("ecumenical") Protestant minority churches played an important role in education and health care. – In a very different regional and colonial context, *Lebanon* – previously a French 'mandate territory' – gained its sovereignty as early as 1943. In 1956, the percentage of Christians in Lebanon was reported at 54% of the population. By distributing the highest state offices among various denominations, the political system sought to secure the balance of power among the country's religious communities. Thus, according to the (repeatedly updated) constitution of 1943, the head of state had to be a Maronite Christian and the head of government a Sunni Muslim.

21.2 Loss of Status and Persecutions under Communist Rule

In 1949, the People's Republic was proclaimed in *China*. The new communist rulers were initially less concerned with extermination rather than with control over the Christian churches. Nevertheless, massive repression soon set in. They intensified with the beginning of the Korean War (1950–1953), in which Chinese units faced American troops. Euroamerican missionaries were expelled from the country in 1951 [Text 90c] and all "imperialist ties" between China's churches and the West were cut.

As early as 1949, "patriotic" Chinese Christians had broken away from the "old" overseas missions in a "manifesto" [Text 90b]. In 1954, the later so-called "Three-Self Patriotic Movement" was founded, which sought to unite the various Protestant communities under the control of the Communist Party [Text 90d]. Dissident groups (and unregistered "house churches") continued to operate underground. In the Catholic context, too, a "patriotic" organization was established. Recognized by the state but rejected by Rome, it faced the underground church of Catholics loyal to Rome since 1958.

For all Christians, however – whether Catholics, Protestants or indigenous communities, whether "patriotically" united or driven underground – a period of horror followed. The two decades from the late 1950s to the late 1970s have been called the "darkest period" in the modern history of Chinese Christianity. Initially, during the so-called "Great Leap Forward" (beginning in 1958), 90% of the churches still open, especially in the countryside, were closed. Clergymen were imprisoned; believers were mistreated or sent to labor camps, where they often did not survive. During this period, "prisons and labor camps became an important place where the gospel was spread."[2] Repression increased again during the "Great Proletarian Cultural Revolution" of 1966–1976, which, combined with an excessive cult of the "Great Chairman" Mao Zedong (1893–1976), aimed to eliminate all "remnants of the bourgeoisie and feudalism" in the party, government, army and society. At the same time, it led to the persecution of the various religious communities and, in particular, to the complete dismantling of all remaining church structures [Text 95]. Nevertheless, Christian communities survived underground and in some cases experienced a rapid upswing in the post-Mao era.

On Korean soil, two states and competing political systems existed since 1948. In communist *North Korea*, dictator Kim Il-Sung (1912–1994) eliminated any potential opposition, including the Christian churches. The latter were combatted as carriers of an imperialist ideology and an extended arm of the Americans controlling the south of the country [Text 91]. A form of socialism developed in North Korea that differed from both the Soviet and Chinese models and established one of the most totalitarian systems of the 20th century. After initial economic successes, the country was almost completely destroyed by the end of the Korean War (1950–1953), triggered by the North's invasion of the South. Externally, it increasingly isolated itself also from its socialist neighbors (China and the Soviet Union). Domestically, along with other freedoms, religious freedom was completely suppressed by 1949. Religious organizations were wiped out, their buildings confiscated, and other social manifestations of religion, such as traditional customs and holidays, abolished. Instead, a quasi-religious cult arose around the "fatherly leader" and the "sun of the nation," Kim Il-Sung, which was even reinforced by his son and successor Kim Jong-il (and his son and successor Kim Jong-un) after his death in 1994.

Vietnam did not escape the fate of division into two parts (and their incorporation into rival power blocs). After the end of French colonial rule in 1954, the country was initially provisionally divided along the 17th parallel at the Indochina Conference in Geneva. However, the elections scheduled for 1956, which were to decide the political orientation of the – hopefully then reunited – nation, never took place. Vietnam was thus divided for the next twenty years into the (Communist-ruled) 'Democratic Republic of Vietnam' in the north and the (Western-backed) 'Republic of Vietnam' in the south. Again, the country's numerous Catholic population, dating back to the activities of Portuguese Jesuits and French missionaries in the 17th and 18th centuries, lived mostly in the north. Again, the division of the country led to a mass exodus from north to south. Among other Christians, about 700,000 Catholics – almost half of the Catholic population of northern Vietnam – emigrated to the south. This included five bishops and 700 priests (and thus two-thirds of the entire North Vietnamese clergy) – despite appeals to the contrary by the Catholic hierarchy [Text 91]. – In 1975, the victory of the communists in the so-called Vietnam War (ca. 1955–1975) triggered a new wave of refugees, this time from the south to neighboring Asian countries as well as to the United States. For the Christian community of the country this meant a new bloodletting. Then, in 1976, all of Vietnam was reunified under communist leadership. The new masters confiscated church institutions now also in the south and sent hundreds of priests to "re-education camps". It was not until the late 1980s that the relationship between church and state gradually began to ease. – In neighboring *Laos* and *Cambodia,* too, the tiny Christian minority was subjected to sometimes massive repression by socialist regimes in the 1970s and 1980s.

21.3 Search for Christian Identity in the "New Asia"

Increased cooperation and networking among the various Christian communities were one form of response to the new challenges in postcolonial Asia. In the Protestant context, the system of interdenominational 'National Christian Councils' (NCC's), some of which had already been established in the 1920s, was further developed. In 1959, as already mentioned, the forerunner organization of the later so-called 'Christian Conference of Asia' (CCA) was founded in Kuala Lumpur. Not only as an organizational structure, but above all as a platform of exchange between Asian Christians from different cultural, ecclesiastical and political contexts, the CCA gained increasing importance. In Catholic Asia, it was impulses from the Second Vatican Council (1962–1965) that led to the formation of the 'Federation of Asian Bishops' Conferences' (FABC) in 1972. Then, in 1998, there was the convening of an (overall) 'Asian Synod'. Other supra-regional and trans-denominational associations (such as the 'Asian Theological Conference' formed in 1979) as well as evangelical or Pentecostal networks formed in the 1970s and 1980s.

In the years following independence, a variety of experiments in *cultural indigenization* proliferated, especially in the Protestant space. In areas such as church architecture, sacred music, liturgy, the design of worship spaces, the performing arts, poetry and various forms of social life, greater use was made of local traditions instead of Western patterns. This happened partly much earlier than in Catholic Asia. Here only the Second Vatican Council brought a breakthrough on a broad front. The idea of Christian ashrams, for example, was already discussed in Protestant India and Sri Lanka at the beginning of the 20th century and realized in 1917 and 1921, respectively [see Text 68]. This happened long before the first hesitant experiments in the Catholic context, which began in the 1940s and were initially eyed with suspicion by the church hierarchy. With the Second Vatican Council, however, the wind changed, and a spirit of optimism spread. For example, the Philippine bishop Julio X. Labayen at the end of the 1970s, looking back on the Council and its impact on the Catholic Church on the continent:

> I am most enthusiastic about the recent growth of the basic Christian communities [in the Philippines] .... I think they will prove to be the major influence in the church of the future. [...] I am also enthusiastic about the growth of all ecumenical activities in Asia and the Philippines—those between the Christian churches, those with the traditional religions of Asia, and those also with dedicated secularists, including Marxists, of good will. Vatican II ... has turned us to closer cooperation with all others who dream and work for the kingdom or for the true liberation of the people. [...] Finally, I am excited about our bishops in Asia and the Philippines, about the growth of so many people in mature spirituality for social action, and about the beginnings of a theology appropriate to Asia. [Text 98]

Not only openness to the traditions of Asian spirituality was now on the agenda. It was also a variety of other aspects of church life – such as the growth of Christian base communities, ecumenical openness, interreligious cooperation, social activities and a theological reorientation – that marked the departure of Asian Catholicism from the ghetto of self-imposed isolation in which it had previously found itself constrained. At the same time, however, this awakening triggered backlash from conservative circles.

21.4 Approaches to New Theological Orientation

The changed situation in revolutionary Asia led at the same time to diverse approaches of theological reorientation. The prominent role that Asian theologians played early on a global ecumenical level is noteworthy. D. T. Niles (1908–1970), for example, a Methodist pastor from northern Sri Lanka, served in various ecumenical functions in Asia and later at the WCC in Geneva, where he headed the Department for Evangelization since 1953. He placed the task of evangelization in the context of the "post-colonial crisis of mission". He assigned the Christian minority in Asia the task of a "prophetic" commitment and critical accompaniment in the process of national reconstruction. M. M. Thomas (1916–1996), representative of the ancient Indian Mar Thomas Church and at the same time member of the communist party of Kerala, already clarified in his biography the field of tension of Christian action in the new Asia. From 1968–1975 he moderated the Central Committee of the WCC. In his activities he combined spirituality with politics and searched for a Christocentric secular community of believers also outside organized churches, with which he connected the idea of a "new humanity". – In postwar Japan, Kazoh Kitamori's (1916–1998) "Theology of God's Pain" temporarily attracted considerable attention also in the wider public. Kitamori combined the Japanese concepts of *itamu* and tsurasa, of natural love and self-sacrifice through death, with biblical insights. Inspired by Luther and his interpretation of the Bible passage Jeremiah 31:20, he in turn had a considerable impact, for example, on the German theologian Jürgen Moltmann.

In 1970, the Filipino theologian Emerito P. Nacpil formulated the "Asian critical principle" as a guideline of theological education for the 'Association of Theological Schools in Southeast Asia' (ATSSEA). Characteristics of this concept were the reference to the religious and cultural plurality of South Asia, its colonial past, the experience of oppression and exploitation as well as the search for a "new worldwide social order". – Quite analogously oriented is also the already mentioned [chap. 20.3] concept of "contextualization" which – formulated in 1972 by the Taiwanese educator Shoki Coe – became formative for the WCC's programs of theological education in the global South. In addition to cultural factors, the socioeconomic upheavals of the time became guiding aspects of situational analysis. – Increasing attention was also paid to the perspectives of feminist theology. The writer Henriette M. Katoppo (1943–2007), for example, has been called "Indonesia's first internationally recognized woman theologian."[3] She was active in many ecumenical associations and since the 1970s has helped to shape the debates about an "Asian theology" from the "perspective of Asian women." In this, she stands in the tradition of other prominent Asian Christian women – such as Pandita Ramabai (1858–1922) or

Lilivathi Singh (1868–1909) from India – who had already received international attention at the beginning of the 20th century [see Figures 38 + 40].

Theology of the "people" was one of the buzzwords that increasingly came into use in the 1970s to give expression to the specific experiences and hopes of marginalized groups. In India, these are in particular the "Dalits," the group of formerly so-called casteless people who make up the majority of the Christian population in various regions. In Korea, it was the 'Minjung theology' that since its first public manifestation in 1973 increasingly shaped the debates of the 1970s and 1980s. This happened amid the experiences of military rule and 'developmental dictatorship'. In this context, Minjung refers to the suffering people who are, however, at the same time actors and subjects of their history. In this concept, biblical traditions are combined with the specific experiences of the Korean history of suffering and oppression [Text 101].

Notes to Chapter 21

1. Seiichi (1991), *Third Generation*, 128 f.
2. Bays (2012), *New History*, 176.
3. Phan (2011), *Christianities* in Asia, 65.

Further Reading for Chapter 21

21.1 (*Christians as a Minority in the Process of Nation Building*)
Phan (2018), *Asia in the 20th Century*, 399ff. 405ff; Aritonang/ Steenbrink (2008), *Christianity in Indonesia*, 187–203; Becker (1996), *Pancasila*; Muskens, M.P.M. (1979), *Partner in Nation Building* (Indonesia); Philips (1981), *Rising of the Sun*, 1–16; Seiichi (1991), *Dritte Generation*, 128–163 (Japan); Kim/Kim (2015), *Korean Christianity*, 157–214.

21.2 (*Loss of Status and Persecutions under Communist Rule*)
Yang (2012), *Survival and Revival under Communist Rule*; Bays (2012), *New History*, 158–182; Wickeri (1988), *Three-Self Movement*; Kim/ Kim (2015), *Korean Christianity*, 162–168.180–186.193–196; Ho Tai (2001), *Country of Memory*; Phan (2018), *Asia*, 404ff.

21.3 (*Search for Christian Identity in the "New Asia"*)
Briggs/ Oduyoye/ Tsetis (2004), *Ecumenical Movement* 3, 495–522 („Regional Ecumenism: Asia"); Weber (1966), *Asia and the Ecumenical Movement*, 220–306; Sonntag (2021), *Early Post-War Japan*, 1–40; Poon (2010), *Christian Movements*;

Phan (2002), *Vatican II in Asia*, 243–258; Kämpchen (1982), *Katholische Ashrams*, 274–287; Baago (1969), *Pioneers of Indigenous Christianity*.

21.4 (*Approaches to New Theological Orientations*)
Phan (2018), *Asia in the 20th Century*, 405ff; England (1981), *Theology in Asia;* Elwood, (1978), *What Asian Christians are thinking*; Briggs/ Oduyoye/ Tsetis (2004), *Ecumenical Movement* 3, 495–522, esp. 498–502 („Theological Responses"); Phan (2011), *Christianities in Asia*, 1–8. 61ff; Kitamori (1972), *Theologie des Schmerzes Gottes*; Lienemann-Perrin (1992), *Politische Verantwortung*, 117–228; Phan (2011), *Christianities in Asia*, 1–8. 61 ff; Furtado (1978), *D. T. Niles;* Thomas (1976), *Christ of the Indian Renaissance*; Kartoppo (1979), *An Asian Woman's Theology;* England et al. (2002–2004), *Asian Christian Theologies* I-III.

CHAPTER 22

Africa in the 1960s

22.1 Church and State in New Africa

At the end of the 1950s, the "wind of change" also reached Africa [Text 194–196]. 1960 is the year in which numerous countries on the continent gained independence in one fell swoop. In addition to populous (British) Nigeria and (Belgian) Congo (Zaire), these were Cameroon, Togo, the Ivory Coast, Senegal, Gabon, Dahomey, Chad, the Central African Republic, Upper Volta, Niger, Mali, Madagascar, Somalia, Mauritania, and Congo-Brazzaville. After Egypt (1952) and Tunisia, Morocco and Sudan (1956), Ghana (1957) and Guinea (1958) were the first black African states to achieve sovereignty. Other countries in sub-Saharan Africa followed in the 1960s. Southern Africa (South Africa, Rhodesia [Zimbabwe] and Portuguese-ruled Angola and Mozambique) initially remained under white rule. In 1975, Portuguese colonial rule on the continent too came to an end.

Political independence initially brought far fewer changes in state-church relations in most sub-Saharan African countries than might have been expected. Earlier tensions between nationalist movements and the missions, for example in central Kenya or Zambia, subsided once independence was achieved. Mass expulsions of Western missionaries (as in 1964 from Arab-dominated southern Sudan) or attacks on Catholic mission stations (as in 1960/61 in Congo) remained the exception. The main Protestant churches quickly Africanized their leadership ranks. For the Catholics, this took somewhat longer. But they too soon had enough indigenous archbishops and bishops to participate in the political processes of the new era. Church institutions in education and health care initially remained irreplaceable even in the postcolonial order. According to UNESCO statistics, more than 60% of Africa's general education was still in the hands of the churches as late as 1961. Moreover, as mentioned earlier [chap. 18.4], the new leaders of independent Africa, especially in Anglophone Africa, had received their education mostly at mission schools [see Text 186–193]. The later presidents of Zambia (Kenneth Kaunda, r. 1964–1991), Kenya (Jomo Kenyatta, r. 1963–1978), or Malawi (Hastings Banda, r. 1964–1985) were Presbyterians (before they partially joined other churches). Kwame Nkrumah (Ghana, r. 1957–1966) and Julius Neyerere (Tanzania, r. 1961–1985) were baptized Catholics. Nmamdi Azikiwe, first president of Nigeria (r. 1963–1966), had attended Catholic, Anglican, and Methodist schools. In Southern Rhodesia

© KLAUS KOSCHORKE, 2025 | DOI:10.1163/9789004699830_023
This is an open access chapter distributed under the terms of the CC BY-NC-ND 4.0 license.

(Zimbabwe), nationalist leaders such as Joshua Nkomo, Ndabaninghi Sithole, George Nyandaro, and Robert Mugabe had previously been Methodist preachers or Anglican or Catholic activists. Many of these men had started out as enthusiastic church members but had later let that connection fall asleep or broken off altogether. But they had repeatedly studied at the same schools as the new African church leaders. Personal relationships mitigated emerging conflicts in many places.

Once the new order was established, however, tensions grew. The contentious issues were the same in different countries. They concerned the control of the school system, the introduction of authoritarian one-party regimes (with the restriction of democratic freedoms and ideological control of youth movements), and the personal glorification of national leaders. The latter could rise to the level of a quasi-religious glorification that used Christian terminology and developed in the direction of a state religion, at the expense of other forms of faith. This was the case in Ghana, where a personality cult formed around *Kwame Nkrumah* (1909–1972) – who had led the country to independence in 1957. Nkrumahism" was declared the "highest form of Christianity" [Text 201] and a "creed to Kwame Nkrumah" was formulated:

> "I believe in the Convention People's Party, the opportune Saviour of Ghana, and in Kwame Nkrumah, its founder and leader, who is endowed with the Ghana Spirit, born true Ghanaian for Ghana, suffering under victimizations: was vilified, threatened with deportation; he disentangled himself from [the decrees of the British government], ... ascended to Political Heights, and sitteth at the Supreme Head of the C.C.P. [Convention People's Party] from whence he shall demand Full Self-Government for Ghana. I believe in Freedom for all peoples ... the Victorious end of our struggle, its glory and pride, and the Flourish of Ghana, for ever and ever" [Text 202].

Kwame Nkrumah had been baptized after attending a Catholic missionary school. He studied in the U.S. (where he also occasionally worked as a lay preacher) and London and, after his return in 1947, organized strikes and mass rallies against British colonial rule in what was then known as the Gold Coast. In doing so, he used the methods of both Gandhi and American campaigners. As the first president of independent Ghana, he made the country a center of pan-African activity. He also sought close ties with the communist world (China, Soviet Union). His rule became increasingly authoritarian, and in 1964 Ghana was transformed into a one-party state. Conflicts with the churches arose from the nationalization of church schools and the para-religious organization of party youth. "Seek first"– as one slogan of "Nkrumahism" read, in a modification of the Bible passage Mt. 6:33 – "the political kingdom, and all things will be added to you." In 1966, Nkrumah was overthrown in a military coup.

His removal from power also ended "the epoch of Nkruhmah as the continent's prime guru ... and that of Nyerere began"[1] From 1961 to 1985, *Julius Nyerere* (1922–1999) was first prime minister and then president of Tanzania (so named since its union with Zanzibar in 1964). His policy was determined by the goal of economic independence. In the 1967 Arusha Declaration, he developed the concept of "African socialism," which was based less on Marxist models than on traditional African ways of life. Central to this was the idea of living together (Ujamaa) and the development of village communities (as an idealized model of society). Nyerere was also inspired by Christian ideas; and he called on the country's churches to participate "in the rebellion against the social structures and economic organizations that condemn people to poverty, humiliation and degradation." Only then could the church effectively "promote its doctrine of love to all men" [Text 204]. – The project of collectivization along the lines of African village communities failed, however, and was abandoned as early as the mid-1970s. In 1985, Nyerere voluntarily stepped down from the political stage – a rare event in contemporareous Africa.

There were two phases of African nationalism, the All African Conference of Churches (AACC) noted in 1968: "In the first, forces are mobilized against the colonial power, leading eventually to independence. The second, far more important stage, is about making a nation out of very different groups and making sure that the ethnic groups live well together. It is at this stage that the most pressing problems arise in our country" [cf. Text 200]. Indeed, the integration of heterogeneous ethnic groups or the establishment of internal unity within the national borders drawn, sometimes arbitrarily, by the former colonial powers represented a crucial challenge for the new states of Africa. This was the cause of numerous conflicts in the 1960s, such as the civil war in Biafra, Nigeria, in 1967 or the so-called Congo troubles. By the end of the decade, the spirit of optimism of the first years of independence had largely faded. It gave way to growing disillusionment and authoritarian rule.

22.2 'Historical' and Independent Churches

The process of decolonization did not lead to the disappearance of Christian churches on the continent. The opposite was the case: "Christianity may never have experienced such a quantitative expansion as in [sub-Saharan] Africa between 1960 and the end of the 20th century," according to Africa historian Adrian Hastings.[2] According to estimates, the number of African Christians rose from 34 million to nearly 200 million between 1950 and 1990. By the turn of the millennium, the Christian share of the continent's total population was reported to be 45.9%, up from 9.2% in 1900. Regional centers were (in descending order) South, Central, East and West Africa.[3]

This enormous growth refers to both the so-called "historical" churches (which emerged from the work of Western missions) and the "independent" churches (which are under African leadership). In Tanzania, for example, the membership of the 'Evangelical Lutheran Church' (ELCT) had increased from about 400,000 in 1963 to about 1.5 million in 1991.[4] The largest independent church in Africa in the 1960s was that of the Kimbanguists, with at least half a million members. Originally an underground religious movement limited to some regions of Belgian Congo, it had increasingly spread to various neighboring countries and by the 1990s had a following numbering in the millions. Evangelization (mainly by Africans themselves), widespread migration, the socioeconomic upheavals and the general population increase of the time were causal factors for the enormous church growth in postcolonial Africa.

As far as the *"historical"* (or former missionary) *churches* are concerned, the transition to legal autonomy in the individual regional churches took place rapidly and simultaneously with the assumption of leadership positions by indigenous Christians. In 1960, for example, the Synod of Mansibou – to cite three prominent examples from the Protestant spectrum – established full autonomy for the Protestant Church of the Congo (Brazzaville). In 1961, the Methodist Church of Ghana gained full autonomy, with its own conference as the governing body. In 1963, seven previously separate Lutheran mission churches in Tanzania merged to form the ELCT mentioned earlier. There was also much discussion in these early years of "national awakening" about the establishment of interdenominational national churches. References to the model of the South Indian Church Union of 1947 [Text 87a; cf. chapter 21.1] played a role. Later, ecumenical enthusiasm waned. But in the individual countries, the National Christian Councils became more and more important as forums of interdenominational cooperation (so initially in Ghana and Kenya). They increasingly included the larger independent churches and established links with the Catholic Church. At a pan-African level, the 'All Africa Conference of Churches' (AACC), established in 1963, became increasingly important [Text 197+200]. An enduring problem was the linguistic division between Anglophone and Francophone churches. African leaders and theologians such as Desmond Tutu (South Africa; Figure 54) and John Pobee (Ghana) also held prominent positions in the WCC.

On the Catholic side, the *Second Vatican Council* (1962–1965) triggered a surge of indigenization in leadership positions. Above all, the number of African archbishops increased by leaps and bounds, although the majority of the episcopate was still white for a long time. Mostly educated in Rome, they held theologically rather conservative positions. Rome thus had little to fear from an Africanization of the hierarchy. In 1969, Pope Paul VI was the first head of the Catholic Church to travel to sub-Saharan Africa (Uganda). Toward the end of the 1970s, "the vast majority of church leaders in all denominations were natives, not missionaries. One consequence was that the contrast between missionary-led 'historic' churches and African-led 'independent' churches diminished. All were now under African leadership, and all took seriously the need for inculturation."[5]

In the 1960s, the number of *African Independent Churches* ('AIC's) grew by leaps and bounds. For South Africa, the 1960 census shows that the membership of the independent churches there had now grown to 2.3 million people. This was 21% of the African population and 31% of the country's African Christians. In Zaire, the previously illegal Church of the Kimbanguists ('Église de Jésus-Christ sur la terre par son envoyé spécial Simon Kimbangu', in short: E.J.C.S.K.) had only been officially recognized in 1959 while still under Belgian colonial administration [see Text 206 + 216c]. New movements were constantly forming, for example in Kenya, the Ivory Coast and Ghana. In Nigeria it was the 'Christ Apostolic Church', which counted about 100,000 members around 1966. Starting in Rhodesia (Zimbabwe), the Vapostori community spread widely. The phenomenon of ecclesiastical independentism was widespread both in rural and urban areas and among different social classes. Initially, Africa's new political leaders met the independent churches with great sympathy. Later, interest cooled as these mostly charismatic-prophetic communities had little to offer in the process of nation-building and the development of a modern education system and other infrastructure projects.

Everywhere, AIC's "mushroomed". In the early 1970s, their number was estimated at between 5,000 and 10,000. Most were very small, with fewer than 100 members. The 95 or so larger among them (with membership of 20,000 or more) developed into well-structured churches. The vast majority of these independent communities had a Protestant background. They repeatedly justified the break with their former missionary mother churches by referring to the example of the Reformation ("We do as Luther did on October 31, 1517"). But there were also splits in the Catholic context. For example, the 'Maria Legio Church' that emerged in Kenya in 1969, with about 75,000–100,000 adherents, lasted about 30 years. It claimed to be "Catholic, but not Roman Catholic. Because we are Catholics in Africa and not Catholics in Rome."[6] Adherence to traditional ways of life (such as polygamy) and religious traditions (great importance of visions, dance, ecstasy) play an important role in many AIC's. In 1969, the Kimbanguist Church (E.J.C.S.K.) became the first AIC to be accepted into the World Council of Churches (WCC) (though it was dispensed again in the early 2000s). Others followed. In 1978, an all-African federation of independent churches was also formed.

Among the pre-colonial or *"Ancient Oriental" Churches* of Africa, *Ethiopia* was of particular importance, especially in the 1960s. Ethiopia – ancient, independent, Christian – also played a prominent role in the Pan-African as well as the Non-Aligned Movement of the 1960s. The headquarters of the 'Organization of African Unity' (OAU), founded in 1963, was Addis Ababa. Emperor Haile Selassie (r. 1930–1936 and 1941–1974), who was temporarily expelled by the Italians, was internationally regarded as a figurehead of anti-colonial resistance. But he also aroused messianic expectations, as among the African-American population of Jamaica during his visit there in 1966. The Ethiopian Orthodox Tewahedo Church was one of the founding members of the WCC in 1948. In 1959, it broke away from centuries of institutional dependence on the Coptic Church. Since then, for the first time, it has had an Ethiopian patriarch at its head. A series of famines led to the fall of the imperial house in 1974. The ensuing socialist military dictatorship lasted until 1991.

The Coptic Church of *Egypt* was also one of the founding members of the WCC in 1948. Under Patriarch Cyril VI (r. 1959–1971), there was a revival of traditional monasticism. Earlier reform activities had been prompted by the lay-led Sunday school movement. Coptic intellectuals had played a not inconsiderable role in the early Egyptian national movement of the 1920s. Under President Gamal Abd' an-Nasser (r. 1954–1970), the influence of the Christian minority, which comprises about 5–10% of the population, was again pushed back more strongly. The broader picture of Coptic Christianity also includes the growing diaspora in the United States and Europe, but remarkably also missionary successes among migrants in sub-Saharan Africa.

22.3 Approaches to African Theology, Interreligious Initiatives

The process of political independence was preceded by a rediscovery of African culture. Léopold S. Senghor, a Catholic and the first president of Muslim-majority Senegal (ruled 1960–1980), had already launched the movement of 'négritude' – pride in one's own black African identity – in the 1950s together with Afro-French intellectuals [see Text 203]. In reaction to the rigid assimilation policy of French colonialism, the intrinsic value of old African traditions was emphasized anew. Initially, it was mainly Catholic theologians from Francophone Africa (such as Bénezét Bujo, DR Congo) who analyzed the religious worldview of traditional Africa and used it to reformulate certain aspects of Christian doctrine. They devoted themselves to the study of the myths, poems, proverbs, rites and sacrificial customs of African peoples and sought to understand them anew from the perspective of ecclesial reflection and practice. In the process, the traditional religions of the continent were also understood as 'praeparatio evangelii' (preparation of the gospel), in which God had already spoken before the arrival of the missionaries.

In the 1960s, there was a growing debate about the goal (and various forms) of an *'African theology'*. It sought to do justice to the cultural traditions of the continent – in distinction from imported Western missionary theological models. Keywords of this debate were the terms 'inculturation', 'adaptation', 'indigenization' or 'Africanization'. The 1960s saw a plethora of university foundations, many with their own departments for religious studies or theology. Christian Baeta in Ghana [Text 207], Harry Sawyer in Sierra Leone, Vincent Mulago in Congo/Zaire, or John Mbiti in Kenya [Text 208] were among this first generation of academically educated theologians. They were followed by Desmond Tutu [Figure 54] and many others in South Africa, John Pobee and Kwame Bediako from Ghana [Figure 53] or Jean-Marc Ela in Cameroon. Protestant voices, especially from Anglophone West Africa, saw their it as their most urgent task to put the Bible and African culture into an appropriate relationship. For James Dickson (Ghana), for example, the only valid approach was to move from biblical revelation to the traditional religions of Africa, and not vice versa. This was also done in critical confrontation with the practice of certain independent churches, which often continued pre-Christian practices and rites unseen. At the same time, since the end of the 1960s, critical voices have been growing, warning against a romanticized transfiguration of the African past. Fixated on past identities, the current problems of the continent – such as poverty, oppression and neocolonial exploitation – would be neglected. This was often accompanied by criticism of the church's own leaders, who had adapted to the new power relations and neglected the church's "prophetic guardianship".

The so-called *"Black theology"*, which began to attract increasing attention in the 1970s, was clearly more politically oriented. Developed primarily in the context of the South African apartheid system, it was at the same time strongly influenced by African-American voices from the USA. Stephen Biko (1946–1977), for example, founder of the 'Black Consciousness' movement in South Africa and repeatedly imprisoned by the apartheid regime there, described it as the task of black theology "to bring God back to black man and to the truth and reality of his situation" [Text 209]. The God of the Bible is the God of liberation and not of oppression, a God of right and not of wrong, according to Allan B. Boesak, another early representative of this movement (and later president of the 'World Alliance of Reformed Churches'). Not only the 'black man', therefore, needed to be liberated – 'black' referring not only to skin color, but more generally to the experience of oppression – but also the gospel wherever it was abused and exploited (by white apologists of the apartheid system). Another early voice was that of Manas Buthelezi, later bishop of the Lutheran Church of South Africa [Text 210]. 'African theology' – more inculturation theology oriented – and 'black theology' – calling for political engagement – often described as opposites, increasingly converged. – In the 1980s, approaches to a black feminist theology were also strengthened.[7] At the same time, however, efforts to formulate an "African Evangelical Theology" were remarkable. They sought to formulate an independent African form of pietistic-evangelical spirituality.

The need for peaceful coexistence between the different religions was repeatedly emphasized, especially in the founding phase of the new states [e.g., Text 203]. Yet *interreligious dialogue* in sub-Saharan Africa (and especially that between Christians and Muslims) was "for a long time a lived rather than a reflected dialogue."[8] An early example of an institutionalized form of dialogue was the 'Islam in Africa Project' (IPA), founded in 1959. Its goal was to "prepare Christians for encounter with and responsibility toward sub-Saharan Muslims" and to "build bridges of mutual understanding." This included the 'Study Center for Islam and Christianity' opened in 1965 in Ibadan (Nigeria) for students from all over Africa. Renamed 'Programme for Christian-Muslim Relations in Africa' (PROCMURA) in 2003, the project has developed into a pan-African Christian organization. It is supported by various Protestant (and also independent) churches, including in Ghana [Text 215].[9] Organized dialogue efforts on the Catholic side existed since 1969, promoted by the Second Vatican Council. The emergence of political Islam in the 1980s led to significantly increased tensions [Text 214] and posed a whole new challenge [cf. chap. 24.2]. In 1989, a 'Circle of Concerned African Women Theologians' was founded in Ghana – with the aim of broadening pan-African and interreligious theological perspectives of African women.

22.4 South Africa: Christians and Churches in the Apartheid State

South Africa requires a separate consideration. For white minority rule did not end here until 1990 (respectively with the first free general elections held in 1994). Moreover, debates about the system of apartheid was a central theme also of the country's Christian history, with different voices from different camps. At the same time, this controversy played an enormous role in global ecumenism, with repercussions also for the churches of the West. In the struggle against apartheid – according to Nelson Mandela in 1992, symbolic figure of the black resistance and later South Africa's first black president (r. 1994–1999) – the "contribution of the broad ecumenical movement in South Africa itself and internationally" was of outstanding importance and "without parallel".[10]

The unequal treatment of the different "racial" groups in South Africa had steadily intensified since the beginning of the 20th century. However, it was not until 1948 that the ideological and legal system of apartheid was officially established, which made racism the basis of the state order and provided for "separate development" for the groups of "whites," "blacks," "coloreds" and "Asians," each classified as a "race," with different rights and access to resources. Public facilities such as park benches, post offices, beaches, train stations, schools, and churches were segregated by "race" [see Photo H02]. Until the 1970s, government expenditures for a white schoolchild were about 20 times as high as for a black one. The latter were to be taught only elementary knowledge. The freedom of movement of the black majority was massively restricted by a perfected passport system. A policy of rigorous segregation of residential areas was intended to keep Africans out of the "white cities. Forced resettlements were the result. The resistance that had been swelling since the Sharpeville massacre of 1960 was brutally crushed.

The policy of apartheid was societally supported in particular by the Boers (or "Afrikaners," as they called themselves), that section of the white population who originally had come from the Netherlands. Their self-image was characterized by a special sense of election – as a "new Israel" in the midst of a hostile environment [Text 212a]. Theologically, it was supported mainly by the Reformed churches of Dutch tradition (such as the 'Nederduitse Gereformeede Kerk' [NGK]). On the opposite side were black Christians and activists from the various communities, but also individuals from the more liberal English-speaking churches (such as the Anglican Trevor Huddleston). The 'Christian Institute for Contextual Theology', founded in 1963, developed into a focal point of the church opposition. Led by Christiaan F. Beyers Naudé (1915–2004) as the most prominent white critic of the apartheid system, it was dissolved by the government in 1977.

Another center was the 'South African Council of Churches' (SAAC), most of whose member churches were also members of the WCC. Under black leadership (with high-profile general secretaries such as Bishop Desmond Tutu [1978–1985; see Figure 54] and Rev. Frank Chikane [1988–1994]), it intensified its activities and international contacts – both with exiled opposition politicians and with the Protestant ecumenical movement. The South African Catholic Bishops' Conference also intensified its cooperation with SAAC. An 'Alliance of Black Reformed Churches' of South Africa formally declared apartheid a "sin" and its justification a "heresy." In 1982, the World Alliance of Reformed Churches confirmed this judgment and expelled the NGK, which continued to be pro-apartheid, from its ranks [Text 213b]. At the same time, it elected the black pastor Allan Boesak as its president. In the South African and ecumenical debates of this time, reference to the experiences of the German church struggle, to Bonhoeffer and the 'Barmen Theological Declaration' of 1934 also played an important role. In German Protestantism, in turn, disputes over the WCC's anti-racism program sparked fierce controversy. Church action groups and calls for boycotts (against goods from South Africa) reached a wider public. In South Africa itself, repression intensified against political opposition, but increasingly also against church opposition. Thousands of activists were arrested, abducted, tortured or murdered.

At the height of state violence in 1985, when no end to the apartheid system was yet in sight, a group of committed Christians – mostly black – called on the country's churches for a decisive "prophetic" witness. Reconciliation, they said, could not be achieved without fundamental change in social and political structures. This call has become known as the *'Kairos document'* and has attracted attention far beyond the country's borders.

> The time has come. The moment of truth has arrived. [...] It is the kairos or moment of truth not only for apartheid but also for the Church. [...] Our present kairos calls for a response from Christians that is biblical, spiritual, pastoral and, above all, prophetic. [...] It would be quite wrong to see the present conflict as simply a racial war. [...] The situation we are dealing with here is one of oppression. [...] Throughout the Bible God appears as the liberator of the oppressed. He is not neutral. He does not attempt to reconcile Moses and Pharaoh ... Oppression is sin and it cannot be compromised with, it must be done away with. [Text 213d]

Five years later, the apartheid system collapsed [see chapter 25.1].

Notes to Chapter 22

1. Hastings (1979), *African Christianity*, 184.
2. RGG4 I (1998) 155. 147–158: „Afrika III: Christentumsgeschichte" (A. Hastings).

3. Iliffe (1995), *Geschichte Afrikas,* 357; Hock (2005), *Christentum in Afrika,* 237 f; Barrett et al. (²2001), *World Christian Encyclopedia* I, 12 gives a significantly higher figure for 1995 of approx. 295 million.
4. Ngeiyamu / Triebel (1994), *Tansania,* 104.
5. RGG4 I (1998) 156. 147–158: „Afrika III: Christentumsgeschichte" (A. Hastings).
6. Quoted from: Baur (1992), *Christianity in Africa,* 354; Hastings (1979), *African Christianity,* 176.
7. Oduyoye/ Musimbi (1992), *The Will to Arise.*
8. Hock (2005), *Christentum in Afrika,* 224.
9. Baur (1994), *Christianity in Africa,* 336f; Hock (1998), *Verantwortung im islamischen Kontext,* 517–527); Pratt (2017), *Engagement with Islam,* 140–164.
10. Walshe (1997), *Anti-Apartheid Struggle,* 387.

Further Reading for Chapter 22

22.1 + 2 (*Church and State in New Africa/ Historical and Independent Churches*)

Iliffe (³2017), *Africans,* 282–315 („Independent Africa, 1956–1995"); Hastings (1979), *African Christianity,* 131–183.184–258; Baur (1994), *Christianity in Africa,* 288–374; Sundkler/ Steed (2000), *Church in Africa,* 901–1037; Isichei (1995), *Christianity in Africa,* 323–352; Marx (2004), *Geschichte Afrikas,* 241–270. 271–293; Reinhard (1988), *Expansion* III, 147–166; Hock (2005), *Christentum in Afrika,* 194–220; Ludwig (1999), *Church and State in Tanzania*; Grohs (1967), *Stufen afrikanischer Emanzipation;* Ngeiyamu/ Triebel (1994), *Tansania*; Hage (2007), *Orientalisches Christentum,* 185 ff.210 ff.; Maxwell (2008), *Postcolonial Christianity in Africa,* 410–421.

22.3 (*Approaches to African Theology, Interreligious Initiatives*)

Kalu (2005), *African Christianity,* 469–493 ("African Christian Theologies"); Dickson (1984), *Theology in Africa*; Parratt (1987), *African Christian Theology*; Kamphausen (2005), „*African Cry*", 77–100; Pemberton (2002), *African Women Theologians*; Bürkle (1968), *Theologie und Kirche in Afrika*; Oduyoye/ Musimbi (1992), *The Will to Arise*; Pratt (2017), *Engagement with Islam,* 140–164; Barron (2023), *African Christian Theology.*

22.4 (South Africa: Christians and Churches in the Apartheid State)
Elphick/ Davenport (1997), *Christianity in South Africa*, 135ff. 347–399; Iliffe (³2017), *Africans*, 267–281, esp. 278ff („The Destruction of Apartheid"); Marx (2004), *Geschichte Afrikas*, 265–269 (Ende of Apartheid); Marx (2024), *Verwoerd;* Walshe (1997), *Anti-Apartheid Struggle*, 383–399; Lienemann-Perrin (1992), *Politische Verantwortung*, 229–414; Lessing et al. (2015), *Contested Relations*, 362–508: Section IV: „Christian Resistance to Apartheid".

CHAPTER 23

Latin America: the 1970s

23.1 Between Social Revolution and State Repression

In the 1960s and 1970s, social antagonisms intensified in numerous Latin American and Caribbean countries. Revolutionary movements spread – inspired by the Cuban Revolution of 1959, which had overthrown the corrupt regime of the dictator Batista. The turnaround in Cuba was hailed by many contemporaries – including church people – as a "historic break" and a "sign of hope ... for the entire continent."[1] At the same time, political repression against reform-oriented forces and opposition figures intensified in many places. In several countries, the military couped itself into power. Brazil made a start in 1964. This was followed by Bolivia in 1972, Uruguay and Chile in 1973, and Argentina in 1976, to name only the most important examples. What followed were the so-called "dirty wars" in many places, with tens of thousands of victims killed and hundreds of thousands of victims "disappeared" forcibly and permanently. This happened in the name of a "doctrine of national security" and the fight against communism.

In this context, an ecclesiastical awakening took place that affected a growing part of the Christian communities. The role of the official Catholic Church remained ambivalent. A part of the Roman hierarchy always stood closely on the side of the respective rulers [Text 300]. Other groups, however, developed a new and comprehensive solidarity with the majority of the poor people, out of the concrete daily experiences of violence and oppression. It inevitably also meant criticism of the conditions of ownership and rule. This awakening found its expression in a theological and pastoral reorientation, which was widely disseminated under the term 'theology of liberation', coined in 1971. On the one hand, this new approach was advocated by churchmen and theologians who found the traditional – post-Tridentine and adopted from Europe – theology inadequate to the realities of the continent. Instead, they developed a growing awareness of the social problems and forms of structural violence on the ground. In particular, lay movements such as the so-called base communities were of great importance. Their members were usually landless farmers (campesinos), agricultural workers, slum dwellers or illiterate people who sought to overcome their everyday problems together.

Widespread in both rural and urban areas, these base communities represented rather independent worship communities under the guidance of a priest or local leader. Given the rampant shortage of priests and the remoteness of regular parishes, base communities were in many places the only accessible form of ecclesial presence. They were not a product of liberation theology, but they provided an important space of resonance and experimentation. They existed before and survived multiple attempts at control.

These diverse renewal efforts received an enormous boost from the Second Vatican Council (1962–1965), which had triggered a broad spirit of awakening in the churches of Latin America. Intensively discussed at the Second All-Latin American Bishops' Conference in Medellín (Colombia) in 1968, liberation theology subsequently developed into a kind of standard theology in many dioceses. The decisive keyword here was the "preferential option for the poor." Since the early 1970s, Latin American liberation theology has been taken seriously not only in Asia and Africa, but also in Europe. At the same time, growing resistance was forming in the political and church establishment. The controversies about liberation theology would go on to shape the church life on the continent throughout the 1970s and 1980s.

23.2 The Second Vatican Council (1962–1965) and the Bishops' Conference of Medellín (1968)

In 1959 – the same year as the Cuban Revolution – Pope John XXIII announced a new council. In its preparation and implementation still almost exclusively European dominated, the *Second Vatican Council* then triggered a global dynamic that was to decisively change the face of Catholicism, especially in Latin America. Two documents from the Council in particular had a strong impact: 'Gaudium et Spes' (which opened the Church to the modern world) and 'Lumen Gentium' (which sought to overcome the traditional barrier between clergy and laity). In it, the Church is seen first as the "people of God," to which all Christians belong as children of God, through the sacrament of Baptism. The consultations were attended by 601 bishops from Latin America (compared to 849 from Europe). They thus represented about 23% of all the participants in the Council. Their contribution, with some exceptions, was initially rather modest. But the Chilean Bishop Manuel Larraín, for example, emphatically stressed the "prophetic function of the people of God" and the need for a "church of the poor" [Text 301]. Another prominent participant was the Brazilian bishop Dom Hélder Câmara (1909–1999). He had gone through – in his own words – a multitude of "conversions" before he developed from a rather conservative churchman into one of the most prominent representatives of liberation theology.

A caesura was then marked by the Second General Assembly of the Latin American Episcopate (CELAM) in *Medellín* (Colombia) in 1968. The theme was "The Church in the Contemporary Transformation of Latin America in the Light of the Council". In an equally creative and independent recourse, the Council texts were related to the current challenges of the continent and further developed. The bishops saw the peoples, "churches and Christian communities" of this continent on the threshold of "a new age". They pleaded for a "holistic development for our continent" as well as for a "liberating education" that anticipates the "new type of society that we seek in Latin America" [Text 303a + b]. Under the leadership of Dom Hélder Câmara, the "enormous social injustices in Latin America" were denounced. Both the liberal-capitalist and Marxist social systems were condemned. Instead, a non-violent and reform-oriented "third way" to liberation was proposed. Following on from Pope Paul VI's 1967 encyclical 'Populorum progressio' [Text 302b], significant sections of the Latin American episcopate, in the presence and with the approval of the Pope, elevated the "preferential option for the poor" to the guiding principle of church action [Text 303c].

23.3 Liberation Theologies: Characteristics, Controversies, Developments

Since the mid-1960s, the debates and activities of socially committed priests, religious and lay people increased. This included, for example, the voluntary relinquishment of church property. Elaborated concepts were formulated in the early 1970s. Gustavo Gutiérrez (Peru), Hugo Assmann (Brazil), Juan Luis Segundo (Uruguay) and Leonardo Boff (Brazil) published, all in the same year 1971 and to a large extent independently of each other, their writings, which were later regarded as the foundation of the 'theology of liberation'. Protestant authors also spoke out. These included the theologians united in the 'Church and Society in Latin America' (ISAL) group in Montevideo, who were in contact with the World Council of Churches in Geneva. Names like Emilio Castro, Julio de Santa Ana, José Míguez Bonino as well as Rubem Alvez [see Text 311] are to be mentioned here.

Characteristics of this quite polyphonic and "new kind of theology" (Gustavo Gutiérrez; see Text 304a+b) were certain leading aspects. Central were the emphasis on the primacy of action over metaphysical speculation; theology as liberating change in past and present; a "holistic" understanding of liberation, redemption understood not as a purely otherworldly promise but as an upheaval already taking place in the present; solidarity with the majority of the "impoverished people living in misery"; social sensitization and awareness-raising. Characteristic also was the focus on specific biblical motifs (such as the Exodus tradition; the prophetic social critique; the Magnificat [with its promise of a reversal of all conditions]; Jesus' inaugural sermon in Nazareth [Luke 4]; and the judgment speech in Matthew 25). The new approach was based on a three-step methodology ("see – judge – act") and the application of certain analytical tools. These included the dependency theory as it had developed in the social science debates in Latin America in the 1960s.

This dependency theory criticized a purely technocratic understanding of "development." The backwardness of Latin American societies was seen not as the result of missing endeavors or endogenous factors (such as a lack of capital, cultural attitudes or mental imprints), but as the result of existing structures of dependency and targeted mechanisms of capitalist exploitation. This in the interplay of international actors (such as multinational corporations) and regional oligarchies that enriched themselves at the expense of the marginalized masses. The dismantling of structures of dependency and oppression therefore appeared to be the necessary consequence. Whether this should be done in a more evolutionary or revolutionary way was answered in different ways. One of the contentious issues in the ensuing disputes was whether the use of Marxist social-analytical categories necessarily entailed the Marxist concept of class struggle. The latter was the constant reproach of conservative critics to liberation theology.

Base church communities became the place for completely new forms of biblical interpretation. This was no longer considered a privilege of the clergy, but a matter for ordinary believers and previously marginalized groups who now discovered the liberating message of the Bible for themselves. Women played a prominent role in this. "The Gospel of the Peasants of Solentiname" also became widely known in Europe. This was a collection of Sunday Bible talks by campesinos from a remote group of islands in Nicaragua, published by Ernesto Cardenal [see Text 304d]. The Bible text just read (Luke 4:16–30), said a woman quoted there, "is a prediction of liberation. And it is also a lesson for us that many Christians have not yet grasped. For one can go to church and sing day and night, ding, dong, ding, dong, without a thought of how much … injustice there still is around us, … how many abuses in this country, how many women who have their eyes full of tears every day …"

The years 1970 to 1975 are considered the peak and most influential phase of Latin American liberation theologies. At the same time, they were increasingly received by Christian action groups in Asia and Africa. They also received increasing attention from the ecclesial (and political) publics in Europe and the USA. In the Association of Third World Theologians (EATWOT), founded in 1976, Latin American voices largely dominated. At the same time, however, resistance within the official church was now intensifying, combined with growing pressure from Rome. The election of a new general secretary of the Latin American Bishops' Council (CELAM) in 1972 marked a turning point. He immediately set about pushing back the influence of liberation theology in the activities of CELAM. Subsequently, conservative bishops were increasingly installed in Latin America. These restorative tendencies intensified under the pontificate of John Paul II (1978–2005). The Polish pope criticized the proximity of many liberation theologians to socialist movements. The official preparation of the Third General Assembly of the Latin American Bishops' Council in Puebla (Mexico) in 1979 also largely resembled a campaign against liberation theology. Nevertheless, its central themes were affirmed there. Thus, in continuity with Medellín 1968, the assembly reaffirmed the "prophetic option expressing preference for, and solidarity with, the poor" and the need for a "conversion of the whole Church" with the goal of "integral liberation (sc. of the poor)" [Text 305]. At the same time, other previously neglected themes of the Council's reception were taken up.

Nevertheless, the *dispute over liberation theology* continued. The controversies intensified after the victory of the Sandinistas in Nicaragua in 1979 (with which a socialist revolution had established itself on the Central American mainland for the first time). Churchmen such as Ernesto Cardenal had participated prominently in this [see Text 307]. In the mid-1980s, the Roman 'Congregation for the Doctrine of the Faith' dedicated two instructions to the theology of liberation. In the first, 'Libertatis nuntius' of 1984, the basic concern of liberation theology was positively appreciated, but at the same time it warned against theological "reductionism" and political messianism. In a disastrous way – so the reproach – thereby "the poor of Scripture are confused with the proletariat of Marx" and the "struggle for the rights of the poor" is transformed into a "class struggle". The church of the poor" is thus misunderstood as "a class church" [Text 308]. The second Instruction, 'Libertatis conscientia' of 1986, emphasized the primacy of the educational and evangelizing tasks of the Church. Prominent representatives of liberation theology such as Leonardo Boff (b. 1938) were banned by the Vatican in 1985 from speaking and teaching, initially for one year. As a result, the Brazilian resigned his priesthood in 1992.

Massive *counterpressure* came, of course, especially from the respective national oligarchies and military dictatorships that had established themselves in various South American countries in the 1970s. Through arrest, torture, deportation and targeted killings, they sought to eliminate all potential opposition forces. This also affected many church activists and socially committed priests. They were suspected of being communist sympathizers and often disappeared from the public. The number of Christian priests, pastors and religious who were killed in the 1970s in various regions of Latin America during the period of the ideology of 'national security' is estimated at over 1,000. This was by no means limited to activists such as Roman Catholic priest Camillo Torres, who died in revolutionary action in Colombia in 1966 [cf. Text 302a]. One of the best known – and now canonized – "martyrs" of this era was the Archbishop of El Salvador Óscar Romero [cf. Text 304 f; Figure. 55+56]. While he was celebrating mass in a hospital chapel in El Salvador on March 24, 1980, he was shot by henchmen of the regime.

In the 1980s, a variety of *pluralizing tendencies* could be observed in the already multifaceted landscape of Latin American liberation theologies. New topics (such as ecological questions or feminist concerns) were taken up, traditional positions were reviewed and sometimes treated in a new and more differentiated way. Who, for example, represented the "people" whose voice liberation theology sought to make heard? What modifications of the theory of dependency were considered necessary to do justice to the changed social realities of the continent? Controversies also arose, for example, around the 'cultura popular', i.e. the intrinsic value of the culture of the people or of Latin American popular religiosity. The latter was highly valued, for example, by representatives of the so-called 'Argentine School'. "Their starting point was not the liberation practice of Christian groups, but the practice of the Latin American peoples, in whose wisdom, cultures and religious expressions the gospel was already inculturated." The majority of liberation theologians, on the other hand, had a more skeptical view of popular piety, which they perceived "as an expression of the oppression and alienation of the poor".[2]

23.4 Protestant and (Neo)Pentecostal Groups, Revitalization of African American Religions

"Liberation theology chose the poor, and the poor chose Pentecostalism," is a frequently quoted dictum. Indeed, the precipitous growth of Protestant (and especially Pentecostal) churches since the early 1970s is among the most striking developments in recent Latin American religious history. According to conservative estimates, by the end of the 1990s some 11 to 15 percent of Latin America's population were Protestants, the majority of them Pentecostals. The increase was particularly dramatic in Brazil. "There are now more than 50 million Protestants in Brazil, the vast majority (41 million) of whom are

Pentecostals or charismatics" – according to a 2004 figure.[3] The strongest force among them, with more than 4 million adherents in 2000, was the 'Assembleias de Deus' ('Assemblies of God'), which is also the largest Protestant church in Latin America. In Brazil, their beginnings date back to 1912. Initially, they found followers mainly in the lower social strata, including blacks and "mulattos" (i.e., the group of mixed African-European origin). The latter still make up the majority of its members today. Latin America is now considered the continent with the strongest Pentecostal presence in the world.

The reasons for the *rapid growth* of the Latin American Pentecostal movement have been intensively discussed by sociologists, ethnologists and theologians. Socioeconomic factors – such as the collapse of the old hacienda system in the countryside and the subsequent migration of former agricultural workers to the slums of the cities – represent an important partial aspect. Faced with the collapse of earlier solidarity structures, Pentecostal churches served as a haven for numerous newcomers in the midst of a hostile world. Pentecostalism thus became the religion of migrants in many places. Deficiencies of the Catholic Church – with its hierarchical structures, persistent lack of priests and close ties to the old feudal system – are cited as further reasons. Pentecostal churches, on the other hand, offered space for a more personal spirituality. With the experience of baptism in the Spirit, they also promised direct access to God. The priesthood of all believers, an important element of the Protestant tradition, was emphatically emphasized. Healing services, the hope of deliverance from the "demonic" evils of the present or the experience of "speaking in tongues" (according to 1 Cor. 12–14) had an attractive effect on the crowd of the socially and religiously uprooted. Central to this (similar to, yet quite different from, the base church communities) was the importance of the Bible, which was accessible to lay people as well. Women played an important role. At the same time, the Pentecostals preserved numerous elements of traditional popular Catholicism in an environment influenced, for example, by Brazilian spiritualism and Afro-American cults. According to the Brazilian historian Martin Dreher, this distinguished them in many ways from official Catholicism, which had taken on a more European face since the end of the 19th century as a result of "Romanization.

Another feature of the early Pentecostal communities in particular has been their often Puritan morality and work ethic. They facilitated survival in the context of advancing urbanization and industrialization (and opened up prospects for social advancement). In many cases, Pentecostals have been characterized as apolitical and conservative. However, there have always been significant counter-examples – as shown by the active participation of Pentecostals in labor struggles and the dispute over land rights. Various congregations initially founded by foreign (mostly American) evangelists soon achieved institutional, personnel and financial independence. Other groups were launched from the beginning by indigenous actors. Through splits, new foundations and adaptation to the local context, the groups grew and differentiated themselves through endogenous dynamics. To a large extent, they present now the image of an indigenous religion.

In the historiography on Latin American Pentecostalism, there is often talk of *successive "waves,"* which are defined differently in detail. In any case, a third type – usually called neo-Pentecostal – has been spreading since the end of the 1970s. It ties in with the classic Pentecostal movement, but increasingly addresses the middle and upper classes of society. Neo-Pentecostal groups are usually organized around a charismatic leader and are characterized by a basic authoritarian concept. They oppose any kind of theological and political liberalism and usually propagate a "theology of prosperity" (prosperity gospel). Personally acquired prosperity is understood as a sign of the kingdom of God. "Enough with the gospel of suffering," proclaimed, for example, the preacher of the Honduran church 'Vida Abundante' (literally: 'abundant life') in 1989. "The Gospel of joy should start to fill every life. … It is about prosperity in all areas. … What is everything? Your shoes, your laundry, … your car, your work, … your hen, your cow … All prosper in God" [Text 312a]. – Probably the best known example of this third wave is represented by the 'Igreja Universal do Reino de Deus' (UCKG, Universal Church of the Kingdom of God). Founded in Rio de Janeiro in 1977, it became the fastest growing church in Brazil in the 1990s, with over 1,000 individual churches and about one million adherents. Its members, mostly poor people, were encouraged to bring money to the church to obtain the blessings of God. The UCKG had its own television station, thirty radio stations, its own newspaper, was linked to a political party active at the national level, and increasingly spread to other countries in South America and Africa (see chapter 25.3). The founder of the UCKG was the bishop (and former employee of the state lottery) Edir Macedo, a highly controversial figure. Heavily criticized by other church leaders, he soon gained the dubious reputation of being the richest pastor in the world.

In any case, Brazil's religious landscape became more diverse with the advance of Pentecostal movements. This picture of growing pluralization also includes the upswing that the *Afro-Brazilian religions* of Candomblé and Umbanda experienced during this period. Previously suppressed by state authorities, they were now legal and present in the public sphere [see Photo K02–06]. In a climate of growing black self-confidence as well as the search for alternatives to Western rationalism, they also gained in attractiveness among whites. Thus, for the first time, quasi-official contacts between representatives of Afro-Brazilian cults and the Catholic episcopate occurred in the 1980s. In 1985, for example, the archbishop of Salvador/Bahia sent a letter of welcome to the local Candomblé cult center on the occasion of the election of a new priestess there [Text 314]. Other groups, however, such as the aforementioned UCKG, took a hostile stance and undertook exorcisms to expel the spirits of Candomblé.

Notes to Chapter 23

1. Thus the Chilean liberation theologian Pablo Richard in 1981; quoted in: Spliesgart 2021, *Kuba,* 35 [cf. Text 299. 307].
2. Silva 2009, *Theologiegeschichte Lateinamerikas,* 47 f.
3. Espinoza (2004), *Pentecostalisation,* 277.

Further Reading for Chapter 23

23.1–3 (Between Social Revolution and State Repression/ Second Vatican Council (1962–1965) and Medellín (1968) / Liberation Theologies)

Strassner (2018), *Latin America,* 314–328; Rowland (²2007), *Companion to Liberation Theology;* Garrard-Burnett/ Freston/ Dove (2016), *Religion in Latin America,* 359–371 ("Intellectual Roots of Liberation Theology", by I. Petrella); ibid., 372–397 ("From Vatican II to Pope Francis", by M.A. Vásques/ A.L. Peterson); ibid., 398–413 ("Catholic Church and Dictatorship", by S. Fitzpatrick-Behrens); Klaiber (1998), *Church, Dictatorships, and Democracy;* Goodpasture (1989), *Cross and Sword,* 243–270 (documents); Mannion (2018), *Vatican II,* 182–219; Prien (2013), *Latin America,* 443–525; Dussel (1992), *Latin America,* 153–184 (Second Vatican Council, Liberation Theology); Boff (1989), *Introducing Liberation Theology;* Boff (1985), *Charism and power;* Prien (1978), *Geschichte,* 995–1062; Prien (1981), *Gesellschaft – Kirche – Theologie* I + II; Collet (1990), *EATWOT,* 121–131; Fornet-Betancourt (1997), *Befreiungstheologie.* I, 71–176 (reception in Latin America, Asia, Africa, USA and Europe). II (Critical debates and new challenges); Silva (2009), *Theologiegeschichte Lateinamerikas,* 29–58; Beozzo (2002), Das *Zweite Vatikanische Konzil,* 219–242; Eigenmann (2016), *Dom Hélder Câmara;* Petrella (2006), *Future of liberation theology;* Büschges, C. et al. (2021), *Liberation theology and the others* (on "Catholic activism in 20th Century Latin America").

23.4 (*Protestant and [Neo-]Pentecostal Groups, Revitalization of African-American Religions*)

Garrard-Burnett/ Freston/ Dove (2016), *Religion in Latin America,* 414–429 ("Latin American Pentecostalism as .. Popular Religion", by A. Corten); ibid., 430–450 ("History ... and Prospects of Pentecostalism", by P. Freston); ibid., 462–479 ("Catholic Charismatic Renewal", by J.E. Thorsen); ibid., 603–632 ("African Diaspora Religions", by S. Selk); ibid., "Afro-Carribean Religious Expressions", by M.A. de la Torre); Anderson (2004), *Pentecostalism,* 63–82; Anderson/ Hollenweger (1999), *Pentecostals after a Century;* Prien (2013), *Latin America,* 285–314; Corten/ Marshall-Fratani (2001), *Between Babel and Pentecost,* 1–61.124–215; Smith (1998), *Pentecostal vs. Catholic;* Freston (2001), *Brasilian Pentecostalism,* 196–215; Bergunder (2000), *Pfingstbewegung und Basisgemeinden*; Haustein/ Maltese (2014), *Handbuch*; Espinoza (2004), *Pentecostalisation,* 262–292; Stoll (1990), *Turning Protestant?*; Martin (1990), *Tongues of Fire*; Van Wyk (2014), *Church of Strangers*; Goodpasture (1989), *Cross and Sword,* 271–292 (documents); Hollenweger, W. (1997), *Pentecostalism*; Kim/ Kim (2008), *World Religion,* 159–171; Blakely et al. (1994), *Religion in Africa,* 135–159 (Candomblé).

CHAPTER 24

"Shift of Centers": Developments in the 1980s

24.1 From a North to a South Majority

"Von der Westkirche zur Weltkirche" ("From the Western Church to the World Church") – this was the title of a 1985 book by Walbert Bühlmann, in which he pointed out – surprisingly for the German public – the dramatic changes in Roman Catholicism in the postwar era. The traditional "heavyweight of Christianity in the Occident," according to the Catholic theologian, had "degraded more and more, and in 1970 it came to a tipping point. Now already 51.86% of Catholics live in southern continents, Latin America, Africa, Asia-Oceania. By 1980, the proportion had already increased to 57.56%." In 1980, Latin America alone had 323 million Catholics (equal to 41.4% of the Catholic Church worldwide), while Europe had only 271 million (equal to 34.6%). By the year 2000, it was predicted, "probably 70% of Catholics will live in the Southern Hemisphere."[1]

Analogous shifts have also been observed in the other denominational families too, since the mid-1980s. For example, in the Anglican world communion, which now probably has more adherents in Nigeria than in Great Britain. From 1900 (with about 35,000 members), the number of its adherents there rose to 2,941,000 in 1970 and to about 14,800,000 in the mid-1990s. "Statistically, the Nigerian church should properly be counted as the heart of Anglican Christianity".[2] Other communions also showed an increasing shift to the South. The Herrnhuter Brüdergemeine (Moravians), for example, which had already spread worldwide in the 18th century, counted 29,837 parishioners throughout Europe in 1998. In the East African country of Tanzania alone, however, the number of members was more than thirteen times higher in 1998, at 411,792. Other Protestant denominational families – Methodists, Baptists, Presbyterians, and finally Lutherans – also made the gradual transition from a northern to a southern majority in the last third of the 20th century. A major factor in the explosive growth of churches in the global South (and especially in sub-Saharan Africa) was the rapid spread of Pentecostalism and other charismatic, post-denominational or independentist groups.

Statistics on religion are often problematic, contradictory and fraught with numerous difficulties in data collection and methodology. However, the basic direction of this "southern expansion" of Christianity in the last third of the

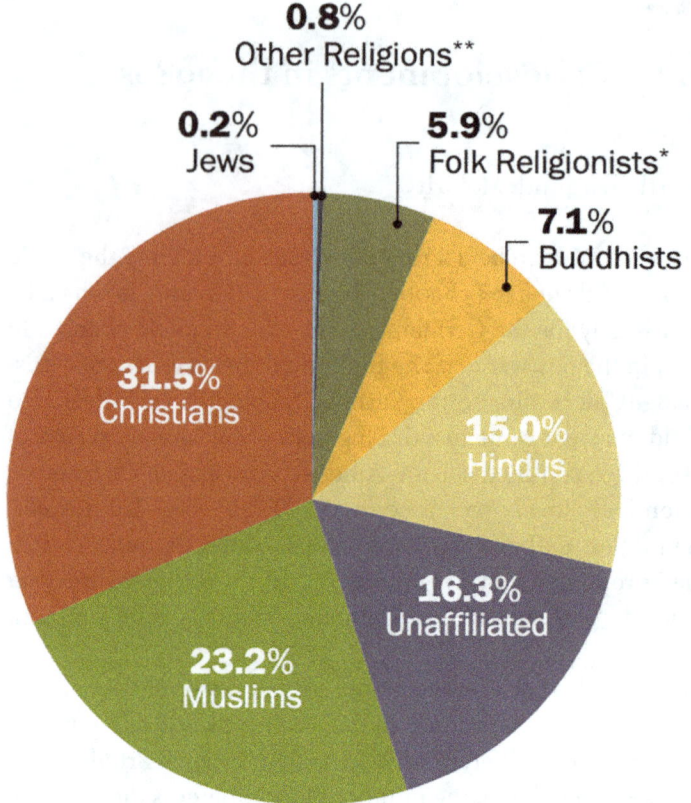

GRAPHIC   World Religions 2010[3]
SOURCE: HTTPS://WWW.RESEARCHGATE.NET/PUBLICATION/264782431
_THE_GLOBAL_RELIGIOUS_LANDSCAPE_A_REPORT_ON_THE_SIZE_AND
_DISTRIBUTION_OF_THE_WORLD'S_MAJOR_RELIGIOUS_ GROUPS_AS_OF_2010
(P. 10, ACCESSED 11/30/2021).

20th century is clear. The 'World Christian Encyclopedia' gives the following figures in a continental comparison:[4]

According to recent data from the renowned Pew Research Center's Forum on Religion and Public Life, the geographic distribution of the world's Christian population in 2010 was as follows: Europe 25.7%, Latin America/Caribbean 24.4%, Sub-Saharan Africa 23.8%, North America 12.3%, Asia/Pacific 13.2%, Middle East/North Africa 0.6%. The figures for the individual regions diverge significantly in some cases.

In view of this development, the Scottish historian and missiologist Andrew Walls (1928–2021) already spoke in the 1980s of a "shift of center[s]

Christain world population	1900	2000
Africa	8756000	335116000
Asia	20758300	307288000
Europe	368210000	536832000
Latin America	60026000	475660000
North America	59570000	212166000
Oceania	4321000	21375000
Total worldwide	521641000	1888437000

of gravity" of Christianity from North to South. With that, he set in motion a debate that continues in the international ecumenical community to this day. What is controversial is not so much the demographic findings – decline, especially in secularized Europe, compared to partly exponential growth rates in the global South – but rather the question of the consequences and new challenges for the contours of world Christianity. For: "the forms and structures for the growth of late 20th-century Christianity could not be contained within either the institutional or the theological frameworks of Western Christianity".[5] Old centers of power in the North were juxtaposed with new demographic majorities in the South. Outdated ecumenical organizational structures (such as the World Council of Churches in Geneva) are increasingly less able to correspond to the cultural diversity and denominational plurality of world Christianity.

The reasons for the partly exponential growth of the southern churches lie on the one hand in the uneven demographic development of the various world regions. In Latin America, for example, the population grew from about 167 million to 511 million people between 1950 and 1999, according to UN statistics. Accordingly, the number of Christians on the continent has increased dramatically – with a relatively constant population share of about 90% (although internally the ratio between Catholics and Protestants/Pentecostals has clearly shifted in favor of the latter). But even in populous countries where Christians live only as a minority (as in Indonesia, with a share of about 9%), general population growth is at the same time leading to a significant increase in the number of believers. In 2000, the number of believers was estimated almost 20 million, out of a total population of about 212.5 million. This is higher than in various European countries.

Elsewhere – in addition to the general population development – a rapid growth of churches began. In South Korea, for example, the proportion of Christians rose from about 3.3% to 26.3% between 1950 and 1995. Even in communist China, there were more Christian believers after the end of the

Cultural Revolution in 1976 than at the time of the communist takeover in 1949. As a result, their numbers increased significantly, according to both state and internal church statistics. Growth in the last third of the 20th century was particularly dynamic in sub-Saharan Africa. This is all the more remarkable because the "new" African nations had only freed themselves from the yoke of European colonialism in the 1960s. But on the one hand, even in the colonial era, the relatively small number of Western missionaries had always been only one factor among others in the spread of Christianity. The decisive factor in this process was rather the role of local actors – laymen, native Bible women or catechists in the service of the established mission churches as well as followers and activists of the independent African churches that sprang up in many places since the end of the 19th century. Moreover, by translating the Bible into numerous indigenous idioms at an early stage, the missionaries themselves had created the preconditions for the genesis of an independent African Christianity. Lamin Sanneh (1942–2019), a religious scholar from Gambia teaching at Harvard (USA), has repeatedly emphasized this. He describes the linguistic and cultural translatability of Christianity as a central condition and factor in the emergence of specifically African versions of Christianity.

At the same time, however, Africa's former mission churches also gained new attractiveness in postcolonial times – but now under indigenous leadership. This can be observed, for example, in Anglicanism in Kenya (and other countries).

> "The new context transformed the liability of being an English religion under a colonial government into the advantage of being a global faith under an independent government. In the 1980s and 1990s. as [sc. Africa's] political and economic institutions began collapsing under corrupt one-party dictatorships, the church became one of the few institutions with the moral authority and international connections to oppose the government, which it did on occasion. In some parts of Africa, the church's infrastructures and international connections provided more stability for supporting daily life than did the government".[6]

The main growth in the 1990s then occurred increasingly through the influx to Pentecostal and charismatic churches. Around 1990, for example, 40% of Christians in South Africa were members of independent African churches.

In the 1980s, not only the demographic relations between the churches in the global North and South changed. There was also a gradual change in the way they were perceived by the European public. In the Catholic context, the enormous travel activities of Pope John Paul II (1978–2005) contributed to the changed image of a church not limited to Europe. While earlier popes hardly ever left Italy, John Paul II visited 127 countries in 104 trips abroad, the majority of which were in Africa [see Figure 52], Latin America and Asia. In January 1995, for example, the pope celebrated mass in Manila in front of four million people with great media attention. At his death in 2005, German television reported live on the sympathy of the faithful worldwide. Broadcasts were made from São Paulo, Mexico, Delhi, Manila and Lagos (Nigeria), among other places.

24.2 "Return of the Religions", Religious Fundamentalisms

In other contexts, too, the last quarter of the 20th century saw an unexpected upsurge and increased public influence of religions. In the 1980–90s, a wave of religious fundamentalisms swept through numerous regions and societies in Asia and Africa, changing the profile of the socioreligious landscapes there. They also affected the coexistence of different faith communities on the ground, sometimes drastically. In the Islamic world, inspired in part by the Iranian Revolution of 1979, the religion of the Prophet was politicized in much of the Near East, Southeast Asia, and West Africa. In Iran, a theocracy (with rule by ayatollahs, or Muslim religious leaders) was established; and in Indonesia-the country with the largest Muslim population, with about 204 million inhabitants in 2000-increasingly, Islamist groups willing to use violence were now making themselves heard. In contrast to the long tradition of religious pluralism and interreligious harmony in the Southeast Asian archipelago, they preached intolerance against non-Islamic groups.

In India, on the other hand, it was militant Hinduism – at the latest since the destruction of the Babri mosque in Ayodya in 1992 – that attracted international attention and, at the same time, drew attention to the deteriorating situation of religious minorities in the multi-ethnic state. To be sure, the development of aggressive Hindu nationalism had begun earlier. In the 1980s, the so-called 'Hindutva' ideology increasingly took hold of other politically influential circles, such as the Bharatiya Janata Party (BJP), founded in 1980, which soon came to power in individual states (and since 1998 also at the national level). Hindutva' refers to the goal of a homogeneous Hindu culture throughout India, to the exclusion of divergent religious traditions. The activities of radical Hindu nationalists were primarily directed against Muslims. Increasingly, however, the Christian minority was also affected by violence. In particular, the Christian Dalits (casteless people) were subjected to a variety of repressive measures.

In Buddhist majority societies such as Sri Lanka in the 1980s, tensions between different ethnic and religious communities intensified, resulting in a bloody and prolonged civil war (1983–2009) between Buddhist Sinhalese and Hindu Tamils. Various initiatives to overcome the interethnic conflict came from the country's Christian community, which includes both Sinhalese and Tamils.

In many places, the advance of fundamentalist currents was also the result of disappointment with corrupt elites, the failure of official development policy and a lack of progress in the process of nation building. This also applies to the spread of political Islam in Africa. "For Islamic Africa," says historian Christoph Marx, "religion was a cultural resource that offered an alternative after the failure of secularist nationalisms. Revolution no longer came in Marxist guise, but in religious guise".[7] In West Africa, conflicts between Christians and Muslims intensified from the 1980s onward. Both faith communities continued to grow there. The number of adherents of traditional African religions, on the other hand, steadily declined. – Finally, in Egypt – the leading nation in the Arab world – Islamic sharia law was established as one source of legislation in 1971, and as its main source in 1980. Head of state Anwar as-Sadat (*r.* 1970–1981), otherwise known in the West primarily for his peace treaty with Israel in 1979, thus opened up to radical Islamic forces. At the same time, he decreed discriminatory measures against the Copts and other churches.

24.3 "Reverse Missions", Impacts on the West

Since the 1970s, the direction of global migration flows has changed. Whereas in the 19th and early 20th centuries millions of Europeans had sought their fortune outside Europe – in the newly conquered overseas colonies, in the less populated areas of South America or in the USA as a land of hoped-for freedom – the last quarter of the 20th century saw an increased influx of people from the global South into the rich industrial societies of the North. They came as migrant workers or later as refugees from the – political, economic and ecological – catastrophes in their home regions. By the mid-1980s, Africa, Latin America, the Caribbean, and Asia had already become net exporters of millions of people to Northern Hemisphere countries. More waves of postcolonial migration there followed.

Many of the migrants from sub-Saharan Africa, for example, were already Christians. They formed diaspora communities in Europe, the USA and other parts of the world and developed a lively religious life – usually more intense and colorful than that of the traditional churches in their new neighborhood. In Europe, the influx initially took place primarily in the former colonial centers (of Great Britain, France, and Belgium, for example), but also in other Western European metropolises such as Milan, Hamburg, Berlin or Copenhagen. In Amsterdam, for example, the number of worshipers in the new migrant congregations (according to a 2008 survey by the World Council of Churches) exceeded those in the city's traditional congregations by a factor of nine. Increasingly, African-led churches also became evangelistically active in their new environments. This was especially true of various charismatic or Pentecostal groups that proliferated in the 1990s. They saw secularized Europe as a continent with a Christian past that needed to be revived spiritually. "Bringing the Gospel back" to the countries from which European missionaries had once departed and whose churches were now languishing spiritually and numerically, they saw as their God-given task. "We are here for a purpose, to awaken the Church in Germany" was how one African church leader described their mission.[8]

The new African-led communities were thus by no means composed solely of migrants. Increasingly, they also appealed to the local population. In 1992, for example, the Nigerian pastor Matthew Ashimolowo founded the Kingsway International Christian Centre in London, which – by its own account – soon gathered more than 10,000 worshipers of different nationalities every Sunday. Even more remarkable is an example from Ukraine, a country with no colonial ties to Africa. Here, in 1993 – after the collapse of the Soviet Union – the 'Embassy of the Blessed Kingdom of God for all Nations' was launched by the West African preacher Sunday Adelaya. It too quickly enjoyed massive attendance from the local population. "Nigerian pastor finds new flock in Ukraine," the Western European press (BBC) described this phenomenon with amazement. In addition to such 'megachurches', there were numerous new foundations of various sizes in various European metropolises by African immigrants, each of which increasingly won "locals" as members as well.

With regard to the USA, the U.S. religious scholar Jehu Hanciles (from Sierra Leone) speaks of a "de-Europeanization" of American Protestantism as a result of massive immigration of African (and Asian) Christians since the 1980s. Despite recent somewhat declining numbers, "the impact of the new immigrants on American Protestantism is considerable. In thousands of churches and Christian communities across the country, the language oof worship, theological orientation, and modes of interaction draw on decidedly foreign elements and seek to replicate non-Western preferences".[9] Along with Protestant immigrants, many from West Africa – as well as an increasing number of Hispanic (or Latino) Protestant congregations – Korean churches represented the fastest-growing communities in American Protestantism.

Even more impressive, Hanciles said, was the impact of new immigrants on American Christianity in the case of Roman Catholicism. By the early 1980s, most Catholic dioceses were losing members and closing schools. Growing immigration (since 1965) helped reverse this trend. In 1996, the top five countries of origin of Catholic immigrants to the U.S. were Mexico (at 27.6%), the Philippines (12.6%), Poland (7.4%), the Dominican Republic (6.1%), and Vietnam (5.5%). More importantly, 42% of new Christian immigrants identified as Catholic-far more than the average for the U.S. population (22%). At the beginning of the 21st century, Latinos made up one-third of all Catholics in the United States. This percentage is expected to increase in the future. – Increasingly, priests and ministers from the Spanish-speaking neighboring countries of Central America also came to serve in Latino Catholic (and Protestant) communities in the United States.

The same applies to the churches of Europe. To remedy the acute shortage of priests, since the 1980s in Catholic Bavaria or French Catholicism, for example, Indian clerics or priests from Francophone Africa have been increasingly recruited. In the Protestant regional churches of Germany, Lutheran pastors from Tanzania or Methodist preachers from Sri Lanka were more likely to be used. Here, however, this takes place mainly within the framework of exchange programs, which, in addition to other bilateral partnerships, seek to establish transregional connections at the congregational level as well.

The ecumenical debates of the 1980s about the apartheid system in South Africa, for example, led also to feedback effects of a completely different kind. They affected not only the churches in the African country itself, but also triggered, for example, profound controversies in German Protestantism and its new self-identification in the context of the global ecumenical movement.

24.4 Regional Developments and Profiles

In *China,* the death of Mao Zedong in 1976 also marked the end of the "Great Proletarian Cultural Revolution" of 1966–1976. It had claimed millions of lives in all strata of the population. Particularly suppressed during this period were all forms of "religious superstition" and especially Christianity – suspected of being the vanguard of the imperialist West [Text 95]. It is all the more astonishing that there were more Christians in China after the end of this period than at the time of the Communist takeover in 1949. In detail, the figures vary, depending on the type of sources available (government statistics, church data, informal estimates). In particular, the number of Protestants increased by leaps and bounds, probably surpassing that of Catholics for the first time in the late 1970s. "While there were 700,000 Protestants in 1949, their number grew to between 12 and 36 million by the end of the century".[10] The number of Catholics developed less dynamically and is estimated to have been between about 7 and 10.5 million around 2000.

Since 1979, Christianity became visible again in the public sphere. The upswing occurred in the slipstream of the economic reforms of Deng Xiaoping, the de facto ruler of China in the post-Mao era. Private property was allowed again, a market economy was introduced, and agriculture was de-collectivized. The state relaxed its control of cultural and social processes. Religious activities were widely decriminalized and believers were encouraged to work for China's modernization. Churches were reopened (as well as later rebuilt in large numbers) beginning in 1978, and theological training centers were reactivated [see Figure 46; Photo B19/20]. The new constitution of 1982 allowed "normal religious activities." In the Protestant sector, growth was initially driven primarily by independent groups that had already existed before 1949. They experienced an enormous boom, first in rural areas and later in the cities. The number of "unregistered" house churches, which were very heterogeneous in themselves, contrasted with an equally growing number of congregations that enjoyed state recognition within the framework of the official "Patriotic Three-Self Movement" [see Chapter 21.2]. This was represented by Bishop K.H. Ting (Ding Guangxun; 1915–2012), who was also president of the post-denominational 'Chinese Christian Council' established in 1980. He also pleaded in the ecumenical movement for an independent path of the Chinese church, free from Western dominance [Text 103].

The divide between an official and an unofficial wing in Chinese Catholicism was even stronger than in Protestantism. Particularly contentious here were the competences in the appointment of bishops or the claim of the communist leadership to be able to do so without a papal mandate. The Vatican always rejected such claims, and in the 1980s a large number of bishops were consecrated without state approval. At the same time, many bishops were consecrated without papal mandate. Parallel structures thus formed of an official – state-approved – church and an "underground" church of Catholics loyal to Rome, both with their own bishops' conference. For decades, China's demand for autonomy for the domestic Catholic Church stood in the way of all Vatican efforts to reach an understanding with the communist state leadership. (It was not until 2018 that a tentative agreement – and one that itself was quite controversial among Chinese Catholics – was reached between the Vatican and the Chinese government on the issue of bishop appointments.)

In the 1980s and 1990s, interest in Christianity also increased by leaps and bounds among Chinese intellectuals. The main motive was the realization that China had an enormous need to catch up with other nations. Christianity was seen as a central aspect of Western culture and modernity. Moreover, it seemed suitable to fill the ideological vacuum after the failure of the Cultural Revolution. Christianity studies were established at state universities. Classics of Christian literature were translated into Chinese and discussed lively in academic circles. Most of these so-called 'cultural Christians' were without church ties; others became believers. They initially understood the program of 'Sino-Christian Studies' primarily as a contribution to the building of China, rather than to the development of a Chinese church theology.

In *sub-Saharan Africa*, the role of the churches changed in many countries in the 1980s. This was a time of economic decline – caused by the collapse of commodity prices, steady population growth, and growing corruption in the ruling one-party regimes. A lack of resources led to the state's withdrawal from many areas (such as education and health care) in which it had previously assumed responsibility. In many places, the Christian churches stepped into this gap once again. The government of Zaire, for example, was no longer able to maintain the schools it had previously nationalized and returned them to the Catholic Church in 1976. The situation is analogous in Tanzania, where formerly church-run hospitals were once again taken over by the Protestant churches. But also "the increasingly numerous independent churches – in Zaire alone, 1300 such churches were founded between 1960 and the early 1980s – ... were more effective than the weakened state, as they formed self-help communities, carried out development projects, created educational institutions, and offered medical or spiritual healing".[11]

In a completely different way, the Roman church became visible to the public in the Ivory Coast, for example. In 1990, the Basilica Notre Dame de la Paix, the largest church in Africa, was inaugurated in the capital Yamoussoukro on the personal initiative of the president. Modeled after St. Peter's Basilica in Rome and partly sharply criticized within the church because of its enormous cost, this house of worship provided space for 11,000 worshippers.

In the *Middle East*, on the other hand, the decline and exodus of Christian minorities continued in the 1980s. In the old countries of origin of Christianity (such as Palestine, Syria, Lebanon, Turkey, Iraq and Egypt), the proportion of Christians in the total population declined continuously – partly due to a lower birth rate, partly as a result of growing emigration. There were many reasons for this development: continuing religious and political discrimination; the rise of Islamic fundamentalism; civil wars and violent conflicts; and higher education among Christians (which facilitated emigration). Lebanon, for example, experienced the net emigration of 990,000 Lebanese, the majority of them Christians, between 1978 and 1989. Many Egyptian Copts left their homeland for North America, Europe, Australia, or the Arab world. In Tur Abdin in the southeast of today's Turkey, about 200,000 Syriac-Aramaic Christians still lived around 1900 – proud to preserve the language of Jesus (in a developed later form). Under the pressure of first Ottoman and then Turkish repression, their numbers had dwindled to about 20,000 by 1980 and subsequently declined even further [see Photo No1–13]. The continuing emigration of Oriental Christians was, among other things, the subject of anxious deliberations of the Middle Eastern Council of Churches in 1999. On the other hand, Arab Christians continued to attain prominent political positions. One example is the Coptic Boutros Boutros-Ghali (1922–2016), who was Egyptian foreign minister for a time and secretary-general of the United Nations (UN) from 199–1996.

Notes to Chapter 24

1. Bühlmann (1985), *Weltkirche*, 14.22 ff.
2. Jenkins (2011), *Next Christendom*, 252. Goodhew (2017), *Growth and Decline*, 45, gives the following figures for 2010:Great Britain 26' 109 000; Nigeria 20' 100 100; Uganda 12' 450 000.
3. https://www.researchgate.net/publication/264782431_The_Global _Religious_Landscape_A_Report_on_the_Size_and_Distribution_of_the _World's_Major_Religious_ Groups_as_of_2010 (accessed 11/30/2021).
4. Figures according to: Barrett et al. (22001), *World Christian Encyclopedia* I, 12 – See Pew Research Center: *Global Religious Landscape* (2012), p. 17f. (https://www.pewforum.org/2012/12/18/global-religious-landscape-exec/-; accessed on 30.11.2021); Johnson/ Ross (2009), *Atlas of Global Christianity*, 110-209 (list by continents). 342-347 (methodology); https://de.statista.com/statistik/daten/studie/256870/umfrage/anteil-der-anhaenger-ausgewaehlter-religionen-an-der-bevoelkerung-in-afrika/; accessed on 30.11.2021). – For the interpretation of this data (and the difficulties of collecting them) see: Ward (2018), *Conclusions*, 501–504; Lehmann (2012), *Christentum im 20.Jh.*, 26–29 („problems with statistics"); Haustein (2011), *Pfingstbewegung als Alternative*, 540–544; Goodhew (2017), *Growth and Decline*; Maxwell (2008), *Postcolonial Christianity in Africa*, 401 f; Cabrita/ Maxwell/ Wild-Wood (2017), *Relocating World Christianity*, 7 ff; Frederiks (2021), *World Christianity*, 15 ff.
5. Robert (2000), *Shifting Southward*, 54.
6. Robert (2000), *Shifting Southward*, 53.
7. Marx (2004), *Geschichte Afrikas*, 353.
8. Währisch-Oblau (2009), *Missionary Self-Perception*, 264.259 ff.5 ff.
9. Hanciles (2008), *Beyond Christendom*, 293 ff.

10. Robert (2000), *Shifting Southwards*, 53; cf. Bays (2012), *New History*, 186 ff; Wenzel-Täuber (2016), *Statistisches Update*, 25.32 ff; Barrett et al. (^{2}2001), *World Christian Encyclopedia* II, 197.
11. Iliffe (1995), *Geschichte Afrikas*, 358.

Further Reading for Chapter 24

24.1 (*From a North to a South Majority*)

Jenkins (2011), *Next Christendom*; Robert (2000), *Shifting Southward*, 50–58; Bühlmann (1985), *Weltkirche*; Walls (2001), *Cross-Cultural Process;* Sanneh (1989), *Translating the Message*; Sanneh (2003), *Gospel Beyond the West*; Carpenter/Sanneh (2005), *Changing Face of Christianity*; Bednarowski (2008), *Twentieth Century Global Christianity*; Davies/ Conway (2008), *World Christianity;* Hanciles (2008), *Beyond Christendom*; Kalu (2008), *Contemporary Christianitiy*; Meyer (2000), *Herrnhuter Brüdergemeine,* 174 f (Moravians); Kim/ Kim (2008), *World Religion*, 210–230; Kim/Kim (2015), *Korean Christianity,* 275 ff; Sunquist (2015), *Unexpected Christian Century;* Cabrita/ Maxwell/ Wild-Wood (2017), *Relocating World Christianity*; Frederiks/ Nagy (2021), *World Christianity*; Ward (2018), *Conclusion*, 501ff.

24.2 (*"Return of Religions", Religious Fundamentalisms*)

Marty/ Appleby (1995), *Fundamentalisms*; Micklewait / Woolridge (2009), *God is Back;* Riesebrodt (2000), *Resurgence of religion,* 266–287; Almond/ Appleby/ Sivan (2000), *Strong Religion*; Iriye/ Osterhammel (2013), *Geschichte der Welt* VII, 631–641; Marx (2004), *Geschichte Afrikas*, 352–357; Bröning/ Weiss (2006), *Politischer Islam*; Kastfelt (2003), *Bible and Koran as Political Models;* Briggs/ Oduyoye/ Tsetsis (2004), *Ecumenical Movement* III, 496 ff.

24.3 (*Reverse Missions, Impacts on the West*)

Cohen (1995), *Survey of World Migration;* Oltmer (2012), *Globale Migration*; Eck (2001), *A New Religious America;* Adogame (2014), *African ‚Retromission'* in Europe, 307–316; Adogame (2005), *African Christian Communities*, 494–514; Adogame/ Gerloff/ Hock (2008), *African Diaspora*; Adogame/ Spickard (2010), *New African Diaspora;* Adogame/ Shankar (2013), *Religion on the Move!*; Hanciles (2008), *Beyond Christendom*, 172–253. Simon (2010), *From Migrants to Missionaries*; Währisch-Oblau (2009), *Missionary Self-Perception*; Suarsana (2010), *Christentum 2.0*, 76 ff; Sunquist (2015), *Unexpected Christian Century*; Heuser (2016), *„Umkehrmission",* 25–54; Im/ Yong (2014), *Global Diasporas*.

24.4 (Regional Developments and Profiles)

Bays (2012), *New History*, 183–208; Chow/ Law (2021), *Ecclesial Diversity*; Lee/ Chow (2021), *Chinese Christianities*, 113–134; Dunn (2015), *Contemporary China*; Poon (2010), *Christian Movements*; Illife (2017), *Africans*, 282–344; Ludwig (1999), *Church and State in Tanzania*, 193–236; Pemberton (2002), *African Women Theologians*; Raheb/ Lamport (2021), *Christianity in the Middle East*; Raheb (2018), *Middle East*, 381–395; O'Mahony/ Loosley (2010), *Eastern Christianity in the Modern Middle East*; Hage (2007), *Orientalisches Christentum*, 457–460; Wessels (1995), *Arab and Christian?*, 189–228; Hildmann (2007), *Christenverfolgung*, 35–92; Badr et al. (2005), *Middle East*, 854–856; Abraham (2013), *Copts of Egypt*; Vogt (2019), *Christen im Nahen Osten;* Womack (2020), *Contemporary Middle East*, 189–213.

Illustrations for Part 5

FIGURE 45   Seoul (Korea): The 'Yoido Full Gospel Church' is considered Asia's first mega-church, with numerous services every Sunday and thousands of visitors each time (photo taken in 2010) [see photo D03–06].

FIGURE 46   Beijing (China): the 'Haidian Christian Church' in the university district (photo taken in 2012) [= photo B19].

ILLUSTRATIONS FOR PART 5

FIGURE 47 Sri Lanka: Morning worship (2019) at the Theological College in Kandy-Pilimatalawa. The worship space is designed with elements of traditional Sinhalese culture [= photo E20].

FIGURE 48 Colombo (Sri Lanka): Chapel in the Anglican Cathedral (built in 1973), example of cultural indigenization [= photo E23].

FIGURE 49   "Wonderful Jesus" – street scene in Ghana (1997) [= photo G03].

FIGURE 50   Ghana: Rural Pentecostal church in Nkawkaw (1997) [= Photo G07].

ILLUSTRATIONS FOR PART 5

FIGURE 51
Albert Luthuli (1898–1967): South African Congregationalist lay preacher, delegate at the Tambaram World Missionary Conference in 1938, president of the African National Congress since 1952, Nobel Peace Prize laureate in 1960.

FIGURE 52
The pope in Africa: John Paul II (1978-2005) was the first pope to visit numerous African countries (here: 1988 in Botswana).

FIGURE 53
Kwame Bediako (1945–2008), prominent West African theologian, emphasized the influence of indigenous cultures on African Christianity.

FIGURE 54
Desmond Tutu (1931–2021): Fighter against apartheid, Nobel Peace Prize laureate (1984), Anglican Archbishop of Cape Town (South Africa).

FIGURE 55
Óscar Romero (1917–1980), Archbishop of San Salvador and prominent proponent of liberation theology, assassinated by the military during a mass on March 24, 1980.

FIGURE 56 San Salvador: Crowds at the 1994 celebrations for the beatification of Óscar Romero, the archbishop of San Salvador who was assassinated in 1980.

ILLUSTRATIONS FOR PART 5

FIGURE 57   Porto Allegre (Brazil): The Crucified and the Junkie (street scene 2019 [= photo K01]). The representation of human suffering in the suffering Christ is a constant motif in the history of Christianity in Latin America (cf. already the pictorial chronicle of Poma de Ayala around 1614 [Figure 10]).

PART 6

On the Threshold of the 21st Century

CHAPTER 25

1989/90 as an Epoch Year in the History of World Christianity

25.1 End of the Cold War, Collapse of Apartheid, Crisis of Liberation Theologies

The year 1989/90 saw a political system change and the beginning of profound upheavals in various regions of the world, triggered by the collapse of the Soviet Union. The Christian communities of the respective countries were also strongly affected, directly or indirectly.[1] On November 9, 1989, the Berlin Wall fell. Shortly thereafter, the apartheid system in *South Africa* collapsed. There is a close connection between the two events. With the dissolution of the Soviet empire and the end of the Cold War, the global postwar order, which had been shaped by the East-West divide, also came to an end. In South Africa in particular, there was no longer any justification for Western governments to continue supporting the already isolated and morally damaged apartheid regime as an alleged bulwark against the "communist threat" in Africa. As a result, negotiations between the white government and the black opposition, which had been conducted in secret for some time, came to a rapid conclusion. In early 1990, the most important apartheid laws were repealed. It took some time until the first free and general elections in 1994 – in which the resistance fighter Nelson Mandela, who was also supported by the ecumenical movement, was elected South Africa's first black president. But already with the release of Mandela and the legalization of the 'African National Congress' (ANC) in February 1990, the end of the apartheid system, which the country's churches had previously partly supported and partly resolutely opposed, was sealed [see chap. 22.4]. In the subsequent phase of peaceful transition, church people like Desmond Tutu, the black Anglican archbishop of Cape Town (1986–1996), Nobel Peace Prize laureate and, since 1995, chairman of the Truth and Reconciliation Commission for dealing with the wounds of the apartheid era, who passed away in 2021, played a prominent role.

In numerous other *African states*, too, autocratic one-party regimes that had previously been supported or kept alive by either the West or the East toppled around 1990. Here, too, churches often played a significant role during the transition period. Historians such as Paul Gifford speak of a "second wave of democratization" (after the process of decolonization in the 1960s) with regard to the years 1989 to 1993.² In many places, 'round tables' were established that sought to organize the transition to a democratic order. They were mostly moderated by Catholic bishops or Protestant church leaders-such as in Gabon, Togo, Zaire, Congo, Madagascar, Malawi, Zambia, and Kenya. In Zambia, too, there was a democratic transfer of power in December 1991, and the winner of the presidential election – Frederick Chiluba – promptly declared the country a "Christian nation." In Ethiopia, on the other hand, the socialist military dictatorship previously supported by the Soviet Union and Cuba, which had overthrown the Christian imperial house in 1974, collapsed in 1991. Churches and monasteries, previously oppressed in many ways, now experienced a new flowering.

For the churches and Christians in *Eastern Europe*, too, the collapse of the Soviet empire in 1989–1991 marked a decisive turning point. It meant the end of decades of oppression and brought religious freedom as well as drastically expanded opportunities for action in the public sphere. Even before that, during the period of transition, Christian activists and groups in many places played an important role as civic actors and advocates of democratic change. In 1989, for example, the Monday demonstrations in East Germany (German Democratic Republic; GDR) – which ultimately led to the fall of the communist SED regime – took their starting point in Leipzig's Nikolai Church. In Romania, the country's political insurgency developed from local expressions of solidarity for the Reformed pastor László Tőkés in Timişoara, who had denounced the Ceauşescu regime's everyday human rights abuses. The demonstrations quickly spread to other parts of the country. In Lithuania (part of the Soviet Union until 1990), members of the opposition in many sites replaced statues of Marx and Lenin with images of the Virgin Mary; and in Poland – where the election of 'Polish Pope' John Paul II in 1978 had contributed significantly to the later success of the country's labor and democracy movements – Catholic bishops moderated the transition from communist to democratic rule. This development reached a significant climax with the election of the first non-communist head of government in August 1989.

The Central 'Round Table' in the *East German GDR* opened on December 7, 1989, under an Advent star in the prayer room of the Herrnhuter (Moravian) Brüdergemeine in the Dietrich Bonhoeffer House in Berlin-Mitte. Protestant church leaders and church-committed personalities found themselves in the leadership of the new democratic parties of the 'Wendezeit' (turnaround era) as well as at the cabinet table of the first freely elected GDR government. Finally, it was a Protestant pastor (Erich Holmer) who temporarily took in the ousted GDR state and party leader Erich Honecker after he had previously been denied asylum in Moscow. In reunified Germany, personalities from the

GDR with a church background – such as former pastor Joachim Gauck as president of the Federal Republic of Germany (2012–2017) or the pastor's daughter Angela Merkel as chancellor (2005–2021) – played prominent roles.

In *Asia,* the situation presented itself differently in various contexts. In socialist China, the role of religions in the revolutionary upheavals of Eastern Europe was carefully observed. As in Vietnam, the Christian churches here were subsequently confronted with a balancing act – between accelerated economic (and limited religious) liberalization on the one hand and increased political and ideological monopoly claims of the ruling CP on the other. The latter was combined with repression of officially unrecognized religious groups. In capitalist or Western-oriented countries such as South Korea and the Philippines, on the other hand, it was above all the increased ideological and religious pluralism, together with fundamentalist counter-movements, that presented the churches with new challenges. In West and Central Asia, as well as in various neighboring regions, the new alliance of religion and nationalism represented a significant factor in the process of disintegration of the Soviet empire. This applies to religious nationalisms of Christian (Armenia, Georgia), Islamic (Central Asia) or, as in the case of Mongolia, Buddhist character. In Armenia, a return to centuries of Christian tradition was an important driving force behind the country's national movement, which declared independence from Moscow in 1991 and completed it in 1992. Signs of the new era included the reconstruction of old churches and monasteries and the construction of new ones, as well as the transformation of the Institute for the Scientific Study of Atheism in the capital, Erivan, into an Orthodox theological faculty. In other post-Soviet societies, however, the Christian minority often found itself confronted with a revitalized (and increasingly aggressive) Islam–as in Uzbekistan and other Central Asian republics.

In *Latin America,* liberation theology lost an important reference model with the end of Eastern European socialism. Contemporary observers as well as conservative critics expressed the assumption that "liberation theology had been buried together with the Berlin Wall". This was also the case with Cardinal Ratzinger, the later Pope Benedict XVI.[3] Its advocates countered that liberation theology could only disappear together with its conditions of origin – the structures of social injustice on the continent. Indisputably, however, it fell into a serious crisis and subsequently underwent manifold modifications and thematic expansions. – In Nicaragua, the Sandinistas lost the presidential elections of February 1990, and with their defeat the dream of a socialist and Christian democracy faded – a dream shared also by many Christians outside the country and the region. Conversely, the last three remaining military dictatorships on the continent, which had also defined themselves as anti-communist, ended in 1989 in Chile, Paraguay and Panama. Elsewhere, such as Brazil and Argentina, the transition from military to civilian rule had been completed earlier. But the devastating legacy of the military dictatorships continued to reverberate for a long time, and church leaders, especially Catholic but also Protestant, played an important role in dealing with them. In Guatemala, for example, Auxiliary Bishop Juan Gerardi Conedera was beaten to death by an assassin hired by the military in 1998 – two days after he had presented a four-volume final report on the victims of the long civil war to the public in the cathedral.

In general, the system breaks and transformation processes of the early 1990s also triggered a *theological paradigm shift* in many societies in Africa, Asia and Latin America. Previously, different forms of a "contextual" theology had developed in numerous churches in these regions in the 1970s and 1980s, which – in the face of political repression and economic exploitation – were mostly confrontational in nature. These also found considerable resonance in global ecumenism and in the social-ethical debates of the WCC. This is especially true of the liberation theologies of Latin America, but also, for example, of the Minjung theology developed in Korea or the "prophetic" respectively Kairos theology of the ecumenical churches of South Africa. Whereas opposition and resistance had previously been dominating issues, now – after the transition from authoritarian to democratic rule had been completed – it was a matter of building up a critical-constructive relationship with the state and seeing oneself as an active member of civil society. From then on, different models of a "public theology" or "theology of reconstruction" increasingly determined the social-ethical debates in many churches of the global South and the ecumenical movement.

25.2 Internet, Digital Globalization, Liberalized Travel

Apart from the end of the Cold War, another important date is associated with the year 1989/90: the invention of the *Internet* (more precisely: the development of the 'World Wide Web' [www] at the CERN research center near Geneva). Initially reserved for a small circle of specialists, it set in motion a media revolution that was also to permanently change the contours of world Christianity. It enabled entirely new forms of religious communication and transregional networking, as well as the simultaneous presence of competing religious digital cultures on the ground. People from a wide variety of backgrounds thus became connected to their respective home regions. Since the mid-1990s, the Internet has also been used as a tool of religious and social transformation.

In the Christian context, it accelerated the growth of (neo)Pentecostal movements and the formation of so-called megachurches. At the same time, it facilitated the trans-regional networking of migrant congregations of all stripes. This applies not only to technologically leading countries in the northern hemisphere (such as the USA), but also – increasingly since the turn of the millennium – to numerous regions in the global south. For Africa, for example, the Ghanaian religious scholar Kwame Asamoah-Gyadu stated in the early 2000s: "The massive growth in African Christian presence since the middle of the last century and the current increasing appropriation of modern media technologies by new African Christian communities constitute two 'important new developments' on the continent".[4]

In terms of its revolutionary impact, the invention of the Internet has often been compared with that of printing in the mid-15th century. Print culture was a key factor not only in the rapid spread of the Reformation movement in 16th-century Europe, but also in the Protestant missionary movement in the 19th century, when it was used not only by Western missionaries to spread their message. At the same time, local Christians came into contact with co-religionists in other parts of the world through reporting in the missionary press. Increasingly, however, these were also journals of their own, in which – as discussed elsewhere [cf. chapter 17.2] – indigenous Christian elites from Asia and Africa articulated their specific concerns from the end of the 19th century and increasingly networked trans-regionally.

The *new media* of the early 20th century were also quickly used by groups outside the religious mainstream. For example, Pentecostal Aimee Sermple McPherson preached over one of the first radio stations in the United States in 1918. In Africa in the 1970s and 1980s, simple technological innovations such as audio cassettes proved to be the most effective medium of evangelism. They were used by various Christian groups. At the same time, however, the same was true of the spread and politicization of Islam in Africa. Television was introduced in Ghana as early as 1963 and in Nigeria at the supraregional level in 1977, but it was subject to a state monopoly for a long time. As a result of the democratization push in the early 1990s, it then became accessible to religious actors (and especially various Christian communities). A thriving religious film industry developed in Nigeria in the 1980s and 1990s. Neo-Pentecostal churches here, as in other African countries, increasingly moved to using movie theaters (rather than church buildings) as meeting places.

Globally, Internet use increased by leaps and bounds in the first years of the new millennium. This is particularly true of certain countries in the so-called global South. Between 2000 and 2007, Internet usage increased by 640% in Africa, 491% in the Middle East, 466% in Latin America and the Caribbean, and 258% in Asia. By 2002, South Korea (rather than the U.S.) was the most Internet-connected country in the world.[5] At the same time, South Korea (after the Philippines) was the Asian nation with the highest percentage of Christian population (of about 30%), as well as a highly active world missionary center. In other "Internet-rich" countries on the continent, such as Singapore, Hong Kong or – predominantly Hindu – India, Christian churches and organizations also established a considerable presence in the digital public sphere and developed into nodes of an emerging "Internet Christianity" in Asia.

In general, the spread of the Internet also spurred the formation of so-called megachurches. These are very large congregations, mostly evangelical or (neo) Pentecostal in character, attended by at least 2,000 worshipers in a weekend. They also expanded their digital presence in various locations. The first megachurch in Asia was the Yoido Full Gospel Church in Seoul, which was founded in 1973 on a more modest scale [see Figure 45; Photo D-03/06]. Since the 1980s and 1990s, such "large churches" (established by local church leaders) have spread to numerous countries in the southern hemisphere, such as Kenya, China, Korea and Nigeria. Besides the 'Yoido Full Gospel Church' in South Korea with (according to its own information) 480000 weekly visitors, the 'Calvary Temple Church' in India (190 000 visitors) and the 'Bethany Church of God' in Indonesia (140 000 visitors) are among the largest megachurches worldwide. Prominent examples from Brazil include the 'Igreja da Cidade' in São José dos Campos or, with numerous offshoots in other countries as well, the aforementioned 'Igreja Universal do Reino de Deus' (Universal Church of the Kingdom of God). In 2018, the 'Glory Dome' in Abuja (Nigeria), the world's largest church building with 100,000 seats, was inaugurated.

But smaller Christian communities also increasingly made use of electronic media. These served not only communication and advertising purposes, but also led to the development of new forms of worship and Christian spirituality. Previously isolated (or underground) Bible study groups now networked through the Internet. Traditional church congregations experienced that celebrating together is possible without a physical presence, through digital mediation – such as in the midst of the Corona pandemic of 2019/20. In Indonesia, for example, urban congregations quickly switched to livestreamed worship services in the midst of this crisis. In rural areas, where many people could only access the internet via mobile networks, sermons were sent as text messages via WhatsApp. What was new (compared to older electronic media) were especially the possibilities of interactive use. This promoted the development of a sense of belonging across locations and new digital forms of community.

This applies in particular to the connections within the various transregional diaspora communities. As recently as the mid-20th century, migration was usually still associated with a lifetime farewell to the country of origin. With the travel facilitation of the 1990s, the possibilities of repeated home visits or reciprocal visits also improved. Above all, however, digital real-time communication intensified the links both between the diaspora communities themselves and with their respective countries of origin and home churches: "Even more than ever before" – according to the Sinobrit historian Alexander Chow – "we have to speak of 'Korean Christianity' or 'Filipino Christianity' or 'Ghanaian Christianity' in transnational categories".[6]

Elsewhere, too, the liberalization of travel in the 1990s, together with drastically falling air fares and the abolition of burdensome visa regulations, had an impact. Increasingly, so-called "short-term missionaries" arrived from the United States for short-term assignments in countries of the global South (for example, during semester breaks). Without longer preparation and cultural sensitization, their commitment often made the situation of older Christian communities on the ground (for example in the Middle East) more difficult.

25.3 Changing Geographies of Religion, Transcontinental Churches, New Dynamics of Polycentrism

It is not only along the former "Iron Curtain" in Eastern Europe that barbed wire and border fortifications have been dismantled since 1990. Elsewhere, too, bloc borders and nation-state barriers have fallen – for example, in Asia between the former Soviet (and Chinese) sphere of power and the neighboring countries in the region. Even South Africa – previously isolated in apartheid times – now opened its borders to people from other African countries. South Korea, which has been relatively homogeneous ethnically, also experienced a significant influx of cheap labor from other countries in the 1990s. Production facilities were moved from expensive Europe first to low-cost China and then to areas with even lower labor costs (such as Vietnam, Cambodia and Bangladesh). American economists propagated unrestricted worldwide trade and celebrated the assumed global victory of neo-liberal capitalism.

Economic liberalization was accompanied by a surge in international labor migration. Regional conflicts, environmental disasters and economic underdevelopment intensified the worldwide migration flows. At the same time, this changed the religious geographies in the respective destination areas. In Europe, for example, the proportion of Muslims increased steadily as a result of continuous migration and successive waves of refugees from the Middle East and North Africa (massively, for example, as a result of the Syrian civil war in 2015 ff). Conversely, however, in the Gulf states, for example, the influx of Filipino (and other) guest workers led for the first time to forms of a significant Christian presence in this region. Around 2010, for example, Christians accounted for 18.5% of the total population in Qatar, 11.9% in Kuwait and 11.9% in the United Emirates.[7]

In the U.S., the process of religious pluralization has been further intensified by immigration from Asia, Africa and Latin America. "How a 'Christian' Country has become the World's most religiously diverse nation" is the (sub)title of a 2001 study by Diana L. Eck, which analyzes this development paradigmatically. At the same time, however, the majority of immigrants to the United States belonged to a Christian community. Within North American Protestantism, the influx of African and Asian Christians, as already mentioned, intensified the process of "de-Europeanization" [see chap. 24.3]. In North American Catholicism, it was the mass immigration of Catholic Latinos from Central and South America that triggered a similar effect there.

In the changed situation of the 1990s, new dynamics of polycentrism developed at the same time. Missionaries from Korea – which had already developed into a new center of Protestant world mission – were now no longer only active in Sri Lanka, Turkey or at Lake Titicaca in the Andes of Peru. After the collapse of the Soviet empire, they were now also to be found in the subway stations of Budapest or on Red Square in Moscow. They also became active in previously closed regions such as Mongolia. Here, in the 1990s, they founded congregations and a theological seminary in Ulan Baator, for example, which subsequently experienced a rapid upswing [see Photo D-22]. – Along with Korea, Brazil was also among the "largest missionary-sending countries in the world," specifically to the Portuguese-speaking communities in Europe and Africa.[8] As noted earlier, Pentecostal missionaries (and Catholic priests) from the U.S.'s Spanish-speaking neighbors in Central America played an important role in the re-evangelization (or pastoral care) of the booming Latino communities in the United States. – African diaspora congregations also became evangelistically active around the globe. In South Asia, the Chinese expatriate diaspora – the largest diaspora community in the world with an estimated 36 million members (circa 2000) – was particularly important. Christians were disproportionately represented in it. From centers such as Singapore, Hong Kong or the urban metropolises of Indonesia, they developed (and continue to develop) considerable evangelistic activities. – The ancient Near Eastern churches are often regarded as static and rather fixated on the past. However, through migration – forced or voluntary – a steadily increasing number of their members live in other regions and contexts, where they develop new forms of Orthodox identity. Indian St. Thomas Christians, for example, are present in the Gulf region, and Copts are also on the move in southern Africa. Syriac Orthodox Christians – once fleeing repeated persecution in the Ottoman Empire and modern Turkey – are making America a new center for their ancient church while seeking to maintain links with their regions of origin.

"From everywhere to everywhere" is one of the catchwords used to propagate (and describe) the ways of multidirectional expansion of different Christianities in the late 20th century. This no longer took place – as in traditional Western mission history – simply from north to south (or vice versa, as in the case of African initiatives for a "reverse mission", from south to north), but increasingly in different directions. At the same time, there was the formation of new transcontinental churches of non-European origin. The 'Igreja Universal do Reino de Deu' ('Universal Church of the Kingdom of God', UCKG) already mentioned several times offers an impressive example [cf. chap. 23.4]. It was founded in Brazil in 1977 – the country with the highest number of Pentecostal believers in the world. By 2000, it had spread to more than fifty countries, including Latin America (first in Paraguay in 1985), the USA (since 1990), Portugal (since 1990), and southern Africa. There, it was initially very strongly represented in Portuguese-speaking Mozambique, and later also in English-speaking South Africa. Figures from 1995 list 75 branch churches in Latin America, 63 in Europe, 52 in Africa, 24 in North America, and 7 in Asia. Overall, the UCKG is gaining support primarily (but not only) in the Portuguese-speaking societies and people of Latin America, Africa, and Europe.[9]

The UCKG represents a special case in many respects. Because of its pronounced ideology of prosperity, it is also viewed critically by other Christian groups. But a general characteristic of the diverse (neo)Pentecostal networks – which boomed in the 1990s, especially in Latin America and sub-Saharan Africa – is their supraregional and transcontinental orientation. It is already noticeable that the adjective "global", "worldwide" or "international" is used more often in the self-designations of different groups such as the 'Gospel Light International Church' or the 'Fountain of Life International Church' (both from Ghana). Also noteworthy is the changing rendering (or "translation") of the "I" in the acronym "AIC". Originally used as an abbreviation for the 'African Independent Churches' (since the beginning of the 20th century), it was later increasingly read as 'African Initiated Churches' and since the 1990s increasingly as 'African International Churches'. This "international" orientation is not primarily a question of numerical size (as with many of the "megachurches" that sprang up in the 1990s). In many cases, it is first and foremost an expression of the self-image of smaller local groups. These groups know that they are connected – in spirit as well as through modern media – with like-minded activists and believers around the globe.

25.4 "The Next Christendom" – Discussions and Expectations around the Turn of the Millennium

Around 1900, missionary circles had looked quite optimistically to the future. The American Methodist and later Nobel Peace Prize laureate J.R. Mott, for example, was convinced of the "evangelization of the (whole) world" still "in this generation". This expectation of a "glorious age" of Christianity, which in particular also had a lasting influence on the debates of the World Missionary Conference in Edinburgh in 1910, was then shattered by the moral catastrophe of the First World War. Nevertheless, the 20th century was characterized by contrary developments: on the one hand, by massive losses of terrain, the horror of the two world wars, and the experience of anti-religious dictatorships in Nazi Germany, Stalinist Russia, and Mao Zedong's China. On the other hand, however, the Christian communities in various southern regions experienced a sometimes almost explosive growth in the second half of the century [see chap. 24.1]. Around 2000, they comprised about one third of humanity – similarly to 1900 – but now with a growing majority of the world's Christian population in the global South.

Less noticed, but highly remarkable in view of the subsequent development, was the vision of Indian Protestant Christians around 1900. They looked back on the 19th century as the time of the – quite meritorious, but now expiring – phase of Western missionary activities. The new 20th century, on the other hand – so their prognosis and at the same time their demand – would be entirely characterized by the "native churches" of Asia (and worldwide), "self-governing, self-supporting and self-extending". Already at the height of Western colonialism, a post-missionary (and post-colonial) perspective was thus formulated, which subsequently had a considerable impact on the ecumenical movement in Asia, among others.[10]

The *debates about "the future of Christianity"* in the global ecumenical community were, of course, particularly intense *around the year 2000*, in view of the upcoming (respectively meanwhile occurred) turn of the millennium. "The Next Christendom. The Coming of Global Christianity," for example, was the title of a highly influential and controversial study in 2000 by Philipp Jenkins, an American historian of religion (who converted to Catholicism from the Anglican Church). The starting point for him, too, was the expectation of a North-South shift in global Christianity that would intensify in the future: "If we imagine a typical Christian back in 1900, we might think of a German or an American; in 2050, we should rather turn to a Ugandan, a Brazilian, or a Filipino".[11] At the same time, Jenkins expected very different characteristics of the Christianities of the North and the South. The (shrinking) churches of the

North would tend to be liberal, rational, and socially engaged, while the (growing) Christianities of the South would tend to be conservative in matters of faith and morals. Strongly biblically oriented, hardly influenced by the Enlightenment, and traditional in forms of social engagement, the many Christians in the South would be more interested in the supernatural and personal salvation than in radical politics.

While the growing importance of the southern churches in global ecumenism was the consensus forecast of different voices in this worldwide debate, the implications of this shift from north to south for the contours of future world Christianity were quite contrarily assessed. Prominent ecumenists and scholars such as Kirsteen and Sebastian Kim questioned the scenario of increased North-South confrontation drawn by Jenkins. In the future, the Korean-British researcher couple said, "the Christianities of the North and South will remain connected in many ways" through "historical relationships, mission, migration, common challenges (such as Islam, secularization)," as well as the fading of denominational boundaries. Indisputably, however, the "worldwide future of Christianity" will be increasingly characterized by "regional differences and commonalities."[12] Other voices, however, articulated concerns about a growing disintegration and fragmentation of the global ecumenical movement through an increasing proliferation of independentist movements and charismatic start-ups. What, for example, would the new Protestant megachurches of Brazil have in common with the independent communities of Africa or the house churches of China, which move in the gray area of tolerated illegality?

Tensions between the churches of the North and the South, even within the same denominational family – so another fear – could go to the limit of a formal schism. A foretaste of this was provided, for example, by the fierce conflicts in the Anglican world communion in the 1990s over the question of homosexual bishops. In any case, institutional ecumenism in Geneva will be confronted with completely new challenges in view of the growing pluralization within the Christian community. These include the need to seek new forms of dialogue with various groups within the Pentecostal spectrum, with whom until now there have been only occasional contacts. Within the Catholic world church, on the other hand, the weight of conservative forces from the South will increase. In the greater Manila region alone, for example, more Catholics live than in the liberal Netherlands. The "unexpected" growth of Christianity in the Global South was mainly the work of local actors, "Koreans, Chinese, Brazilians, Indians, Ghanaians," etc., who, unlike the earlier Western missionary movement, were "hardly supported by secular power". According to the evangelical historian Scott Sunquist, this development will increasingly continue in the 21st century.

Many of these statements on the future of worldwide Christianity in the new millennium were less forecasts than wish lists and visions. As early as 1985, for example, the Catholic theologian Walter Bühlmann, as mentioned above, had analyzed the transformation of Roman Catholicism from a "Western church to a world church" with considerable resonance. As a decisive characteristic of a future "third church" and expected "new church presence" in the year 2001, he named the intensified "exchange" between North and South – in matters of "money, personnel, theology, pastoral experiences, models of life".[13] Quite analogously, authors such as Noel Davies and Martin Conway emphasized in their outlook on the 21st century the necessity of a comprehensive mutuality between Christians of the "First" and "Third World" as well as the connection of local commitment with global responsibility.[14] Pentecostal historians (such as Walter Hollenweger and Allan Anderson) expected a further swelling of Pentecostalism in Africa, Latin America and Asia. As a prerequisite for this, however, they mentioned the "rediscovery" ("back to the roots") of its beginnings among the poor and marginalized also in the new millennium, which threatened to get lost among some representatives of the "Prosperity Gospel".[15]

The voices from – and forecasts for – the individual world regions vary. For sub-Saharan Africa – with its phenomenal growth the starting point for the paradigm of the "shift of center(s) of gravity of Christianity" [see chapter 24.1], which has been intensively discussed since the 1980s – many voices expect a continuing process of Christianization, despite growing competition from Islam (often supported by petrodollars). This growth of Christianity, however, will not take place in its European but African form or as a "renewal of a non-Western religion". So the Ghanaian Presbyterian theologian Kwame Bediako (1945–2008; Figure 53), who at the same time regarded Africa as a "laboratory" for world Christianity. For here an intensive ecumenical intercultural dialogue between the (former) established (missionary) churches and new religious movements is already taking place in the present, which is also inevitable in other regions of the world. – As for Latin America, researchers and historians such as Ondina E. and Justo L. González (Cuba/USA) see wider shifts within the traditional Christian majority in Mexico (from earlier Catholic dominance to Pentecostal-charismatic growth). The decisive question for the future, however, will be to what extent Catholicism and Protestantism can overcome their "two faces" or internal polarization – between a socially progressive and politically reactionary wing – and at the same time integrate elements of the old indigenous and African religions. Also important, so their assessment, is the "challenge posed by post-modernity," or the question of how Christian denominations are able to make the upcoming "leap from a non-modern world to a post-modern one." – For the historic Christianities of the Middle East, the Palestinian Lutheran theologian Mitri Raheb sees a largely black future, as a result of increasing external violence and rising pressure to emigrate: "Christianity may soon no longer exist in the land of its origins. But it will live on in the diaspora."[16]

Asia is home to the majority of the world's population and at the same time the continent with a multitude of – quantitatively, denominationally and culturally – very heterogeneous Asian Christianities. Accordingly, the US American historian Peter Phan, who comes from Vietnam, differentiates very strongly according to individual regions in his overview of the current situation and demographic "Future of Christianity in Asia". In addition to countries with a Christian majority (Philippines, East Timor) and a very strong and growing part of the population (such as South Korea), he names countries with a Christian minority, which also has only little social influence due to limited religious freedom. In other countries, such as India, Sri Lanka, Vietnam, Hong Kong and Macao, Christian communities "remain influential in many sectors of society, especially in education and social services". It is particularly difficult to make a forecast for China, Phan said. Different perspectives are discussed. For example, the option of a further "increase" in the number of conversions to Christianity, which would at the same time find its way into the mainstream of Chinese culture; an "absorption" into Chinese culture, analogous to the fate of Chinese Buddhism; or a future as a "subcultural minority religion in China." In either case, Phan said, the future of Asian Christianity will be characterized by a "threefold dialogue": "with Asian people, cultures, and religions."[17]

Or, in the words of former Sri Lankan Anglican Bishop Kumara Illanghasinghe, what are the prospects for the churches of Asia, which proudly consider themselves the cradle of Christianity: Church growth? A role as a prophetic minority? Or effective as "leaven" in the midst of the social transformation processes of the vast continent?[18]

Notes to Chapter 25

1. The topic of this chapter 25.1 was the subject of the Sixth International Munich-Freising Conference 2008 on the "Year 1989/90 as an Epochal Year in the History of World Christianity", the results of which have been published in: Koschorke (2009), *Falling Walls*, with numerous regional studies and individual examples from Africa, Asia, Latin America and Europe.
2. Gifford (1995), *Democratisation of Africa*; Gifford (2009), „Second Liberation Struggle", 137–156; Maxwell (2008), *Postcolonial Christianity in Africa*, 414–416.

3. Silva (2009), *Theologiegeschichte Lateinamerikas*, 53 FN. 48.
4. Asamoah-Gyadu (2007), *Cyberspace and Christianity*, 227.
5. Kim (2007), *Ethereal Christianity*, 208.
6. Chow (2022), *Digital Culture*, xx.
7. Im/ Yong (2014), *Global Diasporas*, 120.
8. Kim/Kim (2008), *World Religion*, 161.
9. Freston (2001), *Brasilian Pentecostalism*, 198 ff.
10. Koschorke (2019), *'Christian Patriot'*, 99 f.16–21.146 f.
11. Jenkins (2011), *Next Christendom*, xi.
12. Kim/ Kim (2008), *World Religion*, 223.
13. Bühlmann (1985), *Weltkirche*, 135 ff.
14. Davies/ Conway (2008), *World Christianity*, 281–294.
15. Anderson/ Hollenweger (1999), *Pentecostals after a Century*, 203–229; vgl. Miller/ Yamori (2007), *Global Pentecostalism*.
16. Bediako (1995), *Renewal of a Non-Western Religion*; González/ González (2007), *Christianity in Latin America*, 607.
17. Phan (2011), *Christianities in Asia*, 255 ff.166 ff.
18. Personal communication from Bp. Kumara Illanghasinghe to the author

Further Reading for Chapter 25

25.1 (End of the Cold War, Collapse of Apartheid, Crisis of Liberation Theologies)

Koschorke (2009), *Falling Walls*, passim; Lombard (2009), *Fall of the Berlin Wall*, 89–94; Cochrane (2009), *Post-Apartheid Christianity*, 95–116; Gifford (2009), *„Second Liberation Struggle"*, 137–156; Gifford (1995), *Democratisation of Africa*; Silva (2009), *Transformationen der Befreiungstheologie*, 335–351; Von Sinner (2012), *Democracy in Brazil*; Malek (2009), *1989 in China*, 215–242.

25.2 (Internet, Digital Globalization, Liberalized Travel)

Asamoah-Gyadu (2007), *Cyberspace and Christianity*, 225–241; Adogame (2008), *To God be the Glory*, 147–159; Goh (2005), *Internet and Christianity in Asia*, 831–848; Horsfield (2015), *From Jesus to the Internet*, 261–284; Horsfield/ Hess/Medrano (2004), *Media and Christianity*; Kim (2007), *Ethereal Christianity*, 208–222; Campbell (2010), *New Media;* Loveland/Wheeler (2003), *From Meetinghouse to Megachurch;* Meyer (2005), *Pentecostalism*, 290–312; Meyer/ Moors (2005), *Public Sphere*; Währisch-Oblau (2021), *WhatsApp-Predigten*, 63–69; Chow (2022), *Digital Culture*.

25.3 (Changing Geographies of Religion, Transcontinental churches, New Dynamics of Polycentrism)

Koschorke/ Hermann (2014), *Polycentric Structures*, 15–28; 69–72.111–130.307–334.347–376; Castles/ De Haas/ Miller (2014), *Age of Migration*; Im/ Yong (2014), *Global Diasporas*, 89–157; Eck (2001), *A New Religious America*; Adogame/ Gerloff/ Hock (2008), *African Diaspora*; Adogame (2014), *African ‚Retromission'*, 494–514; Thomas (2014), *Christianity in the Persian Gulf*, 117–129; Yeh (2014), *The Chinese Diaspora*, 89–98; Kim (2014), *Korea as a Missionary Centre*, 111–130; Freston 2001, *Brazilian Pentecostalism*, 196–215; Corten/Marshall-Fratani (2001), *Between Babel and Pentecost*; Espinoza (2004), *Pentecostalisation*, 262–292; Anderson (2004), *Pentecostalism*, 63–82. 103–165; Kim/ Kim (2008), *World Religion*, 161.204 ff; Garrard-Burnett/ Freston/ Dove (2016), *Religion in Latin America*, 666–679 (by T. Hartch).

25.4 ("The Next Christendom" – Discussions and Contrary Expectations around the Turn of the Millennium)

Jenkins ([2]2008), *Next Christendom*, passim; Kim/Kim (2008), *World Religion*, 223–230; Ward (2018), *Conclusion*, 501ff. 515–516; Lehmann (2012), *Christentum im 20. Jh.*, 207 ff; Schreiter ([5]2002), *The New Catholicity*; McGrath (2002), *Future of Christianity*; Sunquist (2015), *Unexpected Christian Century*; Stanley (2018), *Twentieth Century*, 357–366; Cabrita/ Maxwell/ Wild-Wood (2017), *Relocating World Christianity*, 7 ff.25 ff.29 ff; Boesak (2019), *Challenges of 21rst Century*.

Outlook, Perspectives

Since the year 2000 – the final date of this survey – dramatic changes have taken place in many places. Unforeseen events have hit the global community. These lines, for example, are being written in December 2023, in the midst of Russia's invasion of Ukraine. A new global Cold War is threatening. Civil wars and religious conflicts are raging around the globe. In Nagorno Karabakh, for example, more than 100'000 Armenians have been forced in September 2023 by the Azeris to flee their centuries old homeland within one week. The long-term effects of the coronavirus pandemic of 2020/22 have not yet been overcome. It has affected the countries in the global South much stronger than those in the northern hemisphere.

Manifold changes and new developments can also be observed in other areas. The worldwide flow of refugees continues to swell, with growing sealing off by the post-industrial societies of the North. At the head of the Roman universal church, the Argentine Jorge Mario Bergoglio has become in 2013 the first non-European pope since the 9th century (with the brief pontificate then of the Syrian Gregory III). By programmatically adopting the papal name Francis, he emphasized the church's solidarity with the poor and marginalized. In various Latin American societies, however, the Christian religious right is on the rise, often with great affinity for authoritarian regimes. In a country like India, Hindu fundamentalists are currently in power, and they are increasingly discriminating against religious minorities (such as Muslims and Christians). In China, on the other hand, religious life is increasingly being regulated and strangled by the state across all religions. At the same time, however, decentralized growth and the spontaneous formation of new Christian communities continue here as elsewhere. Overall, the religious landscapes have become more complex locally and globally, and the picture more diffuse.

Precisely in view of this growing confusion, however, an ecumenically and globally oriented history of Christianity has become increasingly important. It should provide orientation and contribute to the development of a worldwide culture of remembrance of Christianity. For church history and ecumenism are two sides of the same coin, as my academic teacher Alfred Schindler once put it. Ecumenism refers to the current diversity of world Christianity, while church history – as an academic discipline – has the task of analyzing the different stages and historical learning experiences on the way to this current plurality. Schindler himself related his observation primarily to various projects of an 'ecumenical church history' in the 1960s and 1970s, which sought in particular to do justice to the confessional plurality of Christianity (in its main strands of Catholicism, Protestantism, and Orthodoxy). His dictum, however, is equally relevant with regard to the *cultural and contextual diversity of Christianity as a global movement* in the 20th and 21st centuries.

For it is necessary to preserve and share the different experiences of Christians from heterogeneous contexts. At the same time, a growing awareness of a common past should also help to shape the vision of a shared future – in the midst of a dramatically changing world. This can only happen in dialogue, in conversation with people from different regions, cultures and faith traditions. The days are long gone, by the way, when the various forms of World Christianity could simply be divided among different geographical zones. Philippine Catholics, Nigerian Aladura Christians, Brazilian Pentecostals, Chinese Lutherans or Egyptian Copts are no longer to be found only in their respective countries of origin. Increasingly, they are also encountered locally, in the migrant communities of European metropolises or lecture halls of American colleges, each with their own stories, experiences and identities.

The goal of a search for shared experience and unifying hope cannot be the expectation of a quasi-monolithic World Christianity. Rather, I find myself echoing the words with which Kirsteen and Sebastian Kim conclude their book on 'Christianity as a World Religion':

> We do not expect a single world Christianity, a world church or a global theology, but we hope for ongoing conversations between Christians, Churches and theologies from around the world.[1]

In the last days of 2021, former Anglican Archbishop of Cape Town and Nobel Peace Prize laureate Desmond Tutu (b. 1931; see Figure 54) passed away. A national hero in the fight against apartheid and highly respected internationally, Nelson Mandela's companion was also one of the most prominent faces of World Christianity at the end of the second millennium. Tutu was significant not only as a "moral compass and conscience of the nation," as South African President Cyril Ramaphosa paid tribute to him in his eulogy at St. George's Cathedral in Cape Town. His voice was also heard internationally in the fight against racism, social injustice and climate change. Tutu played a decisive role in South Africa's peaceful transition to a multiethnic "rainbow nation" (the term he coined) and headed the Truth and Reconciliation Commission

---

[1] Kim/Kim (2008), *World Religion*, 229.

from 1996 to 1998. This commission sought to heal the wounds of apartheid by openly acknowledging the injustices committed – in this a model for similar undertakings also in other former dictatorships and autocracies. For Tutu, faith was the source of social commitment. "We are prisoners of hope," his words were recalled at the Cape Town funeral service. "We must always, always hope. And if we do not hope, there is no possibility of change in our hearts, and no possibility of change in the world."

Maps

MAP 1   Portuguese on the way around Africa (15th/16th c.)

MAPS

MAP 2   Stages of the Spanish Conquista in America (16th c.).

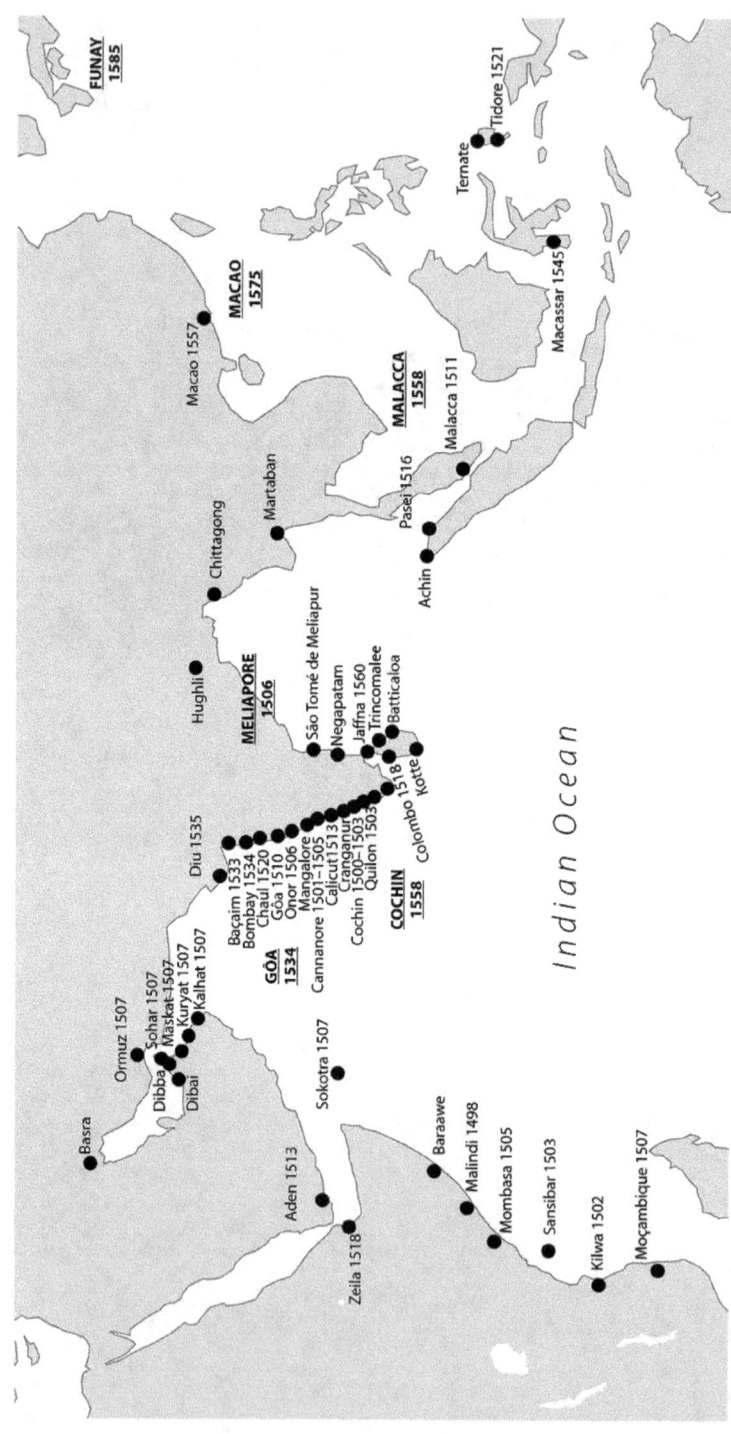

MAP 3   Portuguese colonial expansion (15th/16th c.).

MAPS 317

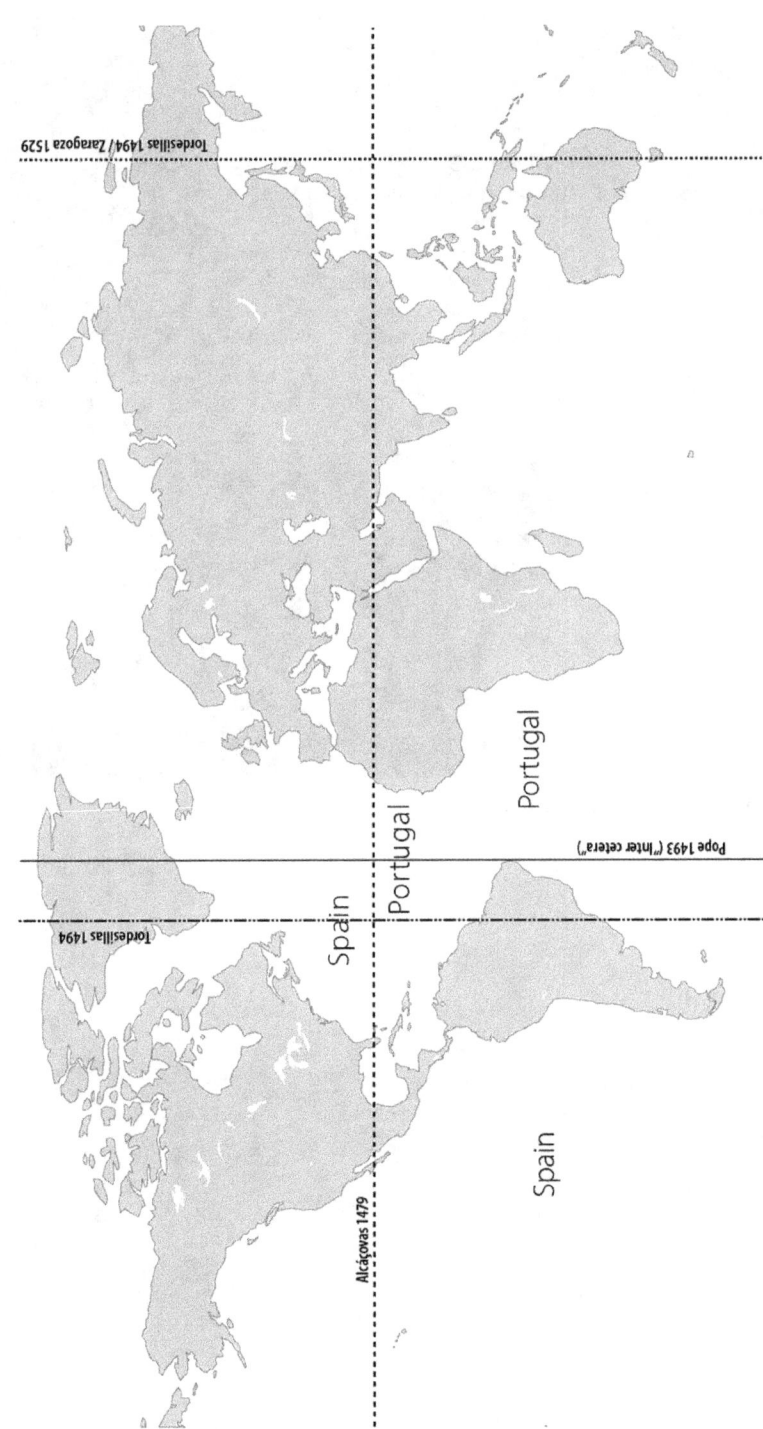

MAP 4   Divided spheres of interest ('Inter Cetera' 1493, Tordesillas 1494).

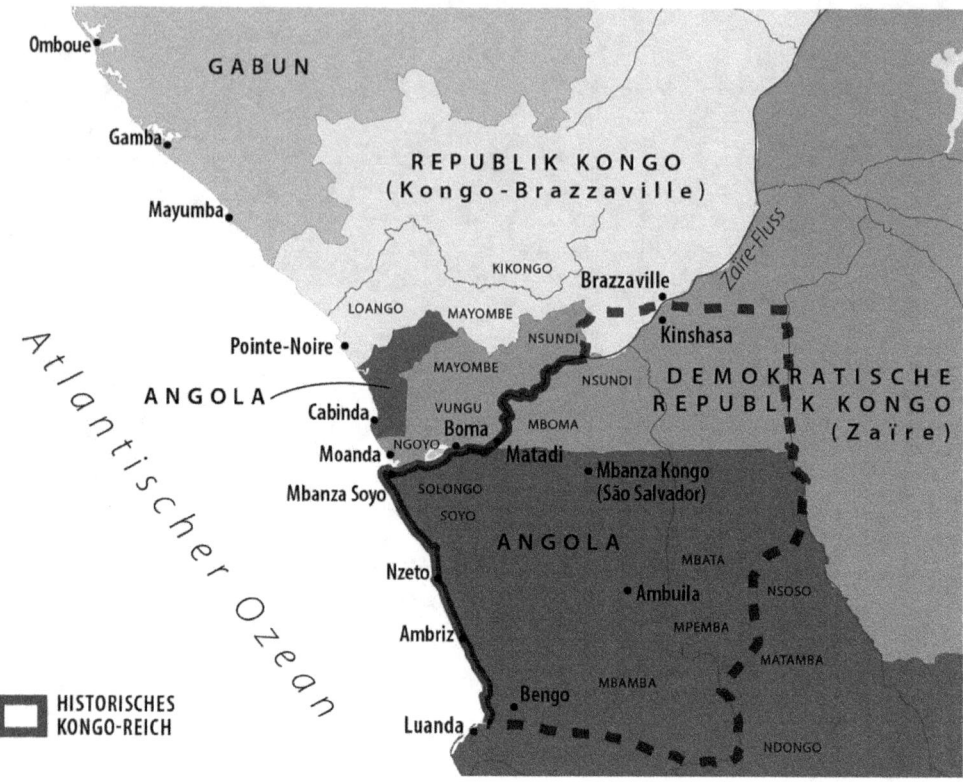

MAP 5 Historical Kongo kingdom (15th–17th c.).

MAP 6   Dioceses in Spanish America (16th/17th c.).

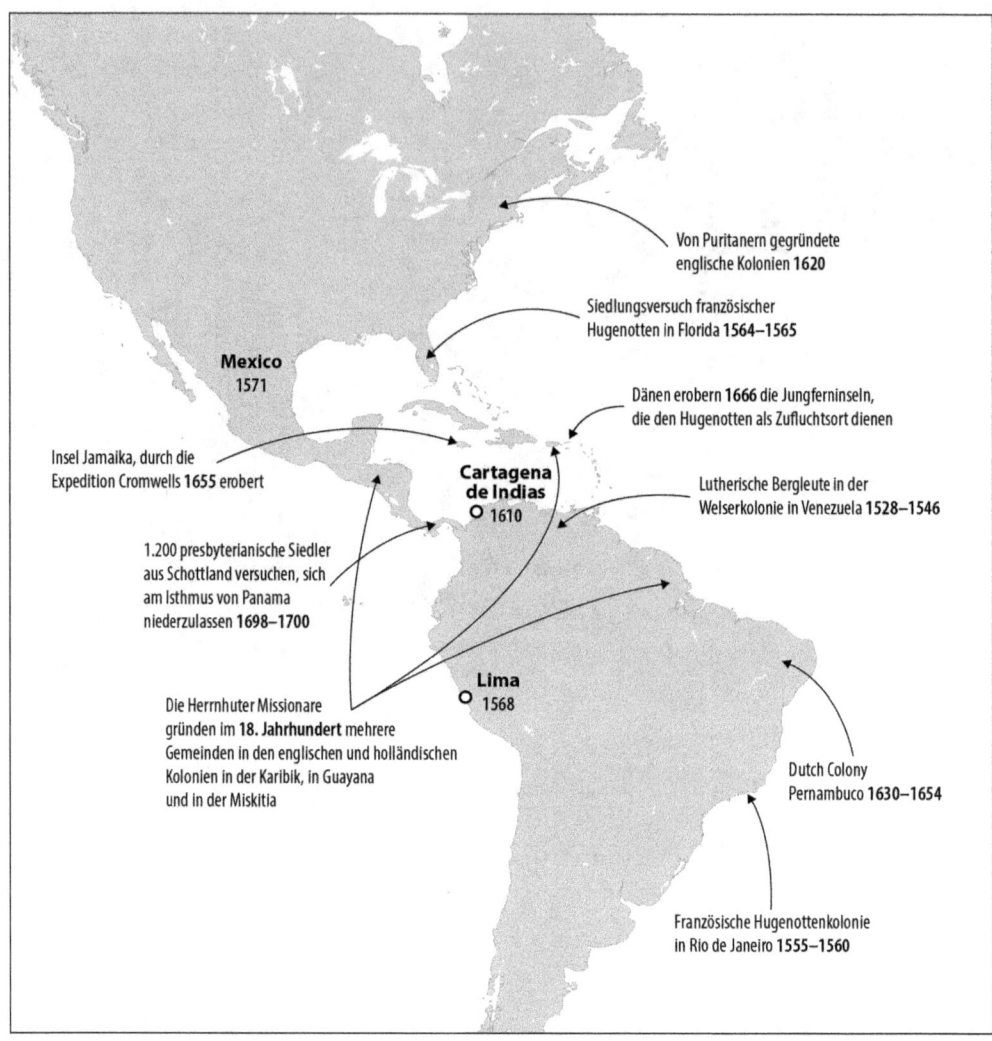

MAP 7   Protestants in colonial Iberoamerica (16th–18th c.).

MAPS 321

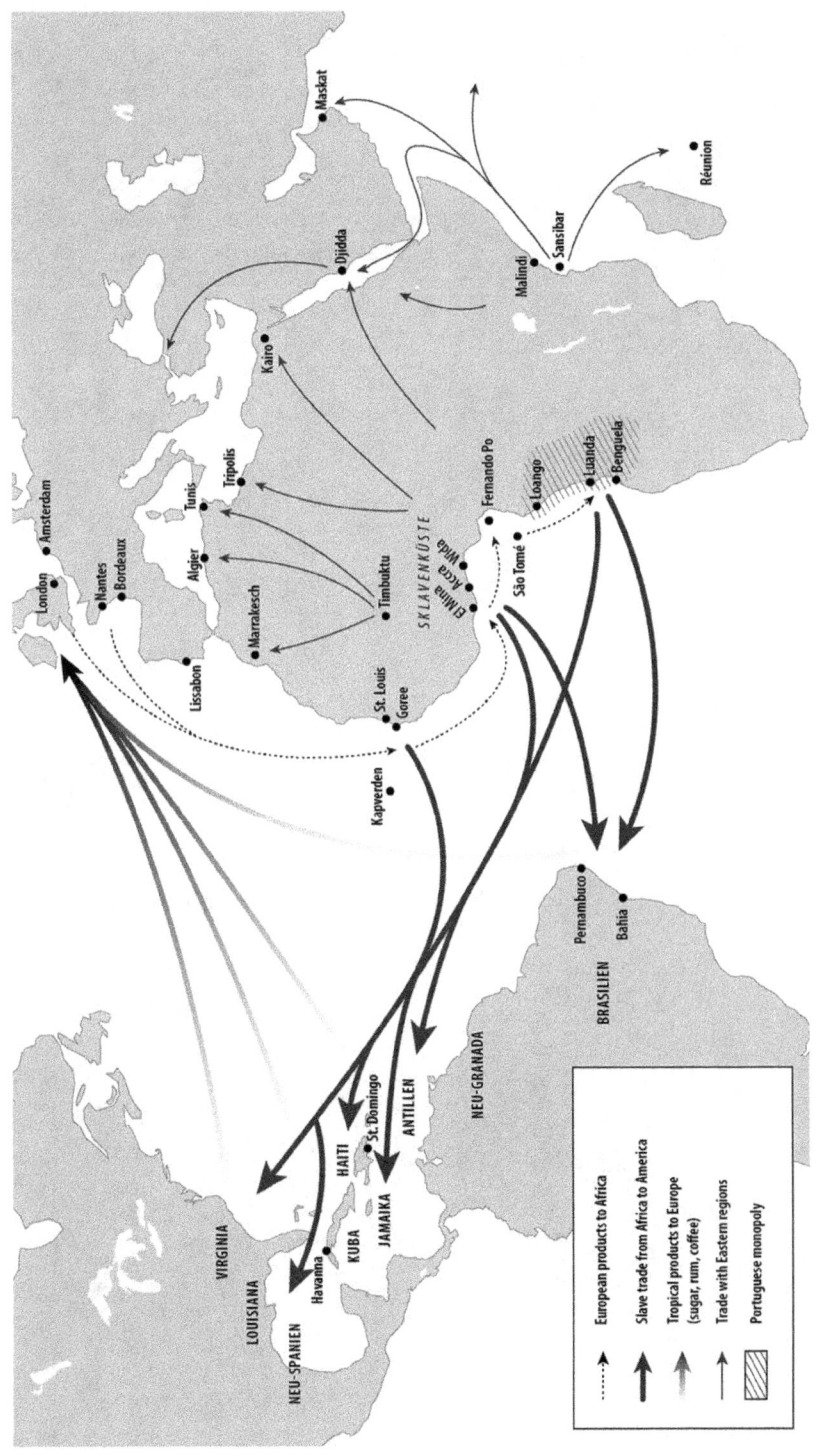

MAP 8   Transatlantic slave trade (16th–18th c.).

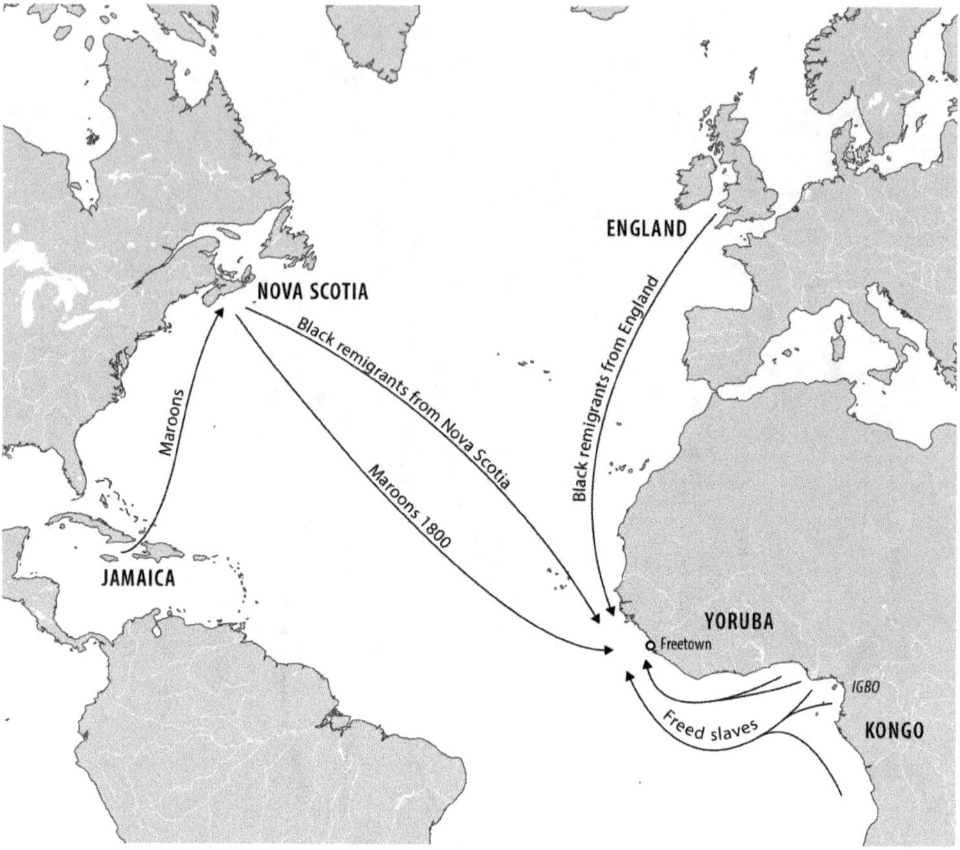

MAP 9   Transatlantic remigration to Africa and the founding of freetown (Sierra Leone) in 1792

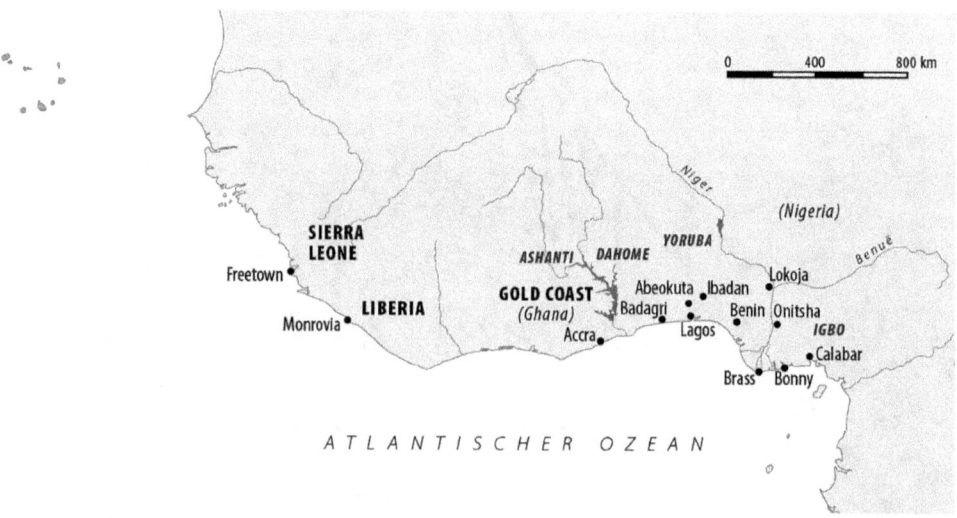

MAP 10   West Africa in late 18th/ Mid 19th c.

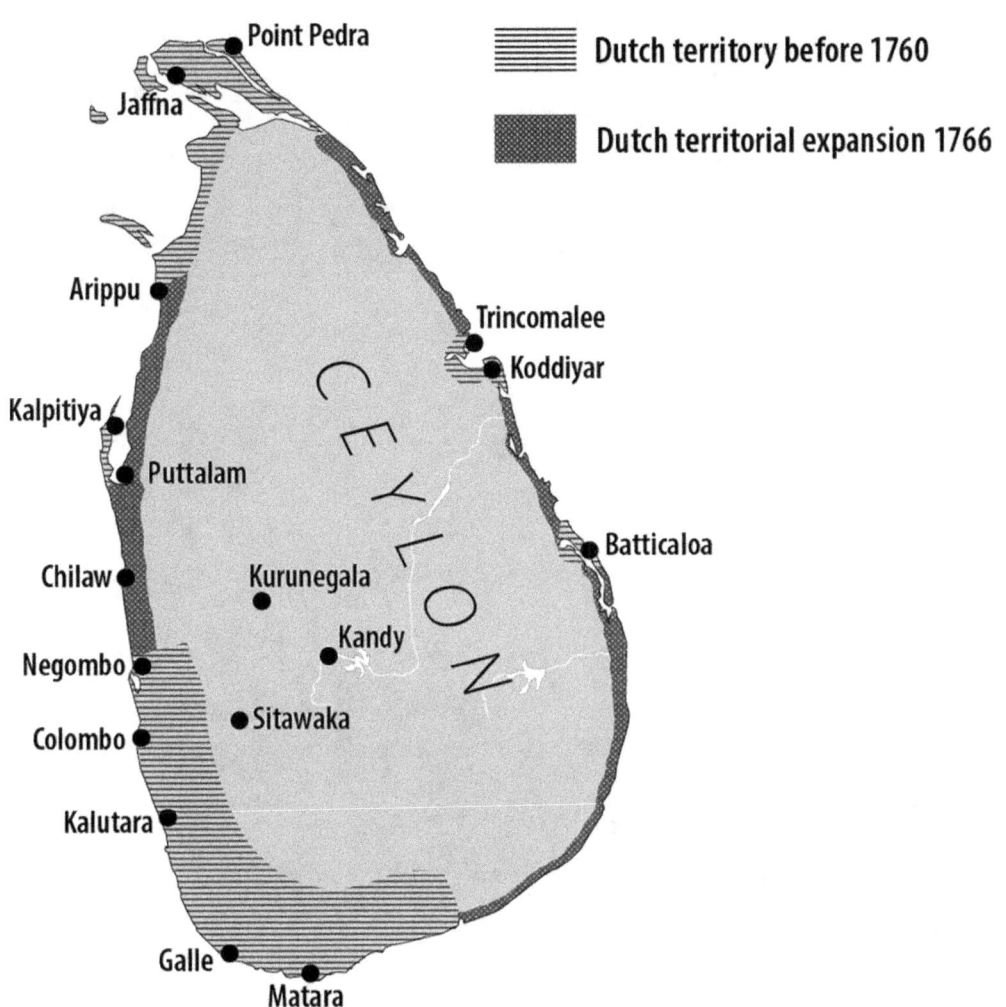

MAP 11 Ceylon (Sri Lanka) under Dutch rule (1658–1796)

MAP 12   Japan in the 16th and 17th Centuries

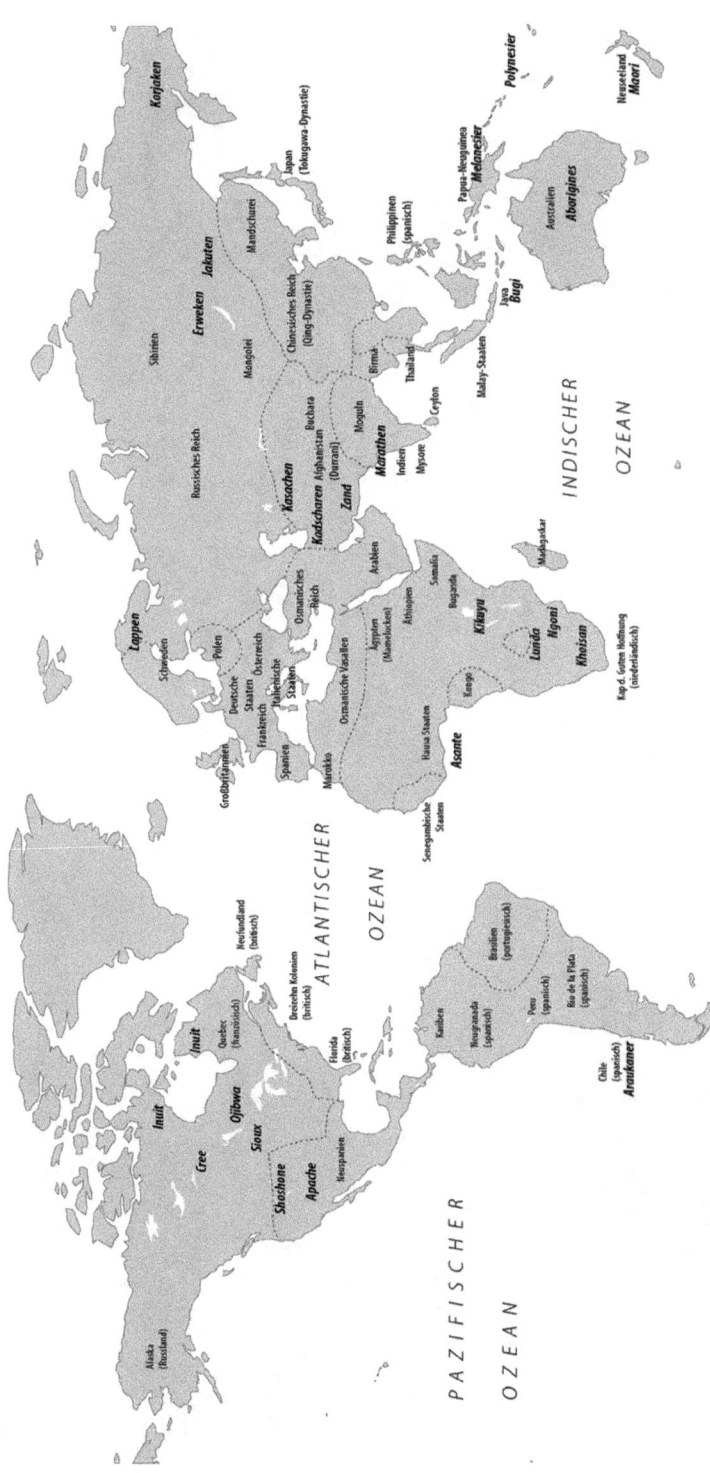

MAP 13   The World around 1750

MAP 14 European colonial possessions around 1830

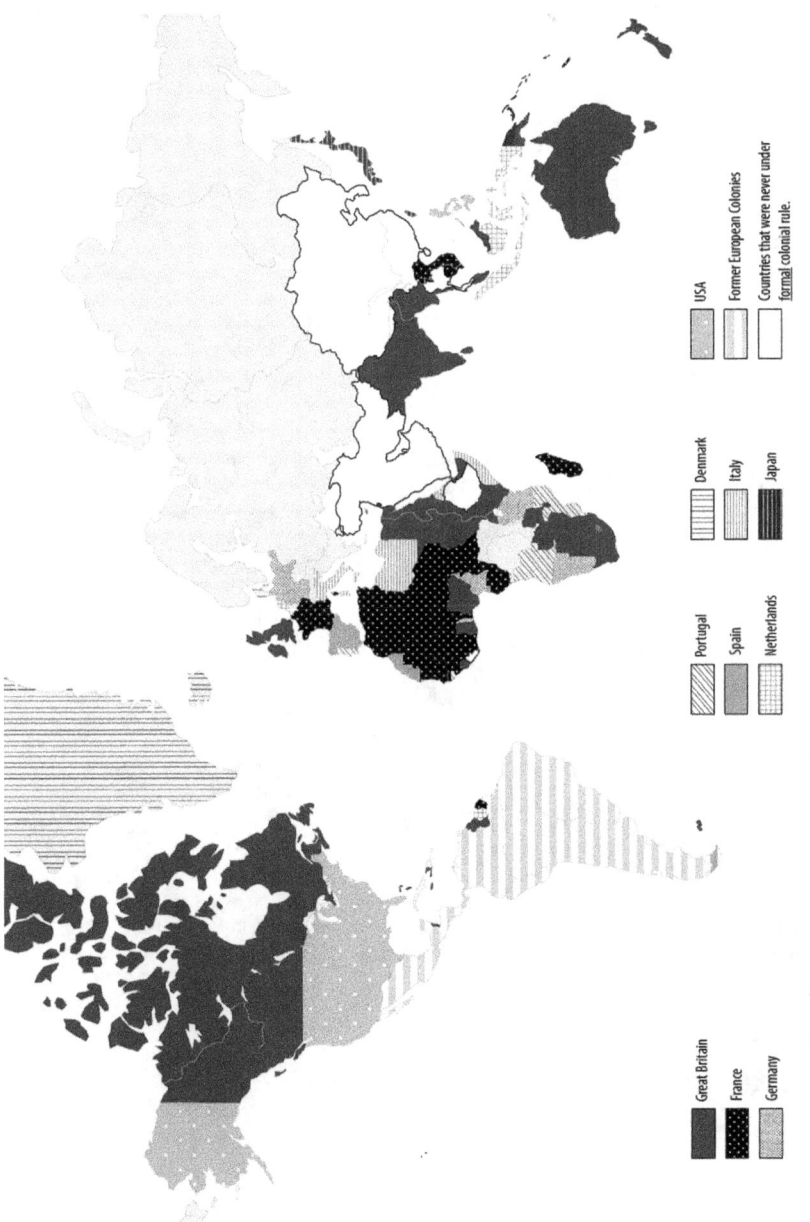

MAP 15 European colonial possessions around 1914

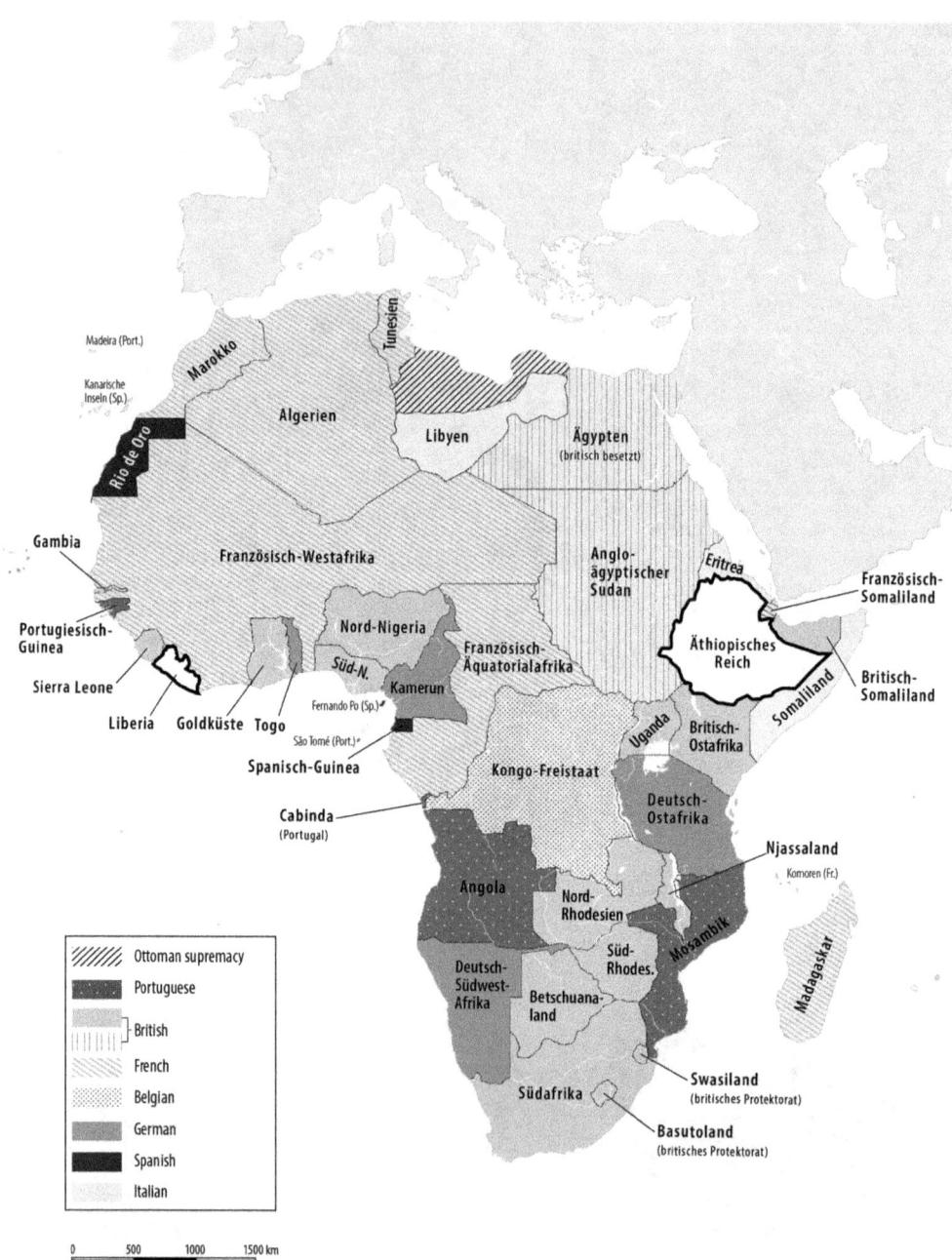

MAP 16 Africa around 1900

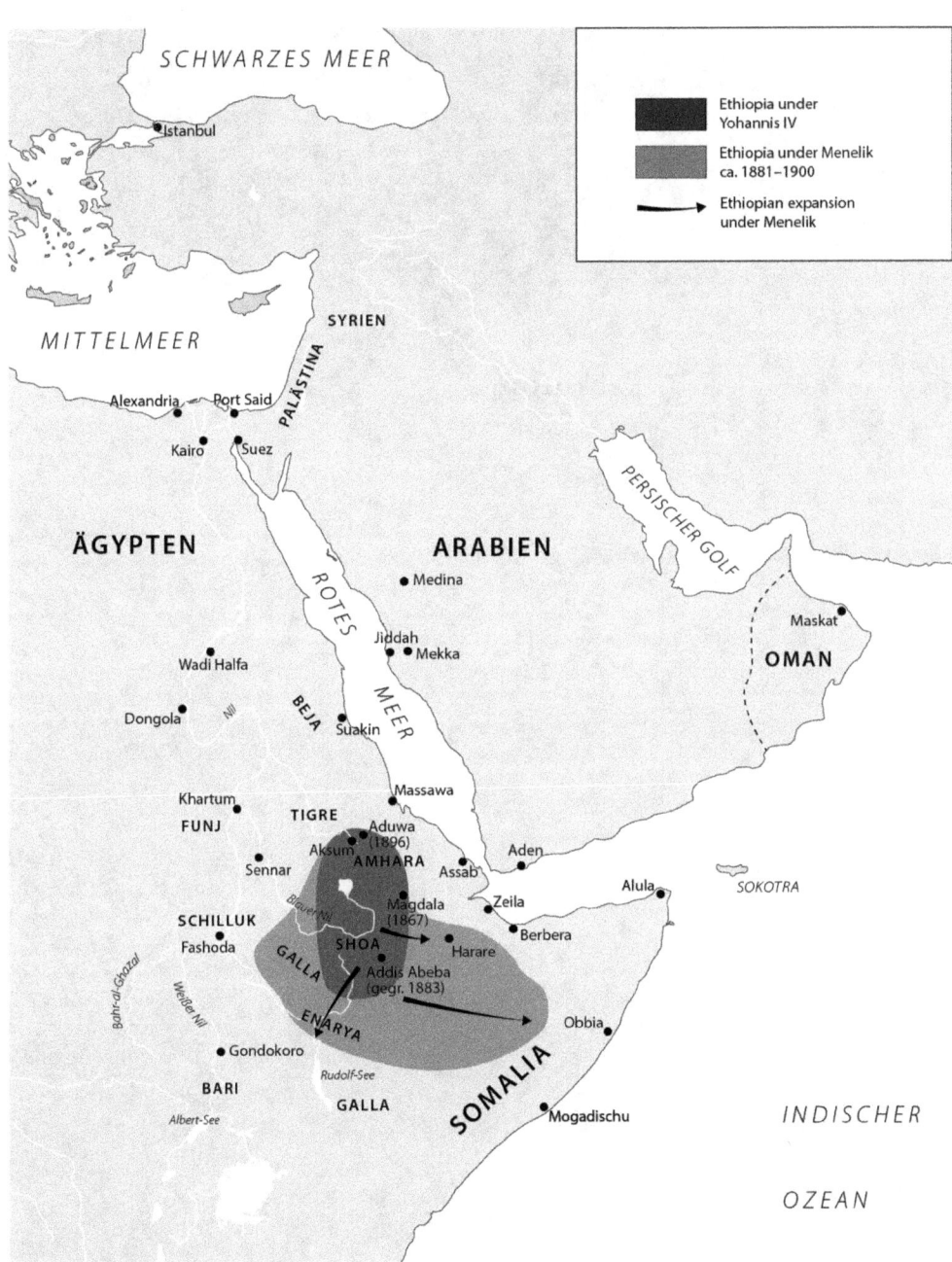

MAP 17　Ethiopia around 1900

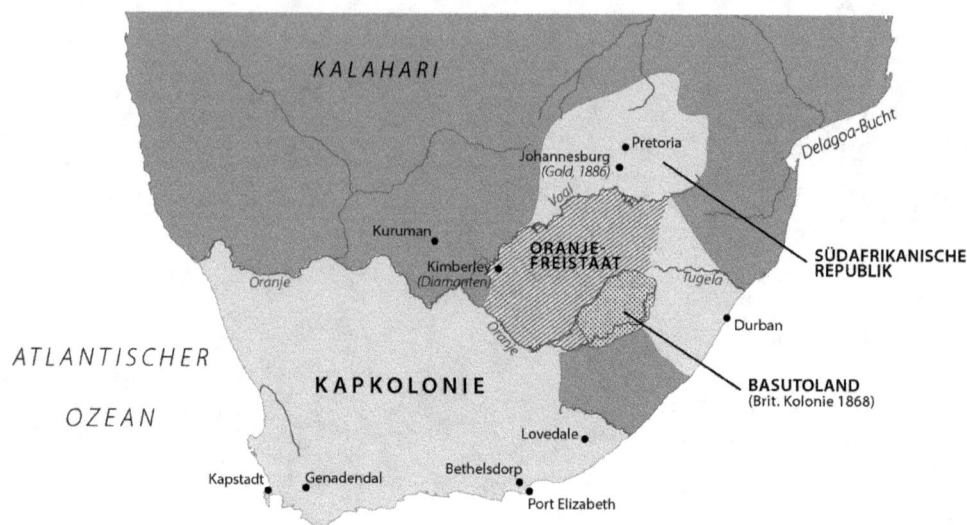

MAP 18 South Africa around 1900

MAPS

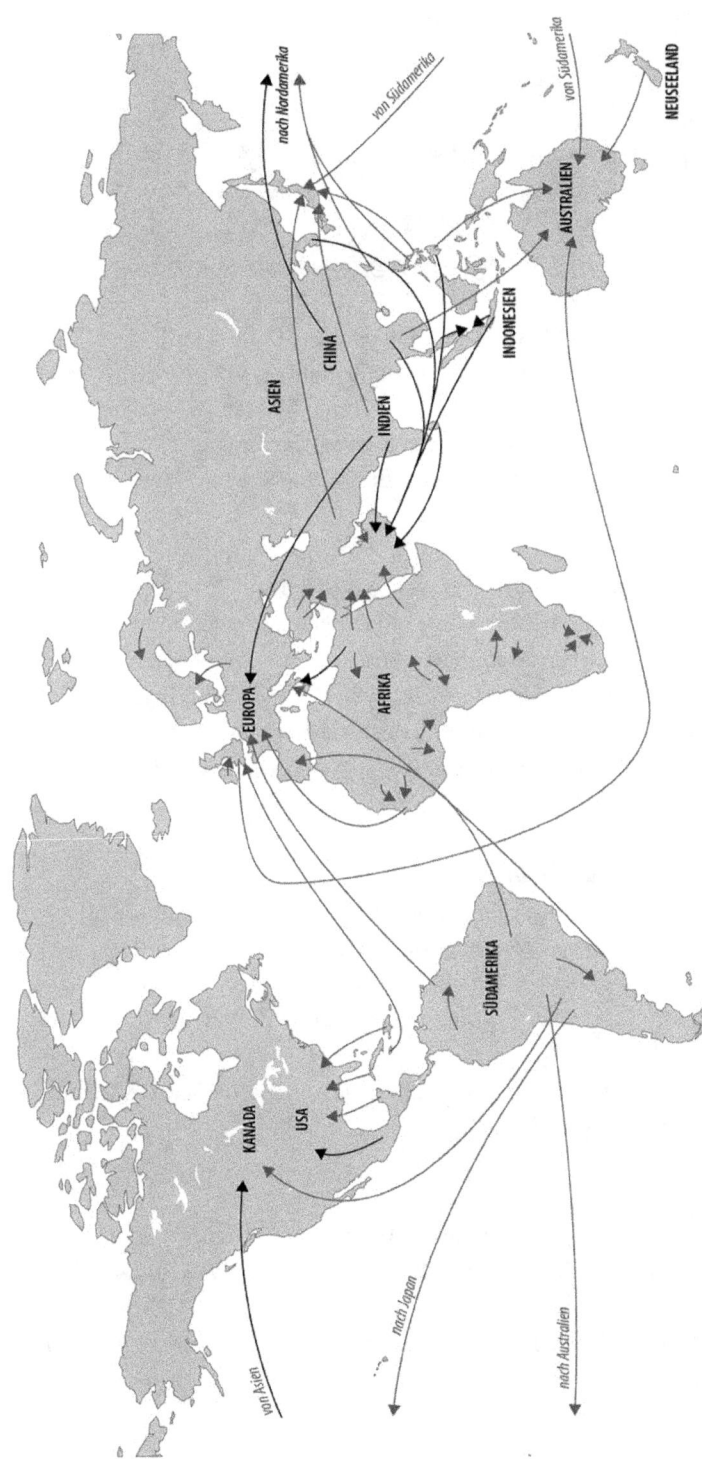

MAP 19   Global migration circa 1975

Bibliography

Bibliography 1: Standard Works, General Surveys

Asia

Moffett, S. H. (1991/2005), A History of *Christianity in Asia.* Vol. I: Beginnings to 1500; Vol. II: 1500–1900 (New York)
Phan, P. C. (2011) (Ed.), *Christianities in Asia* (Malden, MA/ Oxford, UK)
Frykenberg, R. E. (2013), *Christianity in India.* From Beginnings to the Present (Oxford)
Bays, D. H. (2012), A *New History* of Christianity in China (Malden, MA/ Oxford)
Kim, S./ Kim, K. (2015), A History of *Korean Christianity* (Cambridge)
Wilfried, F. (2014) (Ed.), The Oxford Handbook of *Christianity in Asia* (Oxford)

Africa

Hastings, A. (1994), The *Church in Africa,* 1450–1950 (Oxford)
Sundkler, B./ Steed, C. (2000), A History of the *Church in Africa* (Cambridge)
Kalu, O.U. (2005) (Ed.), *African Christianity:* An African Story (Pretoria)
Hastings, A. (1979), A History of *African Christianity* 1950–1975 (Cambridge etc.)
Hock, K. (2005), Das *Christentum in Afrika* und dem Nahen Osten (KGE IV/7; Leipzig)
Blakely, T.D./ Van Beek, W.E.A./ Thomson, D.L. (1994) (Eds.), *Religion in Africa* (London/ Portsmouth, NH)

Latin America, Carribean

González, O.E./ González, J.L. (2008), *Christianity in Latin America* (Cambridge)
Prien, H.-J. (2013), Christianity in *Latin America* (Leiden/ Boston)
Dussel, E. (1992) (Ed.), The *Church in Latin America* 1492–1992 (New York)
Lippy, C.H./ Choqette, R./ Poole, S. (1992), Christianity Comes to the *Americas,* 1492–1776 (New York)
Garrard-Burnett, V./ Freston, P./ Dove, S.C. (2016) (Eds.), The Cambridge History of *Religion in Latin America* (Cambridge)

Oceania

Breward, I. (2001), A History of the Churches in *Australasia* (Oxford)
Ross, K.R./ Tahaafe-Williams, K./ Johnson, T. (2023) (Eds.), *Christianity in Oceania* (Peabody, MA)
Lange, R. (2005), *Island Ministers*: Indigenous Leadership in 19th Century Pacific Islands Christianity (Canberra)

Middle East, Ancient Oriental Churches

Raheb, M./ Lamport, M.A. (2021) (Eds.), The Rowman & Littlefield Handbook of *Christianity in the Middle East* (Lanham)

Angold, M. (2006) (Ed.), *Eastern Christianity* (Cambridge)

Baum, W./ Winkler, D.W. (2003), The *Church of the East*: A Concise History (London/ New York)

Hage, W. (2007), Das *orientalische Christentum* (Stuttgart)

Lange, C./ Pinggéra, K. (2010), Die *altorientalischen Kirchen*. Glaube und Geschichte (Darmstadt)

Transcontinental Links and Entanglements

Koschorke, K./ Hermann, A. (2014) (Eds.), *Polycentric Structures* in the History of World Christianity/ Polyzentrische Strukturen in der Geschichte des Weltchristentums (StAECG Vol. 25; Wiesbaden)

Koschorke, K. (2012) (Ed.), Etappen der Globalisierung in christentumsgeschichtlicher Perspektive/ *Phases of Globalization* in the History of Christianity (StAECG Vol. 19; Wiesbaden

Koschorke, K. (2002) (Ed), *Transcontinental Links* in the History of Non-Western Christianity/ Transkontinentale Beziehungen in der Geschichte des Aussereuropaeischen Christentums (StAECG Vol. 6; Wiesbaden)

World Christianity in 20th/21st Centuries

Stanley, B. (2018), Christianity in the *Twentieth Century*. A World History (Princeton/ Oxford)

Kim, S./ Kim, K. (2008), Christianity as a *World Religion* (London)

Lehmann, H. (2012), Das *Christentum im 20. Jh.*: Fragen, Probleme, Perspektiven (Leipzig)

Jenkins, P. ([2]2011), The *Next Christendom*. The Coming of Global Christianity (Oxford)

Cabrita, J./ Maxwell, D./ Wild-Wood, E. (2017) (Eds.), *Relocating World Christianity*. Interdisciplinary Studies in Universal and Local Expressions of the Christian Faith (Leiden/ Boston)

Frederiks, M./ Nagy, D. (2021) (Eds.), *World Christianity*: Methodological Considerations (Leiden/ Boston)

Johnson, T.M./ Zurlo, G.A. (2023) (Eds.), *World Christian Database* (Leiden/ Boston).

Mission History

Walls, A. (1996), The *Missionary Movement* in Christian History. Studies in the Transmission of Faith (New York/ Edinburgh)

Robert, D.L. (2011), *Christian Mission*: How Christianity Became a World Religion (New York)

Latourette, K. S. (R1980), A History of the *Expansion* of Christianity. Vol. I–VII (Grand Rapids, MI)

Neill, S. (²1990), A History of *Christian Missions* (London)

Gründer, H. (1992), *Welteroberung* und Christentum. Ein Handbuch zur Geschichte der Neuzeit (Gütersloh)

Hsia, Ronnie Po-Chia (2018) (Ed.), A companion to early modern *Catholic global missions* (Leiden/ Boston)

Ward, K./ Stanley. B. (1999) (Eds.), *Church Mission Society* and World Christianity, 1799–1999 (Grand Rapids, MI/ Cambridge, UK)

European Expansion, Colonialism, Decolonization

Osterhammel, J. (1997), *Colonialism*: A Theoretical Overview (Princeton/ Kingston).

Abernethy, D.B. (2000), The Dynamics of Global Dominance: *European Overseas Empires*, 1415–1980 (New Haven)

Benjamin, T. (2006) (Ed.), Encyclopedia of *Western Colonialism* Since 1450. Vol. I-III (Detroit etc.)

Reinhard, W. (1983–1990), Geschichte der europäischen *Expansion* I–IV (Stuttgart etc.)

Schmitt, E. (1986–2003) (Ed.), *Dokumente* zur Geschichte der europäischen Expansion. Vol. I–V (Munich)

Boxer, C.R. (1991), The *Portuguese Seaborne Empire*, 1415–1825 (Manchester)

Porter, A.N. (2016), *European Imperialism*, 1860–1914 (London)

Jansen, J.C./ Osterhammel, J. (2017), *Decolonisation:* A Short History (Princeton)

Rothermund, D. (2006), The Routledge Companion to *Decolonization* (London)

Standard Books, General Surveys

Schjørring, J. H./ Hjelm, N.A. (2017/18) (Eds.), *History* of Global Christianity. Vol. I: Ca. 1500–1800; Vol. II: 19th Century (Leiden/ Boston)

Schjørring, J. H./ Hjelm, N.A./ Ward, K. (2018) (Eds.), *History* of Global Christianity. Vol. III. 20th Century (Leiden/ Boston)

The Cambridge History of Christianity:
- Vol. 5: Angold, M. (2006) (Ed.), *Eastern Christianity* (Cambridge)
- Vol. 8: Gilley, S./ Stanley, B. (2005) (Eds.), *World Christianities* c. 1815–c. 1914 (Cambridge)
- Vol. 9: McLeod, H. (2008) (Ed.), *World Christianities, c.* 1914–*c.* 2000 (Cambridge)

The Edinburgh Companions to Global Christianity
- Ross, K./ Asamoah-Gyadu, J.K./ Johnson, T.M. (2017) (Eds.), Christianity in *Sub-Saharan Africa* (Edinburgh)

- Ross, K./ Jeyaraj, D./Johnson, T.M. (2019) (Eds.), Christianity in *South and Central Asia* (Edinburgh)
- Ross, K./ Alvarez, F./Johnson, T.M. (2019) (Eds.), Christianity in *East and South East Asia* (Edinburgh)
- Ross, K./ Bidegain, A.M. /Johnson, T.M. (2022) (Eds.), Christianity in *Latin America and the Caribbean* (Edinburgh)

Selection of Sources

Koschorke, K./ Ludwig, F./ Delgado, M. (^{R}2021) (Eds.), A History of Christianity in Asia, Africa and Latin America, 1450–1990. A *Documentary Sourcebook* (Grand Rapids, MI/ Cambridge, UK) (will be cited not according to pages, but according to the individual documents as [Text]; see above under "Notes on use" (see p. xviii, fn. 3).

Bibliography 11: Complete List of References

Abernethy, D.B. (2000), The Dynamics of Global Dominance: *European Overseas Empires*, 1415–1980 (New Haven)

Abraham, V. (2013), The *Copts of Egypt*: The Challenge of Modernity and Identity (London)

Adiele, P.O. (2017), The popes, the Catholic Church and the *transatlantic enslavement* of Black Africans 1418–1839 (Hildesheim/ New York)

Adogame, A. (2005), *African Christian Communities* in Diaspora (in: Kalu, *African Christianity*, 494–514)

Adogame, A. (2008), Globalization and *New Religious Movements* in Europe (in: Kalu, *Contemporary Christianity*, 296–316)

Adogame, A. (2008), *To God be the Glory* (in: *Critical Interventions. Journal of African Art History and Visual Culture*, 2:3–4, 147–159)

Adogame, A. (2014), *African „Retromission" in Europe* (in: Koschorke / Hermann, *Polyzentrische Strukturen*, 307–316)

Adogame, A./ Gerloff, R. / Hock, K. (2008) (Eds.), Christianity in Africa and the *African Diaspora* (London / New York)

Adogame, A./ Shankar, S. (2013) (Eds.), *Religion on the Move!* New Dynamics of Religious Expansion in a Globalizing World (Leiden/ Boston)

Adogame, A./ Spickard, J. (2010) (Eds.), Religion on the Move! Transnational Religious and Social Dynamics in Africa and the *New African Diaspora* (Leiden/ Boston)

Adorno, R. (1985), The Rhetoric of Resistance: The Talking Book of *Felipe Guaman Poma* (in: *History of European Ideas* VI.4, Oxford/ New York, 447–464)

Adorno, R. (2000), Guaman Poma: *Writing and Resistance* in Colonial Peru (Austin)

Ahn, Kyo Seong (2014), *Korea as an Early Missionary Center*: Korean Missionaries Around 1910 (in: Koschorke/ Hermann, *Polycentric Structures*, 99–110)

Ajayi, J. (1965), Christian Missions in Nigeria 1841–1891: The *Making of a New Elite* (London)

Akinade, A. (2018), *African Christianity in the 20th Century* (in: Schjørring/ Hjelm/ Ward, *History 343–355*III,

Almond, G./ Appleby, S./ Sivan, E. (2000) (Eds.), *Strong Religion*. The Rise of Fundamentalism around the World (Chicago)

Anderson, A.A. (2001), *African Reformation*. African Initiated Christianity in the 20th Century (Trenton, NJ)

Anderson, A.A. (2004), An Introduction to *Pentecostalism*. Global Charismatic Christianity (Cambridge, UK)

Anderson, A.A. (2014), *Pfingstliche Geschichtsschreibung* in globaler Perspektive. Eine Revision (in: Haustein/ Maltese, *Handbuch*, 135–159)

Anderson, A.A./ Hollenweger, W. (1999) (Eds.), *Pentecostals after a Century*: Global Perspectives on a Movement in Transition (Sheffield, UK)

Anderson, G. (1969) (Ed.), Studies in *Philippine Church History* (Ithaca / London)

Andes, S.J.C. (2012), A *Catholic Alternative* to Revolution. The Survival of Social Catholicism in Postrevolutionary Mexico (in: *The Americas* 68, 529–562)

Andrade, N. (2018), The *Journey of Christianity to India* in Late Antiquity. Networks and the Movement on Culture (Cambridge, UK)

Andrews, E.E. (2013), *Native Apostles*. Black and Indian Missionaries in the British Atlantic World (Cambridge, MA / London, UK)

Angold, M. (2006) (Ed.), *Eastern Christianity* (Cambridge)

Ansprenger, F. (^{4}1981), *Auflösung der Kolonialreiche* (München)

Arbaiza, G. (1964), Peruvian Colonial Art. The *Cuzco School of Painting* (New York)

Ardanaz, D.R. (1992) (Ed.), *Pedro de Quiroga*. Coloquiois de la Verdad (Valladolid)

Aritonang, J.S./ Steenbrink, K. (2008) (Eds.), A History of *Christianity in Indonesia* (Leiden/ Boston)

Armanios, F. (2011), *Coptic Christianity* in Ottoman Egypt (Oxford)

Asamoah-Gyadu, J.K. (2005), „*Born of Water* and the Spirit": Pentecostal/Charismatic Christianity in Africa (in: Kalu, *African Christianity*, 388–409)

Asamoah-Gyadu, J.K. (2007), „Get on the Internet!" Says the Lord: Religion, *Cyberspace and Christianity* in Contemporary Africa (in: *Studies in World Christianity* 13/3, 225–241)

Ayandele, E.A. (1966), The *Missionary Impact* on Modern Nigeria, 1842–1914 (London)

Azzi, R. (1993) (Ed.), *Theologiegeschichte* der Dritten Welt: Lateinamerika (Gütersloh)

Baago, K. (1969), *Pioneers of Indigenous Christianity* (Madras)

Badr, H./Slim, S.A./ Nohra, J.A. (2005) (Eds.), Christianity. A History in the *Middle East* (Beirut)

Bakewell, P. (^{2}2004), A *History of Latin America* (Malden, MA/ Oxford, UK)

Barnet, M. (2000), *Afrokubanische Kulte*. Die Regla de Ocha. Die Regla de Palo Monte (Frankfurt a. M.)

Barreto, R./ Cavalcante, R. / Da Rosa, W.P. (2017) (Eds.), World Christianity as *Public Religion* (Minneaopolis, MN)

Barreto, R.C. (2021), Granting Full Citizenship to *Latin American Christianities* in World Christianity (in: Hanciles, *World Christianity*, 138–157)

Barreto, R.C./ Lamport, M.A. (2024) (Eds.), Engaging Coloniality: The Liberative Story of Christianity in America (Eugene, OR)

Barrett, D.B./ Kurian, G.T./ Johnson, T.M. (^{2}2001), *World Christian Encyclopedia*. A comparative survey of churches and religions in the modern world. Vol. 1+2 (Oxford)

Barron, J. (2020), "Christianity in Japan: *Kakure Kirishitan*: A Bibliography" (https://www.academia.edu/49085724/)

Barron, J.R. (2021), World Christianity and *Global Christian History* — where to start? An introductory readers' guide (https://www.academia.edu/50501629/)

Barron, J.R. (2023), *African Christian Theology*. A Select Bibliography (https://www.academia.edu/50910578/)

Barsch (2003), *Rastafari*. Von Babylon nach Afrika (Mainz)

Bastian, J.-P. (1995), Geschichte des *Protestantismus* in Lateinamerika (Luzern)

Baum, W. (1999), Die Verwandlungen des Mythos vom Reich des *Priesterkönigs Johannes*, (Klagenfurt)

Baum, W./ Winkler, D.W. (2003), The *Church of the East*: A Concise History (London/ New York)

Baumer, C. (2005), Frühes Christentum zwischen Euphrat und Jangtse. Eine Zeitreise entlang der *Seidenstraße* zur Kirche des Ostens (Stuttgart)

Baumgartner, J. (1971/72), Mission und *Liturgie* in Mexiko. Bd. I/II (Schöneck)

Baumgartner, J. (1992), Evangelisierung in *indianischen Sprachen*. Die Bemühungen der Ordensleute um das wichtigste Hilfsmittel zur Verkündigung der Frohbotschaft und zur Unterweisung im christlichen Leben (in: Sievernich, *Conquista und Evangelisation*, 313–347)

Baur, J. (1994), 2000 Years of *Christianity in Africa*. An African History 62 – 1992 (Nairobi)

Bays, D.H. (1996) (Ed.), *Christianity in China*. From the 18th Century to the Present (Stanford)

Bays, D.H. (2012), A *New History* of Christianity in China (Malden, MA/Oxford)

Beck, H. (1981), Brüder in vielen Völkern. 250 Jahre *Mission der Brüdergemeine* (Erlangen)

Becker, D. (1996), Die Kirchen und der *Pancasila*-Staat (Erlangen)

Beckerlegge, G. (2008), Colonialism, Modernity, and Religious Identities. *Religious Reform Movements* in South Asia (Oxford)

Beckmann, J. (1971), *Utopien* als missionarische Stoßkraft (in: Baumgartner, J. [Hg.], Vermittlung zwischenkirchlicher Gemeinschaft; Immensee; 361–407)

Bediako, K. (1995), Christianity in Africa. The *Renewal of a Non-Western Religion* (Edinburgh)

Bednarowski, M.F. (2008) (Ed.), *Twentieth Century Global Christianity* (Minneapolis)

Benjamin, T. (2006) (Ed.), Encyclopedia of *Western Colonialism* Since 1450. Vol. I–III (Detroit etc.)

Beozzo, J.O. (2002), Das *Zweite Vatikanische Konzil* (1962–1965) und die Kirche in Lateinamerika (in: Koschorke, *Transkontinentale Beziehungen*, 203–218)

Bergunder, M. (2000) (Ed.), *Pfingstbewegung und Basisgemeinden* in Lateinamerika (Hamburg)

Beshah, G./ Aregay, M.W. (1964), The *Question of the Union* of the Churches in Luso-Ethiopian Relations (1500 – 1632) (Lisbon)

Besier, G./ Boyens, A./ Lindemann, G. (1999), Nationaler Protestantismus und *Ökumenische Bewegung*. Kirchliches Handeln im Kalten Krieg (1945–1990) (Berlin)

Bitterli, U. (1981) (Ed.), Die Entdeckung und Eroberung der Welt. *Dokumente* und Berichte I+II (München)

Bitterli, U./ Schmitt, E. (1991) (Eds.), Die *Kenntnis beider „Indien"* im frühneuzeitlichen Europa (München)

Blakely, T.D. / Van Beek, W.E.A./ Thomson, D.L. (1994) (Eds.), *Religion in Africa* (London/ Portsmouth, NH)

Boahen, A.A. (1985) (Ed.), *Africa under Colonial Domination* 1880–1935 (Paris/ London/ Nairobi)

Boesak, A.A. (2019), Children of the Waters of Meribah: *Black Liberation Theology* (Stellenbosch)

Boff, L. (1985), *Charism and power*: Liberation theology and the institutional church (London)

Boff, L. (1989), *Introducing Liberation Theology* (Kent)

Böll, V. (1998), *Von der Freundschaft zur Feindschaft*. Die äthiopisch-orthodoxe Kirche und die portugiesischen Jesuiten in Äthiopien, 16. und 17. Jh. (in: Koschorke, „Christen und Gewürze", 43–58)

Böll, V. (2012), Die Jesuiten und die *gescheiterte Katholisierung* der äthiopisch-orthodoxen Kirche (in: Koschorke, *Etappen der Globalisierung*, 157–170)

Boudens, R. (1957), The *Catholic Church in Ceylon* under Dutch Rule (Rom)

Bowser, F.P. (1974), The *African Slave* in Colonial Peru (Stanford)

Boxer, C.R. (1963), *Race Relations* in the Portuguese Empire, 1415–1825 (Oxford)

Boxer, C.R. (1972), The *Dutch Seaborne Empire* 1600 – 1800 (London)

Boxer, C.R. (1978), The *Church Militant* and the Iberian Expansion 1440–1770 (Baltimore / London)

Boxer, C.R. (1991), The *Portuguese Seaborne Empire* 1415–1825 (Manchester)

Boxer, C.R. (1993), The *Christian Century* in Japan 1549–1650 (Manchester)
Breward, I. (2001), A History of the Churches in *Australasia* (Oxford)
Briggs, J./ Oduyoye, M.A./ Tsetis (2004) (Eds.), A History of the *Ecumenical Movement*. Vol. III: 1968–2000 (Geneva)
Bröning, M./ Weiss, H. (2006) (Eds.), *Politischer Islam* in Westafrika: Eine Bestandsaufnahme (Münster)
Brook, T. (1996), Towards Independence: Christianity in China under *Japanese Occupation* (in: Bays, *Christianity in China*, 317–337)
Brown, C.G. (2001), The *Death of Christian Britain*. Understanding Secularisation 1800 – 2000 (London)
Bryner, E. (2004), Die *orthodoxen Kirchen* von 1274 bis 1700 (Leipzig)
Budge, E.A.W. (1932), The *Queen of Sheba* and her only son Menyelek (London)
Bühlmann, W. (1985), *Weltkirche*. Neue Dimensionen – Modell für das Jahr 2001 (Graz / Wien etc)
Buisson, I./ Schottelius, H. (1980), Die *Unabhängigkeitsbewegungen* in Lateinamerika 1788–1826 (Stuttgart)
Burkholder, M.A. / Johnson, L.L. (1994), *Colonial Latin America* (New York/Oxford)
Bürkle, H. (1968) (Ed.), *Theologie und Kirche in Afrika* (Stuttgart)
Burlacioiu, C. (2015), „*Within three years* the East and the West have met each other". Die Genese einer missionsunabhängigen schwarzen Kirche im transatlantischen Dreieck USA – Südafrika – Ostafrika 1921–1950 (Wiesbaden)
Burlacioiu, C. (2022) (Ed.), Migration and *Diaspora Formation*: New Perspectives on a Global History of Christianity (Berlin)
Burlacioiu, C. (2024), West African Christianity and its Transatlantic Trails. *Sierra Leone* in the Late 18th and Early 19th c. (in: Koschorke et al., *South-South-Links*)
Burlacioiu, C./ Hermann, A. (2013) (Eds.), *Veränderte Landkarten*. Auf dem Weg zu einer polyzentrischen Geschichte des Weltchristentums. Fs. für Klaus Koschorke (Wiesbaden)
Büschges, C./ Müller, A./ Oehri, N. (2021) (Eds.), *Liberation Theology* and the Others. Contextualizing Catholic Activism in 20th Century Latin America (Lexington)
Buve, R.T./ Fisher, J.R. (1992) (Eds.), *Handbuch* der Geschichte Lateinamerikas. Bd. II: Lateinamerika von 1760 bis 1900 (Stuttgart)
Cabrita, J./ Maxwell, D./ Wild-Wood, E. (2017) (Eds.), *Relocating World Christianity*. Interdisciplinary Studies in Universal and Local Expressions of the Christian Faith (Leiden / Boston)
Campbell, H.A. (2010), When Religion Meets *New Media* (London / New York)
Campbell, J. (2024), Race, Religion and Repatriation: Ideological *Origins of the Back-To-Africa Movement*, 1770–1820 (in: Koschorke et al., *South-South-Links*)
Campbell, J.T. (1998), *Songs of Zion*. The African Methodist Episcopal Church in the United States and South Africa (Oxford)

Campbell, J.T. (2006), *Middle Passages*. African American Journeys to Africa, 1787 – 2005 (New York)

Cañizares-Esguerra, J./ Maryks, R./ Hsia, R.P. (2018) (Eds.), Encounters between *Jesuits and Protestants* in Asia and the Americas (Leiden/ Boston)

Caraman, P. (1976), *The lost paradise*: the Jesuit Republic in South America (New York)

Castles, S./ De Haas, H./ Miller, M.J. (2014) (Eds.), The *Age of Migration*. International Population Movements in the Modern World (London)

Cayota, M. (1993), Die *indianische Kirche* – Eine Sehnsucht im Werden (in: Rotzetter, *Von der Conquista*, 35–107)

Chenchiah, P. et al. (1941), *Ashrams* Past and Present (Madras)

Chidester, D. (2000), Christianity. *A Global History* (San Francisco)

Chow, A. (2018), *Chinese Public Theology* (Oxford).

Chow, A. (2022), „What has Jerusalem to do with the Internet? World Christianity and Digital Culture" (in: *International Bulletin of Mission Research*. Vol. 47/2)

Chow, A. / Law, E. (2021) (Eds.), *Ecclesial Diversity* in Chinese Christianity (Cham)

Christensen, M.Z. (2014), *Translated Christianities*. Nahuatl and Maya Religious Texts (University Park, PA)

Christ-Von Wedel, C./ Kuhn, T.K. (2015) (Eds.), *Basler Mission*. Menschen, Geschichte. Perspektiven 1815–2015 (Basel)

Clarke, P.B. (1986), *West Africa* and Christianity (London)

Clossey, L. (2006), *Merchants, migrants, missionaries*, and globalization in the early-modern Pacific (in: Journal of Global History 2006/1, 41–58)

Clossey, L. (2008), *Salvation and Globalization* in the Early Jesuit Mission (Cambridge, UK)

Cochrane, J.R. (2009), Reframing the Political Economy of the Sacred: Readings of *Post-Apartheid Christianity*, (in: Koschorke, *Falling Walls*, 95–116)

Cohen, L. (2009), The Missionary Strategies of the *Jesuits in Ethiopia* (1555–1632) (Wiesbaden).

Cohen, R. (1995) (Ed.), The Cambridge *Survey of World Migration* (Cambridge / New York)

Coleman, S. (2004), The Globalisation of *Charismatic Christianity*. Spreading the Gospel of Prosperity (Cambridge, UK)

Collet, G. (1990) (Ed.), Theologien der Dritten Welt. EATWOT als Herausforderung westlicher Theologie und Kirche (Immensee).

Comblin, J. (1979), The Church and the National Security State (Maryknoll)

Cooper, M. (2004), A Mission Interrupted: *Japan* (in: Hsia, *Reformation World*, 393–410)

Corten, A. /Marshall-Fratani, R. (2001) (Eds.), *Between Babel and Pentecost*. Transnational Pentecostalism in Africa and Latin America (Bloomington, IN)

Cox, J. (2008), The *British Missionary Enterprise* since 1700 (New York/ London)

Cracknell, K. / White, S.J. (2005), An Introduction to *World Methodism* (Cambridge)

Cragg, K. (1991), The *Arab Christian*. A History in the Middle East (Louisville)
Crowley, F.G. (1971), *Garcilaso de la Vega*. El Inca and his sources in Comentarios des los Incas (The Hague)
Cushner, N.P. (2000), The *Jesuits in Colonial America*, 1565–1767 (Buffalo, NY)
Daniels, D.D. (2014), *Kongolese Christianity in the Americas* of the 17th and 18th Centuries (in: Koschorke, *Polycentric Structures*, 215–226)
Daniels, D.D. (2019), *Luther and Ethiopian Christianity* (in: Ludwig, *Reformation*, 21–32)
Davies, N./ Conway, M. (2008), *World Christianity* in the 20th Century (London)
De Alva, K/ Jorge, J. (1988) (Eds.), The *Work of Bernardino de Sahagún*: Pioneer Ethnographer of Sixteenth-Century Mexico (Austin)
De Gruchy, J. (2009) (Ed.), Christianity and the Modernisation of *South Africa*, 1867–1936 A Documentary History Vol. I (Pretoria)
De La Rosa, R.V. (1992), *Reinheit des Blutes*? Der verwehrte Zugang zu Priesteramt und Ordensstand (in: Sievernich, *Conquista und Evangelisation*, 271–292)
De Souza, T. (1998), The *Indian Christians* of St. Thomas and the Portuguese Padroado: Rape after a century-long courtship (1498–1599) (in: Koschorke, „Christen und Gewürze", 31–42)
De Souza, T. (2002), The *Council of Trent* (1545–1563): Its Reception *in Portuguese India* (in: Koschorke, *Transcontinental Links*, 189–202)
Del Pomar, F.C. (1964), Peruvian Colonial Art. The *Cuzco School of Painting* (New York)
Delgado, M. (1991), *Gott in Lateinamerika*. Texte aus fünf Jahrhunderten (Düsseldorf)
Delgado, M. (1994/95) (Ed.), Bartolomé de *Las Casas. Werkauswahl* Bd.1+ 2 (Paderborn etc)
Delgado, M. (1996), *Abschied* vom erobernden Gott (Immensee)
Delgado, M. (2002), Die Jungfrau von Guadalupe, der Apostel Thomas und die *kreolischen Emanzipationsbestrebungen* in Mexiko um 1800 (in: Koschorke, *Transkontinentale Beziehungen*, 315–328)
Delgado, M. (2017), *Catholicism* in Spain, Portugal, and their Empires (in: Schjørring/ Hjelm, History I, 17–76)
Demel, W. (1993), Wie die Chinesen gelb wurden. Ein Beitrag zur Frühgeschichte der *Rassentheorien* (Bamberg)
Dennis, J.S. et al. (1911) (Ed.), *World Atlas of Christian Missions* (New York)
Díaz Basera, V. (2005), The Pyramid under the Cross: *Franciscan Discourses* of Evangelization and the Nahua Christian Subject in Sixteenth-Century Mexico (Tucson)
Diaz, H. (1986), *A Korean Theology*. Chu-Gyo Yo-Ji: Essentials of the Lord's Teaching, by Chóng Yak-jong Augustine (1760 – 1801) (Immensee).
Dickson, K.A. (1984), *Theology in Africa* (Maryknoll, NY).
Dilke, C. (1978) (Ed.), *Letter to a King*. A Picture-History of the Inca Civilization by Huamán Poma (London/Boston/ Sydney)
Dohi, A. et al. (1991) (Eds.), Theologiegeschichte der Dritten Welt: *Japan* (München)

Dreher, M. (1978), *Kirche und Deutschtum* in der Entwicklung der Evang. Kirche Lutherischen Bekenntnisses in Brasilien (Göttingen)

Dreher, M. (1998), *Volkskatholizismus* und Pfingstlertum in Brasilien. Widerstand der Armen? (in: Koschorke, „*Christen und Gewürze*", 203–216)

Dreher, M. (2017), *Latin America* and the Caribbean in the 19th Century (in: Schjørring/ Hjelm, History II, 205–222)

Drescher, S. (2009), Abolition: a history of *slavery and antislavery* (Cambridge)

Drummond, R.H. (1971), A History of *Christianity in Japan* (Grand Rapids)

Ducellier, A. (1995) Die Orthodoxie in der *Frühzeit der türkischen Herrschaft* (in: Geschichte des Christentums. Vol. 7, 6–49

Duguid-May, M. (2018), The *Ecumenical Movement* (in: Schjørring/ Hjelm/ Ward, History III, 147–182)

Dunn, E. (2015), Lightning from the East: Heterodoxy and Christianity in *Contemporary China* (Leiden)

Dussel, E. (1992) (Ed.), The *Church in Latin America* 1492–1992 (New York)

Duve, Th. (2010), *Konzilien* im kolonialen Hispanoamerika und frühneuzeitliche „Jurisdiktionskultur" (in: Erdö, P./ Szuromi, A. S. (Eds.), Proceedings of the Thirteenth International Congress of Medieval Canon Law, 2008, Città del Vaticano, 693–698)

EATWOT [Ecumenical Association of Third World Theologians] (Ed.) (1978–2007), *Voices from the Third World* (New York)

Eck, D.L. (2001), *A New Religious America*. How a „Christian Country" has become the World's Most Religiously Diverse Nation (London/New York).

Edmonson, M.S. (1974) (Ed.), Sixteenth Century Mexico: The Work of *Sahagún* (Albuquerque)

Eigenmann, U. (2016), *Dom Helder Câmara* (Luzern)

Elbourne, E. (2002), *Blood Ground*. Colonialism, Missions and the Contest for Christianity in the Cape Colony and Britain 1799–1853 (London)

Ellsberg, R. (1991) (Ed.), *Gandhi on Christianity* (Maryknoll, NY)

Elphick, R. (2012), The *Equality of Believers*. Protestant Missionaries and the Racial Policy of South Africa (Charlottesville / London)

Elphick, R. / Davenport, R. (1997), *Christianity in South Africa*. A Political, Social and Cultural History (Oxford / Cape Town).

Elwood, D.J. (1978) (Ed.), *What Asian Christians are thinking*: a theological source book (Quezon City)

Engel, E. (2015), Encountering Empire. *African American Missionaries* in Colonial Africa, 1900–1939 (Stuttgart)

England, J.C. (1981) (Ed.), Living *Theology in Asia* (London)

England, J.C./ Kuttianimattathil, J./ Mansford Prior, J. et al. (Eds.) (2002–2004), *Asian Christian Theologies*. A Research Guide to Authors, Movements, Source. Vol I-III (Dehli/ Maryknoll, NY

Enzensberger, H.M. (1981) (Ed.), Las Casas. *Bericht von der Verwüstung* der Westindischen Inseln (Frankfurt a.M.)

Espinoza, G. (2004), The *Pentecostalisation* of Latin America and U.S. Latin Christianity (in: *Pneuma* 26/2, 262–292)

Etherington, N. (1976), Mission Station *Melting Pots* as a Factor in the Rise of South African Black Nationalism (in: *The International Journal of African Historical Studies.* Vol. 9, No. 4; 592–605)

Etherington, N. (2009) (Ed.), *Missions and Empire* (Oxford)

Everett, S. (1998), *Geschichte der Sklaverei* (Augsburg)

Fairbank, J.K. (1989), Geschichte des modernen *China* (München)

Fane, D. (1996) (Ed.), *Converging Cultures:* Art and Identity in Spanish America (New York)

Farhadian, C. E. (2012) (Ed.), Introducing *World Christianity* (Chichester)

Fernández-Armesto, F. (1991), *Columbus* (Oxford)

Fey, H.E. (^{3}1993) (Ed.), The Ecumenical Advance. A History of the *Ecumenical Movement* Vol. II: 1948–1968 (Geneva).

Fieldhouse, D.K. (1991), Die *Kolonialreiche* seit dem 18. Jh. (Frankfurt a.M.)

Fornet-Betancourt, R. (1997) (Ed.), *Befreiungstheologie.* Kritischer Rückblick und Perspektiven für die Zukunft. Bd. I-III (Mainz)

Fountain, D.L. (2010), Slavery, Civil War, and Salvation: *African American slaves and Christianity,* 1830 – 1870 (Baton Rouge)

Francois, W./ Soen, V. (2018) (Eds.), The *Council of Trent*: Reform and Controversy in Europe and Beyond. Vol 1–3 (Göttingen)

Frederiks, M. (2021), *World Christianity*: Contours of an Approach (in: Frederiks/ Nagy, World Christianity, 10–39).

Frederiks, M./ Nagy, D. (2021) (Eds.), *Critical Readings* in the History of Christian Mission (Leiden/ Boston)

Frederiks, M./ Nagy, D. (2021) (Eds.), *World Christianity*: Methodological Considerations (Leiden/ Boston)

Freston, P. (1995), *Pentecostalism in Brazil*: A Brief History (in: *Religion* 25, 119–133)

Freston, P. (2001), The Transnationalisation of *Brasilian Pentecostalism*: The Universal Church of the Kingdom of God (in: Corten/ Marshall-Fratani, *Babel and Pentecost,* 196–215)

Friedrich, M. (2022), *The Jesuits*: A History (Princeton)

Frieling, R. (1986), *Befreiungstheologien* (Göttingen)

Frieling, R. (1992), Der Weg des *ökumenischen Gedankens* (Göttingen)

Frost, E.C. (1993), Die Anfänge der Inkulturation – Das *Tlatelolco-Projekt* (in: Rotzetter u.a., *Von der Conquista,* 126–144])

Frykenberg, R.E. (2013), *Christianity in India.* From Beginnings to the Present (Oxford)

Furtado, C.L. (1978), Contribution of Dr. *D.T. Niles* to the Church Universal and Local (Madras)

Fyfe, C./ Walls, A. (1996), *Christianity in Africa* in the 1990s (Edinburgh)

Garrard-Burnett, V./ Freston, P./ Dove, S.C. (2016) (Eds.), The Cambridge History of *Religion in Latin America* (Cambridge)

Gensichen, H.-W. (1976), *Missionsgeschichte* der neueren Zeit (Göttingen)

Gifford, P. (1995) (Ed.), The Christian Churches and the *Democratisation of Africa* (Leiden)

Gifford, P. (2009), Africa's Churches and the „*Second Liberation Struggle*" of 1989–1993 (in: Koschorke, *Falling Walls*, 137–156)

Gilley, S./ Stanley, B. (2005) (Eds.), *World Christianities* c. 1815 - c. 1914 (Cambridge)

Gillman, L./ Klimkeit, H.-J. (1999), *Christians in Asia before 1500* (Ann Arbor, MI)

Gillner, M. (1997), Bartolomé de *Las Casas* und die Eroberung des indianischen Kontinents (Stuttgart etc.)

Goh, R.B.H. (2005), The *Internet and Christianity in Asia*: Cultural Trends, Structures and Transformations (in: *International Journal of Urban and Regional Research* 29/4, 831–848)

Gombrich, R./ Obeyesekere, G. (1988), *Buddhism Transformed*. Religious Change in Sri Lanka (Princeton).

González, O.E./ González, J.L. (2008), *Christianity in Latin America* (Cambridge)

Goodhew, D. (2017) (Ed.), *Growth and Decline* in the Anglican Communion (Abingdon)

Goodpasture, H.M. (1989) (Ed.), *Cross and Sword*. An Eyewitness History of Christianity in Latin America (NY)

Graf, F.W. (2004), Die *Wiederkehr der Götter*. Religion in der modernen Kultur (München)

Graham, J. (2018), Pepper, Padroado and Prester John. *Portuguese-Thomas Christian Relations* and the Creation of an Imperial Patron Saint (in: Almeida, R. [Ed.], A Post-Colonial Society Between Cultures; Goa, 169–193)

Granados, J.J. (2003), *Bild und Kunst* im Prozess der Christianisierung Lateinamerikas (Münster etc.)

Gray, R. (1990), *Black Christians* and White Missionaries (Yale/London)

Greschat, M. (2014), Der *Erste Weltkrieg und die Christenheit*. Ein globaler Überblick (Stuttgart)

Grohs, G. (1967), *Stufen afrikanischer Emanzipation*. Studien zum Selbstverständnis westafrikanischer Eliten (Stuttgart u.a.)

Gross, A./ Kumaradoss, Y.V./ Liebau, H. (2006) (Eds.), Halle and the *Beginning of Protestant Christianity* in India. I-III (Halle)

Gründer, H. (1982), Christliche Mission und *deutscher Imperialismus 1884–1914* (Paderborn)

Gründer, H. (1988), Der „Jesuitenstaat" in Paraguay. „Kirchlicher Kolonialismus" oder Entwicklungshilfe» unter kolonialem Vorzeichen? (in: *Geschichte und Kulturen* 1, 1–25)

Gründer, H. (1992), *Welteroberung* und Christentum. Ein Handbuch zur Geschichte der Neuzeit (Gütersloh)

Gründer, H. (2003), Eine Geschichte der europäischen *Expansion* (Darmstadt)

Gründer, H./ Hiery, H. (^{3}2022), Die Deutschen und ihre *Kolonien*. Ein Überblick (Berlin)

Gumileumilev, L. (1987), Searches for an Imaginary Kingdom. The Legend of the *Kingdom of Prester John* (Cambridge)

Gutiérrez, G. (1973), *Theologie der Befreiung* (München)

Hage, W. (2007), Das *orientalische Christentum* (Stuttgart)

Hamilton, R. (2009) (Ed.), Guaman Poma: *The First New Chronicle and Good Government* (Austin: University of Texas Press)

Hanciles, J. (2005), *Back to Africa*: White Abolitionists and Black Missionaries (in: Kalu, *African Christianity*, 191–216)

Hanciles, J. (2014), The *Black Atlantic* and the Shaping of African Christianity, 1820–1920 (in: Koschorke/ Hermann, *Polycentric Structures*, 29–50)

Hanciles, J.J. (2008), *Beyond Christendom*. Globalization, African Migration, and the Transformation of the West (Maryknoll, NY)

Hanciles, J.J. (2021) (Ed.), *World Christianity*. History, Methodologies, Horizons (Maryknoll, NY)

Hanke, L. (1994), *All Mankind is One*: A Study of the Disputation between B. de las Casas and J. G. de Sepúlveda in 1550 ... (DeKalb)

Harper, S.B. (2000), In the Shadow of the Mahatma. *Bishop V.S. Azariah* and the Travails of Christianity in British India (Grand Rapids).

Hartch, T. (2014), The *Rebirth* of Latin American Christianity (Oxford, UK)

Hartmann, P.C. (1994), Der *Jesuitenstaat* in Südamerika 1609 – 1768 (Weißenhorn)

Hastings, A. (1979), A History of *African Christianity* 1950–1975 (Cambridge etc.)

Hastings, A. (1994), The *Church in Africa*, 1450–1950 (Oxford)

Hastings, A. (1998), The Christianity of *Pedro IV of the Kongo*, „the Pacific" (1695–1718) (in: Koschorke, *„Christen und Gewürze"*, 59–72)

Haustein, J. (2011), Die *Pfingstbewegung als Alternative* zur Säkularisierung? Zur Wahrnehmung einer globalen religiösen Bewegung des 20. Jh. (in: *Archiv für Sozialgeschichte* 51, 533–554)

Haustein, J./ Maltese, G. (2014) (Eds.), *Handbuch* pfingstliche und charismatische Theologie (Göttingen)

Henkel, W. (2006), Die Wirkungsgeschichte des dritten Provinzialkonzils von Lima (in: *Annuarium Historiae Conciliorum* 38, 199–212)

Henkel, W./ Pietschmann, H. (1984), Die *Konzilien* in *Lateinamerika* Teil I: Mexiko 1555 – 1897 (Paderborn)

Henkel, W./ Saranyana, J.-L. (2010), Die *Konzilien in Lateinamerika* Teil II: Lima 1551–1927 (Paderborn)

Hermann, A. (2016) (Ed.), The P*hilippines* (in: Koschorke et al., *Discourses* of Indigenous Christian Elites, 337–446).

Heuser, A. (2015) (Ed.), Pastures of Plenty: Tracing Religio-Scapes of *Prosperity Gospel* in Africa and Beyond (Frankfurt a.M. etc.)

Heuser, A. (2016), „*Umkehrmission*" – Vom Abgesang eines Mythos (in: *Interkulturelle Theologie* 42/1, 25–54)

Heywood, L.M./ Thornton, J. (2007), Central Africans, *Atlantic Creoles*, and the Foundation of the Americas, 1585–1660 (Cambridge)

Higgs, C. (1997), The Ghosts of Equality: The Public Lives of *D.D.T. Jabavu* 1885–1959 (Cape Town)

Hildmann, P.W. (2007) (Ed.), „Sie werden Euch hassen ..." *Christenverfolgung* weltweit (München)

Ho Tai, H.-T. (2001), The *Country of Memory*: Remaking the Past in Late Socialist Vietnam (Berkeley)

Hock, K. (1998), Christliche *Verantwortung im islamischen Kontext* (in: *Ökumenische Rundschau* 47/4, 517–527)

Hock, K. (2005), Das *Christentum in Afrika* und dem Nahen Osten (KGE IV/7; Leipzig)

Hodkin, T. (1975), *Nigerian Perspectives*. An Historical Anthology (London / Oxford / NY)

Hofmann, T. (22006), Annäherung an Armenien. Geschichte und Gegenwart (München)

Hofmeyr, J.W./ Pillay, G.J. (1994) (Eds.), A History of *Christianity in South Africa*. Vol. 1 (Pretoria)

Holland, R.F. (1985), European *Decolonization* 1918 – 1981 (London)

Hollenweger, W. (1997), *Pentecostalism*: Origins and Developments Worldwide (Peabody, MA)

Horsfield, P. (2015), *From Jesus to the Internet*. A History of Christianity and Media (Malden, MA / Oxford, UK)

Horsfield, P. / Hess, M. / Medrano, A. (2004) (Eds.), Belief in Media: Cultural Perspectives on *Media and Christianity* (Aldershot)

Hovannisian, R. (2007) (Ed.), The *Armenian genocide* (New Brunswick, NJ)

Hsia, R. Po-Chia (1995), *Mission und Konfessionalisierung* (in: Reinhard, W./ Schilling, H. [Hgg], Die katholische Konfessionalisierung; Gütersloh, 158–165)

Hsia, R. Po-Chia (2004) (Ed.), A Companion to the *Reformation World* (Malden, MA/ Oxford)

Hsia, R. Po-Chia (2004), *Promise: China* (in: Hsia, *Reformation World*, 375–392)

Hsia, R. Po-Chia (²2005) (Ed.), The World of *Catholic Renewal* 1540–1770 (Cambridge)

Hsia, Ronnie Po-Chia (2018) (Ed.), A companion to early modern *Catholic global missions* (Leiden/ Boston)

Iglehart, C.E. (1960), A Century of Protestant Christianity in *Japan* (Rutland/ Tokyo)

Ileto, R.C. (1979), *Pasyon and Revolution*. Popular Movements in the Philippines, 1840–1910 (Quezon City)

Iliffe, J. (1997), *Geschichte Afrikas* (München)

Iliffe, J. (2002), *Africans*: the history of a continent (Cambridge)

Im, C.H. / Yong, A. (2014), *Global Diasporas* and Mission (Oxford)

Iriye, A./ Osterhammel, J. (2013) (Eds.); *Geschichte der Welt VII*: Die globalisierte Welt. 1945 bis heute (München)

Irvin, D.T. (2008), *World Christianity*: An Introduction (in: *The Journal of World Christianity* 1:1, 1–26)

Irvin, D. T. (2017), The Protestant *Reformation and World Christianity* (Grand Rapids, NY).

Irvin, D.T./ Sunquist, S.C. (2001/2012), History of the *World Christian Movement* I/II (Maryknoll, NY)

Isichei, E. (1995), A History of *Christianity in Africa* from Antiquity to the Present (London)

Jakobbson, S. (1972), *Am I not a Man* and Brother? British missions and the abolition of the slave trade and slavery in West Africa and the West Indies 1786 – 1838 (Uppsala)

Jansen, J.C./ Osterhammel, J. (2017), *Decolonisation:* A Short History (Princeton)

Jedin, H. (1957/1961), A History of the *Council of Trent*. 2 vol. (London)

Jedin, H. (R1985), *Handbuch* der Kirchengeschichte VI/1: Die Kirche zwischen Revolution und Restauration (Freiburg etc),

Jenkins, P(aul) (1998) (Ed.), The Recovery of the West African Past. *African Pastors* and African History in the 19th Century (Basel)

Jenkins, P(hilipp) (2008), The *Lost History* of Christianity (New York)

Jenkins, P(hilipp) (³2011), The *Next Christendom*. The Coming of Global Christianity (Oxford)

Jeyaraj, D. (1998) (Ed.), Ordination of the *First Indian Pastor Aaron* (Madras/ Chennai)

Jeyaraj, D. (2012), Cotton Mather's „India Americana" (1721): *Transcontinental Communications* between Tranquebar in India and Boston in North America (in: Koschorke, Etappen der Globalisierung, 195–213)

John, P. (²2004), A *History of Latin America*: c. 1450 to the present (Oxford)

Johnson, T. M./ Zurlo, G. (³2020), *World Christian Encyclopedia* (Edinburgh)

Johnson, T.M. / Ross, K.R. (2009) (Eds.), *Atlas of Global Christianity*, 1910–2010 (Edinburgh)

Johnson, T.M./ Zurlo, G.A. (Eds.), *World Christian Database* (Leiden/ Boston)

Kalu, O.U. (2005) (Ed.), *African Christianity:* An African Story (Pretoria)

Kalu, O.U. (2008) (Ed.), Interpreting *Contemporary Christianity*. Global Processes and Local Identification (Grand Rapids, MI / Cambridge, UK)

Kämpchen, M. (1982), *Katholische Ashrams* in Indien (in: *Geist und Leben*, Bd. 55/4, 274–287)

Kamphausen, E. (2005). *„African Cry"*. Anmerkungen zur Entstehungsgeschichte einer kontextuellen Befreiungstheologie in Afrika (in: Koschorke / Schjørring, *African Identities*, 77–100)

Kastfelt, N. (2003) (Ed.), Scriptural Politics – the *Bible and the Koran as Political Models* in the Middle East and Africa (London)

Kaufmann, S.B. (1981), A *Christian Caste in Hindu Society* (in: *Modern Asian Studies* 15, 203–234)

Kaufmann, T. (2017), *Latin-European Christianity* in the 16th Century (in: Schjørring/ Hjelm, History I, 149–204)

Keen, B. (1996), A History of *Latin America* (Boston etc.)

Keith, C. (2012), *Catholic Vietnam*: A Church from Empire to Nation (Berkeley etc).

Kellermann, G. (2001), Atlas zur Geschichte des *Islam* (Darmstadt)

Kilcourse, C.S. (2016), *Taiping Theology*: The Localization of Christianity in China, 1843–64 (Basingstoke)

Kim, In Soo (1996), Protestants and the Formation of *Modern Korean Nationalism*, 1885 – 1910 (New York etc).

Kim, K. (2007), *Ethereal Christianity*: Reading Korean Mega-Church Websites (in: Studies in World Christianity 13/3, 208–222)

Kim, K. (2009), South *Korea as a Missionary Centre* of World Christianity: Developments in Korean Protestantism After the Liberation 1945 (in: Koschorke / Hermann, *Polyzentrische Strukturen*, 111–130)

Kim, S. (2014), *„Non-Missionary Beginnings"* of Korean Catholic Christianity in the Late Eighteenth Century (in: Koschorke/ Hermann, *Polycentric Structures*, 73–98)

Kim, S./ Kim, K. (2008). Christianity as a *World Religion* (London)

Kim, S./ Kim, K. (2015), A History of *Korean Christianity* (Cambridge)

Kitamori, K. (1972), *Theologie des Schmerzes Gottes* (Übers. von Tsuneaki Kato und P. Schneiss; Göttingen)

Kitzhoff, M.C. (1996) (Ed.), *African Independent Churches* Today. Kaleidoscope of Afro-Christianity (Lewiston etc.)

Ki-Zerbo, J. (1981), Die *Geschichte Schwarz-Afrikas* (Wuppertal)

Klaiber, J. (1988), The Catholic Church in *Peru* 1821–1985. A Social History (Washington, D.C.)

Klaiber, J. (1998), The *Church, Dictatorship, and Democracy* in Latin America (Maryknoll, NY)

Klaus, S. (1999) Uprooted Christianity: The Preaching of the Christian Doctrine in Mexico Based on *Franciscan Sermons* of the 16th Century Written *in Nahuatl* (Bonn)

Klein, H.S. (1986), *African Slavery* in Latin America and the Caribbean (NY/Oxford)
Kollman, P. (2014), Understanding the *World-Christian Turn* in the History of Christianity and Theology (in: *Theology Today* 2, 164–177)
Konetzke, R. (1991), *Süd- und Mittelamerika* I (Frankfurt a.M.)
Kong, Lee Chee (2001), *Taiping Rebellion* (in: Sunquist, *Dictionary of Asian Christianity*, 814f).
Kopf, D. (1979), The *Brahmo Samaj* and the Shaping of Modern Indian Mind (Princeton)
Koschorke, K. (1998) (Ed.), *„Christen und Gewürze".* Konfrontation und Interaktion kolonialer und indigener Christentumsvarianten (StAECG Vol. 1; Göttingen)
Koschorke, K. (1998), The Dutch Colonial Church and *Catholic Underground Church in Ceylon* in 17th and 18th Centuries (in: Koschorke, *„Christen und Gewürze"*, 106–116)
Koschorke, K. (2002) (Ed.), Transkontinentale Beziehungen in der Geschichte des Außereuropäischen Christentums / *Transcontinental Links* in the History of Non-Western Christianity (StAECG 6; Wiesbaden)
Koschorke, K. (2002), The World Missionary Conference in Edinburgh 1910 and the *Rise of National Church Movements* in Asia and Africa (in: Koschorke, *Transcontinental links*, 203–217)
Koschorke, K./ Schjørring, J.-H. (2005) (Eds.), *African Identities* and World Christianity in the Twentieth Century (StAECG 10; Wiesbaden)
Koschorke, K. (2009) (Ed.), *Falling Walls*. The Year 1989/90 as a Turning Point in the History of World Christianity / Einstürzende Mauern. Das Jahr 1989/90 als Epochenjahr in der Geschichte des Weltchristentums (StAECG 15; Wiesbaden)
Koschorke, K. (2010), *Polyzentrische Strukturen* der globalen Christentumsgeschichte (in: Friedli, R. u.a. [Eds.], Intercultural Perceptions and Prospects of World Christianity; Frankfurt a.M. etc., 105–126)
Koschorke, K. (2011), „When is India to have her own native bishops?" Der schwarzafrikanische *Bischof Samuel Ajayi Crowther* (ca. 1806–1891) in der christlichen Publizistik Asiens und Afrikas im 19. Jh. (in: Delgado, M./ Sievernich, M. [Eds.], Mission und Prophetie in Zeiten der Interkulturalität; St. Ottilien, 315 – 324)
Koschorke, K./ Mottau, S.A.W. (2011) (Ed./ Tr.), The *Dutch Reformed Church in Colonial Ceylon* (18th Century) (Wiesbaden)
Koschorke, K. (2012) (Ed.), Etappen der Globalisierung in christentumsgeschichtlicher Perspektive / *Phases of Globalization* in the History of Christianity (StAECG 19; Wiesbaden)
Koschorke, K. (2012), *Edinburgh 1910 als Relaisstation*. Das „Erwachen großer Nationen", die nationalkirchlichen Bewegungen in Asien (und Afrika) und die Weltchristenheit (in: Koschorke, *Phases of Globalisation*, 273 – 284)
Koschorke, K./ Hermann, A. (2014) (Eds.), *Polycentric Structures* in the History of World Christianity / Polyzentrische Strukturen in der Geschichte des Weltchristentums (StAECG Vol. 25; Wiesbaden)

Koschorke, K. (2014), *Polycentric Structures* in the History of World Christianity (in: Koschorke/ Hermann, *Polycentric Structures*, 15 – 28)

Koschorke, K. (2016), *Religion und Migration*. Aspekte einer polyzentrischen Geschichte des Weltchristentums (in: *Jahrbuch für Europäische Überseegeschichte* 16, 123 – 144)

Koschorke, K./ Hermann, A. / Burlacioiu, C. / Mogase, P. (2016) (Eds.), *Discourses of Indigenous Christian Elites* in Colonial Societies in Asia and Africa around 1900. A Documentary Sourcebook from Selected Journals (Wiesbaden)

Koschorke, K. (2016), *Transcontinental Links*, Enlarged Maps, and Polycentric Structures in the History of World Christianity (in: Hermann, A. / Burlacioiu, C. / Phan, P.C. [Eds.], The „Munich School of World Christianity". Special Issue of *The Journal of World Christianity* Vol. 6/1, 28–56)

Koschorke, K. (2017), *Asia* in the 19th and Early 20th Centuries (in: Schjørring/ Hjelm, History II, 267–300)

Koschorke, K./ Hermann, A./ Ludwig, F./ Burlacioiu, C. (2018) (Eds.), *„To give publicity to our thoughts"*. Journale asiatischer und afrikanischer Christen um 1900 und die Entstehung einer transregionalen indigen-christlichen Öffentlichkeit (StAECG 31; Wiesbaden)

Koschorke, K. (2018), *Christliche Internationalismen um 1910* (in: Koschorke/ Hermann, „To give publicity to our Thoughts", 261–282)

Koschorke, K. (2018), *Dialectics of the Three Selves*. The Ideal of a „self-governing, self-supporting, self-extending Native Church" – from a missionary concept to an emancipatory slogan of Asian and African Christians in 19th and early 20th centuries (in: Hofmeyr, H./ Stenhouse, J. [Eds.], Essays in honour of Prof. G. Pillay; Centurion, 127 – 142).

Koschorke, K. (2019), „Isn't Germany a Christian Country?". Der *Erste Weltkrieg* als *moralische Katastrophe* und Ende des Christianity-Civilization-Modells in den Debatten asiatischer und afrikanischer Christen (in: Van der Heyden, U./ Wendt, H. [Eds.], Mission und dekoloniale Perspektive, Stuttgart, 123–142)

Koschorke, K. (2019), „Owned and Conducted entirely by the Native Christian Community". Der *„Christian Patriot"* und die indigen-christliche Presse im kolonialen Indien um 1900 (StAECG 34; Wiesbaden)

Koschorke, K./ Ludwig, F./ Delgado, M. (^{R}2021) (Eds.), A History of Christianity in Asia, Africa and Latin America, 1450–1990. A *Documentary Sourcebook* (Grand Rapids, MI/ Cambridge, UK)

(*This sourcebook is not cited according to pages, but according to the individual documents or texts as [text]; see below p. xviii*)

Koschorke, K./ Hermann, A. (2023), „Beyond Their own dwellings": The Emergence of a Transregional and Transcontinental *Indigenous Christian Public Sphere* in the Late 19th and Early 20th Centuries (in: *Studies in World Christianity* 29/2, 177–221)

Koschorke, K. (2024), *Transatlantic Ethiopianism*: Ethiopia as a Symbol f Redemptions and Independency among Black Christians on Both Sides of the Atlantic (in: Koschorke et al., *South-South-Links*, 97-112)

Koschorke, K./ Burlacioiu, C./ Kuster, P. (2024) (Eds.), Early *South-South Links* in the History of World Christianity (16th-18th Centuries) (Wiesbaden)

Kpobi, D.N.A. (2005), *African Chaplains* in 17th Century West Africa (in: Kalu, *African Christianity*, 140–170).

Lam, J./ Thurston, N. (2023) (Eds.), *Moltmann and China*. Theological Encounters from Hongkong zo Beijing (Leiden)

Lange, C./ Pinggéra, K. (2010), Die *altorientalischen Kirchen*. Glaube und Geschichte (Darmstadt)

Lange, R. (2005), *Island Ministers*: Indigenous Leadership in 19th Century Pacific Islands Christianity (Canberra)

Langley, J.A. (1973), *Pan-Africanism* and Nationalism in West Africa 1900 – 1945 (Oxford)

Latourette, K.S. (R1980), A History of the *Expansion of Christianity*. Vol I-VII (Grand Rapids, MI)

Lee, J.T. / Chow, C.C.S. (2021), Study of *Chinese Christianities* (in: Frederiks/ Nagy, *World Christianity*, 113–134)

Lehmann, H. (2012), Das *Christentum im 20. Jh.*: Fragen, Probleme, Perspektiven (Leipzig)

Lehmann, W. (1949) (Ed.), *Sterbende Götter* und christliche Heilsbotschaft. Wechselreden indianischer Vornehmer und spanischer Glaubensapostel in Mexiko 1524 (Stuttgart)

León-Portilla, M. (2002), *Bernardino de Sahagún:* First Anthropologist (Norman)

Leon-Portilla, M. / Heuer, R. (1986) (Eds.), *Rückkehr der Götter*. Die Aufzeichnungen der Azteken über den Untergang ihres Reiches (Frankfurt a.M.)

Lessing, H. et al. (2011) (Eds.), *Deutsche evangelische Kirche* im kolonialen südlichen Afrika (Wiesbaden)

Lessing, H. et al. (2012) (Eds.), The *German Protestant Church* in colonial Southern Africa (Pietermaritsburgh)

Lessing, H. et al. (2015) (Eds.), *Contested Relations*. Protestantism between Southern Africa and Germany from the 1930s to the Apartheid Era (Wiesbaden)

Li, Tiangang (2020), Towards a Glocal Sinology: The "Chinese *Rites Controversy*" Revisited (in: *News. Institute of Sino-Christian Studies*, 1–2)

Liebau, H. et al. (2010) (Eds.), The *World in World Wars*. Perceptions and Perspectives from Africa and Asia (Leiden)

Lienemann-Perrin, C. (1992), Die *politische Verantwortung* der Kirchen in Südkorea und Südafrika. Studien zur ökumenischen politischen Ethik (München).

Lienhard, M. (2003) (Ed.), *Titu Kusi Yupanki*: Der Kampf gegen die Spanier (Düsseldorf)

Lindenfels, D. (2021), World Christianity and *Indigenous Experience*. A Global History, 1500 – 2000 (Cambridge)

Lippy, C.H. / Choquette, R. / Poole, St. (1992), Christianity comes to the *Americas*, 1492–1776 (New York)

Lloyd, T.O. (1996), *The British Empire* 1558–1995 (Oxford)

Lockhart, J. (1992), We People Here: *Nahuatl Accounts* of the Conquest of Mexico (Berkeley)

Lombard, C. (2009), The *Fall of the Berlin Wall* and the End of Apartheid in South Africa (in: Koschorke, *Falling Walls*, 89–94)

Loveland, A.C. / Wheeler, O.B. (2003), *From Meetinghouse to Megachurch:* A Material and Cultural History (Columbia, MO).

Ludwig (2002), *African Independent Churches* in West Africa around 1900 (in: Koschorke, *Transcontinental Links*, 259–273)

Ludwig, F. (1992), *Kirche im kolonialen Kontext*. Anglikanische Missionare und afrikanische Propheten im südöstlichen Nigeria 1879–1918 (Frankfurt a.M. etc.)

Ludwig, F. (1993), *Elijah II*: Radicalisation and Consolidation of the Garrick Braide Movement 1915 – 1918 (in: *Journal of Religion in Africa* 23, 296–317)

Ludwig, F. (1999), Church and State in *Tanzania*. Aspects of a Changing Relationship, 1961–1994 (Leiden/ Boston)

Ludwig, F. (2000), Zwischen Kolonialismuskritik und Kirchenkampf. Interaktionen afrikanischer, indischer und europäischer Christen während der Weltmissionskonferenz *Tambaram* (StAECG 5; Göttingen).

Ludwig, F. (2020) (Ed.), The *First World War as a Turning Point* (Berlin)

Ludwig, F. et al. (2019) (Eds.), *Reformation in the Context of World Christianity*. Theological, political and social interactions between Africa, Asia, the Americas and Europe (Wiesbaden)

Lutz, J.G. (2010) (Ed.), Pioneer *Chinese Christian Women*: Gender, Christianity, and Social Mobility. (Bethlehem)

Lynch, J. (2012), New Worlds. A Religious History of *Latin America* (New Haven / London)

Malek, R. (2009), Das Jahr *1989 in China* (in: Koschorke, *Falling Walls*, 215–242).

Mannion, G. (2018), *Vatican II:* How the First Global Council Transformed Catholicism (in: Schjørring/ Hjelm/ Ward, History III, 182–219)

Marcus, H.G. (1995), The Life and Times of *Menelik II*, Ethiopia 1844–1913 (Addis Ababa etc)

Martin, D. (1990), *Tongues of Fire*: The explosion of Protestantism in Latin America (Oxford, UK)

Martin, J.L. (2020) (Ed.), *Theology Without Walls*. The Transreligious Imperative (London / New York)

Martin, L./ Pettus, J.A.G. (1973) (Eds.), *Scholars and Schools* in Colonial Peru (Texas)

Martin, S.D. (1989), *Black Baptists and African Missions*. The Origin of a Movement 1880–1915 (Macon)

Martin, S.D. (2002), African American Christians and the *African Mission Movement* during the 19th Century (in: Koschorke, *Transcontinental Links*, 56–72)

Marty, M.E./ Appleby, R.S. (1995), *Fundamentalisms* Comprehended (Chicago)

Marx, C. (2004), *Geschichte Afrikas*. Von 1800 bis zur Gegenwart (Paderborn etc.)

Marx, C. (2008), Pelze, Gold und Weihwasser. *Handel und Mission* in Afrika und Amerika (Darmstadt)

Marx, C. (2024), The Anxieties of White Supremacy. *Hendrik Verwoerd* and the Apartheid Mindset (Oldenburg)

Mauntel, C. (2021), *Geography and Religious Knowledge* in the Medieval World (Berlin/ Boston)

Maxwell, D. (2008), *Postcolonial Christianity in Africa* (in: McLeod, World Christianities, 410–421)

Mcgrath, A. E. (2002), The *Future of Christianity* (Oxford)

McGrath, A./ Russell, L. (2022), The Routledge Companion to *Global Indigenous History* (London/ New York)

Mcleod, H. (2006) (Ed.), *World Christianities*, c. 1914 – c. 2000 (Cambridge)

Meier, J. (1991), Die *Anfänge* der Kirche auf den Karibischen Inseln (Immensee)

Meier, J. (1993), „… dem zerfallenden und dem verderbenden *Katholizismus Brasiliens* Hülfe bringen" (in: *Zeitschrift für Missionswissenschaft und Religionswissenschaft* 77, 3–24)

Meier, J. (1998), Ein Grenzgänger zwischen altandiner Kultur und spanisch-amerikanischem Christentum: Felipe Guamán *Poma de Ayala* in Peru (ca. 1534–1619) (in: Lüddeckens, D. [Hg.], Begegnung von Religionen und Kulturen; Dettelbach, 145–155).

Meier, J. (1998), Religiöse Entwicklungen in den *Chiquitos-Reduktionen* (Bolivien) seit der Ausweisung der Jesuiten (in: Koschorke, „Christen und Gewürze", 117–131)

Meier, J. (2018), Bis an die *Ränder* der Erde. Wege des Katholizismus im Zeitalter der Reformation und des Barock (Münster)

Meier, J. (2018), Die Stimme erheben. *Studien* zur Kirchengeschichte Lateinamerikas und der Karibik (StAECG 30; Wiesbaden)

Meier, J./ Langenhorst, A. (1992), *Bartolomé de las Casas*. Der Mann – das Werk – die Wirkung (Frankfurt a.M.)

Meier, J./ Strassner, V. (2009) (Eds.), *Kirche und Katholizismus* seit 1945. Bd. 6 (Paderborn)

Meltzer, D.J. (2009), *First Peoples* in a New World: Colonizing Ice Age America (Berkeley).

Menegon, E. (2009), *Ancestors, Virgins and Friars*. Christianity as a Local Religion in Late Imperial China (Cambridge/ London)

Mérida, J.L.M. (1994), Hispanoamerika. *Kirche und Mission* (in: Pietschmann, *Handbuch 1*, 376–399)

Merkel, F.M. (1920), G.W. von *Leibniz und die China-Mission*. Eine Untersuchung über die Anfänge der protestantischen Missionsbewegung (Leipzig).

Merrim, S. (1999) (Ed.), Feminist perspectives on *Sor Juana Inés de la Cruz* (Detroit)

Mettele, G. (2009), Weltbürgertum oder Gottesreich. Die Herrnhuter *Brüdergemeine als weltweite Gemeinschaft* (Göttingen)

Metzler, J. (1971) (Ed.), Sacrae Congregationis de *Propaganda Fide* Memoria Rerum I/1 (1622–1700) (Rom etc)

Metzler, J. (1980), *Synoden in China, Japan und Korea* 1570–1931 (Paderborn etc.)

Meyer, B. (2004). Christianity in Africa: From African Independent to *Pentecostal-Charismatic Churches* (in: *Annual Review of Anthropology* 33, 447–474)

Meyer, B. (2005), Impossible Representations: *Pentecostalism*, Vision, and Video Technology in Ghana (in: Meyer/ Moors, *Public Sphere*, 290–312)

Meyer, B./ Moors, A. (2005) (Eds.), Religion, Media, and the *Public Sphere* (Indiana University Press)

Meyer, D. (2000), Zinzendorf und die *Herrnhuter Brüdergemeine*, 1700 – 2000 (Göttingen)

Meyer, J. (2013), *La Cristiada*. The Mexican People's War for Religious Liberty (New York)

Meyer-Herwartz, C. (1979), Die *Rezeption des Antirassismus-Programms* in der EKD (Stuttgart)

Micklewait, J. / Woolridge, A. (2009), *God is Back*. How the Global Revival of Faith is Changing the World (New York)

Milhou, A. (1994), Die Neue Welt als geistiges und moralisches Problem (1492–1609) (in: Pietschmann, *Handbuch I*, 274–296)

Miller, D.E./ Yamori, T. (2007), *Global Pentecostalism*. The New Face of Christian Social Engagement (Berkeley etc)

Mills, K./ Taylor, W.B. (1998) (Eds.), Colonial Spanish America. A *Documentary History* (Wilmington)

Minamiki, G. (1985), The *Chinese Rites Controversy* from its Beginnings to Modern Times (Chicago)

Moffett, S.H. (1991/ 2005), A History of *Christianity in Asia*. Vol. I: Beginnings to 1500; Vol. II: 1500 – 1900 (New York)

Molina, J. M. (2013), To Overcome Oneself: The Jesuit Ethic and *Spirit of Global Expansion*, 1520–1767 (Berkeley, CA)

Mormando, F. (2006) (Ed.), *Francis Xavier* and the Jesuit Missions in the Far East (Chestnut Hill, MA)

Morris, J.H. (2018), Rethinking the History of Conversion to *Christianity in Japan*, 1549 – 1644 (PhD St. Andrews)

Müller-Krüger, T. (1968), Der *Protestantismus* in *Indonesien* (Berlin)

Mullins, M. R. (1998), *Christianity Made in Japan*. A Study of Indigenous Movements (Honolulu):

Mullins, M.R. (2003) (Ed.), Handbook of *Christianity in Japan* (Leiden).

Mundadan, A.M. (1967), The *Arrival of the Portuguese* in India and the Thomas Christians under Mar Jacob 1498–1552 (Bangalore)

Mundadan, A.M. (1984), History of *Christianity in India I*: From the *Beginning* up to the Middle of the Sixteenth Century (up to 1542) (Bangalore)

Mungello, D.E. (1994), The *Chinese Rites Controversy.* Its History and Meaning (Nettetal)

Muskens, M.P.M. (1979), *Partner in Nation Building*. The Catholic Church in Indonesia (Aachen)

Nebel, R. (1983), *Altmexikanische Religion* und christliche Heilsbotschaft. Mexiko zwischen Quetzalcóatl und Christus (Immensee)

Nebel, R. (1992), *Missionskatechismen*. Evangelisation im Kontext indianischer Kulturen (in: Sievernich, *Conquista und Evangelisation*, 242–270)

Nebel, R. (1992), Santa María Tonantzin *Virgen de Guadelupe*. Religiöse Kontinuität und Transformation in Mexiko (Immensee)

Nebel, R. (2006), Mestizische und *indigen-christliche Autoren im kolonialen Mexiko* (in: *Periplus* 16, 142–161)

Negel, J./ Pinggéra, K. (2016) (Eds.), *Urkatastrophe*. Die Erfahrung des Krieges 1914–1918 im Spiegel zeitgenössischer Theologie (Freiburg).

Neill, S. (1984/1985), A History of *Christianity in India*. Vol. I: The Beginnings to AD 1707; Vol. II: 1707 – 1858) (Cambridge etc.)

Neill, S. (^{2}1990), A History of *Christian Missions* (London)

Ngeiyamu, J./Triebel, J. (1994) (Eds.), Gemeinsam auf eigenen Wegen. Evang.-luth Kirche in *Tansania* nach 100 Jahren (Erlangen)

Noll, M. (2009), The *New Shape of World Christianity*. How American Experience Reflects Global Faith (Downers Grove)

Novak, M. (1987), Liberation Theology and the *Liberal Society* (Lanham, MD / London)

Ntageli, S. /Hodgetts, E. (2011), *More than one Wife*: Polygamy and Grace (Kampala)

O'Mahony, A./ Loosley, E. (2010) (Eds.), *Eastern Christianity* in the Modern Middle East (London)

Oduyoye, M.A./ Musimbi, R.A.K. (1992), *The Will to Arise*. Women, Tradition, and the Church in Africa (Maryknoll, NY).

Oltmer, J. (2012), *Globale Migration*. Geschichte und Gegenwart (München)

Olupona, J.K. (2014), *African Religions*: A Very Short Introduction (Very Short Introductions), Oxford 2014

O'Malley, J.W. (2000), *Trent and all that*. Renaming Catholicism in the Early Modern Era (Cambridge/ London)

O'Malley, J.W. (2013), *Trent:* What Happened at the Council (Cambridge, MA)

O'Malley, J.W. (2017), *The Jesuits*: A History from Ignatius to the Present (Lanham)

Osterhammel, J. (1997), *Colonialism*: A Theoretical Overview (Princeton/ Kingston)

Osterhammel, J. (2009), Die *Verwandlung der Welt*. Eine Geschichte des 19. Jh. (München)

Paiva, J.P. (2019), The *Impact of Luther* and the Reformation in the Portuguese Seaborne Empire: Asia and Brazil, 1520–1580 (in: Journal of Ecclesiastical History Vol. 70/2, 283–303)

Pakenham, T. (1998), The *Scamble for Africa* (London)

Pappe, I. (³2014), The *Modern Middle East*: A Social and Cultural History (London/ New York)

Paquette, R. et al. (2010) (Ed.), The Oxford *handbook of slavery* in the Americas (Oxford)

Parratt, J. (1987), A Reader in *African Christian Theology* (London)

Parratt, J. (2004) (Ed.), An introduction to *Third World theologies* (Cambridge)

Parry, J.H. (1990), *The Spanish Seaborne Empire* (Berkeley etc.)

Paulau, S. (2021), Das andere Christentum. Zur transkonfessionellen *Verflechtungsgeschichte* von äthiopischer Orthodoxie und europäischem Protestantismus (Göttingen)

Paulau, S./ Tamcke, M. (2022) (Eds.), *Ethiopian Orthodox Christianity* in a Global Context. Entanglements and Disconnections (Leiden/ Boston)

Pemberton, C. (2002), Circle Thinking: *African Women Theologians* (Leiden)

Perera, S.G. (1942), Life of the Venerable Father *Joseph Vaz* (Galle)

Petrella, I. (2006), The *future of liberation theology*: an argument and manifesto (London)

Phan, P.C. (2002), The Reception of *Vatican II in Asia* (1972–1998). Historical and theological Analysis (in: Koschorke, *Transcontinental Links*, 243–258)

Phan, P.C. (2011) (Ed.), *Christianities in Asia* (Malden, MA / Exford, UK)

Phan, P.C. (2018), Christianities in *Asia in the 20th Century* (in: Schjørring/ Hjelm/ Ward, History III, 396–421)

Phan, P.C. (2020) (Ed.), Christian Theology in the *Age of Migration* (Lanham).

Phelan, J.L. (1956), The Millennial Kingdom of the Franciscans in the New World. A Study of the Writings of *Geronimo de Mendietta* (1525–1604) (Berkeley).

Philips, J.M. (1981), From the *Rising of the Sun*. Christians and Society in Contemporary Japan (Maryknoll)

Pietschmann, H. (1994) (Ed.), *Handbuch* zur Geschichte Lateinamerikas. Bd. 1: Mittel-, Südamerika und die Karibik bis 1760 (Stuttgart)

Pillay, G.P. /Hofmeyr, J.W. (1991) (Eds.), *Perspectives* on Church History. An Introduction for South African Readers (Pretoria)

Poole, C.M.S. (1995), Our *Lady of Guadalupe*, The Origins and Sources of a Mexican National Symbol, 1531 – 1797 (Tucson).

Poon, M. Nai-Chiu (2010), *Christian Movements* in Southeast Asia (Singapore)

Porter, A.N (2003), The *Imperial Horizons* of British Protestant Missions, 1880–1914 (Grand Rapids, MI)

Porter, A.N. (2016), *European Imperialism*, 1860–1914 (London)
Pratt, D. (2017), Christian *Engagement with Islam*. Ecumenical journeys since 1910 (Leiden etc:).
Prien, H.-J. (1978), Die *Geschichte* des Christentums in Lateinamerika (Göttingen)
Prien, H.-J. (1981) (Ed.), Lateinamerika. *Gesellschaft – Kirche – Theologie*. Bd. I + II (Göttingen)
Prien, H.-J. (2002), Das *Trienter Konzil* (1545–1563) und der Rückgang lokalkirchlicher Experimente in Spanisch-Amerika (in: Koschorke, *Transcontinental Links*, 163–188)
Prien, H.-J. (2007), Das Christentum in *Lateinamerika* (KGE IV/6; Leipzig)
Prien, H.-J. (2013), Christianity in *Latin America*. Revised and Expanded Edition (Leiden/Boston)
Provost, F. (1991), *Columbus*: an annotated guide to the scholarship on his life and writings (Detroit)
Raheb, M. (2018), Christianity in the *Middle East*, 1917–2017 (in: Schjørring/ Hjelm/ Ward, History III, 375–395)
Raheb, M./ Lamport, M.A. (2021) (Eds.), The Rowman & Littlefield Handbook of *Christianity in the Middle East* (Lanham)
Raison-Jourde, F. (1995), The *Madagascan Churches* in the Political Arena and their contribution to the change of Regime 1990–1993 (in: Gifford, *Democratisation of Africa*, 292–301)
Raupp, W. (1990) (Ed.), *Mission in Quellentexten* (Erlangen)
Reinhard, W. (1983–1990), Geschichte der europäischen *Expansion* I-IV (Stuttgart etc)
Reinhard, W. (1996), Kleine Geschichte des *Kolonialismus* (Stuttgart)
RGG[4]: Religion in Geschichte und Gegenwart (Vierte Auflage, hg. von H.D. Betz u.a., Bd. I-VIII, Tübingen 1999– 2005. Zitiert wird nach Band, Seite, Artikel, Autor)
Riesebrodt, M. (2000), Fundamentalism and the *resurgence of religion* (in: Numen 47, 266–287)
Rivera-Pagán, L.N. (2008), *Pentecostal Transformation* in Latin America (in: Bednarowski, *Twentieth-Century Global Christianity*, 190–210)
Robert, D. (2000), *Shifting Southward*: Global Christianity since 1945 (in: *International Bulletin of Missionary Research* 24/2, 50–58)
Robert, D.L. (2005), *American Women in Mission*. A Social History of their Thought and Practice (Macon)
Robert, D.L. (2011), *Christian Mission*: How Christianity Became a World Religion (New York)
Roberts, J.D. (2005), Bonhoeffer and King. Speaking Truth to Power (Louisville, KY)
Ross, A.C. (2002), *David Livingstone*: Mission and Empire (London / New York)
Ross, C. (1994), A *Vision Betrayed*. The Jesuits in Japan and China (Edinburgh)
Ross, K. / Bidegain, A.M./ Johnson, T.M. (2022) (Eds.), Christianity in *Latin America and the Caribbean* (Edinburgh)

Ross, K./ Alvarez, F./ Johnson, T.M. (2019) (Eds.), Christianity in *East and South East Asia* (Edinburgh)

Ross, K./ Asamoah-Gyadu, J.K./ Johnson, T.M. (2017) (Eds.), Christianity in *Sub-Saharan Africa* (Edinburgh)

Ross, K./ Bidegain, A.M./ Johnson, T.M. (2022) (Eds.), Christianity in *Latin America and the Caribbean* (Edinburgh)

Ross, K./ Jeyaraj, D./ Johnson, T.M. (2019) (Eds.), Christianity in *South and Central Asia* (Edinburgh)

Ross, K.R./ Tahaafe-Williams, K./ Johnson, T. (2023) (Eds.), *Christianity in Oceania* (Peabody, MA)

Rothermund, D. (2006) (Ed.), The Routledge Companion to D*ecolonization* (London)

Rotzetter, A. u.a. (1993) (Eds.), *Von der Conquista* zur Theologie der Befreiung (Zürich)

Rowe, E.K. (2020), *Black Saints* in Early Modern Global Catholicism (Cambridge/ New York)

Rowland, C. (²2007) (Ed.), The Cambridge *Companion to Liberation Theology* (Cambridge)

Russel, H.O. (2000), The Missionary Outreach of the West Indian Church: *Jamaican Baptist Missions* to West Africa in the 19th Century (New York)

Russel-Wood, A.J.R (1992), A *World on the Move*: the Portuguese in Africa, Asia and America 1415 – 1808 (Manchester)

Sahlberg, C.-E. (1987). From Krapf to Rugambwa. A Church History of *Tanzania* (Nairobi)

Salvadore, M. (2017), The African Prester John and the Birth of *Ethiopian-European Relations*, 1402–1555 (London/ New York)

Samir, S.K. (2007), *Arabisch-christliche Kulturgeschichte* im Übergang zur Moderne (in: Kreikenbom, D. et al. [Eds.], Arabische Christen – Christen in Arabien; Frankfurt a.M. etc, 133–148)

Sanderlin, G. (1993) (Ed./Tr.), *Bartolome de Las Casas*: Witness: Writing of Bartolome de Las Casas (Maryknoll, NY)

Sanneh (1999), *Abolitionists Abroad*. American Blacks and the Making of Modern West Africa (Cambridge, MA/ London)

Sanneh, L. (1983), *West African Christianity*. The Religious Impact (New York)

Sanneh, L. (1989), *Translating the Message*. The Missionary Impact on Culture (New York)

Sanneh, L. (1999), The CMS and African Transformation: Samuel Ajayi *Crowther and the Opening of Nigeria* (in: Ward/ Stanley, *Church Mission Society*, 173–197)

Sanneh, L. (2003), Whose Religion is Christianity? The *Gospel Beyond the West* (Grand Rapids, MI)

Sanneh, L.O./ Carpenter, J.A. (2005) (Eds.), The *Changing Face* of Christianity in Africa, the West, and the World (Oxford)

Sanneh, L.O./ McClymond, O. (2016) (Eds.), The Wiley-Blackwell Companion to *World Christianity* (Chichester)

Saranyana, J.-I. (1986), *Catecismos hispanoamericanos* des siglo XVI (in: *Scripta Theologica* 18:251–264)

Scharf da Silva, I. (2017), *Umbanda.* Eine Religion zwischen Candomblé und Kardezismus. (Berlin)

Schilling, H. (2017), *1517:* Weltgeschichte eines Jahres (München)

Schilling, H. (2020), *Karl V.* Der Kaiser, dem die Welt zerbrach (München).

Schilling, H./ Seidel Menchi, S. (2017) (Eds.), The Protestant *Reformation in a Context of Global History* (Bologna/ Berlin)

Schjørring, J.H. (2018), Christianity in the *First World War* (in: Schjørring/ Hjelm/ Ward, History III, 19–40)

Schjørring, J.H./ Hjelm, N. A. (2017/18) (Eds.), History of *Global Christianity.* Vol. I: Ca. 1500–1789; Vol. II: 19th Century (Leiden/ Boston)

Schjørring, J. H./ Hjelm, N.A./ Ward, K. (2018) (Eds.), *History* of Global Christianity. Vol. III. 20th Century (Leiden/ Boston)

Schmitt, E. (1986–1988) (Ed.), *Dokumente* zur Geschichte der europäischen Expansion. Bd I-IV (München)

Schmitt, E./ Beck, T. (2003) (Eds.), *Dokumente* zur Geschichte der europäischen Expansion. Bd. V (Wiesbaden)

Schreiter, R.J. (^{5} 2002), *The new Catholicity.* Theology between the Global and the Local (Maryknoll, NY)

Schumacher, J.S. (1981), *Revolutionary Clergy.* The Filipino Clergy and the Nationalist Movement 1850 – 1903 (Quezon City).

Schurhammer, G. (1963), Die *Bekehrung der Paraver* (1535–1537) (in: ders., Gesammelte Schriften Bd. 2, Rom, 215–254).

Schurhammer, G. (1973), *Francis Xavier: his life, his times* (Rome)

Seiichi, Y. (1991), Die *dritte Generation*: 1945 – 1970 (in: Dohi, *Japan*, 128–163).

Sensbach, J. (2005), *Rebecca's Revival*: Creating Black Christianity in the Atlantic World (Cambridge, MA).

Shaull, R./ Cesar, W. (2000), Pentecostalism and the *Future* of the Christian Churches: Promise, Limitation, Challenges (Grand Rapids, MI)

Sievernich, M. (1992) (Ed.), *Conquista und Evangelisation* (Mainz)

Silva, S. (2009), *Theologiegeschichte Lateinamerikas* seit 1945 (in: Meier/ Strassner, *Kirche und Katholizismus*, 29–58)

Silva, S. (2009), *Transformationen der* lateinamerikanischen *Befreiungstheologie* in den 1990er Jahren (in: Koschorke, *Falling Walls*, 335–351)

Simon, B. (2010), *From Migrants to Missionaries*: Christians of African Origin in Germany (Frankfurt a.M.)

Sinner, R. (2017), Theologie in Lateinamerika – *neuere Entwicklungen* (in: *Theologische Literaturzeitung* 142/6, 589–602)

Skreslet, S.H. (2023), Constructing Mission History. Missionary Initiative and *Indigenous Agency* in the Making of World Christianity (Minneapolis)

Smallwood, A.D. (1998), The Atlas of *African-American History* and Politics: From the Slave Trade to Modern Times (New York).

Smith, B.H. (1998), Religious Politics in Latin America. *Pentecostal vs. Catholic* (Notre Dame, IN)

Soen, V. u.a. (Eds.) (2018) The *Council of Trent*. Reform and Controversy in Europe and Beyond (1545–1700) (Göttingen)

Sonntag, M. (2018), *Christian Patriotism and Japanese Expansionism*. „God's Kingdom" in Debates of Christian Intellectuals in Modern Japan (in: Koschorke et al., „*To Give Publicity*", 285–298)

Sonntag, M. (2021), The Reception and Reinterpretation of Christian Socialism as an Antidote to Communism in *Early Post-War Japan* (1945–1972) (in: *Kirisutokyōgaku* 63, 1–40)

Specker, J. (1974), *Missionarische Motive* im Entdeckungszeitalter (in: Rzepkowski, H. [Hg.], Mission – Präsent – Verkündigung – Bekehrung?; Steyl, 80–91)

Spence, J.S. (1996), *God's Chinese Son*. The Taiping Heavenly Kingdom of Hong Xiuquan (New York)

Spliesgart, R. (2006), „*Verbrasilianerung*" und Akkulturation. Deutsche Protestanten im brasilianischen Kaiserreich am Beispiel der Gemeinden in Rio de Janeiro und Minas Gerais (1822–1889) (StAECG 12; Wiesbaden)

Spliesgart, R. (2021), Yoruba – Santería – Jazz Batá. Lateinamerikanische Befreiungstheologie und sozialistischer Realismus in *Kuba* (in: *Zeitschrift für Mission* 1/2021, 35–67)

Standaert, N. (2001) (Ed.), Handbook of *Christianity in China*. Vol. I: 635–1800 (Leiden)

Stanley, B. (1990), The *Bible and the Flag*: Protestant Mission and British Imperialism in the 19th and 20th Centuries (Leicester)

Stanley, B. (2005), *Christian missions, antislavery* and the claim of humanity (in: Gilley/Stanley, World Christianities, c.1815 - c. 2000, 443–457)

Stanley, B. (2009), The World Missionary Conference, *Edinburgh 1910* (Grand Rapids, MI / Cambridge, UK)

Stanley, B. (2018), Christianity in the *Twentieth Century*. A World History (Princeton / Oxford).

Steiner, M. (1992), Guaman *Poma de Ayala* und die Eroberer Perus. Indianischer Chronist zwischen Anpassung und Widerstand (Saarbrücken)

Steiner, N. (2012), Globales Bewusstsein und Heiligenverehrung – Spuren eines weltweiten Kults der *japanischen Märtyrer von 1597* (in: Koschorke, *Etappen der Globalisierung*, 135–156)

Stoll, D. (1990), Is Latin America *Turning Protestant*? The Politics of Evangelical Growth (Berkeley etc.)

Strassner, V. (2018), Christianity in *Latin America* and the Caribbean in the 20th Century (in: Schjørring/ Hjelm/ Ward, History III, 298–342)

Suarsana, Y. (2010), *Christentum 2.0*? Pfingstbewegung und Globalisierung (Würzburg)

Sundkler, B./ Steed, C. (2000), A History of the *Church in Africa* (Cambridge)

Sunquist, S.W. (2015), The *Unexpected Christian Century*. The Reversal and Transformation of Global Christianity, 1900 – 2000 (Grand Rapids, MN)

Sunquist, S.W. et al. (2001) (Eds.), A *Dictionary of Asian Christianity* (Grand Rapids, MI/ Cambridge, UK).

Sylvest, E.E. (1975), *Motifs* of Franciscan Mission Theory in 16th Century New Spain (Washington)

Tavárez, D. (2017) (Ed.), Words and Worlds Turned Around. *Indigenous Christianities in Colonial Latin America* (Boulder)

Tekkedath, J. (1982), History of *Christianity in India* II: From the Middle of the 16th to the End of the 17th Century (1542 – 1700) (Bangalore)

Terraciano, K. (2014), Religion and the Church in *Early Latin America* (in: Hsia, *Companion*, 335–352)

Thaliat, J. (1958), The *Synod of Diamper* (Rome)

Thelle, N.R. (1987), *Buddhism and Christianity in Japan*. From Conflict to Dialogue, 1854 – 1899 (Honolulu).

Thiemer-Sachse, U./ Kunzmann (2004) (Hg./Tr.), Felipe *Guamán Poma de Ayala*: Die neue Chronik und gute Regierung / El Primer Nueva Corónica Y Buen Gobierno: Faks.-Ausg. u. Übersetzung auf CD-ROM (Berlin)

Thomas, G. (1979), *Christian Indians and Indian Nationalism* 1885–1950 (Frankfurt etc.)

Thomas, G. (1994), *Das portugiesische Amerika* (1549 – 1695) (in: Pietschmann, *Handbuch* I, 597–662)

Thomas, M.M. (1976), The Acknowledged *Christ of the Indian Renaissance* (Madras)

Thomas, M.M. (1990), *My Ecumenical Journey* (Trivandrum)

Thomas, T.V. (2014), South Asian Diaspora *Christianity in the Persian Gulf* (in: Im/ Yong, *Global Diasporas*, 117–129)

Thornton, J.K. (1984), The Development of an *African Catholic Church* in the Kingdom of Kongo, 1491 – 1750 (in: *Journal of African History* 25, 147 – 167)

Thornton, J.K. ([2]1998), Africa and Africans in the Making of the *Atlantic World*, 1400 – 1800 (Cambridge).

Thornton, J.K. (1998), The *Kongolese Saint Anthony*. Dona Beatriz Kimpa Vita and the Antonian Movement 1684–1706 (Cambridge)

Thornton, J.K. (2023), The *Correspondence of Afonso I* Mvemba a Nzinga (Indianapolis)

Thornton, J.K. (2024), Early Kongo Christianity in its *Transatlantic connections* (in: Koschorke et al., South-South Links)

Thrupp, S.L. (1962) (Ed.), *Millenial Dreams* in Action (The Hague)
Tobler, H.W./ Bernecker, W.L. (1996), *Handbuch* der Geschichte Lateinamerikas. Bd. III: Lateinamerika im 20. Jh. (Stuttgart)
TRE: Theologische Realenzyklopedie (Studienausgabe, ed. by G. Müller et al., Vol. 1–36, Berlin etc. 1993–2004 (is cited according to volume, page, article, author)
Tschuy, T. (1978), Hundert Jahre *kubanischer Protestantismus* (1961–1761) (Frankfurt a.M.)
Tyrell, H. (2004), Weltgesellschaft, *Weltmission* und religiöse Gesellschaften (in: Bogner et al. [Eds.], Weltmission und religiöse Organisationen. Protestantische Missionsgesellschaften im 19. und 20. Jh.; Würzburg, 13–136)
Van Laak, D. (2005), *Über alles in der Welt.* Deutscher Imperialismus im 19. und 20. Jh. (München)
Van Wyk, I. (2014), The Universal Church of the Kingdom of God in South Africa: A *Church of Strangers* (Cambridge, UK)
Villa-Vicensio, C./ Grassow, P. (2009) (Eds.), Christianity and the *Colonisation of South Africa*, 1487–1883. A Documentary History Vol. I (Pretoria)
Villegas, J. (1971), Die *Durchführung* der Beschlüsse des Konzils von Trient in der Kirchenprovinz Peru 1564 – 1600 (Köln)
Vischer, L. (1983) (Ed.), Towards a *History of the Church in the Third World*. The Issue of Periodisation (Bern)
Von Albertini (²1985), Europäische *Kolonialherrschaft* 1880–1940 (Stuttgart)
Von Sinner, R. (2012), The Churches and *Democracy in Brazil* (Eugene, OR)
Wagner, H.R./ Parish, H.R. (1967), The Life and Writings of *Bartolomé de Las Casas* (Albuquerque, NM)
Wagner, R. G. (1982), Reenacting the Heavenly Vision. The Role of Religion in the *Taiping Rebellion* (Berkeley).
Währisch-Oblau, C. (2009). The *Missionary Self-Perception* of Pentecostal / Charismatic Church Leaders from the Global South in Europe (Leiden)
Währisch-Oblau, C. (2021), *WhatsApp-Predigten* und Nothilfepakete (in: EMW [Hg.], Online durch die Pandemie. Jahrbuch Mission 2021, 63–69)
Walls, A. (1993), David *Livingstone* (in: Greschat, M. [Hg.], Gestalten der Kirchengeschichte. Bd. 9,2, Stuttgart etc., 140 – 152)
Walls, A. (1996), The *Missionary Movement* in Christian History. Studies in the Transmission of Faith (Maryknoll, NY)
Walls, A. (2001), The *Cross-Cultural Process* in Christian History (Maryknoll, NY)
Walls, A. (2002), *Sierra Leone*, Afroamerican Remigration and the Beginnings of Protestantism in West Africa (18th -19th Centuries) (in: Koschorke, *Transcontinental Links*, 45–56)
Walshe, P. (1997), Christianity and the *Anti-Apartheid Struggle*: The Prophetic Voice within Divided Churches (in: Elphick/ Davenport, *Christianity in South Africa*, 383–399).

Walvin, J. (1998), An African's Life. The Life and Times of *Olaudah Equiano* 1745–1797 (London/ New York)

Ward, H.N. (2009), *Women Religious Leaders* in Japan's Christian Century, 1549–1650 (Ashgate)

Ward, K. (1998), African Culture, Christianity and Conflict in the Creation of *Ugandan Identities* (in: Koschorke, „Christen und Gewürze", 158–170)

Ward, K. (2006), A History of *Global Anglicanism* (Cambridge)

Ward, K. (2017), *Christianity in Africa*, 1500–1800 (in: Schjørring/ Hjelm, History I, 129–148)

Ward, K. (2017), Christianity in Africa: The *Late 18th Century* to 1914 (in: Schjørring/ Hjelm, History II, 121–144

Ward, K. (2017), The Protestant *Missionary Movement* in the 19th Century (in: Schjørring/ Hjelm, History II, 223–246

Ward, K. (2018), African Christianity in the *20th Century* (in: Schjørring/ Hjelm/ Ward, History III, 356–374)

Ward, K. (2018), *Conclusions* (in: Schjørring/ Hjelm/ Ward, History III, 501–516)

Ward, K. /Wild-Wood, E. (2012), The *East African Revival* (Kampala/ Farnham)

Ward, K./ Stanley, B. (2000) (Eds.), The *Church Mission Society* and World Christianity, 1799–1999 (Grand Rapids, MI/ Cambridge, UK)

Warneck, G. (1880), Warum ist das 19. Jahrhundert ein *Missionsjahrhundert*? (Halle)

Warneck, G. (⁴1898/ ¹⁰1913), *Abriss* einer Geschichte der protestantischen Missionen von der Reformation bis auf die Gegenwart (Berlin)

Weber, H.-R. (1966), *Asia and the Ecumenical Movement* 1895 – 1961 (London)

Wendt (1997), *Fiesta Filipina*. Koloniale Kultur zwischen Imperialismus und neuer Identität (Freiburg i.B.)

Wendt, R. (2007), Vom Kolonialismus zur *Globalisierung*. Europa und die Welt seit 1500 (Paderborn etc.)

Wenzel-Teuber, K. (2016), *Statistisches Update* zu Religionen und Kirchen in der Volksrepublik China (in: *China heute* XXXV, 2016/1, 24–37)

Wessels, A. (1995), *Arab and Christian?* Christians in the Middle East (Kampen)

Whelan, C. (1996), The Beginning of Heaven and Earth. The Sacred Book of *Japan's Hidden Christians* (Honolulu)

Wickeri, P. (1988), Seeking the Common Ground: Protestant Christianity, the *Three-Self Movement* and China's United Front (Maryknoll)

Wicki, J. (1976), Die unmittelbaren *Auswirkungen des Konzils* von Trient auf Indien (ca. 1565–1585) (in: id., Missionskirche im Orient; Immensee, 213–229)

Wijsen, F./ Schreiter, R. (2007), *Global Christianity*. Contested Claims (Amsterdam)

Wild-Wood, E. (2001), The Interpretations, Problems and Possibilities of *Missionary Sources* in the History of Christianity in Africa (in: Frederiks/ Nagy, World Christianity, 92–103).

Wilfried, F. (2014) (Ed.), The Oxford Handbook of *Christianity in Asia* (Oxford)

Williams, R.A. (1990), The American Indian in Western Legal Thought: The *Discourses of Conquest* (Oxford)

Williams, W.L. (1982), *Black Americans* and the Evangelization of Africa, 1877–1900 (Madison)

Wissmann, H. (1981), Sind doch die Götter auch gestorben. Das *Religionsgespräch der Franziskaner mit den Azteken* von 1524 (Gütersloh)

Womack, D.F. (2018), Christian Communities in the *Contemporary Middle East*: An Introduction (in: *Exchange* 49, 189–213)

Yang, F. (2012), Religion in China: *Survival and Revival under Communist Rule* (New York)

Yasutaka, H. (2021), *Senpuku Kirishitan* o shiru jiten (Dictionary on the Senpuku Kirishitan) (Tokyo) in Southeast Asia (Singapore)

Yates, T.E. (2004), The *Expansion* of Christianity (Downers Grove)

Yeh, A. (2014), *The Chinese Diaspora* (in: Im/ Yong, *Global Diasporas*, 89–98)

Yeo, K.K.. (2021) (Ed.), The Oxford Handbook of the *Bible in China* (Oxford)

Zeuske, M. (1998), *Kuba* 1492–1902 (Leipzig)

Zeuske, M. (2004), *Schwarze Karibik*. Sklaven, Sklavereikultur und Emanzipation (Zürich)

Zeuske, M. (2022), Afrika – Atlantik – Amerika : *Sklaverei und Sklavenhande*l in Afrika, auf dem Atlantik und in den Amerikas sowie in Europa (Berlin/Boston)

Zhang, Qiong (2015), Making the New World their own: *Chinese encounters* with Jesuit science in the age of discovery (Leiden/ Boston).

Županov, I.G. (2019) (Ed.), The Oxford *Handbook of the Jesuits* (New York, NY)

Županow, I.G. (2005), "One Civility, but Multiple Religion": *Jesuit Mission* among St. Thomas Christians in India (16th-17th c.) (in: *Journal of Early Modern History* 9.3–4, 284–325)

Županow, I.G./ Fabre, P.A. (2018) (Eds.), The *Rites Controversies* in the Early Modern World (Leiden/ Boston)

Zurlo, G. (2023), *Women in World Christianity*: Building and Sustaining a Global Movement (Chichester)

Illustration Credits

1   Figures

Adveniat.de: 56; The Akrofi-Christaller Institute of Theology, Mission and Culture (courtesy): 53; Archivio 'De Propaganda Fide': APF, SOCG 576, fol. 314: "Antoniano colla corona in testa" (courtesy): 15; Campbell (1998), Songs of Zions [see p. 330] (courtesy): 36, 37; Gründer (1992), Welteroberung [see p. 334] (edited original: MS Egerton 2898, British Museum; courtesy): 5; Heiligenlexikon.en: 39; Klaus Koschorke (photo): 1, 2, 4, 6, 7, 9, 12, 13, 18, 20, 21 (copy in Macao Museum, Macao), 30, 31, 35, 42, 43, 45, 46, 47, 48, 49, 50, 57; McManners, J. (1990), The Oxford Illustrated History of Christianity (Oxford): 29, 52; Prien (1978), Geschichte [see p.344] (courtesy): 10, 11; Thomas Ruhland (photo): 25; Studienzentrum A. H. Francke Halle, Signature 131 F22 (photo: Daniel Jeyaraj): 24; Unitätsarchiv Herrnhut, GS.393: 17; WCC Archives, D7233–00 (courtesy): 44; Wikimedia Commons/ public domain: 3, 8, 14, 16, 19, 22, 23, 26, 27, 28, 32, 33, 34, 38, 40, 41, 51, 54, 55.

2   Maps

The maps were taken with kind permission and/ or redrawn from: Bastian (1995), *Protestantismus in Lateinamerika*: 7; Bayly (2008), *Geburt der Modernen Welt:* 13; Castles/ De Haas/ Miller (2014), *Age of Migration* (Red Globe Press/Bloomsbury Publishing): 19; Hock (2005), *Christentum in Africa*: 1, 5, 9, 10, 16, 17, 18; Ki-Zerbo (1981), *Geschichte Schwarzafrikas* 8; Koschorke/ Mottau (2011), *Dutch Reformed Church in Colonial Ceylon*: 11; Meier (2018), *Ränder* 12; Pietschmann (1994), *Handbuch I*: 6; Reinhard (1983/1985/1988), *Expansion* I–III: 2, 3, 4, 14, 15; Tobias Stäbler: 5.

Survey of the Digital Appendix: Photos from Selected Regions

A   Silk Road (Ancient Oriental Christianities along the Continental and Maritime "Silk Roads").
B   China
C   Japan
D   Korea
E   Sri Lanka
F   Ethiopia
G   Ghana
H   South Africa
J   Peru
K   Brazil
L   Jamaica
M   Mexico
N   Tur Abdin (Turkey)

Photos by Klaus Koschorke (copyright)

This appendix can be accessed via the "Bonus Material" button at https://doi.org/10.6084/m9.figshare.27623484.v2

Index

1. Countries, Regions, Places

Andes   34, 53, 81
Armenia   XXIV, 7–9, 63, 192, 194, 197, 297, 311, 346
Azusa   189f, 222, 239

Bolivia   82, 119, 165, 170, 217, 263
Brazil   IX, XVI, XXIII, **15**, 20f, 24, 26, 41, 51, 56f, 71, 75, 78–80, 82, 84f, 93f, 119, 124f, 148, **163–166**, 168–170, 182, 187, 189, **217–219**, 220–224, 237–239, 263–265, 267–271, 291, 298, 300, 302–305, 308f, 312, 343, 356, 362, **366** (-> Photo Appendix)

California   XXII, 198
Caribbean   XIV, XXI, XXIII, XXIV, 13, 20–22, 31, 35, 51, 71f, 75, 84, 92–95, 111, 119, 125, 147, 163, 182, 208, 222, 234, 263, 274, 299, 335, 355f, 349, 361, 366
Ceylon. *See* -> Sri Lanka
Chile   20f, 32, 119, 122, 125, 163–165, 169, 187, 191, 217, 222, 237, 239, 263f, 271, 298
China   VI, VII, VIII, XIV, XV, XVI, XXIII, XXIV, 5f, 8f, 10, 12, 17, 43, 44–47, 73, 75f, **98–100**, 102, 106, 114, 121, 123f, 126, 129, **135–137**, 141, **144–146**, 154, 172f, 181–183, 186, 189–191, 195, 197–200, 202, 204, 226, 231, 233, 235, **244–246**, 252, 275, **280–282**, 285f, 297, 300f, 304f, 307f, 311, 332, 337, 339, 342f, 346, 348, 352–354, 357f, 360, 363f, **366** (-> Photo Appendix)
Congo/ Kongo (historical kingdom) / Zaire   VI, XIII, XVII, XXIII, 11f, 42, 50f, 54f, 56, 75f, 86, **91f**, 111, 127, 149, 154, 181f, 205f, 210, 212, 232, 251, 253f, 255–257, 282, 296, **318**, 341, 345, 361
Cuba   IX, XXII, 13, 21, 31, 25, 119, 163, 182, 217, **218–220**, 223f, 232, **263f**, 296, 306

Egypt   XXIV, 4f, 8f, 38, 147, 158, 251, **256**, 278, 282f, 285, 312, 335f
Ethiopia/ Abyssinia   VI, VII, VIII, XIII, XV, XVII, XXI, XXIV, 4, **6–9**, 10, **38–40**, 46, 56f, **61–64**, 65, **89f**, 156, **158f**, 162, 176, 181f, 205, 213, 256, 296, **329**, 338, 340f, 350, 352, 356, 358, **366** (-> Photo Appendix); *Ethiopianism/ Ethiopian Movement*   xxi, 95, **126–128**, 161, **177**, 189f, **208f**, 216, 223

Georgia (Caucasus region)   XXIV, 8, 297
Ghana/ Gold Coast   IV, XIV, XVI, 12, 41, 71, 74f, **92**, 111f, 149, 160, 209, 211, 213f, 236, **251–253**, 254f, 257f, 288, 299, 301, 303, 305f, 354, **366** (-> Photo Appendix)
Goa   VI, **42–47**, 49, 56, 60, 74, 90, 92, 101, 119
Guam   119, 163, 182
Guatemala   31, 82, 169, 298
Guinea   40, 53, 182, 251
Gulf states   301

Hawaii   XXII, 137, 198
Honduras   13, 165
India   V, VI, XIII, XIV, XV, XVI, XX–XXIII, XXIV, 4–9, 10f, 13, 16, **17–19**, 21, 39f, **42–44**, 47, **48–50**, 54f, 60f, 64f, 72f, 92f, 104–107, 115, 119, 121, 123, 125, **129–134**, 142, 146, 155, 160, 162, 181, 183, 185–189, 190–193, **195–199**, 200, 203f, 213, 222, 225, 227, 232, 234, 236f, 242, 247–250, 254, 277, 300, 302, 304f, 307, 311, 336, 341, 343–347, 349, 355, 361, 364
Indonesia   VIII, 4, 44, 71f, 76, 119, 123, 126, 135, **141f**, 146, 181, 202, 202, 204, 231f, **243f**, 248f, 277, 300, 302, 336, 355
Iran/ Iraq/ Persia/ Mesopotamia: 4, 7–9, 18, 60, 181, 277, **282f**

Jamaica   72, 84, 95, 126, 128, 223, 256, 358, **366** (-> Photo Appendix)
Japan   VI, VII, VIII, XIII, XV, XVII, XXII, XXIV, 29, 43, **44–46**, 47, 56, 67f, 74, 76, 97f, 102, 106, 121, 135, **137–141**, **142–144**, 146, 174, 181, 185f, 188f, 195, **198–203**, 204, 222, 225f, 231, 233, **243f**, 248f, **324**, 337, 339–342, 347, 354–361, 363, **366** (-> Photo Appendix)

Kenya 11, 90, 153, 155, 212, 251, 254f, 257, 276, 296, 300
Kongo (historical kingdom). *See* -> Congo
Korea VII, VIII, XV, XVI, XXII, XXIV, 102–104, 107, **135**, **139–141**, 145f, 189, 193, 198, **201f**, 204, 226, 231, 233, 235, 238f, 245, 249, 275, 279, 284, 286f, 298, 300–305, 307, 309, 332, 335, 341, 348, 351, 354, **366** (-> Photo Appendix)

Lebanon 7, 244, 282
Liberia 12, 127, 147, **149**, **159f**, 181, 191, 205, 209

Macao XIV, 43, 113, 119, 307, 376
Madagascar VIII, 93, **156–158**, 162, 206, 251, 296
Malawi/ Nyasaland 154f, 191, 206, 214, 251, 296
Malaysia, 43, 71, 135, 232, 234
Medellín x, 264f, 267, 271
Mexico V, IX, XIII, XXII, 14, 20f, 24–26, **28f**, 31–36, 52f, 56, **58**, 66, 74, 77–79, 85f, 110, 119, 122, 124, **163–165**, 169, 182, 187, 198, 218, **219f**, 221, 224, 267, 277, 280, 306, 336, 341f, 348, 252, **366** (-> Photo Appendix)
Mexico City 33, 78f
Mongolia 6, 231, 233, 297, 302
Mozambique 11, 91f, 121, 153f, 206, 232, 251, 303
Myanmar/ Burma 9, 129, 131, 181, 186, 195, 198, 231f, 235

Namibia/ German East Africa 11, 41, 151, 155, 182, 207, 211
Nicaragua 29, 31, 165, 232, 267, 297
Nigeria VIII, XIV, 12, 41f, 47, 90f, 94, 96, 111, 127, 148f, **159f**, 162, 187, 205, 209–211, 214f, 223, 232, 236, 251, **253**, 255, 258, 274, 277, 279, 283, 299f, 312, 336, 346, 352, 358

Oceania XXIV, 123, 273, 275, 332

Pakistan 232, 234, 242
Palestine 4, 7, 282, 307
Panama 13, 21, 170, 173, 187, **190**, 193, **222**, 298
Paraguay 20, 74, 82–85, 119, 222, 298, 303, 345
Peru XIII, XXII, 20f, 24, 32, 34, **52–54**, 63, 74, 80–83, 97, 109, 119, 163, 165, 170, 221, 236, 265, 302, 335f, 338, 341, 348, 352f, 360, 362, **366** (-> Photo Appendix)

Philippines VII, VIII, 15, 44, 56, 74, 100–102, 107, 139, **141**, 146, 163, 182, 187, 198, **202**, 231–234, **247**, 280, 297, 300, 307, 310, 347
Puerto Rico 119, 163, 182, 187, 232

Rwanda 205, 211

Senegal 251, 256
Serampore **129–133**, 189, 197
Siberia XXII, XXIII, 8, 198
Sierra Leone VIII, XVII, XXIII, 11, 95, 126–128, **147–149**, **159f**, 161, 192, 257, 279, 322, 339, 362
Singapore 135, 231, 300, 302, 364
South Africa VIII, IX, XV, XVI, **XVI**, XXI, XXIV, 11, 72, 76, 119, 125, 127, 149, **150–153**, 154, 160f, 177, 188f, 198, 203, 207f, 210–214, 232, 238f, 251, 254f, 257f, **258–260**, 262, 276, 280, 289, **295**, 301, 303, **312f**, **330**, 339, 341–346, 352, 356, 362, **366** (-> Photo Appendix)
Sri Lanka VI, VII, XII, **XVI**, 9, 43, **48–50**, 54, 71f, 74, 76, **100f**, 107, 119f, 123, 125, 131, 152, 160, **185f**, 191, 195, 198, 232, **234f**, 242, 247f, 277, 280, 287, 302, 307, **323**, 344, 349, 351, **366** (-> Photo Appendix)
Sudan/ Nubia 8, 251
Syria XXIII, XXIV, 4f, 7–9, 301, 311

Taiwan 198, 202, 233, 235, 248
Tanzania/ Tanganyika/ German East Africa **154f**, 182, 205, 211, 214, 251, 253f, 261, 273, 280, 282, 285, 352, 358
Thailand/ Siam 9, 126, 135, 181, 186, 195, 233
Togo 12, 182, 205, 211, 251, 296
Tranquebar VII, XIV, 72f, 75, 92, **104–107**, 115, 347
Tur Abdin 282, **366** (-> Photo Appendix)
Turkey XXII, 8, 192, 282f, 302f, 305, 366
Tuskegee 212

Uganda/ Buganda VIII, **156–158**, 162, 206, 211, 234, 255, 283
Uruguay 82, 119, 165, 222, 263, 265

Vietnam VIII, **141f**, 146, 186, 191, 195, 231f, **245f**, 280, 297, 301, 317, 348

Zaire. *See* -> Congo

11. Persons, Groups, Movements

Aaron nee Arumugun (first Indian Protestant pastor)   XIV, 105, **115**, 347
Agbebi, Mojola (Nigerian Baptist minister and nationalist) 187, 208
Anderson, Rufus (American missiologist) 124, 146, 198
Azariah, Vedanayakam Samuel (Indian ecumenical pioneer)   XV, 133, 196, 199, 203f, **225**, 345
Azikiwe, Nnamdi (first Nigerian president) 214, 216, 251

Baeta, Christian G. (West African church leader)   213, 257
Base church movements   247, 266, 269
Bediako, Kwame (West African theologian)   XVI, 257, **289**, 306, 308, 338
Biko, Stephen (anti-Apartheid activist)   257
Bolívar, Simón   164
Bonhoeffer, Dietrich (global reception)   238f, 260, 296, 357
Braide, Garrick Sokari (African Christian prophet)   191, 209f, 352
Buthelezi, Manas (South African church leader)   258

Câmara, Hélder (liberation theologian and Brazilian archbishop)   221, 264f, 271, 342
Capitein, Jacobus Eliza J. (West African pastor)   XIV, 92, **112**
Cardenal, Ernesto (Nicaraguan priest)   266f
Carey, William (Baptist pioneer missionary to India)   129f
Chao Tzu-ch'ens (Chinese ecumenist)   237
Chilembwe, John (Baptist minister, Malawian revolutionary)   191, 214
Coe, Shoki (Taiwan educationalist and ecumenist) 235
Columbus, Christopher   V, XX, 4, 6, 9, 11–14, 17, 18–21, 30, 343, 357
Christeros (revolutionary movement in Mexico)   214f
Creoles   55, 85, 163, 346
Crowther, Samuel Ajayi (first Black African bishop in modern times)   VIII, XV, 149, 159–163, 176, 186, 196, 208, 211, 214, 349, 358
Cruz, Juana Inés de la (Mexican nun, poet)   XIII, 33, 48, 78f, 87, 110, 354

Ding, Guangxun (Chinese church leader)   281
Dom Afonso I / Nzinga Memba (Christian Kongo ruler)   42, 50f, 361

Equiano, Olaudah (West African author, abolitionist)   XIV, 94–96, **111**, 128, 148, 161, 363
Ethiopianism/ Ethiopian Movement   XXI, 95, **126–128**, 161, 177, 189f, 208f, 216, 223

Fa, Liang (Chinese evangelist)   XIV, 126, 144, **172**
Fabri, Frederick (German colonial propagist)   182, 205
Fasilidas (Ethiopian king)   VI, 61–64, 89, 90

Galawdewos/ Claudius (Ethiopian king)   39, 63
Gama, Vasco da   V, XX, 6, 9, 11, 13, 17–19, 39, 42
Gandhi, Mahatma   203f, 233, 252, 342
Guadalupe, Virgin of,   55, 86, 219, 341, 356
Gutiérrez, Gustavo (Peruvian liberation theologian)   221, 265, 345
Gützlaff, Karl   124, 135f, 144

Hidalgo, Miguel (Mexican priest, revolutionary)   XV, 164, 175
Hong Xiuquan (Taiping leader)   XIV, 142, 144f, **172f**, 360
Hurtado, Alberto   221

Isabella of Castile I (Spanish queen)   11, 13f, 32

Jabavu, John Tengo   (South African publicist)   153, 346
Johnson, James (African Anglican bishop, nationalist)   215
Johnson, Samuel (African pastor and historian)   236

Kakure Kirishitan/ Sempuku Kirishitan   98, 138, 142, 144, 146, 337
Katoppo, Henriette M.   248
Kenyatta, Jomo   251
Kimbangu, Simon / Kimbanguism   210, 216, 254f
Kimpa Vita, Doña Beatriz (Kongolese prophetess)   XIII, 74, 91, **111**, 361
Krapf, Johann Ludwig (German missionary to East Africa)   153, 358

Las Casas, Bartolomé de (Dominican, human rights activist)   V, XIII, 23f, 24, 27, 29–36, 58, **66**, 82, 164, 341, 343–345, 353, 358, 362
Lebna, Dengel (Ethiopian emperor)   38
Lee Seung-Hoon, Peter (Korean pioneer)   102f
Livingstone, David (British missionary and explorer)   VIII, 153–155, 161f, 357, 362
Luthuli, Albert John (South African politician)   XVI, 153, 203, 214, **289**

Macaulay, Herbert   214
Magellan, Ferdinand   21
Mandela, Nelson   259, 295, 312
Maria Kannon   98, 143
Mbiti, John S.   257
Mendieta, Gerónimo de   27, 34, 37, 356
Mendouça, Lourenço da Silva   75
Menelik II (Ethiopian emperor)   159, 162, 352
Mina Soga   (South African women activist)   203
Moctezuma (Aztec ruler)   14, 21f
Mokone, Mangena Maake (South African church founder)   XV, 127, 177, 189, 208
Montesinos, Antonio (Dominican, human rights activist)   V, XXIII, **29–31**, 36
Morelos, José María   164
Morrison, Robert   (missionary to China)   XIV, 135, 172
Mott, John R. (ecumenist)   304
Mwanga (Kabaka of Uganda)   157f

"Nestorians", East Syrian Christians   XXIII, 8f, 17f, 60f, 192
Niijima Jo (Joseph Hardy Neesima)   XV, 139, 174

Nkrumah, Kwame   233, 251–253
Nyerere, Julius Kambaragene   253

Olcott, Henry S. (Theosophist)   195

Paravars (South Indian fisher caste)   VI, 48, 49, 54
Philip II (King of Spain)   XII, 92, 151, 304
Pieris, Aloysius   235
Poma de Ayala, Felipe Guamán (Peruvian chronicler)   XIII, XVI, 53, 55, 81, 87, 108, 236, 291, 335, 341, 345, 353, 360f
Popes: *Alexander III*: 6; *Alexander VI*: 14; *Benedict XIV*: 100, 200; *Benedict XV*: 200, 211; *Benedict XVI*: 297; *Clement XI*: 100; *Clement XIV*: 121; *Gregory XVI*: 73; *Hadrian VI*: 24; *Innocent XI*: 75; *John XXIII*: 264; *John Paul II*: 276f, 289, 296; *Leo XII*: 164; *Leo XIII*: 200, 220; *Nicholas V*: 40; *Paul III*: 16; *Paul VI*: 255, 265; *Pius II*: 4; *Pius V*: 32; *Pius VIII*: 165; *Pius IX*: 167; *Pius XI*: 211, 213; *Pius XII*: 221
Prophetic movements. See -> Prophecy (on p. 374)
Protten Africanus, Christian Jakob (West African pastor)   XIV, 75, 92, **111**
Protten, Rebecca (Caribbean evangelist)   XIV, 75, 92, **111**

Quaque, Philip   92
Quiroga, Pedro de   54, 55, 336

Radama I (King of Madagascar)   156
Ramabai, Pandita (Indian social and education activist)   XV, 133, **225**, 248
Ranavalona I (Queen of Madagascar)   156
Rhodes, Cecil (British imperialist)   183
Ricci, Matteo (Jesuit missionary to China)   XIV, 14, 9, 98f, 103, **114**
Romero, Oscar Arnulfo (liberation theologian, archbishop)   XVI, 238f, 268, **290**
Roy, Ram Mohan (Indian religious reformer)   132f

Sahagún, Bernadino de   25, 28, 34, 36, 55, 57f, 341f, 351

INDEX

Schmidt, Georg   93, 151 (Moravian missionary)
Senghor, Leopold   233, 256
Sepúlveda, Juan Ginés de   33, 345
Shembe, Isiah (South African prophet)   210
Singh, Lilivathi (Indian education pioneer)   15, **225**, 249
St. Thomas Christians   V, VI, XIII, XX, XXI, XXIV, 9, 17–19, 38, 42, 60f, 64f, 75, 131f, 142, 196, 302, 341
Sukarno, Achmed (Indonesian president)   242
Sun Yat-Sen (revolutionary, Chinese president, Christian)   126

Taiping (Chinese revolutionary Christian inspired movement)   XIV, 136, **144f**, 146, **172f**, 348f, 360, 362
Torres, Camilo 268
Tupac Amaru II. (José Gabriel Condorcanqui)   86, 88

Tutu, Demond (South Africa archbishop, fighter against apartheid)   XVI, 254, 257, 259, **289**, 295, **312f**

Uchimura Kanzo (Japanese theologian)   XV, 139, 186, 198, **225**

Vega, Garcilaso de la   52, 341
Venn, Henry (British missiologist)   124, 160, 198

Wilson, Woodrow (US American president)   191, 201

Xavier, Francis (Jesuit missionary to Asia)   VI, XIII, XXIII, **43–47**, 49, 56, 67, 98, 354, 359,

Zapata, Marcos (Peruvian Christian artist)   XIII, 53, 81, **109**, 219
Ziegenbalg, Bartholomaeus (Lutheran missionary to India)   XIV, 104f, **115**

III. Subjects, Topics, Themes

Accommodation (concept)   98f, 106
African Independent Churches (AIC's)   XXV, 187, 193, **207–211**, 255, 303
African traditional religions / religiosity   208f, 235, **256f**
African Methodist Episcopal Church (AME)   126f, 177, 189, 208, 339
African-American/ Afro-Brazilian religions   37, 75, 78, 223, **269–271**
Ancient Oriental Churches   7–9, 10, 63, 256, 333, 366 (*See also* -> Armenia, Egypt, Ethiopia, Lebanon, East Syrians, St. Thomas Christians)
American-Indian religions 20f, 28f, 57
Apartheid,,   IX, X, XVI, 152, 232, 238, 257f, **258–260**, 261f, 280, 289, **295**
Architecture   33, 82, 89, 186, 196, 234, **247**
Art, performing / painting   XIII, XV, **53**, 55, 77, **81**, 89, **109**, 247,299, 336, 341
Ashrams, Christian   186, 196, **247**, 250, 340, 348

Baptism   18, 25, 34, 41f, 45, 48, 50, 62, 98, 103, 143, 154, 157, 222, 264, 269
Barmen Theological Declaration, reception   260
Base church movements   247, 266, 269
Bible: *interpretation/ reception*: 28, 30, 58, 65, **98**, 104ff, 122, 131, **133**, **144f**, 148, **149f**, 151, 152, 154f, 168, 208, 215, 248, 253, **257–260**, 266, 276, 300; *dissemination, smuggling*: 135ff, 168f, 276; *criticism*: 152; *translations*: **XIV**, 104, **115**, **122ff**, **129**, 131, 136, 140, **149f**, 172, **276**
Buddhism   29, 45f, 56, 98f, 101, 103, 123, 139f, 143, 146, 152, 185f, 191, 195f, 203, 222, 231, 242f, 277, 297, 307, 344, 361; *Buddhist revival*: 185f, 195ff; *"Protestant Buddhism"*: 123, **195**, 203.

Church assemblies, councils, pan-continental: 188, 190, 233, 246, 265, 253

Church assemblies, councils/synods, regional: 58f, 60, 199, 246, 254
Church and social question   220f
"Christianity and Civilization" (concept)   VIII, **154f, 160, 190ff,** 350
Colonialism: *stages*: 11–17, 21f, 71ff, 117f, 160f, 177–179, 206, 225f; *forms of colonial rule*: 15–17, 71f, 117f, 177, 200; *anti-colonial resistance*: 25, 80, 85f, 100, 118, 120, 138f, 209, 249; *neo-colonialism*: 212, 220f, 250; *colonialism, Japanese*: 236f. (*See also* -> Decolonisation; Independence movements, political; Independence movements, ecclesiastical; Third World)
Confession, confessionalisms/ denominationalisms   IX, XXII, 3, 11, 33, 39, 57, 60, 63, 71, 73, 105, **123–125, 131f,** 137, 140, 151, 155, 168f, 184f, **186–188, 196–199, 206f,** 212, **221–224,** 233f, 237f, 243f, 246f, 254, 273, 275, 281, 305, 307, 312 (*See also* -> Ecumenical movement)
Councils: *Trent* (1545–1563): **56–64,** 167, 341, 343, 347, 355, 360; *Vatican I* (1869–1870): **167f;** *Vatican II* (1962–1965): 235, 237f, 241, 246f, 250, 254, 258, **264f,** 271. 352, 356
Communism   IX, XXIV, 219, 221, 231, 233, 243, 244–246, 248f, 252, 263, 268, 275f, 280f, 295–297, 360, 364 (*See also* -> socialism)
Confucianism   XXII, 99f,102f, 104, 137, 139–141, 145, 196, 201, 22, 235
Conversion   31f, 41–43, 51, 90, 95, 97, 129, 134, 169, 195, 264, 267, 307, 354; *mass/ group conversions*: 25, 134, 142, 158, 209
Contextualization (concept)   235, 248, 259, 298, cf. 312, 339

Dance   51, 208, 255
Decolonisation, stages   84ff. **119f. 163ff.** 175. 231f. 242ff. 251ff
Democratisation, role of Churches   295f, 307f, 344, 357
Dependency theory   233, 266
Diasporas, ethnic   XIV, XXI, XXII, XXIII, 7f, 95, 102, **126,** 135, 137, 148, 172, 188, 198, 210, 220, 256, 272, 278, 284, 300–302, 307–309, 335

EATWOT ('Ecumenical Association of Third World Theologians')   233, 236, 240, 266, 271, 340, 342
Ecumenical movement, modern/ anti-denominationalism   VII, IX, XV, XVI, XXV, 8, 105, 130, 153. 184, **187ff,** 193, 203, 213, 225, 227, 234, 236–239, 241, **247ff,** 249ff, 258f, 275; *church unions* 199, 237, 242, 254; *ecumenism from below*: VIII, 186, 188f, **197–199,** 203f, 215, 225, 234 (*See also* -> Edinburgh 1910, Tambaram 1938, WCC)
Education / schools / colleges/ universities   40, **78f,** 83, 90, 103, 110, 122, **130–134,** 135, **136–138,** 140, 150, 152, 160, 167, 169, 186, 201, 207, **211, 214,** 217f, 220, 222, **235,** 244, 248, 251, 255, **265f,** 282, 307.
Egalitarianism/ 'equality of believers'   145, 151, **153,** 161, 192f, 208, 342, 346; *See also* -> racism, Ethiopianism
Emancipation   VIII, IX, XV, XXI, XXV, 86, **147–150,** 161., 163, 176, 189, 213f, 231f, **233–236,** 240, 242
Enlightenment   73–76, 105, 119, 138, 163, 305
Ethiopianism/ Ethiopian Movement   XXI, 95, **126–128,** 161, 177, 189f, 208f, 216, 223

Fundamentalisms, religious   239, **277f,** 282, 284, 297, 311, 336, 353, 357

Healing/medicine/hospitals/medical mission   30, 43, 90, 122, **132,** 137f, 140, 156, 169, 184, 208f, 210, 268f, **282**
Hinduism   XX, 17, 42f, 45, 48f, 54, 60, 72, 101, 105, 120. 125, 129f, 132–134, 185f, 195f, 222, 242f, 277, 300, 311, 348
Homosexuality   45, 305

Independence movements, ecclesiastical/ religious   IX, XV, XXII, XXV, 12, 38, 42, 48, 50, 59, 61, 86, 124, 126f, 134, 137, 144, 159ff, 159f, 177, 186f, , 191, 193, 197f, **207–211,** 231ff (*See also* -> African Independent Churches, Ethiopianism, National Church movements)
Independence movements, political   VII, VIII, IX, XV, XXII, 53, **84f,** 119–122, 141, 147, 149, 156, 159, **163–166,** 170, 175, 201f, 213ff, 220, 231ff

INDEX 373

Indigenization: *as program:* VIII, 186ff, 195ff, 203, **235**, 247f, 257, 287; *indigenous clergy, native bishops, "indigenous leadership":* 40, 58, 72, 141, **159ff, 186ff, 196**, 200, 211, 254, 276, 332; *"native agency", indigenous actors:* XI, XX-XXIII, 186; *local versions of Christianity:* 56, 91, 142ff, 256ff; *voices of indigenous Christians:* 52-55, 80-82, 142-145; *native press, indigenous Christian journalism:* 152, 188f, 208, 213f, 291, 350; *indigenous missionary initiatives:* 129ff, **189**, 193, **198**, 216, 342; *cultural adaptation and pluralization:* 185ff, 190ff, 233ff, 246ff, 251ff; demand for self-governance, autonomy (see under -> "Three-Selves")
Interreligious dialogue/debates IX, **28f, 45f**, 56, 73f, 76f, 105, 129, 237, 247, **256-258**, 261, 277, 306f, 361
Inculturation (concept) 235, 255, 257f, 268
Islam, Muslims 4f, 6-10, 11f, 17f, 30, **39f**, 42, 44, 56, 62, 90, 130, 150, 157, 195, 205, 212, 242f, 258, 261, 277f, 282, 284, 297, 299, 305f

Judaism/ Jews XXIII, 8f, 22, 39, 43, 231

Language, vernaculars, translations 5, 8, 13f, 16f, 20f, 28, **33**, 38, 49, **58f**, 66, 73, 80, 83, 95, **99**, 101, **103f**, 122, **129f**, 131, 135f, 140, 144. **149f**, 168, 172 (*See also* -> Bible
Liberation theology. *See* -> theologies
Liturgy 61, 143, 186, 196, 223, 247

Mega-churches XVI, 279, 286, **299-303**, 305, 308, 348, 352
Migration VII, XVII, XXI, 22, 95, **124-128**, 149f, 155, 168f, 188, 217, 221f, 254, 269, 278f, 282ff, 300ff, **322, 331**, 339 (*See also:* -> Remigration, Diaspora, Black Atlantic)
Missionary movement: *Stages:* 24-27, 72f, 120-123, 185-187, 253ff; *Roman Catholic:* 11ff, 14ff, **22ff, 28ff**, 40ff. 56ff, 72ff, 77ff, 118-120, 141, 166ff, 190**4**ff, 206ff; *Protestant:* 11, 72f, 92f, **104ff**, 119, 122ff, 129-140, 147ff, 159ff, 168ff, 183ff, 268ff; *Orthodox:* 7, 132, **138f, 189**, 208, 234, 256, 303; *Pentecostal:* 138f, 189, **239ff, 303f**; *Indigenous missionary initiatives, societies:* 129ff, **189**, 193, **198**, 216, 342; *African-American missionaries:* **124-127**, 147-150, 189, 193, 216; *Reverse missions:* 278ff

Missions: religious orders, societies, actors (in selection): *Dominicans:* **23-25**, 40, 52, 59, 75, 92, 100; *Franciscans:* XIII, 6, 17, 22, **24f, 28f**, 28, **33f**, 36, 40, 42f, 52f, 57-59,66, 80, 100, 122. 166; *Jesuits:* XIV, XXI, XXII, 9, 19, 24, 29, 39f, 42, **44-47**, 52, 56f, 60, **61-64**, 73-75, 77, 79f, 82-87, 89, 97f, 102, **113f**, 121, 131, 141, 157, 167, 211, 221, 235, 246, 340f, 343; *Pietism (Halle, Moravians):* **71-73**, 75f, 84, 90, **92f, 111, 104-107**, 151, 273, 296, 344; *Basel Mission:* XXIII, 123, 131, 141, 149, 184, 238; *Baptists:* 95, **123f**, 126, 128, **129f**, 131, 147-149, 191, 193, 210, 222, 273, 353; *'Church Missionary Society' (CMS):* 90, 123f, 147f, 153, 157, **159f**, 184, 207, 358; *Congregationalists (ABCFM):* XVI, 124, 131, 151, 157, 214, 234, 289; *White Fathers:* 155, 157, 211; *Indigenous missionary societies:* 189, 198

Mission methods / strategies / concepts: 24ff, 32ff, 40, 44ff, 98ff, 98f, 104ff, 129ff, 233f, 253ff
Missionary conferences: Edinburgh 1910: 130, 137, **185f**, 188, **190f**, 193, 196, **199**, 204, 304; Panama 1916: 187, 190, 193, 222; Tambaram 1938: XVI, 193, 203f, 213-215
Mission and colonialism, colonial ethical debates: 12f, 20-27. **29-33**, 38ff, 72f, 77ff, 92f, **104f**, 119ff, 122ff, 153ff, **183ff**, 205f, 213-216, 233ff
Military dictatorships 236, 263ff, 256, 267, **296-298**
Music 45, 51, 53, 77, 81, 83, 186, 196, 247

Nationalism, anti-colonial national movements VIII, 139, 146, 155, **185-187**, 191, 193, 195f, 203, 214, 219, 242, 251-253, 277f, 297, 343, 348
National church movements/ aspirations VIII, XX, 5, 141, 165, 186f, 193, **197-199**, 204, 212, 218, 234, 254, 349
'National Church of India' 134, 186, 197

Patronage/ Padroado   VI, 15, 15f, **38–42**, 91, 94, 121, 341, 344

Pentecostalism, (neo-)Pentecostalism   X, XVI, 125, 189f, 211, **222–224**, 237, **239–241**, 247, 268–272, 273, 275f, 279, 288, 299f, 302–306, 308f, 336, 340

Persecution of Christians, martyrs   VI VII, XIII, **48–50**, 54, 68, 74, 76, 97, **102–104**, 107, 140, **142–144**, 156f, **239**, 268, 360

Polycentrism in the history of world Christianity   X, XI, **XXII, XXIII**, 293, 222, 239, 301–303, 309, 333, 349

Polygamy   152, 154, 203, **209f**, 212f, 355

Printing press, journals, media, internet   XIV, 14, 33, 104, 122, 129. **131f**, 137, 150, 152, 156, 172, **188**, 277, **298f**, 300, 308, 336, 340, 344, 346, 350

Propaganda Fide   16, **73**, 75f, 94, 121, 200, 354

Prophecy, prophetic movements   XIII, 22, 31, 74, 91, 111, 156, 187, **191**, 209f, 212, 243, 255, 257, 260, 264, 267, 298, 307

Racism/ paternalism/ social Darwinism   XXV, 82f, 160, 183, 206f, 238, 259f, 312

Remigration, transatlantic   XVII, 93f, **95**, 126, 322, 362 (*See also* -> Sierra Leone)

Requerimiento   V, 16, **22f**, 27, 29–33

Rites controversy   91, **99f**, 106f, 121, 204, 351f

Slavery   VI, XIV, XV, **35**, 37, 93f, 96,   125, 150, 155, 161, 166, 342f, 347, 349, 356; *transatlantic slave trade*: VII, XIV, XVII, 35, 37, 41f, 51, 75, 91, **93–96**, 112, 123, 143, 148, 154f, **321**; *abolition, Christian abolitionism*: XIV, XV, 95f, 111, 148, 150, 154f, 161, **175**, 184, 342, 360

Socialism   191, 220, 222, 233, 245f, 253, 256, 267, 296f, 346, 360; *See also* -> communism

South-South connections/ transregional, transcontinental networks   XXII, XXIII, 50–52, 74–76, 93–96, 124–128, 187–189, 301–303

Taiping movement   XIV, 136, **144f**, 146, **172f**, 348f, 360, 362

"Third World"   IX, **232f**, 235–237, 240, 306, 356, 362 (*See also* -> EATWOT)

Theologies: *Liberation theologies*:   233, 263–266, 271, 290, **295ff**; *Contextual theologies*: xi, 235, 259, 298; *Minjung theology*: 235, 244, 249, 298; *Dalit theology*: 249, 277, cf. 134, 277; *Kairos theology*: 260, 298; *Feminist theology*: 248, 258, 268, 354; *Theology of Reconstruction*: 248, 298; *Prosperity Gospel*: 270; *Theologies in Asia*: 248–251; *Theologies in Africa*: 256–258; *Theologies in Latin America*: 265–268, 295ff

"Three Selves"/ "Three-Self"-movement   VIII, 124, 140, **159f**, 160, 189, 193, 196, 198, 216, 244, 249, 281, 350, 363

Urbanisation   217, 221, 269

Women/ female education/ right to knowledge/ as religious leaders   22, 49, 51, **78f**, 81, 103, 106, 110, **124**, 127, **133**, 136, 140, 146, 183, **203**, 222, **225**, 248, 258, 261, **266**, 269, 276, 285, 352, 355f, 363f (*See also* -> Juana I. de la Cruz, Beatriz Kimpa Vita, Pandita Ramabai, Lilivathi Singh)

World Council of Churches (WCC)   237–239, 248, 254–256, 259f, 298

World War I   VIII, IX, 71, 134, 141, 188, **190–194**, 200, **201ff**, 21, 218, 304

World War II   IX, XXII, 199, 203f, 213, **231ff**, 240, 243f, 304, 351f, 359

www.ingramcontent.com/pod-product-compliance
Lightning Source LLC
Chambersburg PA
CBHW050526300426
44113CB00012B/1970